Management Accounting for Healthcare Organizations

James D. Suver, DBA, CMA, FHFMA
and Bruce R. Neumann, PhD

NEW REVISED EDITION

⁈HFMA
Healthcare Financial
Management Association

pluribus
press Inc.

Library of Congress Catalog Card Number:
85-62675

International Standard Book Number:
0-931028-71-X

Second printing—1986

Healthcare Financial Management Association
1900 Spring Road
Oak Brook, Illinois 60521

Pluribus Press, Inc., Division of Teach'em, Inc.
160 East Illinois Street
Chicago, Illinois 60611

Printed in the United States of America

To
Jean and Mary
and all our
other students

About the authors

James D. Suver, DBA, CMA, FHFMA, is Professor of Accounting and Health Administration and Director of the Program in Health Services Administration at the University of Colorado at Denver. Previously he was Professor of Health Policy and Administration and Director of the Masters Program in the Department of Health Policy and Administration, School of Public Health, University of North Carolina at Chapel Hill. A frequent speaker at healthcare meetings around the nation, Dr. Suver is actively involved in bringing the problems of the practitioner to the classroom and the concepts of the academic world to the practitioner. He was one of the initial faculty members in the Executive Graduate Program in Healthcare Financial Management sponsored by the Healthcare Financial Management Educational Foundation. He is author or coauthor of three books and over 35 articles in professional journals.

Dr. Suver received his MBA and DBA from the Graduate School of Business Administration at Harvard University and is a Certified Management Accountant. Research activities include nursing productivity models and cost-sharing models for merged institutions. He was co-winner of the Association of Government Accountants' Research Award (1978) for his work in zero base budgeting.

The author has served as chairman of the local Health Planning Council and as a member of the Project Review Committee of the Health Systems Agency. He was a judge and game referee in the first national competition conducted by the American College of Hospital Administrators. Dr. Suver is currently involved in several projects with local hospitals which include coaching seminars for the Fellowship exams of the Healthcare Financial Management Association.

Bruce R. Neumann, PhD, is Professor of Accounting and Health Administration in the Graduate School of Business Administration, University of Colorado at Denver. Dr. Neumann is one of the founders of the University of Colorado's Executive Graduate Program in Health Care Financial Management and is on its faculty.

The author earned his doctorate at the University of Illinois, where his dissertation research pioneered the concept of peer grouping for hospital cost reimbursement and for performance evaluation. His undergraduate and master's degrees are from the University of Minnesota. Dr. Neumann has taught at Northwestern University and the State University of New York at Albany.

Dr. Neumann is author or coauthor of numerous articles as well as two monographs on mergers and shared services of healthcare organizations. He designed and published a uniform chart of accounts for medical group practices, as well as a system for paying hospitals for prospective capital costs. He has also served on the board or as president of several community groups.

Contents

Preface to second edition

During recent years, the financial condition of healthcare providers has been receiving considerable attention from external and internal sources. Strong cost containment pressures are forcing hospital managers to try new techniques in order to survive. Many of these new ideas and methods require the use of management accounting.

Management accounting is concerned with the uses and the users of accounting information for decision-making. Both uses and users are the primary focus of this text. It is expected that readers will have some previous exposure to basic financial accounting concepts, either in an introductory accounting course or through various work experiences.

Therefore, this text was designed to meet the needs of two distinct groups of individuals. One group includes healthcare managers who need more information on how accounting can be used by a manager. Managers who are not accountants generally require a complete coverage and explanation ranging from a basic foundation to the more sophisticated techniques. Each chapter is designed and arranged to meet this need.

The second group includes those accountants and financial managers who must try to satisfy the information needs of the first group. This second group typically will be more selective in requiring a reference source that is readily available as problems or opportunities occur. Each chapter can stand alone in this respect. The questions and problems, along with additional references cited at the end of each chapter, help meet this objective.

The second edition has been revised significantly to improve the flow and transitions between chapters and to include new material on prospective payment systems and product-line cost accounting. The first seven chapters now represent a cohesive and complete discussion of planning and control in healthcare organizations. This set of integrated materials provides an essential foundation for a thorough understanding of management accounting and control in a wide variety of healthcare delivery systems. The last seven chapters deal with specific topics and provide detailed decision tools that can be used to implement the concepts identified in the first seven chapters. Many of the appendices in the first edition are now incorporated into appropriate chapters while others have been revised as part of selected problems or discussion materials. Two new chapters have been added, one on pricing strategies and rate setting and the other on management information systems.

The second edition has been substantially revised to specifically reflect prospective payment concerns and DRG-based cost accounting systems. In hindsight, the first edition provided an effective framework for health care providers to use as a means of restructuring their cost accounting systems at the time that DRG's were adopted. The authors have made every effort to insure that this new edition provides a conceptual framework that will work not only with current Federal and State payment systems, but also with future revisions in reimbursement and prospective payment. It provides tools that managers can use to make effective and efficient decisions for their organizations as they face prospective payment pressures.

The authors have developed and used this text in graduate executive continuing education courses and in formal Master of Health Administration (MHA) programs. It can be used effectively to meet the requirements of both group and individual study plans. In particular, this text can enhance preparation for the Healthcare Financial Management Association (HFMA) Fellowship examination because it is a major reference in the bibliography of the Study Guide.

We would like to thank our students in the Executive Graduate Program in Healthcare Financial Management and the students in the MHA program at the University of Colorado. They suffered through the early drafts and offered many suggestions used in the final revisions.

Certain key individuals affiliated with HFMA must be acknowledged. In publication of the first edition, Bob Shelton encouraged and supported our efforts throughout the long process; Mary Berry deserves special acknowledgment for her careful review, her penetrating questioning and persistence in meeting due dates, and the review panel of Ronald Horwitz, Herman Kohlman, Bill Nelson, and Bill Fill patiently read draft copies and made excellent recommendations which were incorporated into the final draft. Our thanks too for the assistance given by Ron Keener and Don Dignam who facilitated the logistics of publication on the second edition.

A special acknowledgment must be given to Hans Kleyn, Vice President, Fiscal Affairs, of St. Joseph's Hospital in Denver, Colorado. His experience and counsel were instrumental in the design of several chapters.

As any author knows, no book is ever completed without the help of a dedicated administrative staff. We owe a special thanks to Sharon Bratcher and Judy Strong for typing assistance. They played a vital part in bringing this text to print. John Mills, University of Nevada at Reno, and

Glen Tellock, Ernst & Whinney contributed some of the questions and problems for several chapters.

Finally, we must recognize our wives and families, who sometimes lacked our companionship during the years of development, testing and revision of this book. We hope the final product reflects the sacrifices they made.

All of these individuals deserve credit for helping complete this book. However, the authors alone must take responsibility for any errors and omissions which remain.

James D. Suver, DBA CMA FHFMA
Bruce R. Neumann, PhD
Denver, Colorado
October, 1985

CHAPTER 1

Introduction to management accounting for healthcare organizations

Objectives of accounting

Accounting systems provide most of the quantitative information available to hospital managers. In the past, accountants, as custodians of the system, were primarily involved in accounting for payroll costs, payables and receivables, and supply costs. Recently, however, accountants have become increasingly involved in determining departmental costs, calculating costs per unit (such as cost per laboratory test) and in assisting hospital administrators in evaluating alternative decisions.

This represents a shift in the primary role of the accountant. Historically, accounting in health care organizations has had four major objectives:

1. Internal reporting to hospital managers of information concerning routine planning and control decisions.
2. Internal reporting to hospital managers of information concerning nonroutine planning and control decisions.
3. External reporting to providers of capital and other resources of information about the financial condition and performance of the hospital. Providers of capital resources include bankers, private donors, physicians, unions, government agencies and others who do not actively participate in hospital management.
4. External reporting to third parties and other providers of operating resources of information about the performance of the hospital relative to other hospitals. Providers of operating resources are external agencies that purchase, through some kind of reimbursement process, healthcare services rendered to a constituent of the external agency. Such external agencies are becoming increasingly concerned with the relative performance

of hospitals that receive reimbursement through the third-party agency.

Most economic organizations are finding that external parties are becoming more interested in information prepared for internal managers. They are requiring detailed information about the internal operation of the organization. At the same time, internal managers are becoming more actively involved in preparing information for external parties. It is no longer the sole province of the controller or chief accountant. Outside CPAs often review and attest to the fairness of financial statements that satisfy the third objective mentioned above. To meet the fourth objective, the same CPAs or management consultants may use a computerized allocation program to help prepare cost reports for Medicare or other reimbursement purposes. Different health systems agencies (HSAs), state regulatory agencies, and other providers of operating resources have unique reporting forms and accounting requirements; because the emphasis is on external reporting, it becomes exceedingly difficult for healthcare organizations to maintain an internal accounting viewpoint. This book is designed to help carry out this reporting function.

Fulfilling the third objective referred to earlier is usually considered financial accounting. Financial accounting requires that certain principles of disclosure and external reporting be followed in order to obtain a "clean" or unqualified opinion regarding the fairness of the financial statements. This objective will be further discussed later in this chapter. The first two objectives are the topic and focus of management accounting. Most of the cost accounting activities found in a large manufacturing organization will also be found in a hospital. The preparation of cost reports and other internal reports all require the tracing and/or allocation of costs to units of service. Management accounting encompasses these cost determination activities and includes the preparation of any information that will assist managers in making more informed decisions.

Regardless of the type of system a hospital employs, hospitals need two kinds of information from a cost accounting system. According to John Eresian, vice president, finance, and treasurer, Northwestern Memorial Hospital, Chicago, "First, hospitals need information for strategic pricing of their services and products, product-line management, profit-and-loss information, and other marketing-oriented needs. Second, they need information for managing operating costs through standard cost systems, flexible budgeting, and performance reporting. The common building block for both of these is a system that helps determine the variable and fixed costs of doing a procedure."[1]

---

[1]Jo Ellen Mistarz, "Cost Accounting: A Solution, But a Problem," *Hospitals,* October 1, 1984, p. 96.

In fact, the major purpose of this book is to show how accounting information can be effectively used to improve the decision process. The authors develop the principles for preparing and using information to make decisions in healthcare organizations. The intent of the book is to illustrate, both normatively and descriptively, how accounting information can be extended into new frontiers of managerial decision-making. Managers will discover more effective budgeting and cost control techniques. New approaches to capital budgeting are discussed. Each chapter focuses on the "how" of decision-making. Theoretical concepts are discussed in order to support the practical mechanics that are used to implement each concept.

Therefore, the objectives of this book coincide with the objectives of accounting. Accounting can be defined as "the process of identifying, measuring, and communicating economic information for the purpose of permitting informed judgment and decisions to be made by the users of that information."[2]

Building upon a decision-oriented definition of the accounting process, this book will assist managers of healthcare organizations to improve the identification, measurement and communication of managerial accounting information. The book will show how that information can be used to improve managerial decisions.

The management control process

Management control relies on accounting information. It is concerned with how efficiently resources are used. For example, does a particular nursing unit with 90 percent occupancy use too many, or too few, hours of nursing care? How much waste exists in the dietary department? What travel schedule (location or routes) is assigned to the rural public health nurse? All of these questions require comparison of the resources actually used with the resources that should have been used to accomplish the same objective. This is an efficiency question. Could the same result have been accomplished with fewer resources? With a different mix of resources? Two analogies follow:

1. A fly swatter accomplishes its purpose very efficiently compared to a sledge hammer that might also be used to destroy the fly—and anything else nearby. Both tools are effective, but the fly swatter is more efficient.
2. A four-cylinder car might be more efficient than an eight-cylinder car, and both may be able to get from one city to another in the

---

[2]Price Waterhouse Foundation, *A New Introduction to Accounting: Report of the Study Group,* New York: Price Waterhouse Foundation, 1971.

same amount of time. Both cars are effective, but the four cylinder auto will save gasoline.

Similarly, management control must also assure that the organization is effective in accomplishing its objectives. Effectiveness compares the organization's strategic objectives with its actual accomplishments. Efficiency concerns the efforts necessary to reach some objective. Effectiveness evaluates whether the objective was actually accomplished and, if not, why not? In the analogies above, the fly was killed in both cases and the traveler reached the intended destination. In the nursing department, an appropriate level of care was supplied; high quality food was prepared by the dietary department, and the public health nurse reached her patients. In each case, the actual results must be compared with the expected results.

The management control process is diagrammed in *Exhibit 1—1*. This figure shows that both effectiveness and efficiency must be evaluated at the conclusion of each phase of operations. The results of effectiveness evaluations have an impact on both the strategic planning process and the establishment of new programs, products or departments. The results of efficiency evaluations are usually linked to an operating budget—or perhaps to the next phase of operations—without any effect on the budget. This link is called a feedback loop because lessons learned from the results of past operations can best be used to affect future operations. Assuming that the activity is operating effectively, the feedback loop portrays the immediate adjustment of the next period's operating activities.

In the case of the dietary department, the required adjustment may be as immediate as the next meal. In the case of the nursing unit, it may come next week or next month. In the case of the public health nurse's routes, adjustment may not be feasible until some redistricting or realignment of jurisdictional boundaries can occur. The point is that the timing of the actions indicated by an efficiency evaluation should occur as close as possible to the point of recognition. On the other hand, the timing of changes in strategic plans or programmatic decisions tends to be long-range. Most hospitals do not make immediate and/or temporary changes in their basic mission and objectives. The shift from general service care to specialty care (e.g., becoming a children's hospital) usually takes years. It would be counterproductive for most healthcare organizations to constantly or regularly evaluate the health maintenance organization issue, for example. In most cases, information about changes in programs or strategic plans usually occurs much less frequently than does the efficiency determination component of management control.

Performance reporting

Note that reporting and analyzing the results of operations is the basis for both effectiveness and efficiency comparisons in *Exhibit 1—1*. This is such an important element of management control that it needs to be discussed separately. Two problems emerge in the area of performance reporting. One of these is the output measurement problem. What units should be used to measure the results of operations? In one case it may be hours of nursing time. In another, it may be pounds of waste or excess miles traveled. In each case, there is an identifiable physical measure of output. Such measures usually exist for efficiency evaluations because efficiency compares the quantity of inputs with the quantity of outputs. In both dimensions, quantities are important.

Exhibit 1-1
Management control cycle

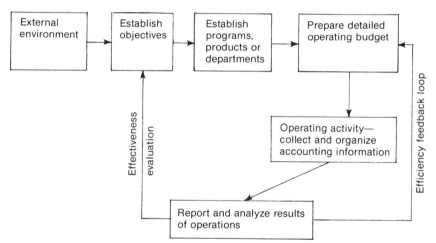

However, output measurement is much more difficult in effectiveness comparisons. What are the units of measurement for quality of care? What unit measures health status or physical wellbeing? In such cases, the authors will consistently recommend comparison of the actual results with a predetermined standard of accomplishment. In other words, the units of measurement are not as important as identifying whether the targeted level of results was actually achieved. In most cases, this resolves into a dichotomous "yes or no" decision.

Therefore, output measurements are not as difficult a problem for intrahospital decision-making. They become much more difficult when two or more hospitals are being evaluated for either efficiency or effectiveness because the standards or the units of measure may not be defined or measured uniformly. However, within a single healthcare institution, time series comparisons are valid as long as the accounting definitions or basic standards of performance do not change.

The second problem alluded to above is that of behavioral responses to performance reports. Ideally, a report on a department's performance will lead to some favorable impact on that department's decisions. If the department's costs are out of control—either in terms of effectiveness or efficiency—some cost-reducing activity would ideally occur. If the department's performance level is acceptable, one would hope that a performance report would lead to the continuation of whatever activities contributed to the results achieved. In other words, if a manager has done something good, a report on that performance should help to induce similar behavior in the future. If unfavorable results are observed, performance reporting should lead to a change in decisions or managerial behavior that will help achieve better results in the future.

Unfortunately, the ideal results that are expected to occur as part of performance reporting do not always happen. Performance reports may be ignored. They may not be distributed on time to the right people. They may induce behavior in a direction opposite of that intended by top management. In such cases, performance reports may have no effect on decision behavior, or they may have negative effects. Ignoring or misusing performance reports may have deleterious consequences.

Research in this area suggests that management accounting must embrace the objective of goal congruence. That is, all parts of the management control system should lead to an increased congruence between organizational objectives and the objectives of individual managers and participants in the organization. Performance reporting can help the organization move toward a higher level of goal congruence. Again, research in this area suggests that increased participation in decision-making will help to avoid the negative consequences of performance reports. Reports on a department's performance should avoid emphasizing noncontrollable costs. For example, nursing service supervisors cannot control the costs incurred in maintenance and dietary. Although these costs are a part of providing healthcare to the patient, they are not the responsibility of the nursing supervisor. Although the nursing service supervisor can often influence these costs and should be aware of them, all indirect or allocated costs should be separated from direct costs such as nursing salaries, etc. Performance reports should not include significant amounts of allocated costs that cannot be controlled by the responsible manager. In a similar manner, performance reports should reflect the impact of volume on the incurred costs. This concept of cost behavior is especially vital in healthcare organizations, where many of the costs are fixed. Performance reports should reflect the relationship between managerial decisions and the behavior of costs.

Many of the ways to improve performance reporting and the behavioral impact of performance reporting are described in more detail in subsequent chapters of this book. Recognition of a potential behavioral impact is the first step to improving performance reporting. Alternative formats should be tested in the hospital or in the individual department. Each manager must be aware of the potential behavioral impact of performance reporting and take action to avoid negative consequences.

One of the major purposes of this book is to show how that objective may be achieved in many different areas of management accounting.

Underlying accounting criteria

The overall objective of accounting that was discussed earlier in this chapter concerns the interaction between accounting data and decision-making. Accounting systems and accounting reports must provide data that are useful for decision-making. This principle can also be called the relevance criterion. Accounting data must be relevant to the decisions that are made. These data must be appropriate for their intended uses.

Independent auditors express relevance in terms of full disclosure and fairness of presentation. The CPA's test of relevance is whether the financial statements fairly represent the results of operations and the financial position of the healthcare organization. If so, the auditor can issue an unqualified opinion on the financial statements. If, in the auditor's opinion, the fairness criterion is not met, the auditor has several options which range from a qualified opinion to no opinion at all. The requirements and criteria for all of these possibilities are beyond the scope of this text. For a fuller discussion of them, the reader can refer to any standard intermediate accounting text or to the American Institute of Certified Public Accountants' (AICPA's) *Statement on Auditing Standards.* In any event, fair presentation includes an evaluation of:

1. the extent to which *full disclosure* is obtained,
2. the extent to which *consistency* between years is obtained and
3. the extent to which all material transactions or events are properly recorded (materiality).

A second major principle that also has an impact on the relevance criterion is whether the accounting data and reports are understandable. Can the information be interpreted by a reasonably informed decision-maker? Accounting information is almost worthless if it is not relevant and understandable. Understandability implies minimal usage of technical terms and specialized jargon in accounting reports presented to non-accountants. Understandabilty requires that the accountant consider the communication process and whether the intended message is actually transmitted and received. It involves the encoding and decoding of signals between the accounting system (sender) and the decision-maker (recipient).

Relevance and understandability also involve timeliness. Accounting reports received after a decision has been made are worthless. Timely data is of the essence in most situations. Waiting two or three months for the books to be closed almost insures that the resulting statements will be filed and forgotten. Timeliness may require greater reliance on estimates. It may require some sacrifice of accuracy and completeness. In such cases, the accountant should provide a range of probable results and indicate the level of risk (or dispersion) associated with each estimate.

A fourth major principle of accounting that concerns healthcare organizations is comparability. Accounting data are often compared with some standard; that standard may be management's expectation, a criterion legislated by a regulatory agency, or results reported by a competing department or hospital. Accounting data that are not comparable are like half of a football score (21). In this era of HSAs and peer grouping, healthcare organizations must be increasingly concerned with the comparability of accounting data and reports.

The final major principle that must be satisfied is the reliability criterion. Reliability involves 1) verifiability and objectivity and 2) neutrality and freedom from bias. Verifiability is a subjective test of whether substantially the same results are reached by different accountants, with the same general qualifications, working independently with the same data base. Objectivity tests whether the results obtained by independent accountants are essentially similar and whether each fairly presents the results of operations and the financial position of the organization. Objectivity and verifiability both require that each transaction or event be properly supported by some form of underlying evidence in the form of source documents, statistics, analyses, etc. Both require that approximately similar conclusions be reached in similar circumstances by similar analysts.

The neutrality principle recognizes that most accounting data and reports must be designed for communication to a variety of decision-makers. Consequently, accounting data and reports must not be slanted or biased to favor a particular group of people. Any known bias must be explicitly disclosed so that the decision-maker can adjust or eliminate such bias. Neutral and unbiased accounting reports are probably never achieved. Bias must be minimized within the cost/benefit resource constraints, and the reports must be as neutral as possible within such constraints. Both management accountants and financial accountants (and independent auditors) must be aware of potential biases; such biases must be removed, if possible, or disclosed at a minimum.

In summary, accounting in healthcare organizations must be simultaneously concerned with providing relevant, reliable, understandable, timely and comparable data and reports. In some cases, reliability may be somewhat reduced to increase relevance and timeliness. In most cases, all five of these principles or criteria must be jointly satisfied at an acceptable level. There are other, less important principles that may be sacrificed to achieve the five major criteria that we have identified. For example, the principles of materiality, conservatism, realization, matching and going concern all rank lower than the five primary criteria identified earlier. The management accountant must be aware of Gresham's Law, where lower-order principles "drive out" or supersede higher-order criteria. In other words, the possibility exists that objective criteria may overwhelm subjective criteria. The five primary criteria that we have identified in this section are all subjective in nature. Since there are no numerical standards that would indicate acceptable levels of relevance, reliability, understandabilty, timeliness or comparability, the management accountant must be responsible for assessing whether these criteria have been satisfied.

Relationship between financial and managerial accounting

Management accounting must be oriented toward decisions made by managers within the organization. The focus is internal and it is on decisions. Consequently, the information prepared for, and used by, internal decision-makers must be relevant to that decision. Different cost information is accumulated for different purposes. Performance reports now have different objectives than budgets. Yet both may be prepared from the same data base. Therefore, the outputs of the management accounting process are usually unique and depend on the decision to be made.

On the other hand, the outputs of financial accounting are usually oriented toward external decision-makers. Bankers, government agencies, other auditors, third-party reimbursers, employees and community representatives all have a stake in the financial condition of the hospital. Such individuals need information that is presented in summary form and annually verified by independent CPAs. It usually must meet standards set by the Financial Accounting Standards Board (FASB) or standards that may be set by state authorities, HSAs or other types of regulatory agencies. In most cases, the standards prescribed by external agencies do not restrict the scope or type of information that can be used for internal decision purposes. For example, uniform charts of accounts only apply to reports prepared for the agency which is imposing the chart of accounts. They need not be used internally. In this age of computers, any computerized information system can be programmed to translate information into a variety of "uniform" formats. Commercial firms routinely prepare tax reports and financial statements according to different standards. For example, the information used for Medicare reporting and reimbursement has a different emphasis and format than the organization's annual audited financial statements.

It is suggested that a similar attitude may be adopted toward any set of uniform reporting or accounting requirements. In other words, the information system should be maintained in a manner that is most useful for managerial decision-making. Periodic performance reports can automatically be prepared to include the effects of particular decisions on reimbursable amounts from particular agencies. The computer can then be programmed to prepare the agency's particular financial statements in whatever detail and format the agency demands. Therefore, the health service organization's information system should first meet its own requirements. Secondly, it should have the flexibility to aggregate information according to the various standards of reporting that may be imposed on it.

The same philosophy can be applied to fund accounting requirements. Many hospitals use the AICPA *Hospital Audit Guide* as a basic guide to the preparation of annual and monthly financial statements. It is suggested that fund accounting is not particularly appropriate for managerial decision-making. Fund accounting may aggregate, or mask, the effects of managerial decisions. Fund transfers can distort the performance of any sector of the institution. The information that is usually appropriate for managerial decision-making depends on the authority and responsibility of individual managers. Department managers should receive information about their particular departments and areas of operations. Assistant or associate administrators should receive information about the group of departments for which each is responsible. The chief executive officer or administrator should have access to information about the entire organization. However, the partitions imposed by fund accounting may not conform to the decentralized locus of decision-making. If not, the accountant, and particularly the management accountant, must match the type of information available with the authority and responsibility of the particular manager. At the top levels of administration, it is suggested that different funds be consolidated and that the effects of inter-fund transactions be eliminated. This is a subject for advanced accounting that cannot be explored in this book. In any event, a CPA or certified management accountant (CMA) should be able to assist in solving this problem.

Total financial requirements

One of the major problems encountered in using accounting information is that most accounting systems do not report on the total financial requirements of healthcare organizations. Many valid financial requirements such as working capital needs, contingency reserves and replacement of existing assets are not routinely shown in the financial statements. Yet identifying and fulfilling these needs is an important part of the hospital management function. One example of displaying total financial requirements is shown in *Exhibit 1-2*. The total financial requirements concepts expressed in *Exhibit 1-2* remain valid in the context of prospective payment systems and discussions about cost shifting. Any healthcare organization must generate financial capital in sufficient amounts to assure long-run financial solvency and continued

Exhibit 1-2
Total financial requirements

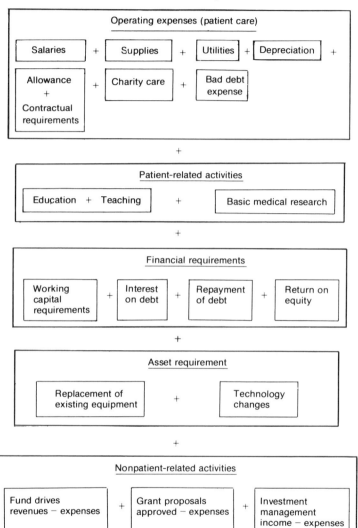

Operating expenses (patient care)

Salaries + Supplies + Utilities + Depreciation +

Allowance + Contractual requirements + Charity care + Bad debt expense

+

Patient-related activities

Education + Teaching + Basic medical research

+

Financial requirements

Working capital requirements + Interest on debt + Repayment of debt + Return on equity

+

Asset requirement

Replacement of existing equipment + Technology changes

+

Nonpatient-related activities

Fund drives revenues − expenses + Grant proposals approved − expenses + Investment management income − expenses

+

Planning requirements
Contingency reserves

=
Total financial requirements

effectiveness. The components of the total financial requirements diagram merely identify the different needs and application for financial capital. While each healthcare organization has recurring needs for financial resources in each of these areas, some needs are more critical at varying time periods. For example, fund drives occur sporadically, as does debt repayment. On the other hand, working capital needs and operating expenses occur daily.

This approach to determining total financial requirements is based on identifying the major areas of cost incurrence. There is usually general agreement on the necessity of meeting the current operating needs except in the categories of education and research. There is more disagreement among major cost-based reimbursers on how to handle credit losses and charity write-offs. In a similar manner, the debt retirement component of the capital cost area creates disagreement on whether repayment provisions must be recognized. Debt is usually repaid by most organizations by the excess of revenues over expenses. It seems clear that in a nonprofit hospital, this requirement must be covered explicitly instead of implicitly as is currently done.

The last area, appropriate levels of reserve and net income, usually involves the most disagreement in terms of inclusion in total financial requirements.

Except for the return on equity for investor-owned hospitals, the amounts needed for the various cost components are not typically recorded in the accounting records. There must be funds set aside for expansion and replacement of services and facilities. Adequate working capital is also a "sine qua non" for any organization which offers services before payment is made. Finally, unless the hospital management can predict the future perfectly, there must be a recognition of the uncertainty involved in the determination of total requirements. A contingency reserve provides this recognition. Determining total financial requirements presents a challenge to the hospital management accountant to provide adequate information for the decision-maker. The tools described in the remainder of the text will help meet this challenge.

Summary

The objective of this book is to improve managerial decision-making. Management accounting should provide information that will improve the efficiency and effectiveness of the use of economic resources. Many issues and problems will be discussed that cannot be fully solved. Therefore, each chapter contains a list of recommended readings. As particular issues arise, the reader is advised to refer to as many of the recommended readings as necessary to help solve the problem. Appendices at the end of the text contain related materials or excerpts from journal articles to provide additional insight into particular topics.

In many cases, the problems in each chapter, along with their solutions, provide additional specific guidance for using the recommended techniques.

It is intended that this book will help the reader develop specific techniques that can be implemented in his/her hospital or department. These techniques should lead to more relevant managerial accounting data. As the quality of information improves, the quality of decisions *can* improve. Whether it does is up to the decision-maker. The mere presence of information will do nothing. It must be used in the decision process. If used correctly, it will help to improve managerial decisions. Generally, the cost of implementing any of these techniques will be minor compared to the benefit that can be obtained.

Questions and problems

1. Define the management control cycle for a healthcare organization.

2. Explain the four major objectives of accounting information for healthcare managers.

3. Define the concept of efficiency in healthcare organizations.

4. Define the concept of effectiveness in a healthcare organization.

5. Can an overemphasis on effectiveness interfere with the efficiency objective? Explain.

6. Why should hospital administrators be concerned with the format of the performance reports for their organizations?

7. Name several examples of output measurements for a healthcare organization.

8. Explain the concept of goal congruence in a healthcare organization.

9. Explain some of the difficulties that may occur when accounting statements prepared for external users are used for internal decision-making.

10. Define total financial requirements for a healthcare provider.

References

Anthony, Robert N. and David W. Young, *Management Control in Nonprofit Organizations,* Homewood, IL: Richard D. Irwin, 1984.

Anthony, Robert N. and James S. Reese, *Management Accounting,* 5th ed., Homewood, IL: Richard D. Irwin, 1978.

Fetter, Robert D., John D. Thompson, and John R. Kimberly, *Cases in Health Policy and Management,* Homewood, IL: Richard D. Irwin, 1985.

Hepner, James O. and Albert D. Ameiss, "Managerial Accounting: Keystone to Accounting Curriculum," *Hospital Financial Management,* February, 1979, pp. 47-52.

Long, Hugh W., "Valuation as a Criterion in Not-For-Profit Decision Making," *Health Care Management Review,* Summer, 1976, pp. 34-46.

Mistarz, Jo Ellen, "Cost Accounting: A Solution, But a Problem," *Hospitals,* October 1, 1984, pp. 96-101.

Silvers, J.B., "Identity Crisis: Financial Management in Health," *Health Care Management Review,* Fall, 1976, pp. 36-40.

Suver, James D., Charles N. Kahn, III, and Jan P. Clement, *Cases in Health Care Financial Management,* Washington, D.C.: AUPHA Press, 1984.

Young, David W. and Richard B. Saltman, "Prospective Reimbursement and the Hospital Power Equilibrium: A Matrix-Based Management Control System" *Inquiry* Vol. 20, Number 1, Sp. 83, pp. 20-33.

CHAPTER 2

Cost behavior patterns

Introduction

One of the most vital inputs into the effective use of management accounting techniques is an understanding of cost behavior patterns. The word "cost" itself can be a formidable barrier. For example: most costs can be defined in several ways, and the definition depends on the purpose to which the costs are applied. "How much does this service really cost?" is an extremely difficult question to answer. Do charges or fees measure costs? Usually not, depending on how the rate was developed. Charge rates do not generally provide an accurate measure of the full cost of providing hospital services. Cross-subsidization can occur in many departments. It is also not clear what the term "full cost" represents. It can and does have a different meaning depending upon its use. In this chapter, we will examine the components of the term "full cost" and develop a common foundation of cost terminology.

We will also examine the relationship of cost behavior to volume of services provided by the hospital. This chapter shows how hospital managers may answer the question, "How do costs vary as volume changes?"

Elements of cost

The basic elements of cost are materials, labor and administrative services (typically called overhead or support costs). These elements are usually expressed as either direct or indirect costs. Separation of direct and indirect costs is important in establishing a rate or charge structure for a particular service. Full costs are usually defined as the direct costs of providing a service plus some share of any indirect costs incurred by the hospital or the department. This relationship is shown in *Exhibit 2-1*.

Exhibit 2-1
Full cost components

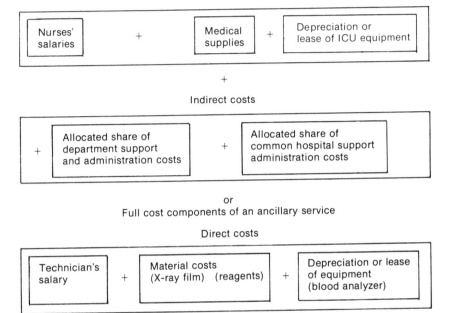

Full cost components of intensive care service

Direct costs

| Nurses' salaries | + | Medical supplies | + | Depreciation or lease of ICU equipment |

+

Indirect costs

| + | Allocated share of department support and administration costs | + | Allocated share of common hospital support administration costs |

or
Full cost components of an ancillary service

Direct costs

| Technician's salary | + | Material costs (X-ray film)   (reagents) | + | Depreciation or lease of equipment (blood analyzer) |

+

Indirect costs

| Allocated share of department's support administration | + | Allocated share of common hospital administration support cost |

Direct and indirect costs

Direct costs are generally defined as those costs which can be specifically traced to or identified with a specific procedure or service. An example would be the salary and fringe benefits of the professional and support personnel who contribute directly to the providing of a service or the monitoring of the equipment in an intensive care unit. In most hospital departments, this type of cost constitutes the major operating expense. Also included in the category of direct costs are materials such as lab supplies, special materials, etc., which are directly related to the providng of a service. It should be stressed here that the concept of direct costs is a function of the procedure under consideration. What is a direct cost for the entire hospital may not be a direct cost for an individual procedure or service. The salary of the administrator would be a direct cost of the hospital. However, it would not be a direct cost to individual services in the laboratory or surgery areas.

The salaries of nursing personnel would be a direct cost to a nursing unit and also to the entire hospital. Basically, one major criterion in deciding whether an item is a direct cost or not is whether the cost would be eliminated if the service were no longer provided. For example, if the intensive care unit were closed, the staff costs would no longer be incurred, hence, these costs are direct costs of the intensive care unit.

Indirect costs, on the other hand, are those costs which cannot be specifically traced to an individual service or procedure. Indirect costs will continue even if the particular service is no longer provided. Indirect costs include any cost that cannot be classified as a direct cost for the individual department. Some examples are office supplies and equipment, rent, general insurance and most management costs. Again, the definition of what is a direct or indirect cost depends upon the level of aggregation desired. Almost all costs could be considered direct at the hospital level; however, at the individual department level there are fewer direct costs and many more indirect costs. *Exhibit 2-2* indicates some possible cost categories for a laboratory department.

Exhibit 2-2
Typical cost categories in a laboratory department

Generally direct costs	Generally indirect costs
Individual supplies used for patient services	Secretaries' salaries
	Administration supplies
Laboratory personnel	Administration's salary
	Financial services
Equipment depreciation	Receptionist
	Library expenses
Equipment repair	Rent
	General insurance
	Fund raising
	General depreciation

The difference between direct and indirect costs is important to the administrator and to the department supervisor. There is generally no argument that direct costs of providing a service should be included in charges for that service. However, there is no such clear relationship for indirect costs. How much of the cost of hospital administration is caused by the patient care procedure? There is no cause/effect relationship; therefore, some method of allocation must be used to calculate full cost. For example, the cost of utilities will probably not vary directly with the volume of service provided, yet it is a cost of providing service. One method used in the case of utilities is to allocate the total utility cost on the basis of the square footage of the space used to provide the service. The choice of an allocation base will naturally influence the allocated portion of full costs. Allocation problems will be discussed in greater detail in later chapters, as allocation of indirect costs is a troublesome issue in rate-setting and management decision-making.

Many managers tend to ignore the existence of indirect costs and base their charges on direct costs. If indirect costs are small, or if the costs are aggregated at a high level in the organization, the resulting charges may approximate the full cost of providing that service. However, in most departments there are many different procedures or services, each with its own direct cost structure. Because the supervisory costs and other department administration costs support all services, they are not a direct cost of any specific service and, therefore, must be treated as an indirect cost and allocated to responsibility centers.

Cost/volume relationships

One key to the effective use of management accounting techniques is an understanding of how certain costs react to changes in volume. How does the number of patients affect costs? If more laboratory tests are performed, how will costs change? The relationship of costs to volume is an important concept for managers to understand. If hospital administrators want to be able to control costs as volume of services changes, they must be able to use this concept analytically and to incorporate it into their decision models.

Generally, costs can be divided into two categories: fixed and variable. Variable costs are those costs which vary directly and proportionately with volume. For example, if costs associated with a certain procedure increase 10 percent with a 10 percent increase in volume, those costs would be classified as variable. Many direct costs, such as supplies, are examples of pure variable costs since they increase in proportion to the number of services performed.

Conversely, fixed costs are those costs that do not vary with volume. Most indirect costs such as rent, insurance or taxes, are examples of fixed costs. A good example of a fixed cost would be a professional staff or supportive personnel who are paid on a salary basis. In other words, their salaries do not increase directly with the number of services provided. The word "fixed" should not imply that the costs cannot be changed, but rather that they do not change as a result of volume. The salary of a clerk typist may be changed, but this change would be caused by a specific management decision, not by any increase in volume of patients or services provided. On the other hand, the number of clerk typists may increase as the volume of typing goes up. Therefore, these salaries are variable in relation to typing volume.

A third type of cost category is semivariable cost. These costs vary in the same direction as volume, but not proportionally. For example, if the number of procedures changes by 10 percent, costs in the semi-variable category would increase, but they would increase less than 10 percent. Nursing costs can fall into this category, along with some maintenance, clerical and utility costs. *Exhibit 2-3* illustrates an example of this type of cost. Semivariable costs can usually be separated into their variable and fixed components by techniques discussed in Chapters 4, 12 and 13. Once this separation is made, they can be treated the same as other fixed and variable costs.

Exhibit 2-3
Semivariable costs for nursing supervisors

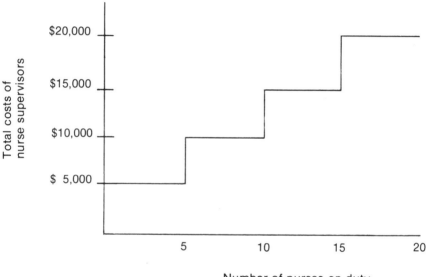

Number of nurses on duty

Several key points should be made here. Most variable costs (per procedure) are assumed to be linear. That is, if the variable cost of one procedure is $8, the variable cost of the second procedure is also $8, and the total variable cost for two procedures is $16. One can test this by checking what the total variable cost would be for three procedures. Does the cost per procedure change? Variable cost behavior is graphically portrayed in *Exhibit 2-4*.

Two key points should be stressed concerning fixed costs: 1) total fixed costs do not vary with volume, and 2) as *Exhibit 2-5* indicates, the average fixed cost per patient decreases as the number of patients increases. This occurs because a fixed amount is divided by a larger number of patients as volume increases. *Exhibit 2-6* displays the data from *Exhibit 2-5* in tabular form.

Exhibit 2-4
Variable costs

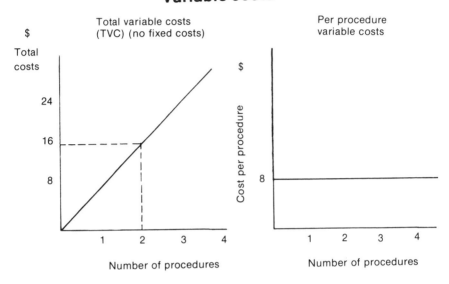

Exhibit 2-5
Fixed costs

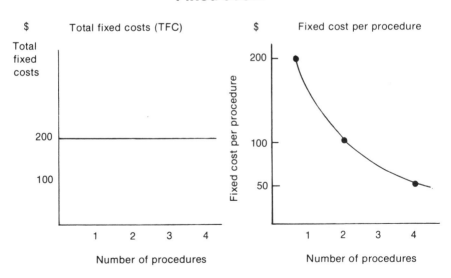

Exhibit 2-6
Total fixed costs $200
Average fixed cost per procedure

(1) Number of procedures	(2) Average fixed costs	(3) Total fixed cost (1 x 2 = 3)
1	$200	$200
2	100	200
3	67	200
4	50	200

The declining average fixed cost per procedure highlights an important cost concept for managers. For example, with the data in *Exhibits 2-4* and *2-6*, what price should be established to cover the full cost? It should be apparent that the estimate used for the number of procedures expected is vital in determing a fair price. Let us assume the laboratory has a variable cost of $8 per visit and fixed costs of $200. The results shown in *Exhibit 2-7* would be obtained.

Exhibit 2-7
Full cost determination

(1) Estimated number of procedures	(2) Average variable cost	(3) Average fixed cost	(4) Full cost per procedure (2 + 3 = 4)
1	$8	$200	$208
2	8	100	108
3	8	67	75
4	8	50	58
5	8	40	48
6	8	33	41

In another example, consider the difficulty of determining the full cost of operating an emergency room. Most of the costs are usually fixed, with the exception of medical supplies and some recordkeeping. In a typical emergency room, the fixed costs probably approximate 90 percent of the total cost of this service. The estimate of the number of patients using the emergency room will be crucial in determining the cost per visit. Assume the following facts:

1. Total emergency room fixed cost is $60,000 per month.
2. Variable costs per unit are $1.
3. Estimated number of patient visits is 5,000.

The cost per patient visit would be:

$$\frac{60,000}{5,000} + \$1 = \$13.$$

If the estimated number of patients to be seen is changed to 4,000, the cost becomes:

$$\frac{60,000}{4,000} + \$1 = \$16.$$

It is generally more conservative, from a hospital's point of view, to estimate volume on the low side. For example, in our previous problem, the patient volume is estimated to be 6,000 visits. Given this estimate, the cost per patient visit becomes:

$$\frac{60,000}{6,000} + \$1 = \$11.$$

If charges are based on the high volume estimate (6,000 visits) and the low volume (4,000 visits) actually occurs, the hospital could run into difficulty with reimbursement based on the lower of cost or charges.

It is imperative to stress that direct and variable costs are not necessarily synonymous. Direct costs are those that can be traced to a single procedure or program. Variable costs are costs that vary with the change in volume of procedures. Most variable costs are also direct costs, but not all direct costs are variable.

For example, the laboratory materials used in a procedure are a variable cost because the costs increase proportionately with the number of procedures. The cost of these materials would also be a direct cost. The cost of the equipment used in the procedure would also be a direct cost, but it would not be a variable cost because the total cost of the machine is not affected by the number of procedures performed (unless it is leased on a units of service basis or the capacity of the equipment is exceeded).

A determination of which costs are direct is very useful in assigning responsibility for cost control, as will be discussed in Chapter 7. At the same time, the separation of cost categories into fixed and variable is absolutely necessary to determine the full cost of a given number of procedures or services.

Estimating the variable cost component

The determination of the variable cost component can be accomplished by several methods. The most obvious one is direct inspection of the cost category. For example, the chemicals used in a lab test, the film for an X-ray scan and the fee charged for a physician's visit are all variable costs in relation to the volume of activity performed. It is also usually possible to separate the costs which are entirely fixed such as administrative salaries, plant depreciation and housekeeping.

The difficult task is estimating the costs that have both a fixed and variable component. Nursing salaries can fall into this category. So can telephone service that has a flat rate plus so much per call. Dietary costs are usually mixed or semivariable. Several statistical methods for estimating the variable costs associated with providing a specific service will be discussed in detail in Chapters 3 and 13. These techniques include regression analysis, statistical sampling and exploratory data analysis.

A simple assumption that can be used to estimate the variable cost component relative to the levels of volume is that only the variable costs should change. For example, given the information in *Exhibit 2-8*, the variable costs could be estimated by using the high-low technique.

Exhibit 2-8
Variable cost determination

Volume	Nursing hours	Total costs
July	2,200	$14,650
August	1,200	11,350
September	2,500	17,050
October	3,000	17,650
November	1,700	13,100
December	1,600	12,900

High volume	Low volume	Difference
(Oct.) 3,000 hrs.	(Aug.) 1,200 hrs.	1,800 hrs.

Related total costs		
(Oct.) $17,650	(Aug.) $11,350	$ 6,300

Difference in total costs/difference in hours
= variable cost per hour
or
$6,300/1,800 = $3.50 variable cost per hour

The amount of total fixed costs (TFC) can be determined in the following manner:

Total costs = TFC + total variable costs
Total costs at volume of 3,000 hours = $17,650
Total variable costs = 3,000 × $3.50 = $10,500
Therefore: $17,650 = TFC + $10,500
TFC = $17,650 − $10,500 = $7,150

Using either the high or low volume total will yield the same fixed cost estimate. The reader may easily verify this assertion.

In this type of estimating, the high and low volume points are selected as representative totals of the entire distribution; this may not always be the case. A technique which offers a visual presentation of the cost behavior is called a scatter diagram. In a scatter diagram, the various volume/total cost relationships are plotted as shown in *Exhibit 2-9*. A straight line is visually fitted to the data points with the total fixed costs being indicated at the intersection of the curve and the y-axis. Once the fixed costs have been determined, the variable costs can be estimated using the methodology shown in *Exhibit 2-8*.

Exhibit 2-9
Volume/total cost relationships

Volume of service	Total costs
1,000	$2,000
2,000	3,000
3,000	4,000
4,000	5,000
5,000	6,000
6,000	7,000
7,000	8,000

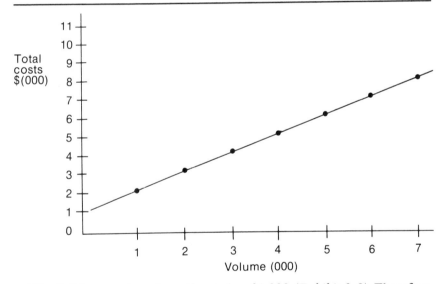

The "y" intercept can be estimated as $1,000 *(Exhibit 2-9)*. Therefore, fixed costs are estimated at $1,000. Given this information, the variable costs can be determined using the same methodology as the high-low method. In this example, the variable costs are $1 per unit of service. The least squares method discussed in Chapter 13 would provide a much more accurate determination.

Differences in the terminology and application of fixed and variable costs exist in different healthcare organizations. The following debate, reported by Mistarz (1984), illustrates these various views:

> How much detail is needed in breaking down costs, and how far a hospital should go in constructing a matrix of costs, can be debated. But in order to

break down costs to the procedure level, Truman Esmond, president of Truman, Esmond & Associates, advises that hospitals should first break down operations. For example, laboratories could be one unit, and they could be broken down into discrete subunits. Tests can be broken down, he says, because certain tests are for hematology, some are for chemistry, and others for nuclear medicine.

"You may or may not be able to break these down into discrete sorting units in your laboratory," Esmond says, but the goal is to create discrete costing units not based on averaging. After breaking down operations into discrete units, he explains, the laboratory example can be broken into fixed and variable components. Costs are allocated to the laboratory, to radiology, and to other places. Ultimately, these costs are allocated to a procedure.

Not all panel members agreed with the total methodology. Neil Bennett, vice-president and regional director, Pacific Southwest region, American Medical International, Inc. (AMI), stated that AMI "firmly does not use the term 'fixed'. That hospital is not fixed. That executive director is not fixed. Nothing is fixed."

He explains that a laboratory manager may be regarded as a fixed cost at other hospitals. But that manager's responsibilities could be changed, and that person could become the manager of both laboratory and radiology departments. "So I don't have a fixed cost in the laboratory department," he says.

Regardless of variations in terminology and methodology, the need for a costing system remains. "Basically, what we're talking about is modeling to develop the impact of change on the institution by changes in mix or volume. Hospitals really need to use a number of grids, or matrixes, because the whole product-line format changes. At one point we may be talking about DRGs; at another, about physical organizations or subspecialties; and at still another, the major service categories," Esmond explains.

Esmond comments that "in terms of where we are in costing, there's a possibility of going way overboard." But, he adds, many hospitals do not go far enough. "A focus on DRGs seems to be the only horizontal breakdown in most places. At many institutions, you see that not all patients are included in the matrix. Medicare patients are on the matrix, for example, and other patients are not. In some cases, we're still talking about DRGs, and in some cases it's general," he observes. What's appropriate depends upon the institution and its circumstances, he notes.

Five years ago, Esmond continues, the technology was not available. "Today, a hospital manager can ask, 'Why do I need this information? This system?' The choice involves what a hospital needs and what it wants a system for. Once it answers the questions, a match can be made with a system," he says.

Summary

In this chapter, cost behavior patterns have been identified. A thorough understanding of cost behavior patterns can help in establishing charges or rates based on full costs. It can also help to improve management analysis and cost containment. In Chapter 4 we will further develop the concept of fixed and variable costs in terms of the flexible budget concept.

Questions and problems

1. Are costs described in this chapter identical to revenues for a hospital? Discuss.

2. Define each of the following as a direct or indirect cost of the operation of the hospital's physical plant.
   a. Supplies used for maintenance of facilities.
   b. Supervisory salaries.
   c. Costs of electrical power for the hospital.
   d. Costs of electrical power for the maintenance department.
   e. Liability insurance premiums paid for any injuries by people coming to the hospital.
   f. A two-year lease for lawn maintenance equipment.
   g. Maintenance on the physical facilities.
   h. Depreciation on facilities.
   i. Telephone expenses for the maintenance department.
   j. Employer's share of social security taxes paid by the department.

3. Using the list above, determine whether these activities represent fixed or variable expenses.

4. Do total variable costs remain constant with changes in volume? Discuss.

5. Costs are fixed or variable only in relationship to a given time period. Discuss.

6. Do the providers of hospital care and third-party reimbursers use the same definition of costs? Discuss.

7. In many hospitals, a radiologist is contracted to provide services and receive a percentage of gross revenues. Would we classify this as a fixed or variable cost? As a direct or indirect expense? Discuss.

8. A group of doctors formed a group practice. In their efforts to determine a price to charge their patients they want to break all costs into fixed and variable costs. While they agree that rent represents a fixed cost, there is considerable debate about whether the power bill should be a fixed or variable expense. Discuss.

9. The present practice in hospitals is to define costs in terms of patient days. There is currently a growing movement toward the development of the concept of costs per case mix. Discuss the type of problems encountered in the use of these concepts.

10. Unit costs decrease as volume increases. Explain. Is this statement always true? Provide examples.

11. How can an analysis of each item of a budget be used to separate the semivariable costs into their fixed and variable elements?

12. The supervisor of the diagnostic radiology department furnished the following information concerning cost behavior in his department:

Volume	Total cost
5,000 procedures	$100,000
7,000 procedures	116,000

Determine the fixed and variable costs per procedure for the department.

13. The laboratory department had the following costs for the preceding six months:

	Jan.	Feb.	Mar.	Apr.	May	June
total tests	2,000	2,800	2,600	3,000	2,400	2,600
Total costs	$8,000	$9,600	$9,300	$9,900	$8,700	$9,500

Required:
a. Estimate fixed and variable costs by the high-low method.
b. Estimate fixed and variable costs by drawing a scatter diagram.
c. If tests in a certain month are estimated to be 2,500 units, what is your estimate of total costs?

14. Community Hospital has an average occupancy rate of 80 percent per month based on 100 licensed beds. At this level of occupancy, the hospital's per diem costs are $120 per occupied bed per day assuming a 30-day month. This per diem rate includes both a fixed and variable cost element. During the month of April, the occupancy rate was 70 percent and actual costs were:

fixed costs	$180,000
semivariable costs	$102,000

Required:
a. Determine the total fixed costs for the month of April.
b. Determine the variable cost per occupied bed per day.
c. What would you have expected the total per diem costs to be for the 85 percent occupancy level?

15. The number of X-rays taken and X-ray costs over the last twelve months in Beverly Hospital are given below:

Month	X-rays taken	X-ray costs
January	6,250	$28,000
February	7,000	29,000
March	5,000	23,000
April	4,250	20,000
May	4,500	22,000
June	3,000	17,000
July	3,750	18,000
August	5,500	24,000
September	5,750	26,000
October	6,100	27,000
November	6,350	28,500
December	6,200	28,000

Required:
a. Using the high-low method, determine the formula for X-ray costs.
b. What X-ray costs would you expect to be incurred during a month in which 4,600 X-rays are taken?
c. Prepare a scattergraph using the twelve month data. Plot cost on the vertical axis and activity on the horizontal axis. Fit a regression line to your plotted points by visual inspection.
d. What is the approximate monthly fixed cost for X-rays? The approximate variable cost per X-ray taken?
e. Scrutinize the points on your graph, and explain why the high-low method would or would not yield an accurate cost formula in this situation.

16. Speedy Laundry Service operates a fleet of delivery trucks in a large metropolitan area. A careful study by the company's costs analyst has determined that if a truck is driven 120,000 miles during a year, the operating cost is 11.6 cents per mile. If a truck is driven only 70,000 miles during a year, the operating cost increases to 14.0 cents per mile.

    a. Using the high-low method, determine the variable and fixed cost elements of the annual cost of truck operation.

    b. Express the variable and fixed costs in the form Y = a + bX.

    c. If a truck were driven 100,000 miles during a year, what total costs would you expect to be incurred?

17. Perkins Hospital experiences considerable fluctuation in its utilities costs from month to month according to the number of machine-hours worked in its energy center. The company has plotted utilities costs at various levels of activity on a graph, and the plotted points indicate that total utilities cost is a mixed cost in the form Y = a + bX. Machine-hours of activity and total utilities cost over the last six months are given below:

Month	Machine-hours (000)	Total Utilities Cost
January	9	$14,000
February	12	17,000
March	16	20,000
April	21	23,000
May	18	21,000
June	14	19,000

Using graphs and the high-low method determine the cost formula for utilities cost.

18. The data below have been taken from the cost records of the Atlanta Hospital. The data relate to the cost of operating one department at various levels of activity:

Month	Units processed	Total cost
January	8,000	$14,000
February	4,500	10,000
March	7,000	12,500
April	9,000	15,500
May	3,750	10,000
June	6,000	12,500
July	3,000	8,500
August	5,000	11,500

    a. Prepare a scattergraph by plotting the above data on a graph. Plot cost on the vertical axis and activity on the horizontal axis. Fit a regression line to your plotted points by visual inspection.

   b. What is the approximate monthly fixed cost? The approximate
       variable cost per unit processed? Show computations.

19. Long-term Corp, Inc., has a total of 2,000 rooms in its nationwide
    chain of nursing homes. On the average, 80 percent of the rooms are
    occupied each month. The company's operating costs are $7 per
    occupied room per day at this occupancy level, assuming a 30-day
    month. This $7 cost figure contains both variable and fixed cost
    elements. During October, the occupancy rate was only 65 percent.
    Some $316,000 in operating costs were incurred during the month.
    a. Determine the variable cost per occupied room per day.
    b. Determine the total fixed operating costs per month.
    c. Assume an occupancy rate of 70 percent. What total operating
        costs would you expect the company to incur?

References

Cleverley, William O., *Essentials of Hospital Finance,* Germantown, MD: Aspen
    Systems Corporation, 1978, Chapter 5.
Herkimer, Allen G., Jr., *Understanding Hospital Financial Management,*
    Germantown, MD: Aspen Systems Corporation, 1978, Chapter 3.
Mistarz, Jo Ellen, "Cost Accounting: A Solution, But a Problem," *Hospitals,*
    October 1, 1984, pp. 96-101.
Silvers, J.B. and Colombatore K. Prahalad, *Financial Management of Health
    Institutions,* Flushing, NY: Spectrum Publications, Inc., 1974.

Identification of cost behavior patterns

Introduction

This book repeatedly emphasizes the concept that knowledge of cost behavior in healthcare organizations will usually improve the managerial decision-making in such organizations. An increased understanding of cost behavior can improve the quality and effectiveness of management control in healthcare organizatons. It can lead to improved efficiency and better cost control. At the highest level, managers who obtain and use information about the behavior of hospital costs can improve their efforts to achieve cost containment without sacrificing quality of care objectives.

As emphasized previously, the concept of cost behavior requires relating changes in costs to changes in some activity. Cost behavior relies on understanding the association or relation between costs and activities or services. In most cases, the activities, services or outputs are observable, often tangible, events. They can be objectively counted and recorded. Costs are recorded in the organization's information system according to the chart of accounts. They may be departmental costs, administrative costs or patient costs.

A healthcare organization that is first attempting to develop information about cost behavior patterns may be required to revise its chart of accounts. Perhaps the existing cost data are so aggregated, or contain so many arbitrary overhead cost allocations, that no usable cost behavior patterns could possibly be identified. If so, the techniques described in this chapter must be preceded by the necessary revisions in the accounting system. Revising or refining the accounting system is beyond the scope of this book. The current chapter presumes that the cost data are accurately recorded in elemental units of direct and indirect costs. If the cost data are in a highly summarized format, or if they contain costs allocated from other departments or responsibility centers, any resulting cost behavior patterns must be used with extreme caution. For example, cost data that have passed through a stepdown cost allocation process may only reflect the allocation techniques rather than an underlying relationship with health services activities.

As indicated above, the purpose of identifying cost behavior relationships is to improve decision-making. The primary improvement in decision-making that can occur is to improve a manager's prediction of future costs. Prediction of future costs is relevant to planning and budgeting. Cost predictions are used in the determination of standard costs. Better cost predictions will also improve management control because they make the feedback comparison of actual costs to budgeted costs more meaningful. Better cost predictions make it possible to find out why deviations occurred; this can lead to making changes in operating policies and procedures. In other words, as the prediction of expected costs improves, so also do management planning and control. Knowledge of cost behavior patterns is essential to better cost prediction.

Cost predictions should be as accurate as feasible. Managers should spend time and money to improve cost predictions so that the extra benefit of better cost predictions approximates the extra costs of obtaining better information. This is a cost-benefit criterion applied to the analysis of cost behavior. Managers should use the set of techniques described in this chapter to determine cost behavior patterns so that the analysis does not cost more than it is worth. The implicit question that must be asked about many of these techniques is: Will more accurate information change the decision I would have made with the information that is now available? If more accurate information will not reduce the risk or uncertainty, or if it will not change a recommended solution, the currently available information is probably sufficient. If not, additional techniques must be used to obtain more accurate cost predictions. Since more accurate cost predictions are a function of how much managers know about cost behavior patterns, the techniques described in this chapter can be used to identify the relevant cost behavior relationships. The remainder of the chapter describes different ways of identifying cost behavior patterns.

General guidelines

The purpose of cost behavior models is to identify and reflect the relationship between costs and activities in the hospital. The financial manager can never hope to uncover an exact and true relationship. If this relationship can be approximated or estimated with a low degree of error, the particular cost behavior pattern can be used with reasonable confidence.

As noted earlier, the basic goal is to be able to predict the costs if the activities are known or planned. A desirable state of affairs would be to identify a cause-and-effect relationship. If the manager knows that the activities cause the costs to occur, a cost behavior model that incorporates the causal variables is probably the most usable model that could be identified. However, causal relationships are not essential to the identification of cost behavior patterns. All a cost behavior model really has to accomplish is the accurate prediction of costs given a knowledge of the activities that will simultaneously occur. If a good long-term relationship can be shown between season of the year and administrative costs, that knowledge can be used to accurately predict future administrative costs. Many cost behavior patterns that are not causally related can be identified and used to good advantage by managers of healthcare organizations.

There are several important prerequisites to the identification of a cost behavior model. One obvious first step is to select the cost that is to be predicted. The cost that serves as the object of the cost behavior model is often called the dependent or criterion variable. The financial analyst wishes to predict costs that are dependent on some other activity or observable event. It may be called the criterion variable because the ultimate criterion of the goodness of the model depends on how well the actual costs match the predicted (criterion) costs.

The second step is to choose an action, or a set of actions or events, that will permit prediction of the dependent variable. The actions or events are called independent variables or predictor variables because they are used to predict the criterion or dependent variable. Most cost behavior models can be expressed in a form indicated by the following functional relationships:

$$\text{costs} = f(\text{activities}),$$
$$\text{dependent variable} = f(\text{independent variables}) \text{ or}$$
$$\text{criterion variable} = f(\text{predictor variables}).$$

If there is only one predictor variable, the cost behavior model is a univariate model. If there is more than one independent variable, the model is multivariate in dimension. Managers in healthcare organizations should try to identify a variety of possible predictor variables and select the set of predictor variables that provides the best cost behavior model. In other words, the starting point in identifying cost behavior models is to choose a cost to be predicted and a set of possible predictor variables. By refining the set of predictor variables, the cost behavior model can usually be successively improved. The optimal set of predictor variables is that set of independent variables that results in the best possible prediction of the cost.

Having identified the variables that will be used in the cost behavior model, the next step is to identify possible forms of the model. Cost behavior models are either linear or nonlinear. A linear cost behavior model can be expressed as a straight line. The equation for a straight line is usually of the form:

$$y = a + bx$$

In this case, "y" represents the criterion variable, "x" represents the predictor variable and "a" and "b" are the coefficients of the model. A straight line can be graphed as shown in *Exhibit 3-1*. This graph shows that "a" is the intercept of the line on the "y" axis and "b" is the slope of the line. The slope can be intuitively thought of as "rise" over "run," or the difference in the "y" values for any two points divided by the difference in the "x" values for the same two points. The slope of the line in *Exhibit 3-1* is calculated as:

$$\text{slope} = \frac{y_2 - y_1}{x_2 - x_1} = \frac{\text{rise}}{\text{run}} = \frac{3 - 2}{4 - 2} = \frac{1}{2}$$

Exhibit 3-1
Graph of a straight line

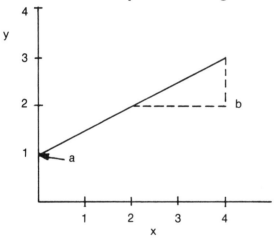

$$\text{Slope} = \frac{3 - 2}{4 - 2} = \frac{1}{2}$$

For every increase in x, y increases by half the increase in x.

The slope can be interpreted as any increase in "x" of two units results in an associated increase in "y" of one unit. The criterion variable in this case increases half as fast as the predictor variable. A slope of 3.0 would indicate that every increase in "x" is accompanied by a corresponding threefold increase in "y". Similarly, an increase of 100 manhours (x) would be associated with a $300 increase in supply costs (y).

Nonlinear cost behavior models can be expressed as univariate or as multivariate. A typical univariate nonlinear model would be an exponential model of the form $y = b^x$.

This model is illustrated in *Exhibit 3-2*. However, univariate nonlinear models have not been identified as useful or relevant to healthcare organizations. Of more relevance is a whole set of linear multivariate models; we will discuss those in more detail in Chapter 13. Note that any cost behavior model with more than two dimensions cannot be graphed on a flat surface; therefore, we will not attempt to graphically illustrate more complex nonlinear models.

Exhibit 3-2
Graph of an exponential model

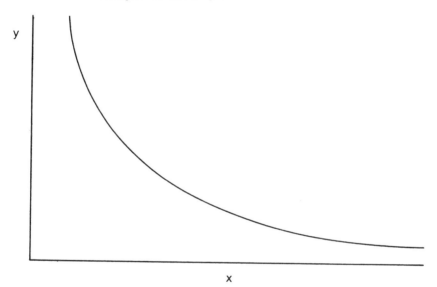

Another important step in the process of identifying cost behavior models in healthcare organizations is to evaluate the input data that will be used as the basis for the cost behavior model. The GIGO principle (garbage-in, garbage-out) can be a significant problem unless the healthcare financial manager takes time to evaluate and understand the input data. A scatter diagram of the input data is the single most important factor that can be used to evaluate the input data.

A scatter diagram is nothing more than a plot of the data. Usually the cost data are plotted against each of the potential predictor variables. For example, a scatter diagram of supply costs versus time is contrasted with a scatter diagram of supply costs versus surgical procedures in *Exhibit 3-3*. These relationships show that time will not be very useful in predicting supply costs, although season obviously has some effect.

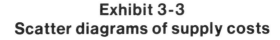

Exhibit 3-3
Scatter diagrams of supply costs

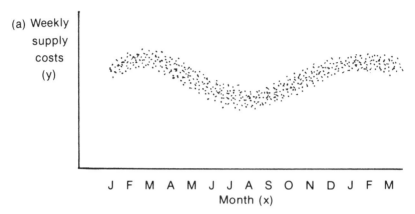

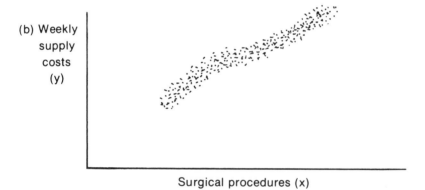

Exhibit 3-3b illustrates a scatter diagram for a variable cost relationship that could be expressed simply as the equation of a straight line. In this case supply costs have a definite linear relationship with surgical procedures. The techniques described later in this chapter will develop the specific methodologies for identifying this type of single predictor variable cost behavior model. On the other hand, the pattern of costs shown in *Exhibit 3-3a* would require a nonlinear cost behavior model. Without more data observation, it is hard to determine whether the cyclical (seasonal) patterns repeat themselves with enough regularity to justify pursuing the search for a relationship between supply costs and time.

Exhibit 3-3 illustrates the fact that one of the important contributions of a scatter diagram is to identify the form of alternative cost behavior models. Scatter diagrams help the manager discard unimportant predictor variables; they also help identify possible nonlinear relationships. Since one of the objectives of a cost behavior model is to make the best possible cost predictions at the lowest possible cost, the healthcare analyst is well advised to first pursue linear cost behavior models and to avoid nonlinear relationships unless they become absolutely necessary.

The second important contribution of a scatter diagram is to help identify the relevant range for the cost behavior model. The relevant range may be restricted to specific quantities of activities or to specific time periods. For example, very few hospitals would like to build cost behavior models for either 20 percent or 150 percent occupancy levels. However, some departments may have wide fluctuations in utilization, and a 40 percent utilization factor may be typical in those departments. Another example would be two hospitals that merged a year ago; very little of the data pertaining to the premerger period would be consistent with observations from the postmerger period. The point is that a scatter diagram can help isolate the relevant range of utilization that is expected to be most typical. It helps identify the activity levels that will serve as inputs to the identification of the cost behavior model.

Scatter diagrams also can be used to jointly identify a linear model over the relevant range. The scatter diagram in *Exhibit 3-4* illustrates two nonlinear segments and one linear segment. If the relevant range happens to coincide with the linear segment, the cost behavior model can be estimated with much greater reliability than if some model had to be identified that fit all three segments.

Exhibit 3-4
Linear and nonlinear scatter diagrams

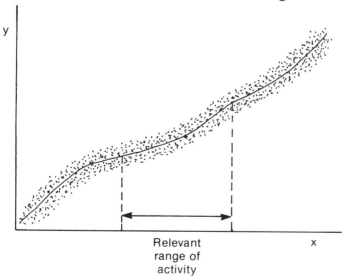

A final role that scatter diagrams have in the determination of cost behavior patterns is to help identify and eliminate erroneous or inconsistent data. In most cases, scatter diagrams will include several extreme observations; usually these extreme points are called outliers. *Exhibit 3-5* is an exact replica of *Exhibit 3-3b* except that several outliers have been added as asterisks.

Exhibit 3-5
Scatter diagram with outliers

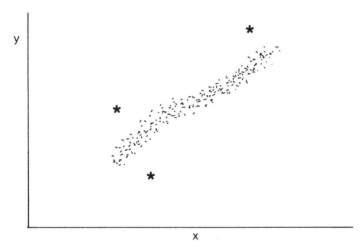

Each of the three outliers in *Exhibit 3-5* must be investigated to determine if it is either the result of erroneous data or if it reflects some event that will not be repeated (or expected to be repeated). If an outlier is a function of an identifiable error, the error should be corrected if at all possible. If the error cannot be corrected, the outlier should be discarded from the data base. If the outlier is a result of some nonrecurring event, it should also be eliminated. In some cases, outliers can be used to help predict what will happen under the same conditions that originally occurred. However, in most cases outliers that are due to random, nonrecurring events, or to events that are not part of the normal operations of the hospital (e.g., a strike, a boiler explosion or some other natural disaster), should be eliminated from the data base. Scatter diagrams should then be redrawn without the outliers.

In summary, the healthcare financial manager must be aware of several potential data problems that can affect cost behavior patterns. Scatter diagrams help identify the nature of the problem and permit the analyst to estimate the severity of the problem. A number of potential data problems are listed in *Exhibit 3-6*.

The final problem that complicates identification of cost behavior patterns is the need to make sure that appropriate techniques are being

Exhibit 3-6
Potential data problems affecting cost behavior patterns

1. Data not in the relevant range.

2. Data pertaining to time periods that reflect abnormal or nonrecurring operations.

3. Data stated in incompatible units; for example, pounds and ounces, kilowatts and kilowatt hours, quarts and liters, "paid" hours and "worked" hours, full-time equivalent employees and "head count" employees, etc.

4. Cost data that have been grossly affected by changing rates of inflation. In this case, price-level adjusted data should be considered.

5. Data that reflect clerical errors.

6. Data that reflect anomalies or other nonrecurring events.

7. Data that reflect significant cost allocations.

8. Data that are misclassified into the wrong accounts and/or the wrong departments.

9. Data that are misclassified according to cost behavior; for example, fixed costs classified as variable costs or vice versa. Another example would be fixed costs that have already been allocated on some basis (per hour, per patient or per patient day)* so that the costs now appear to be variable with some activity factor.

10. Data that have been recorded during start-up or transition phases. The learning curve effects on cost data must be anticipated, and cost behavior patterns should not be identified until any learning phenomena have stabilized.

used. For example, visual methods should not be used if precision and accuracy are critical. Complex mathematical models should not be used if simpler models can provide acceptable results. In addition, the assumptions inherent in the model must be consistent with the data base. This last caveat pertains primarily to statistical techniques that can be used to identify cost behavior patterns. If the statistical assumptions or conditions of the data base are not met, the results may be so distorted as to be useless or deceiving. We will discuss these assumptions later in Chapter 13 in conjunction with the different statistical techniques.

Other types of nonlinear costs that may cause concern for healthcare financial managers are step-function costs. Step costs are usually fixed costs that have discrete increments, or steps, as activity increases. For example, each step may represent the employment of an additional employee. Alternatively, the steps may be salary increments as specified in union agreements. *Exhibit 3-7* illustrates three types of step-function costs.

Exhibit 3-7
Step-function costs

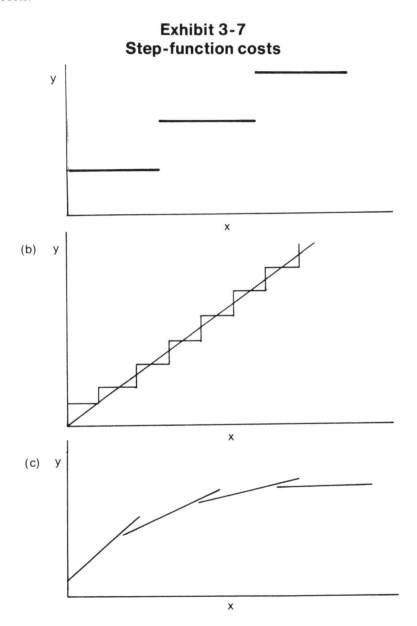

In each of the cost behavior patterns illustrated in *Exhibit 3-7,* costs (y) jump to a different level for small changes in activity (x). The step costs shown in *Exhibit 3-7b* can easily be approximated by a straight line because each step is of uniform height and width. The other two step cost patterns are much more irregular, and any straight-line approximation will yield grossly incorrect cost predictions at many different levels of activity. The pattern shown in *Exhibit 3-7c* is an obvious candidate for a nonlinear relationship; the shape of that relationship could be easily determined. However, the step costs in *Exhibit 3-7a* are all fixed costs that cannot be approximated by a single cost equation. On the other hand, the step costs in both 3-7a or 3-7c can be conveniently expressed by a straight line, as long as the manager can operate within the volume of activity (relevant range) embodied by any single line segment. For example, if the manager can be reasonably sure that operations will be at the extreme right side of either 3-7a or 3-7c, the appropriate cost behavior pattern is simply a fixed cost. That fixed cost relationship will provide accurate cost predictions only if operations continue at the upper levels of (x) activity. As activities contract, other line segments will become relevant, and cost predictions must rely on different cost equations. The point to remember is that any cost behavior pattern is accurate and useful only within a limited relevant range of volume. As operations move outside of that relevant range, new cost behavior patterns may supersede the original cost equations.

Physical observation of cost behavior patterns

The next three sections of this chapter will describe different ways of identifying cost behavior patterns. The three techniques are physical observation, logical observation and statistical analysis. No single technique is suitable under all conditions. Rather, each technique should be used wherever it can lead to the best prediction of costs at the least effort. In addition, these techniques may be used in combination with each other where the results from one phase of the analysis can be used to confirm results from earlier phases. One of the three major ways to identify cost behavior patterns is to observe and measure the relationship of costs to activities. Physical observation is the most direct, and usually the most costly, way to identify cost behavior patterns. It is the technique best suited to identifying causal relationships because the accountant or engineer conducting the analysis can actually verify the direction of causality.

Physical observation can also be called the industrial engineering approach because it includes work measurement and time-and-motion studies. It is also normative in the sense that engineers search for the best possible way to accomplish each objective. The industrial engineering approach to cost behavior patterns may involve all the techniques noted below. However, the factor that differentiates it from these other techniques is that one of the initial steps is to physically monitor the existing process.

In healthcare organizations, the physical monitoring may also take place at other sites. For example, the industrial engineering programs develop normative productivity standards for nursing, housekeeping, dietary, laundry, etc. These productivity standards, initially determined by physical observation, are continuously revised and updated as a result of ongoing monitoring in a few hospitals. After extensive testing of these normative standards, industrial engineers may generalize productivity standards to a variety of hospital and healthcare organizations. Different standards have been established for individual institutional sites and organization structures.

The physical observation technique is also used to identify and determine standard costs. It starts by reviewing the actual supplies, labor and other overhead elements that are presently used to provide healthcare. Time-and-motion studies and other evaluations of people's capabilities and skills serve as inputs to the development of normative task specifications. Each task is first outlined in terms of its physical requirements (hours, skill levels, supplies, space, equipment, etc.). These physical requirements are then transformed into dollars by applying appropriate unit prices and costs. Expected units of output are then estimated, and the standard costs per unit of output are calculated for material, labor and variable overhead by dividing the input cost data by the expected output. The resulting standard costs are then used for performance evaluation as described in earlier chapters.

In all cases the physical observation approach should include discussions with the department head and responsible supervisors. They can help with the proper selection of time and persons to be observed; they are in a better position to judge when the resulting standards are reasonable.

In the event that the healthcare organization doesn't want to obtain standard cost data from the industrial engineering approach, it can halt the process at the point where flexible budget formulas can be established. That is, the input price data can be used to prepare flexible budget formulas that relate input costs to units of activity. These cost behavior relationships then serve as inputs to the planning and control process. The major disadvantage with the industrial engineering approach is that it cannot be applied where the service activities cannot be physically observed. The analyst must be able to trace the costs to input or outout units of activity. If that link is not feasible, then physical observation and the industrial engineering approach are not applicable.

Logical knowledge of cost behavior patterns

The second approach to identifying cost behavior patterns relies on a logical knowledge of the operations of the healthcare organization. The manager or analyst applies expert judgment in determining a representative cost behavior pattern. The physician applies this type of logic in administering treatments to patients with observable disease conditions. A physician can usually make a preliminary diagnosis with knowledge of a set of symptoms and some background information about the patient's history. This preliminary diagnosis then leads to a set of recommended treatments.

The logical approach to identifying cost behavior patterns proceeds in an analogous fashion. The analyst, based on previous knowledge of similar operations, has some idea about how certain costs typically relate to activities or services. The analyst then estimates a cost behavior equation and confirms it with a small sample of information.

The small sample of confirmatory information can be derived by three different techniques. The analyst first identifies the appropriate variables and the relevant range over which the cost behavior relationship is expected to apply. One of these techniques is called account analysis. Account analysis then proceeds to examine the costs recorded in the organization's accounts. These costs are then classified, on the basis of the analyst's judgment, as fixed or variable costs. The cost behavior equation is judgmentally determined. In some cases, the costs cannot be fit into any known linear pattern, and the analyst must discard or ignore costs that cannot be classified on a linear basis.

The second way to confirm logical relationships with limited information is by using the high-low method. Account analysis is very subjective; the high-low method reduces this subjectivity by identifying cost behavior patterns as a function of the highest cost and the lowest cost. The pair of data points with the most extreme costs, over the expected relevant range, becomes the basis for the predictive cost equation. These two points are then input to the rise-over-run calculation discussed earlier. For example, consider the data in *Exhibit 3-8*. The months with the highest cost and the lowest cost are the only basis for the cost behavior equation.

The coefficient calculated by the high-low method is the slope of the line that connects these two points. It can be interpreted as predicting that supply costs will increase by $10.53 for each hour of activity. There is no information about whether this is a representative relationship. There is no statistical information on the relationship's goodness to fit for more than the original two data points. We shall investigate these issues in the next section on statistical techniques.

Exhibit 3-8
High-low method

Month	Supply cost (y)	Hours of activity (x)
1	$200	19
2	400	41
3	300	32
4	100	11
5	500	49

High-low cost behavior equation $= \dfrac{y_2 - y_1}{x_2 - x_1} = \dfrac{500 - 100}{49 - 11} = \dfrac{400}{38}$

$= \$10.53$ per hour

In any event, the high-low method relies on limited information. If that information is distorted or biased, the entire cost behavior relationship may be unusable. Consider the scatter diagram in *Exhibit 3-9.* The two points with the highest and lowest costs are completely atypical of the other data. The cost relationship, predicted from the two outlier points (*) in *Exhibit 3-9,* is completely different from the relationship that would have been predicted from the balance of the available observations. Perhaps, as outliers, they should have been eliminated from the data base. If the relevant range does not include such high (x) volumes, the outliers definitely should have been eliminated. Blind faith in the high-low method will rarely lead to acceptable cost behavior patterns.

Exhibit 3-9
Scatter diagram with extreme outliers

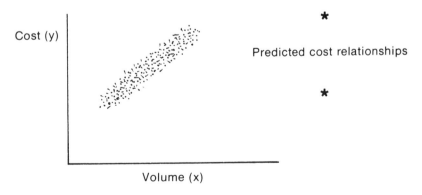

The third technique that can be used to confirm logical relationships is a derivative of the high-low method. It is called representative cost analysis or incremental cost analysis. In this case, two data points are selected that are *representative* of the expected cost behavior pattern with the prespecified relevant range. The two points are selected on the basis of how well they represent the incremental cost behavior pattern. In other words, this technique is used only to estimate the variable cost coefficient; it yields no direct information about fixed cost. At least under the high-low method fixed costs can be indirectly estimated. If the analyst is interested in both fixed and variable cost behavior patterns, the representative or incremental cost behavior technique should be avoided. In addition, it has all the other disadvantages of the high-low method except that the possibility of choosing two unrepresentative data points is minimized.

In summary, the logical approach to identifying cost behavior patterns relies on the manager's judgment. We recommend that these concepts be used to evaluate the results of either of the two techniques. Logic and managerial judgment can be used best to evaluate whether a particular cost behavior pattern is reasonable. Is it plausible? Does it reflect the way in which the department has been operated in the past? Are the results of these "quick and dirty" techniques consistent with the results derived from more elaborate cost behavior models? In our opinion, logical techniques serve as final tests of reasonability and plausibility. They should rarely be used as the sole means for identifying cost behavior patterns.

Statistical techniques for cost behavior identification

Statistical techniques should be an integral element of cost behavior identification. Statistical techniques are techniques that combine the scatter diagrams discussed earlier in the chapter with a statistical analysis of the dispersion shown in the data. Statistical techniques permit the analyst to obtain the best possible fit between the data and the cost behavior equation. In addition, they provide objective measures of the error that may be associated with the predicted costs. If the assumptions are met that permit statistical analysis, managers in healthcare organizations can use this powerful tool to complement other, more intuitive approaches.

When the appropriate assumptions hold, statistical techniques are superior to the other cost behavior identification techniques discussed earlier in this chapter. They are superior because of the objective estimates of potential error that are obtained and because the extent to which each of the statistical conditions (assumptions) is met can be tested. Furthermore, statistical techniques can be used where more than one predictor variable is required. The techniques discussed earlier in this chapter are only appropriate for univariate cost behavior models.

Statistical techniques rely on the premise that historical cost behavior patterns can be used to predict similar relationships in the future. There is nothing normative about the results of statistical analyses; nor is there necessarily anything logical about these results. Statistical models simply extrapolate historical patterns and apply them to some future period. To the extent that operating conditions are changing, or to the extent that the past does not serve as a valid predictor of the future, the benefits ascribed above to statistical techniques are reduced. In other words, statistical techniques are most valid when operating conditions are stable and when future costs are expected to be influenced by the same factors that affected costs in previous periods. Chapter 13 describes a statistical approach based on regression analysis. Regression analysis is the most common statistical approach, and a complete understanding of both Chapters 3 and 13 is essential to the use and interpretation of regression analysis.

Summary

One of the preliminary steps, identified above as part of any cost behavior identification process, was to construct or obtain scatter diagrams of costs as a function of a variety of predictor variables. Once the manager has selected the most logical predictor variable, a line may be visually fit to the observed scatter diagram. The visual fit technique can actually be used to obtain a cost behavior equation. This course of action is not recommended because the results are so subjective and because, for a minor incremental cost, statistical techniques can be applied and a much more accurate equation can be obtained. As noted above, the visual fit technique is useful for identifying potential nonlinearities. It is also useful as a preliminary criterion for selecting (or rejecting) possible predictor variables. In other words, the visual fit technique is a cheap and expedient step that should be used before statistical techniques. Visual fit techniques help the analyst focus attention on promising cost behavior relationships and they help avoid wasting time and effort on analyses that have little hope of success.

Questions and problems

1. What is the advantage of understanding cost behavior in healthcare organizations?

2. How can management improve its decision-making by knowing more about cost behavior patterns?

3. Why is the prediction of future costs important?

4. What criterion must first be applied when analyzing cost behavior?

5. Name five steps in the identification of a cost behavior model.

6. What is the difference between univariate and multivariate models?

7. Describe what a slope of 2 in a linear cost behavior model means.

8. Describe the usefulness of a scatter diagram.

9. What do the following scatter diagrams indicate? What is the preferred relevant range? Are there any potential problems?

(a) Supply costs

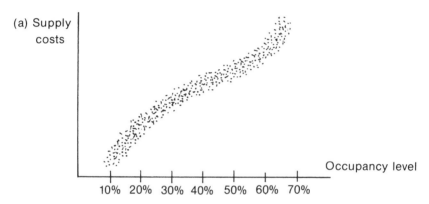

Occupancy level

10% 20% 30% 40% 50% 60% 70%

(b) Heating costs

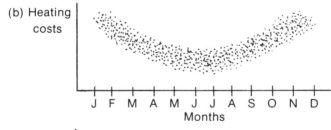

J F M A M J J A S O N D
Months

(c) Laboratory costs

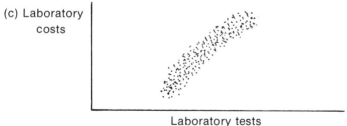

Laboratory tests

(d) Radiology cost

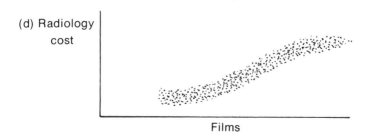

Films

10. Name some potential data problems affecting cost behavior patterns.

11. What are step costs? How can they be approximated?

12. Name three approaches to identifying cost behavior patterns.

13. What are the advantages and disadvantages of the industrial engineering approach to cost behavior patterns?

14. What is another application of the industrial engineering approach?

15. Describe the three techniques for confirming an analyst's estimates of cost behavior.

16. Describe three advantages of statistical techniques for identifying cost behavior patterns.

17. When are statistical techniques most valid?

18. Given the following budget line, determine the 1) slope, 2) fixed cost, 3) variable cost and 4) budget equation.

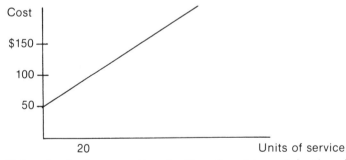

19. Using the budget equation in Question 18, explain the effect of a 100-unit increase in units of service.

20. Given the data below, use the high-low method to calculate the budget equation.

Quarter ended	Supply costs	Patient level
3/31	29,420	23,000
6/30	44,900	32,000
9/30	36,210	28,000
12/31	21,100	15,000

21. Draw scatter diagrams representing each of the following situations:
    a. Variable costs following a linear pattern with usage up to 80 percent utilization, beyond which the variable costs continue to be linear but at a smaller slope.
    b. Both linear and nonlinear variable cost, with a linear relevant range between 20 percent and 70 percent.
    c. Curvilinear relationship between cost and usage.

22. Determine the budget equation from the following budget line:

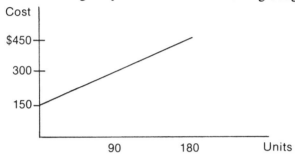

23. Determine the budget equation from the following data using "high-low" analysis.

Month	Costs	Patient level
Jan.	$213,856	4,321
Feb.	259,452	4,695
Mar.	307,222	4,922
Apr.	201,709	3,972
May	198,327	3,825

References

Dahl, N. Tor, "Finding a Standard for Rate Review Comparisons," *"Hospital Financial Management,* January, 1973, pp. 23-25, 28-31, 48.

Horngren, Charles T., *Cost Accounting: A Managerial Emphasis,* 4th edition, New York: Prentice-Hall, 1982, Chapter 24.

Kilpatrick, S. James, Jr., *Statistical Principles in Health Care Information,* 2nd ed., Baltimore, MD: University Park Press, 1977, Chapters 14 and 15.

Michela, William, "Defining and Analyzing Costs — A Statistical Approach," *Hospital Financial Management,* January, 1975, pp. 36-41.

Rowley, C. Stevenson, "Which Is Best to Find Cost Behavior?" *Hospital Financial Management,* April, 1976, pp. 18-28.

CHAPTER 4

Flexible budgeting and breakeven analysis

Introduction

Chapter 2 introduced the concept of fixed and variable costs. Separating costs into these two categories enables the administrator to effectively forecast costs wherever patient volume or other quantities of service have a significant effect on total costs. In this chapter we will continue to develop the concept of budgeting as part of planning; in addition, we will explain the management control function of the budget. Knowledge of fixed and variable cost patterns enables managers to compare actual costs with expected costs and take corrective action if needed. Flexible budgets can play an important part in both the planning and control function.

Static budgets and average costs

Most hospitals or healthcare organizations currently use a planning technique which involves estimating the level of services to be performed during the next operating period. Once the level of services is forecasted, the expected level of cost required to accomplish these tasks can be estimated. The forecasted costs comprise a static budget if the underlying cost relationships are not made explicit. The example in *Exhibit 4-1* illustrates a static budget for one department of a hospital. If the volume or quantity of services changes, the static budget may no longer be relevant or accurate.

The static budget approach is generally satisfactory for the planning process except where the management wants to include the effects of volume changes on total costs. For example, what should be the costs if patient volume decreases or increases by 10 percent? One technique currently used is called the average cost method. The average cost method requires an estimate of total costs for performing a certain number of procedures. Dividing this total cost by the number of procedures will result in the average cost as shown in *Exhibit 4-2.*

Exhibit 4-1
Mercy Hospital
Statement of income and expense for period ending March 1978
Emergency room

Cost center
Budget—year-to-date (YTD)

Cost center	Budget YTD 1978	Actual YTD 1978	Variance dollar	%	Actual March 1977	Actual March 1978	Variance dollar	%
						Budget—Month		
Total revenue	$255,885	$250,885	$(5,000)	(01.9%)				
Total salary expenses	143,126	145,626	2,500	.017				
Total professional fees	36,000	36,500	500	.013				
Total drugs	8,097	9,000	903	.110				
Total supplies	48,306	48,100	(206)	(.004)				
Total repairs & maintenance	7	7	0	0				
Total utilities	69	76	7	.100				
Total education expense	281	281	0	0				
Misc. expense	7	10	3	.428				
Total operating expense	$235,893	$239,600	$ 3,707	.015				
Net after expenses	19,992	11,285	(8,707)	.435				
Indirect expenses	15,065	15,065	0	0				
Net after all expenses	$ 4,927	$ (3,780)	$(8,707)	.435				

(Data omitted from exhibit. Monthly data would typically be included.)

Statistics
Number of visits   (year-to-date)

Emergency	14,351
Nonemergency	3,624
Total	17,975

Exhibit 4-2
Mercy Hospital — Emergency room average cost

$$\frac{\text{Total cost (direct + indirect)}}{\text{Volume of output (procedures or services)}} = \frac{\text{Average cost}}{\text{per unit of output}}$$

$$\frac{\$235,893}{17,975} = \$13.12 \text{ average cost per unit}$$

Exhibit 4-3
Average cost computation

Planned budget for the month of January	$35,000
Estimated number of procedures	5,000
Average cost per procedure	$ 7.00

This average cost can be used to forecast the change in cost when the volume of output changes. Average costs can be used for planning and control purposes; however, it must be understood that average costs are only accurate for the volume used in the calculation. For example, the data in *Exhibit 4-3* can be used to illustrate this type of problem.

Most supervisors would argue correctly that average costs do not reflect the true relationship between cost and volume changes. The data presented in *Exhibit 4-4* lead to a variance analysis based on the adjusted budget.

Exhibit 4-4
Static budget variance analysis

Actual number of procedures	Actual costs	Planned budget	Variance	
4,000	$30,500	$35,000	$ 4,500	F
5,000	34,500	35,000	500	F
6,000	41,000	35,000	6,000	U

Actual number of procedures	Actual costs	Adjusted* budget	Variance	
4,000	$30,500	$28,000	$ 2,500	U
5,000	34,500	35,000	500	F
6,000	41,000	42,000	1,000	F

F = Favorable or under budget
U = Unfavorable or over budget

*Budget adjusted for actual number of procedures times average cost of $7 per procedure.

Should the department supervisor be praised or cautioned for his/her performance if the actual volume was 4,000 or 6,000 procedures? It is impossible to decide without more information. The concept of fixed and variable costs can be useful in answering this type of question. Note that the adjusted budget does not differentiate between fixed and variable cost behavior. Consider the same situation with the following additional information:

$$\text{fixed costs} = \$10,000$$
$$\text{variable costs} = \$5 \text{ per test.}$$

How does this information influence the analysis?

In only one case (volume = 5,000) did the supervisor control costs as planned. Clearly, the fixed costs should not change with the volume changes. The relationships expressed in *Exhibit 4-5* stress this factor.

The data in *Exhibit 4-5* illustrate how a flexible budget may be prepared. The fixed and variable cost relationships are used to compute the budgeted cost data. In planning, a flexible budget can be used to create a series of different levels of costs appropriate to different levels of volume. For example, if the budgeted volume could vary as much as ± 20 percent, how would that affect the budgeted costs? *Exhibit 4-5* illustrates the difference in planned costs that can be determined under a flexible budget.

Exhibit 4-5
Flexible budget variance analysis

Actual volume	Actual costs	Flexible budget	Variance	
4,000	$30,500	$10,000 + $5(4,000) = $30,000	$ 500	U
5,000	34,500	10,000 + 5(5,000) = 35,000	500	F
6,000	41,000	10,000 + 5(6,000) = 40,000	1,000	U

Estimated number of procedures: 5,000
Cost function: $10,000 + $5 per procedure
Budget for 4,000 procedures is: $10,000 + $5(4,000) = $30,000
Budget for 5,000 procedures is: $10,000 + $5(5,000) = $35,000
Budget for 6,000 procedures is: $10,000 + $5(6,000) = $40,000

Flexible budgeting

It is usually more effective to control expenditures before they occur rather than to affix blame after the fact. The development of a flexible budget can help solve this management problem. For example, using the format developed in *Exhibit 4-5,* the manager can easily forecast the impact of volume changes on total costs. A flexible formula is then used for both planning and control.

Given these relationships, department supervisors can monitor their own spending patterns as volume changes. Most supervisors recognize that costs should be reduced as volume declines. Conversely, costs should increase as volume increases. However, unless fixed and variable costs are determined during the budget process, the amount of change is uncertain. The flexible budget concept will help resolve these controversies for both parties.

Exhibit 4-6
Flexible budget — Month of January 1980
Emergency room services —
based on number of patient visits

Cost category	Budget formula Fixed	Variable	Jan. budget (1,500 visits)
Salary expenses	$12,000	$2.00	$15,000
Employee benefits	9,000	—0—	9,000
Professional fees	4,000	—0—	4,000
Drug expense	—0—	.70	1,050
General supplies	—0—	3.00	4,500
Repairs and maintenance	60	—0—	60
Telephone	18	—0—	18
Miscellaneous expense	—0—	1.00	1,500
January budget based on 1,500 visits			$35,128

The format of a flexible budget would resemble that presented in *Exhibit 4-6*. Other variations are possible, depending on the organization structure and the types of controls that have been implemented in the hospital.

Administrators and department managers may question the accuracy of fixed and variable cost components determined for individual services or departments. The important concept is to recognize that these categories exist and to approximate their relative amounts. Some hospitals estimate costs to be 75-80 percent fixed and 20-25 percent variable. The key is intelligent use of the concept in decision-making.

Formula approaches to flexible budgeting techniques

Cost behavior can be a very useful management tool in decision-making. For example, how many patients do I have to see to cover my costs? How many lab tests do I have to perform, etc.? It is possible to estimate answers to these questions by using diagrams and financial statements. However, it is usually quicker and simpler to use mathematical (formula) approaches. In this chapter we will concentrate on the cost relationships (formulae) that may aid in decision-making. Based on the cost behavior concepts developed in Chapter 2, these relationships can be identified.

Definitions

1. TC = total cost or expenses
2. Q = quantity of services or procedures
3. VC_T = total variable costs (VC_T expressed as dollar amount)
4. VC_U = per unit variable cost
5. R_U = charge or rate per individual service or procedure
6. VC_R = ratio of per unit variable cost to individual rate expressed as percentage
7. FC_T = total fixed costs
8. FC_U = per unit fixed costs
9. P = excess of revenue over expenses
10. TR = total revenue (expressed in dollars)
11. BE_R = revenue point at which total revenue equals total costs (TR = TC)
12. BE_Q = breakeven point expressed in units of output rather than dollars
13. $TR = (R_U) \times (Q)$
14. $VC_T = (VC_U) \times (Q)$ or $VC_U = \dfrac{VC_T}{Q}$
15. $TC = FC_T + VC_T$
16. $TR = TC + P$
17. $FC_U = \dfrac{FC_T}{Q}$

The preceding definitions are important in understanding the basic cost and revenue relationships:

1. $TR = (FC_T) + (VC_T) + P$

This can also be expressed as:

2. $(R_U)\,(Q) = (FC_T) + (VC_U)\,(Q) + P$

The breakeven point is generally defined as the point where total revenues (TR) equal total costs (TC) or when profit (P) is zero. This point can be expressed in either dollars or units of service as shown in Formulae 3 and 4 (below).

3. $BE_R = (FC_T) \div (1 - VC_R)$
4. $BE_Q = (FC_T) \div (R_U - VC_U)$

The problem shown in *Exhibit 4-7* illustrates the use of the cost formulae in a typical situation.

Exhibit 4-7
Use of breakeven models to solve
for excess of revenues over expenses

Given: Q = 1,500 procedures performed
R_U = $25 charge per procedure
VC_U = $5 variable cost per procedure
FC_T = $10,000 fixed cost for department

Using formulae 13, 14, 15 and 16 the following results would be obtained:

13. TR = $(R_U \times Q)$ or ($25 × 1,500) = $37,500
14. VC_T = $(VC_U \times Q)$ or ($5 × 1,500) = $7,500
15. TC = $(FC_T + VC_T)$ or ($10,000 + $7,500) = $17,500
16. TR = (TC + P) or $37,500 = $17,500 + $20,000
Therefore   P = $20,000

More examples of this type of problem will be demonstrated in the following pages. These basic relationships are important in effective use of many management accounting techniques which will be used extensively throughout the text.

Contribution margin techniques

One of the many questions a manager has to answer is what will happen to a department's financial position if the volume of service is increased. Coupled with an understanding of cost behavior, a very effective management accounting tool is the concept of *contribution margin*. The contribution margin is the difference between the rate or fee charged for the service performed and the variable costs incurred in providing the service. For example, if the charge for a specific procedure is $20 and the variable costs associated with the service are $8, the contribution margin is $12. Contribution margin represents the resources available to meet fixed expenses that will occur regardless of volume, working capital needs and expansion of services.

For example, let's assume 2,000 patients will demand services during the next month. If the charge is $20 per patient, total revenues are $40,000. Assuming out-of-pocket or variable expenses are $8 per patient, total variable expenses are $16,000. This means $24,000 is available to cover other expenses and profit requirements. These data are summarized in *Exhibit 4-8*.

Exhibit 4-8
Contribution margin computation

Total revenues	$40,000	(2,000 x $20)
Total variable expense	16,000	(2,000 x $ 8)
Total contribution margin	$24,000	(2,000 x $12)

From this understanding of the contribution margin concept, we can find out how many procedures are necessary to cover full costs. This type of analysis, typically called cost/volume/profit (CVP) analysis or breakeven analysis, further expands our knowledge of the decision variables that can be controlled by hospital managers who are aware of the relationship between volume and costs.

For example, the manager may want to know what level of revenues will just cover all the department's costs. This point is called the breakeven point. Following the previous discussion of cost behavior and contribution margin, the breakeven point can be determined by dividing fixed costs by contribution margin.

Exhibit 4-9
Computation of breakeven point

Given: $20   Average revenue per patient visit
          8   Average variable cost per patient visit

        $12   Contribution margin (CM) per patient visit

Total fixed costs (TFC): $240,000

$$BE_Q = \frac{TFC}{\text{contribution margin}} = \frac{\$240,000}{12} = 20,000 \text{ patient visits}$$

This can easily be proved by the following financial statement:

Total revenue	20,000 × $20.00	=	$400,000
Total variable costs	20,000 × $8.00	=	160,000
Total contribution margin	20,000 × $12.00	=	$240,000
Total fixed costs		=	240,000
Excess of revenue over expenses			0

Exhibit 4-9 indicates that 20,000 patients are needed each month to meet the total costs. This model can be developed further to cover any additional amounts needed to repay debt, meet profit objectives or replace equipment. For example, assume that in the preceding situation

Exhibit 4-10
Volume required to cover additional requirements

Contribution margin ($12) remains the same because price and variable costs did not change.

Fixed costs	$240,000
Additional funds required	60,000
Total funds required	$300,000

Substituting in the CVP model we obtain the following results:

$$\frac{\$300,000}{\$12} = 25,000 \text{ patient visits}$$

This can also be easily verified in the following income statement:

Total revenue	$500,000	($20 × 25,000)
Total variable costs	200,000	($ 8 × 25,000)
Total contribution margin	$300,000	($12 × 25,000)
Total fixed costs	240,000	
Net income	$ 60,000	

Exhibit 4-11
Computation of charges

Let CM = contribution margin:

$$\frac{\$300,000}{CM} = 15,000 \text{ patient visits}$$

Solving this equation, 15,000 (CM) = $300,000
CM = $20

With a required contribution margin of $20 and a variable cost per patient visit of $8, we can develop the required price which is equal to the sum of contribution margin:

$$R_U - VC_U = CM$$
$$R_U = CM + VC_U = 20 + 8 = 28$$

The following revenue and expense statement verifies that $28 is the price that satisfies the stated objectives.

Total revenues	($28 × 15,000)	$420,000
Total variable costs	($ 8 × 15,000)	120,000
Total contribution margin	($20 × 15,000)	$300,000
Total fixed costs		240,000
Excess of revenues over costs		$ 60,000

we wanted to generate an additional $60,000 for debt repayment. The only element of the model that changes is the level of additional revenue (cash) that must be generated to cover fixed requirements (*Exhibit 4-10*).

The same model can also be used to develop the price that must be charged if the number of procedures is known. It can also identify the variable cost relationship if the number of procedures and the price are known. For example, if only 15,000 patients can be seen, what price must be established to meet the cost objective of $200,000? In this case, we can substitute terms in the CVP equation as shown in *Exhibit 4-11*.

In some cases, the variable cost relationships are not known. However, even under these circumstances, the maximum level of variable costs can be estimated using the breakeven model. Knowledge of this maximum would help managers determine the level of variable costs or efficiency factors in their own departments. *Exhibit 4-12* illustrates these concepts.

Exhibit 4-12
Computation of maximum variable costs

Maximum price	$33
TFC	$300,000
Maximum volume	10,000

What is the maximum level of variable costs that will permit the department to break even at maximum volume?

$TR - (VC_U)(Q) = TFC$

$(33)(10,000) - VC_U(10,000) = 300,000$

$330,000 - 10,000\ VC_U = 300,000$

$30,000 = 10,000\ VC_U$

$3 = VC_U$

Cost-volume-profit relationships under cost-based reimbursement

The preceding discussion was based on a non-cost-based reimbursement environment. In this type of environment, all patients would pay charges. Graphically this is shown in *Exhibit 4-13*.

In a cost-based reimbursement environment, the CVP model must be modified to show that the cost-based third-party payers will pay only cost above that point. This behavior is based on the practice of paying costs or charges, whichever is lower. Below the breakeven point, charges are lower than costs; therefore, the cost-based payer will reimburse on the basis of charges. If a hospital had 100 percent cost-based patients, then the

Exhibit 4-13
Cost-volume model
(no cost-based reimbursement)

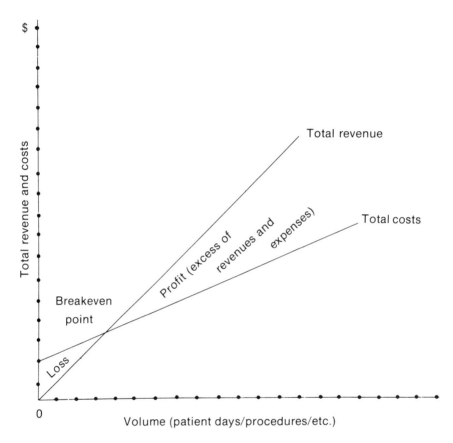

hospital would only recover its costs (as defined by the payer), and the model would appear as shown in *Exhibit 4-14*.

Although the preceding analysis has concentrated on the concept of a single type of patient or service, it is recognized that most departments offer a number of procedures.

Since most hospitals have less than 100 percent cost-based patients, the CVP relationship for most hospitals is probably a line segment between the 50 percent and 100 percent cost-based reimbursement levels shown in *Exhibit 4-15*.

The practice of basing reimbursement on costs clearly has an impact on the financial structure of the hospital and the ability to generate the funds needed to continue to provide quality healthcare. The use of CVP models

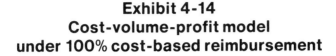

Exhibit 4-14
Cost-volume-profit model
under 100% cost-based reimbursement

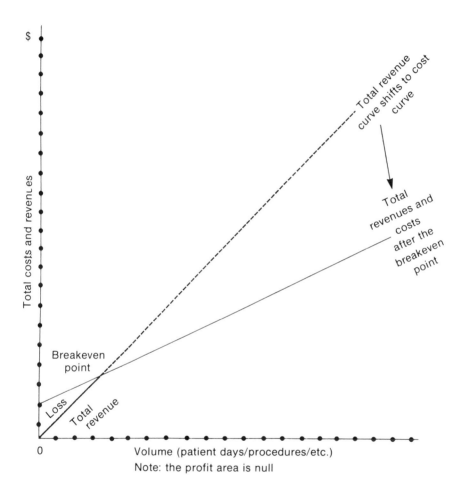

very effectively demonstrates the impact of an increasing number of cost-based patients on the hospital's financial position.

Multiproduct breakeven analysis incorporating changes in patient mix

This chapter has assumed that there was only one primary source of patient revenue. However, there are at least four, and usually more,

Exhibit 4-15
Cost-volume-profit model
under 50% cost-based reimbursement

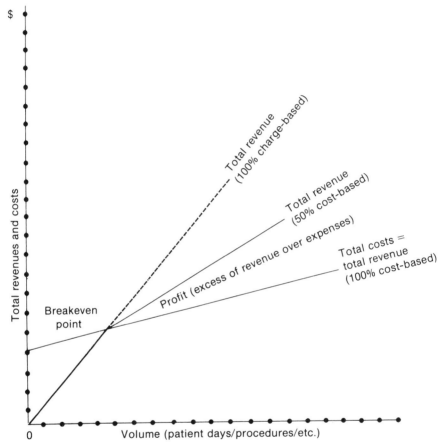

patient (payment) categories. For example, the following categories are usually found:

1. self-pay patients
2. private insurance
3. Medicare plans
4. Medicaid plans.

Each of these plans would probably pay different proportionate amounts of the total patient charges. However, this complication is the same problem faced by industrial companies who produce or sell more than one product. Breakeven analysis can be utilized in these types of environments by using a *composite* contribution margin. For example, consider a hospital with the following cost structure and patient mix:

Patient mix		Reimbursement basis
a) self-pay	20%	total charges
b) private insurance	25%	greater of total charges or DRG rates
c) Medicare	30%	prospective rates (DRG)
d) Medicaid	25%	reimbursable costs only
Fixed costs =	$800,000	
Other necessary costs =	200,000	
Daily charges =	120	per patient day
Variable costs =	40	per patient day (out-of-pocket costs are assumed to be the same for each patient, regardless of the method of payment)

The following schedule is used for reimbursement purposes:

a) self-pay	$120
b) private insurance	$120
c) Medicare	$110 (DRG - based rates)
d) Medicaid	$100 (to the point where costs are greater than charges)

Given the above data, what level of total revenue must be achieved to break even? In order to determine this point, a composite contribution margin can be developed in the following manner:

Method of payment	Patient mix	Contri-bution margin	Weighted contribution margin	Reimburse-ment rate	Weighted reimburse-ment rate
self-pay	20%	(120 − 40) = $80	$16	$120	$24
private insurance	25%	(120 − 40) = $80	20	120	30
Medicare	30%	(110 − 40) = $70	21	110	33
Medicaid	25%	(100 − 40) = $60	15	100	25
		Composite contribution margin =	$72	Composite average daily charges =	$112

Composite contribution margin is .64 ($72/$112). Therefore, variable costs are 36 percent because variable costs plus contribution margin sum to unity. Using these data in our original formula:

$$TR = \$800,000 + .36\ TR + \$200,000$$
$$TR - .36\ TR = \$1,000,000$$
$$TR = \$1,562,500$$

This projected level of total revenue can be used to determine the number of patient days of each type needed from each reimbursement source. This is obtained by mulitplying the projected revenue ($1,562,500) by the patient mix in percentage terms.

Method of payment	Patient mix	Revenue
self-pay	20%	$ 312,500
private insurance	25%	390,625
Medicare	30%	468,750
Medicaid	25%	390,625
	Total revenue =	$1,562,500

The average number of patient days in each category is obtained by first determining the total number of expected patient days. The projected revenue ($1,562,500) must be divided by the composite average daily charges ($112).

$$\$1,562,500 \div \$112 = 13,951 \text{ patient days}$$

This relationship indicates an expected level of volume, in terms of patient days. The number of patient days in each category is determined by multiplying the projected volume (13,951) by the patient mix.

Method of payment	Patient mix	Patient days
self-pay	20%	2,790
private insurance	25%	3,488
Medicare	30%	4,185
Medicaid	25%	3,488
	Total patient days =	13,951

The analysis indicates that 13,951 patient days are needed to operate at the breakeven point if costs and patient mix are at the planned levels.

Multiproduct breakeven applications

Using this concept, hospital management can determine if the forecasted revenue is realistic and, if not, take action to change cost patterns or patient mix to achieve the hospital goals. In addition, the same techniques can be used at the end of an accounting period to determine why actual performance did or did not meet the budgeted goals. This technique is called variance analysis.

It should be obvious that any of the calculations illustrated above depend on the patient mix actually achieved. As patient mix changes, the breakeven level of revenue changes. The analysis can also be used to evaluate changes in the patient mix. For example, if the hospital were able to eliminate Medicare and Medicaid patients and obtain an adequate volume of self-pay and privately insured patients, what volume of patients is required to break even? Assume:

Method of payment	Patient mix	Contribution margin
self-pay	50%	$80
private insurance	50%	$80

The composite contribution margin is now $80 and the breakeven volume of total revenue is obtained:

$$TR = \$800,000 + (40/120)TR + \$200,000$$
$$2/3\ TR = \$1,000,000$$
$$TR = \$1,500,000$$

Using the projected level of total revenue ($1,500,000), the number of patient days in each category can be determined:

Method of payment	Patient mix	Revenue	Patient days
self-pay	50%	$ 750,000	6,250
private insurance	50%	750,000	6,250
		$1,500,000	12,500
$1,500,000 ÷ 120 = 12,500 required patient days			

This analysis shows that if the number of patients in each category (self-pay and privately insured) can be approximately doubled, the hospital can break even under these conditions. It also shows that, under these conditions, the hospital will be able to cover its fixed costs and its other necessary costs at a volume of 12,500 patient days.

These brief examples indicate that patient mix is a significant and crucial variable that cannot be ignored in cost-volume-profit analysis in the healthcare industry. Assumptions about patient mix are extremely critical in planning for the future. It would be very misleading to ignore the effects of a change in patient mix.

These methods would also permit the hospital to engage in separate breakeven calculations for each type of patient. A breakeven analysis for each type of patient would require knowledge of the fixed costs that could be attributed to each type of patient. The authors suspect that a proper analysis of this question would indicate that twice as many patients (or patient days) might be required to cover all related costs for patients covered by government reimbursement programs versus private (self-pay or privately insured) patients. This question should be investigated by the hospital planner in determining the hospital's commitment to serving all types of patients. The authors further suspect that hospitals that have chosen to reject Medicare patients have performed analyses such as those outlined above.

In summary, patient mix must be included in the hospital's planning models. It is essential to be able to identify and separate the effects of changes in patient mix. Managerial information that must be available includes composite contribution margins and composite average daily charges. This information should be incorporated into the cost-volume-profit model and used to estimate the effects of patient mix on the cost and volume of operations.

Summary

Flexible budgeting is a management accounting tool which offers considerable potential for establishing budgets, incremental cost decisions, price-setting and expenditure control. It involves separating the costs of each department into fixed and variable components. Once costs have been separated, breakeven analysis and contribution margin can be used to evaluate the impact of many decisions before actual dollars are involved. A basic familiarity with these tools offers considerable flexibility in the financial management of healthcare organizations.

Questions and problems

1. Given that most hospitals are nonprofit organizations and are reimbursed on a cost basis, is there any need to worry about such concepts as breakeven analysis or contribution margins?

2. What underlying assumptions need to be made when using cost-volume-profit analysis?

3. Explain the differences between flexible and static budgets.

4. Cost per patient day or cost per case are two measures of output for a hospital. What problems are associated with these measures of cost per output?

5. Average cost per unit of output for the hospital is typically based on patient days. What *is* usually used as a measurement device on a

departmental basis for the following departments? What *should* be used to measure performance for these departments?

a. Dietary
b. Laundry and linen
c. Accounting
d. Pharmacy
e. Medical school
f. Operating room

6. If a hospital prepares a fixed budget based on an estimate of 100,000 patient days, and only 80,000 patient days actually occur, what effect will this have on hospital costs?

7. Management prepared a fixed budget based on 100,000 patient days and arrived at total costs of $2,000,000 for the coming year. During the year actual patient days came to 80,000 and costs totalled $1,850,000. Did management do a good job of containing costs for the year? Discuss.

8. There is considerable talk of placing a ceiling on patient charges which would limit charge increases to nine percent a year. Assume this ceiling goes into effect and that your total costs increase by 10 percent per patient. Is it possible for the hospital to still be better off and have a higher fund flow than the previous year? Discuss.

9. A clinic estimates that its breakeven point is 500 patients per month. If its volume of patients falls, will it affect the breakeven point? Profits?

10. A clinic invests $500,000 a year in a CAT scanner. What effect will this have on the clinic's breakeven point in terms of patients?

11. Hospitals find that they are reimbursed at different rates for different types of patients. State and federal programs reimburse at one rate, Blue Cross reimburses at a different rate and private insurance and self-paying patients pay another rate. How would this information be integrated into the cost-profit-volume analysis?

12. St. Anthony's Hospital experienced wide variations in patient days from a low of 8,500 days in December to a high of 13,000 days in July. Total costs at the lowest activity level were $39,250 and at the highest level were $53,900.

a. What are the variable and fixed costs if fixed costs are constant?

b. Prepare a flexible budget for these two months.
c. Using the flexible budget developed, determine total costs at 10,000 patient days.
d. Discuss how reliable these figures might be.

13. A radiologist has the following cost structure:

Fixed costs per period	$15,000
Variable costs per X-ray	$ 25
Units processed per period (budget)	3,000
Charges per unit	$ 60

Required:
a. Calculate the breakeven point in units.
b. Calculate the profit or loss at the budget volume.
c. Compute the income which would result at the budget volume if both the variable cost per unit and the charge per unit increased by 20 percent.

14. The pharmacy department of St. Mary's Hospital is expected to price its drugs to provide a 25 percent return above its actual costs.

The department employs two pharmacists who are paid $20,000 each. The department also has several clerks whose total salaries equal $20,000. The department is allocated $25,000 for costs such as maintenance, depreciation, heating and lighting.

The department averages around 250,000 prescriptions a year with an average cost of $4 per prescription.

Required:
a. What price should be charged per prescription to obtain the necessary return?
b. What would the net income per year be?
c. Calculate the breakeven point in units.

15. A hospital has total fixed costs of $750,000 and average variable costs of $50 per patient day. The hospital charges $100 per patient day.
a. How many patient days are needed to break even?
b. If the hospital has 75 beds, what occupancy rate would be required to break even?
c. If the hospital estimates it will have 18,000 patient days, how much income would be generated?

16. A hospital has total fixed costs of $750,000 and average variable costs of $50 per patient day. The hospital has 100 beds and estimates

patient days to be 30,000. Medicare patients will represent half of the total patient days and are reimbursed for actual costs only.

Required:
a. What is the total cost for the year?
b. What amount would Medicare patients be charged?
c. The hospital wants to earn $200,000. What charges must non-Medicare patients pay?

17. Dr. Anderson started a health prevention clinic in 19X0. For this purpose he rented a building for $400 per month. He hired a receptionist, a clerk and a nurse. In addition, an outside accountant was hired at $300 per month to do tax and bookkeeping work. The necessary furniture and equipment for the clinic were purchased with cash. Dr. Anderson has noticed that expenses for utilities and supplies have been fairly constant.

The clinic volume has increased between 19X0 and 19X3. Profits have more than doubled since 19X0. Dr. Anderson does not understand why his profits have increased faster than his volume.

A projected income statement for 19X4 prepared by the accountant is shown below.

Dr. Anderson Clinic **Projected income statement** **for the year ended Dec. 31, 19X4**		
Clinic revenue (11,875 visits at $8.00)		$95,000
Cost of tests performed	$28,500	
Wages and benefits of receptionist & clerk	15,150	
Wages and benefits of nurse	10,300	
Rent	4,800	
Accounting services	3,600	
Depreciation of equipment	5,000	
Depreciation of furniture	3,000	
Utilities	2,325	
Supplies (medical)	1,200	$73,875
Net income before taxes		$21,125
Income taxes (30 percent of net income)		6,338
Net income		$14,787

Required:
a. What is the breakeven point in terms of the number of visits that must take place?

  b. Revenue is what dollar level at the breakeven point?
  c. Dr. Anderson would like an after-tax net income of $20,000. What volume must be reached in order to obtain the desired income?

18. The following are examples of cost-volume-profit graphs for three separate hospitals. Analyze each graph and answer the following questions about them. All measures are in hundreds of thousands (R = revenue.)

Required:
  a. Are the fixed costs in Hospital X considerably more than in Hospital Y? Explain.
  b. Are the breakeven units smaller for Hospital Y than for Hospital Z? Explain.
  c. If volume is at the 400,000 level, will Hospital X produce more profit than Hospital Z at the same level? Explain.

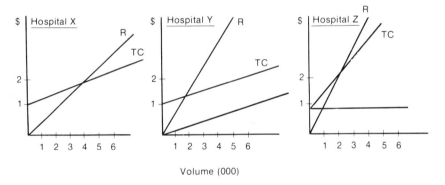

Volume (000)

19. The Glass Laboratories Incorporated plans to organize a company to provide testing facilities to physicians. A marketing study has provided them with the following studies on price/volume relations.

Amount charged per test	Volume per month
$10	25,000
15	15,000
20	8,000

Budgeted fixed costs per month are $100,000 and variable costs were budgeted at $3 per test.

Required:

a. What is the breakeven point in units for each price?
b. Which price would provide the highest income for the company?
c. If variable costs actually turn out to be $4, would the decision made in "b" still represent the best decision?
d. If fixed costs increase to $125,000, which decision would be the best?
e. What other factors might be considered in the pricing decision process?

20. The pharmacy at Memorial Hospital currently has three different prescriptions that can be sold for a certain ailment. The selling price and cost data by product are:

	A	B	C
Selling price	$20	$10	$ 5
Variable costs	8	3	3
Contribution margin	$12	$ 7	$ 2
Contribution margin %	60	70	40
Percentage of total sales dollar mix	40	40	20

Below are the income statements for two recent months for the pharmacy department.

Sales	$80	$60
Costs	60	52
Income	$20	$ 8

Required:

a. Using the income statements for April and May, find fixed and variable costs as a percentage of sales dollars.
b. Determine the breakeven point in dollar sales.
c. Which product is most profitable per unit sold?
d. Which product is most profitable per dollar sales?
e. What sales dollars are needed to earn $35,000 per month, and how many units of each product will be sold at that figure if the usual mix is maintained?

f. In June, sales were $100,000 with a mix of 40 percent A, 30 percent B and 30 percent C. What is the income?

21. Consider a hospital with the following data:

Patient mix		Reimbursement basis (per patient day)
Self-pay	20%	$120 (total charges)
Private insurance	25%	120 (total charges)
Medicare	30%	110 (cost or charges, whichever is lower)
Medicaid	25%	100 (reimbursable costs only)
Fixed costs		$800,000
Other necessary costs		$200,000
Daily charges		$120 per patient day
Variable costs		$ 40 per patient day

Given the above data, what level of total revenue must be achieved to operate at breakeven?

22. Determine the fixed portion of a semi-variable expense for the first three months of 1984, using the high-low method. Information for the first three months of 1984 is:

	Direct Labor Hours	Semi-variable Expense
Jan. 1984	34,000	60,000
Feb. 1984	31,000	58,500
Mar. 1984	32,000	61,000

23. Freedom Hospital plans to discontinue a department with a contribution to overhead of $117,000 and allocated overhead of $141,000 of which $123,000 cannot be eliminated. What would be the effect of this discontinuance on Freedom's profit (before taxes)?

24. Hampton out-patient clinic budgeted revenue from flu vaccinations at $20 per shot. Fixed costs total $5 per unit based on 4000 shots and remain unchanged within the relevant range of 1500 shots to a total capacity of 6500 shots. Variable shots are $10 per shot. After revenue was budgeted at $70,000, the clinic received a request from the local school district for flu vaccinations of its 1000 students at a reasonable cost. If Hampton Clinic wants to increase operating income by $2,000, what should Hampton charge for the shots?

25. Fox Creek Hospital has variable costs of $840 for every arthroscope it performs. Fixed costs total $750,000, allocated on the basis of the number of arthroscopes performed. Revenue is calculated by adding a 10% mark-up to cost. How much should Fox Creek charge for an arthroscope based on a budgeted 7500 arthroscopes?

26. Ely Memorial Hospital is planning to add a new birthing wing to its existing OB/GYN department. This wing is to simulate the environment of one's home. Ely Memorial prepared the following forecast concerning the new wing:

Revenue	$750,000
Revenue per delivery	$ 1,500
Variable Costs	$400,000
Fixed Costs	$200,000

Further studies by an outside consulting firm found that revenue per delivery could be increased by 20% with an expected volume decrease of only 10%. What would Ely Memorial Hospital operating income be if these changes were used?

27. Mount Mary Hospital operates several eye clinics around the state. Although many different procedures are performed at the clinics, the majority of revenue comes from routine eye examinations. Mount Mary is determining the feasibility of opening a new clinic in a rural town. The following estimated revenues and expenses for the new clinic are available to Mount Mary.

Revenue per visit	$20.00
Cost per visit	5.00
Physician Professional Fee	5.00
Total Variable Expenses	$10.00
Fixed Expenses:	
Rent	$ 7,500
Salaries	$17,500
	$25,000

Required:
a. What is the breakeven point in revenue and in units?
b. If the number of examinations (eye tests) performed is estimated at 2000, what would be the net income or loss to the clinic?

c. Determine the annual breakeven point in revenue and in units assuming that Mount Mary decides to discontinue the physician professional fee in favor of a fixed salary increase of $15,000.

d. Suppose the physicians earned $5 for every eye examination performed in excess of the breakeven point (units). Determine the clinic's net income (loss) if 3500 tests are performed.

28. Fill in the blanks for the 4 unrelated cases:

	Sales	Var Exp.	Fixed Exp.	Total Costs	Net Profit	Cont. Margin Ratio
a)	$1000	700	(4)	1000	(8)	(10)
b)	1500	(2)	300	(6)	(9)	.30
c)	(1)	500	(5)	800	1200	(11)
d)	2000	(3)	300	(7)	200	(12)

29. Looking at the information for Oakridge Clinic given below:
   a. What must revenue be to achieve a net income of $5,500 after taxes?
   b. By what percentage must revenue increase over 1983 to achieve a net income of $20,000 before taxes?

Oakridge Clinic	
12/31/83 Income Statement	
Revenue	$40,000
Operating VC	15,000
Operating CM	$25,000
General VC	10,000
Net CM	$15,000
FC-Operating 5000	
FC-General 5000	$10,000
Net Income Before Taxes	$ 5,000
Tax	2,500
Net Income	$ 2,500

30. S.T. EmergiCenter specializes in emergency outpatient care and has experienced steady growth in revenue for the past 5 years. However, increased competition has led the administrators to believe that an aggressive advertising campaign will be necessary next year to

maintain sufficient growth. The following data was presented to the administrator for the current year:

Revenue per visit	$ 25.00
Expected Revenue, 1983 (20,000 visits)	$500,000
Variable cost/visit	$ 13.75
Fixed Costs	$135,000

The administrator has set the revenue target for 1984 at a level of $550,000 (22,000 visits).
a. What is the breakeven point in units for 1983?
b. The administration believes an additional selling expense of $11,250, for advertising in 1984, will be necessary to attain the revenue target (all other costs constant). What will be the breakeven point in revenue for 1984 if the additional $11,250 is spent for advertising?
c. If the additional $11,250 is spent for advertising in 1984, what is the required revenue in dollars to equal 1983's after-tax net income?

31. St. Elizabeth Hospital is a general hospital, however, it rents space to separately owned entities rendering specialized services such as psychiatric and alcohol rehabilitation units. St. Elizabeth charged the following costs to the psychiatric unit for the year ending December 31, 1983.

	Patient Days (variable)	Bed Capacity (fixed)
Dietary	$ 300,000	
Janitorial		35,000
Laundry	150,000	
Lab	225,000	
Pharmacy	225,000	
Repair/Maintenance		15,000
G & A		650,000
Rent		750,000
Billing & Collections	150,000	
Totals	$1,050,000	$1,450,000

For the year ending December 31, 1983, the psychiatric department charged each patient an average of $150 per day and had a capacity of 30 beds and had revenue of $3,000,000 for 365 days.

The psychiatric unit operated at 100% capacity on 90 days during the year ending December 31, 1983. It is estimated that during these

90 days the demand exceeded 10 patients more than capacity. St. Elizabeth has an additional 10 beds available for rent for the year ending December 31, 1984. Such additional rent would increase psychiatry's fixed charges based on bed capacity.

   a. Calculate the minimum number of patient days required for the psychiatric unit to break even for the year ending December 31, 1984, if the additional beds are not rented (Use 1983 information).

   b. Prepare a schedule of increase in revenues and increase in costs for the year ending December 31, 1984, in order to determine the net income or decrease in earnings from the additional 20 beds if the psychiatric unit rents this extra capacity from St. Elizabeth.

32. The Chapel Hill Home Health Agency operates a semi-skilled hotel type facility for patients needing more than home health type care but less than the short term acute hospital type care. Custodial supply expense and patient days of occupancy over the last 6 months were:

	Supply Expense	Patient days
July	$12,000	$10,500
August	8,250	6,500
September	7,500	4,000
October	9,750	7,500
November	10,750	9,000
December	13,500	12,000

   a. Determine the cost formula for supply expense.

   b. Estimate the supply expense for 11,000 patients days.

33. Paradise Hospital produces and sells highly technical services directed toward the teenage market. A new product has come onto the market which the company is anxious to produce and sell. Enough capacity exists in the company's plant to produce 15,000 units each month. Variable costs to manufacture and sell one unit would be $1.60, and fixed costs would total $16,000 per month.

The marketing department predicts that demand for the product will exceed the 15,000 units which the company is able to produce. Additional production capacity can be rented from another company at a fixed cost of $3,500 per month. Variable costs in the rented facility would total 1.75 per unit, due to somewhat less efficient operations than in the main plant. The product will sell for $2.50 per unit.

Required:
a. What is the monthly breakeven point in units and dollar amount?
b. How many units must be sold in order to make a profit of $3,750 each month?
c. If the sales manager receives a bonus of 10 cents per unit sold in excess of the breakeven point, how many units must be sold each month in order to earn a return of 10 percent on the monthly investment in fixed costs?

34. The Bauer Aspirin Company manufactures a high quality aspirin product which is distributed throughout the western part of the United States. The company sells an average of 250,000 bottles of aspirin each month, with the following cost relationships:

	Per bottle
Selling price	$ 0.50
Variable expense	0.15
Contribution margin	$ 0.35
Fixed monthly cost:	
Building rental	$12,250
Equipment depreciation	8,000
Salaries	20,000
Advertising	25,000
Other fixed cost	15,250
Total	$80,500

Required:
a. Prepare a contribution-type income statement showing the company's monthly profits. Include total, per unit, and percent columns.
b. What is the monthly breakeven point in bottles of aspirin? In total sales dollars?
c. Suppose that the company would like to earn a monthly profit of $10,500. How many bottles of aspirin would have to be sold?
d. If the building rental were doubled, what would be the monthly breakeven point in bottles of aspirin? In total sales dollars?
e. Refer to the original data. If salespersons are given a 2-cent bonus commission for each bottle sold over the breakeven point, what would the company's net income be if 260,000 bottles were sold? (Use the incremental approach.)

f. Refer to the original data. The president is confident that an additional $5,000 in advertising each month would generate a 10 percent increase in sales. Would you recommend the increased advertising? (Use the incremental approach.) Would your answer be the same if the contribution margin was 15 cents per bottle rather than 35 cents? Explain.

35. Memorial Hospital has a licensed bed capacity of 450 beds. An average occupancy rate of 90% is used for most cost estimation. At this level of occupancy, the hospital's operating costs are $16 per occupied bed per day, for a 30-day month. During March, the occupancy rate was only 80 percent. The following costs were incurred during the month:

Fixed operating costs	$ 79,350
Mixed operating costs	105,600

a. Determine the variable costs per occupied bed on a daily basis.
b. Determine the total operating costs per month.
c. Assume an occupancy rate of 86%, what are the estimated total costs?

36. University General is responsible for budgeting and controlling the fleet of ambulances owned by the city. Hospital administrators have determined that an ambulance driven 105,000 miles a year has an average operating cost for fuel, oil and supervision of 11.4 cents per mile. If the ambulance is driven only 70,000 miles, the operating costs increase to 13.4 cents per mile. The budget analyst believes some of the costs are linear for the range of 50,000 to 120,000 miles. The next year's estimate of miles to be driven is 80,000. Determine the total budgeted cost for fuel, oil and supervision for the prepared budget.

37. Memorial Medical Corporation has hospitals in Seattle and Dallas. The hospital in Dallas is a Childrens Hospital while the facility in Seattle specializes in sports medicine (sports injuries). The following revenues and costs were budgeted for the year ending December 31, 1984. (Estimated revenue of $200 per day)

Due to the budget operating loss of the Seattle facility, Memorial Medical Corp. is considering the possibility of closing down. If this alternative is chosen, fixed overhead costs of $100,000 would not be eliminated. (Any proceeds from sale of any assets would exceed book value and exactly cover all termination costs.)
The home office costs referred to are fixed and allocated on patient

	Total	Seattle	Dallas
Revenue	3,000,000	1,100,000	1,900,000
Variable costs:			
Lab	750,000	275,000	475,000
Dietary	805,000	330,000	475,000
Billings & collections	505,000	220,000	285,000
Fixed overhead costs	800,000	350,000	450,000
Fixed regional			
promotional costs	100,000	50,000	50,000
Allocated home office			
costs	150,000	55,000	95,000
Total Costs	3,110,000	1,280,000	1,830,000
Operating income (loss)	(110,000)	(180,000)	70,000

days. Fixed regional promotional costs are discretionary advertising costs.

Memorial Medical Center is considering the following alternatives:
1. The prime location and excellent facilities offered by the Seattle hospital, can allow Memorial Medical Center to lease the facility to another hospital specializing in sports medicine. The lease agreement would call for a fixed payment of $75 per patient day. Fixed overhead costs would remain the same, while promotional costs would be reduced by 50%. It is believed the 5500 patient day is attainable.
2. Close the Seattle facility and expand the operation at the Dallas hospital to attain the budgeted total patient days. This alternative would increase Dallas' fixed regional promotional costs by $50,000.
3. Expand Seattle's operation from the budgeted 5500 patient days to 8000. This would increase promotional costs by $50,000.

Required:
a. Compute the number of patient days required by the Seattle facility to cover its fixed factory overhead costs and fixed regional promotional costs. (Without considering the effects of implementing plans 1, 2, or 3.)
b. Prepare a schedule by hospital, and in total, computing budgeted contribution margin and operating income resulting from the implementation of each of the following plans:
   1) Plan 1
   2) Plan 2
   3) Plan 3

References

Bennington, James L., George E. Westlake and Gordon E. Louvau, *Financial Management of the Clinical Laboratory,* Baltimore, MD: University Park Press, 1974, Chapters 10 and 11.

Brandeau, Margaret L. and David S. P. Hopkins, "A Patient Mix Model for Hospital Financial Planning," *Inquiry* Vol. XXI, Number 1, Spring 1984, pp. 32-44.

Cleverley, William O., "Cost/Volume/Profit Analysis in the Hospital Industry," *Health Care Management Review,* Summer, 1979, pp. 29-36.

Cleverley, William O., "One Step Farther—The Multi-Variable Flexible Budget System," *Hospital Financial Management,* April, 1976, pp. 34-44.

Fitschen, Fred, "Contribution Margin Relates Change in Volume/Activity to Revenue/Expense," *Hospital Financial Management,* March, 1974, pp. 32-38.

Herkimer, Allen G., Jr., *Understanding Hospital Financial Management,* Germantown, MD: Aspen Systems Corporation, 1978, Chapters 7, 9, 10, 11.

Houser, Richard, "How to Build and Use a Flexible Budget," *Hospital Financial Management,* August, 1974, pp. 12-20.

Long, Hugh W. and J.B. Silvers, "Medicare Reimbursement is Federal Taxation of Tax-Exempt Providers," *Health Care Management Review,* Winter, 1976, pp. 9-24.

Needles, Belverd E., Jr., "Budgeting Techniques: Subjective to Probabilistic," *Management Accounting,* December, 1971, pp. 39-45.

CHAPTER 5

Standard cost systems

Introduction

In our discussion of cost behavior, we introduced the concept of fixed and variable costs. These concepts were vital in our development of management accounting techniques such as contribution margin and breakeven analysis. Now we turn to another important tool, the standard cost concept.

In the development of a flexible budget, we were in effect using the concept of a standard cost although we did not label it as such. Basically, a standard cost represents what a procedure or service *should* cost. It is a detailed estimate of the amount of resources required to provide a specific procedure, test, or service within professionally determined quality of care constraints.

The use of standard costs can provide several important benefits:

1. The development of standard costs is a vital part of the flexible budgeting process. Because they are carefully predetermined, future oriented costs, standard costs are the vital building blocks for preparing budgets.
2. Standard costs provide a basis for measuring management performance by permitting the comparison of the actual costs incurred with the planned standard costs. Information can be obtained to explain differences between these two costs. Managers can determine why the differences occurred and isolate the effects of decisions that are designed to affect those differences.
3. Standard costs can be useful in making future decisions where the analysis is dependent on cost estimates.
4. Standard costs provide a more rational and useful basis for inventory valuation. They can also simplify accounting systems and/or procedures, especially concerning inventory management. Inventory items can be carried or transferred out at standard, not actual, cost. In high volume areas such as pharmacy, this could simplify record keeping and billing to patients.

5. Standard costs can be very useful in establishing charges for procedures or services.

Development of standard costs

A standard cost is composed of two key factors—the amount and type of resources required to provide the test, service, and/or procedure, and the per unit cost of each of the resources. The amount and type of resources is properly a function of the medical professional, who has the necessary medical background and experience to insure that quality of care concerns are met. The determination of the cost of the service is influenced by management decisions such as equipment cost, salary schedules, and financial decisions. Management personnel have an obligation to provide the required resources in an effective and efficient manner. The development of standard costs requires a joint effort of the medical staff and management personnel. It is not properly the responsibility solely of the accounting department, even though they play an important role in the process. *Exhibit 5-1* indicates possible sources of data in establishing standards in a health care provider.

Exhibit 5-1
Source of Standards

Cost Determination

● External Authoritative Source

● Internal Industrial Engineering

● Averaging (RCC, RVU, per unit from accounting records and case-mix data)

Resource Use Determination

● Medical Staff

● Allied Health Professionals

● Medical Records

● Regulatory Agencies

In developing the standard costs for a lab procedure, it is necessary to estimate the time required, by type of equipment, as well as the time it takes technicians to take the sample and read the results. The amount of lab supplies required would also be estimated. These labor and material costs are combined to obtain the total cost, which becomes the standard cost for the particular test. An example of these calculations is shown in *Exhibit 5-2.*

These calculations include as direct costs the variable costs of labor as well as the fixed cost of depreciation on the equipment used. Indirect costs, which would include the depreciation on the building and other general fixed assets, are not directly traceable to this particular test, but are

Exhibit 5-2
Standard cost for one lab procedure
Chemistry examination (Type A1)

Estimated direct technician's time	10 minutes	
Estimated direct lab materials		$ 2
Equipment time	5 minutes	
Total department fixed overhead (excluding depreciation)		$100,000
Planned hourly salary of technician		$ 6
Monthly depreciation expense on equipment used in exam		$ 2,000
Estimated number of tests to be performed monthly on Equipment A	10,000	
Estimated total number of procedures to be performed in lab during the month	50,000	

The standard cost for the procedure Type A would be:

Direct labor $(\frac{10}{60} \times \$6.00) =$	$1.00	
Direct materials $=$	2.00	
Total direct variable costs	$3.00	
Equipment charge		
(*depreciation $\frac{\$2.00}{10,000}) = \frac{total\ costs}{total\ units} =$	.20	
Total direct costs	$3.20	
Indirect costs $\frac{\$100,000}{50,000} =$	2.00	
Chemistry procedure Type A1 standard cost	$5.20	

*Depreciation may be calculated on the basis of time or the units processed.

also included in the total standard cost. Note that both the depreciation and the other overhead costs are fixed costs in this case. A standard cost includes both direct and indirect costs. In some cases, indirect costs may be omitted from the standard cost; this is not recommended because of the importance of determining the *full* cost of providing a service.

The information developed in *Exhibit 5-2* indicates the standard cost for performing a chemistry procedure Type A should be $5.20. Once this type of procedure has been costed, the resulting standard can be used in budgeting for the laboratory. Once computations similar to that in *Exhibit 5-2* have been performed for all or most procedures, the responsible supervisor has all the information necessary to develop the appropriate flexible budget. The allocated portion of the general indirect expenses of the hospital may be added to the departmental costs in order to obtain the full costs of providing lab services. However, in establishing a budget for the laboratory, it is not necessary to include all allocated costs for budgeting and control purposes. The general indirect costs of the hospital are not under the control of the laboratory supervisor. Under responsibility accounting, they should not be included in the manager's performance evaluation.

It should be stressed at this point that budgets are in reality guidelines for approved projects or programs within the department during the budgetary period. Budgets reflect future costs. However, it is customary to associate the term "standard" with *individual* services or procedures and the word "budget" with *total* department costs. We will follow that practice in this text, noting that a budget may or may not be based on standard costs for individual services.

Standards can also be developed for discharge or case-mix systems such as DRGs. *Exhibit 5-3* illustrates an example of a standard cost approach for DRG 154.

Exhibit 5-3
Standard cost (e.g. DRG 154)
Stomach, esophagus and duodenum procedures

Resources Required:

Inpatient Care	7 Days
Radiology	3 Diagnoses
Laboratory	3 Procedures
Pharmacy	4 Prescriptions
Medical	2 Procedures

Resource Cost:	*Per Unit*	*Per DRG*
Inpatient	$210.30	$1,472.10
Radiology	41.00	123.00
Laboratory	10.50	31.50
Pharmacy	20.10	80.40
Medical	45.00	90.00
Other Direct Costs	$20 per pat. day	140.00
	Direct Costs Subtotal	$1,937.00
Indirect Costs	45%	871.65
	Total Cost	$2,808.65

To summarize, standard costs represent what a service "should cost" in an "effective" and "efficient" health care provider. They require: estimated types of resources, estimated quantity of resources by type, estimated cost per unit of resource. The estimated cost per unit requires: fixed and variable costs components, direct and indirect categories of costs, an estimate of the volume of services to be provided.

Types of cost standards

Given the importance of meeting standards and a supervisor's expectations, it is very important that the standards established reflect the objectives of the health care management. For example, standards may reflect average performance based on past results, target performance level for expected operating conditions, or target performance level for optimum operating conditions. Each of these approaches have a different motivational impact on the organization.

In some hospitals, the objective might be to have the standards reflect what the costs should be if everything were accomplished at maximum levels of efficiency. This type of standard represents an *ideal* standard; that is, all employees would work at maximum efficiency, equipment would never break down and there would be no time delays in obtaining patients or resources. Clearly, this type of standard will generally be impossible to meet and sizeable variances will occur. The strength of an ideal standard (also called a theoretical standard) is that it sets an example for employees to strive for.

However, if a standard is clearly impossible to meet, employees may become disenchanted and lose their motivation to reach it. The "ideal" standard may be ignored, or employees may sabotage the whole performance reporting process in their attempts to "meet" or "beat" the budget.

A more realistic standard would be based on the degree of efficiency that the department is expected to achieve. This type of standard would make allowances for spoilage and waste, slack time and human limitations. Standards of this type are usually called currently attainable standards. They generally result in more meaningful variances than the ideal standard and are more useful in planning for employee/staffing and materials requirements. They result in more predictable cash flows and shorter turnaround times for reporting results.

Given the difficulty and time consumed in establishing accurate standards, some managers incorporate a long-term orientation (learning and/or startup factors) in the standard cost computation. For example, the rate of usage is expected to be low during the first year a new service such as the CAT scan is offered. A standard could be established, based on projected volume for the third or fourth year. Thus, the sizeable variances during the startup periods would be expected. However, these variances would be expected to decrease as the service reached projected usage rates. In other words, these variances may be controllable only by increasing utilization levels. Note also that expected variances are treated differently in the control process.

In another situation where the expected level of services fluctuates widely over several budget periods, a projected long-run average volume of services could be used in establishing the standard cost. Such a standard, called a "normal" standard, minimizes the impact of volume changes on fixed cost allocations. The favorable and unfavorable variances would be expected to offset each other over several budget periods. Such variances are not currently controllable; they are controllable only in the long run. Consequently, "normalized" standard costs are not appropriate in most healthcare organizations. It may also be useful to separate the type of standards by resource cost and resource utilization. *Exhibit 5-4* presents an example of how this approach might be used in the setting of standards.

Exhibit 5-4
Guidelines in establishing standards

Price Levels

- Ideal (goal to shoot for)
- Normal (average over one or more years)
- Current (market approach)
- Base (Beginning of year)

Performance Levels

- Theoretical (maximum potential)
- Attainable (engineered estimate)
- Past performance (last years results)
- Normal performance (management estimate)

Standard cost systems and the control process

Most hospital accounting systems are based on actual costs; that is, as salaries are paid and supplies utilized, the actual costs are collected in the accounting records. Because most managers have less than perfect forecasting and estimating capabilities, the actual costs will usually differ from the planned standard costs. This difference is called a variance. If the actual costs are less than the standard, a favorable variance is said to have occurred. Conversely, actual costs higher than the standard are considered an unfavorable variance. The type and relative amount of the variances can suggest how much attention should be devoted to a particular department. Questions of the department manager would include the cost to correct the situation, the probability of another similar variance and an assessment of whether the variance was caused by random, uncontrollable or exogenous factors.

A general approach to variance analysis

Most hospital supervisors are confronted with two major types of decisions in their attempts to control costs. One concerns the price to be paid for labor and material; the other relates to the quantities of these resources used. Further complications occur when the materials are purchased before their actual use (e.g., inventories). There are also different degrees of controllability over the prices paid. In some hospitals,

Exhibit 5-5
Total material variances for Department A

Key definitions

Actual costs (AC) = Total units of materials purchased (AQ) × actual price paid for
materials purchased (AP); AC = AQ × AP

Standard costs (SC) = Standard amount of materials that should have been used for
the actual number of procedures performed (SQ) × standard
price for materials (SP); SC = SQ × SP

Standard allowance (SA) = Actual quantities of materials used × standard price for
the materials

Actual costs (AC) − standard costs (SC) = total materials variance
(AQ × AP) − (SQ × SP) = total materials variance

Exhibit 5-6
Department A operating results

Actual materials purchased (AQ) 2,000 gallons
Actual price paid (AP) $2.20 per gallon

  Total costs (AC) $4,400
Standard materials allowed for 20,000 procedures actually completed,
  based on .075 gal. per procedure (SQ);
                    (20,000 × .075) =   1,500 gallons
Standard price per gallon of material (SP) $2.00 per gallon

  Total standard costs (SC) $3,000
Therefore, the total materials variance is
    AC − SC = $4,400 − $3,000 = $1,400 unfavorable materials variance

Exhibit 5-7
A general framework for price analysis

Actual quantity times standard price = AQ × SP = SA for actual quantities
Actual quantity times actual price = AQ × AP = AC
AC − SA = (AQ × AP) − (AQ × SP) = price variance*

*This is called a price variance for materials, a rate variance for labor and a spending
variance for overhead.

a purchasing agent is responsible for the prices paid and the materials ordered. Department heads may also not be able to control the salaries paid to their employees since this may be a function of hospital (or union) salary schedules. In other cases, the department manager may be responsible for placing purchase orders, controlling input prices and negotiating departmental wage levels.

It seems clear that in order to properly evaluate the differences between the actual costs incurred and the standards established, some separation of the different effects of price and quantity must be obtained. The remainder of this chapter will concentrate on developing such a model. Price changes and quantity changes are usually the most important factors that affect cost containment. If other factors are also important, a variance analysis model can be developed to reflect these factors. An expanded model for multi-product variance analysis is illustrated in Appendix 1 of this chapter.

The variance model

The hospital administrator is interested in the total variance that occurs in a specific department, that is, the difference between the actual costs and the budgeted costs. However, in order to determine if, and what, corrective action is needed, more information is required. *Exhibit 5-5* displays the basic calculation of the total variance for materials and supplies.

Given the definitions in *Exhibit 5-5* let's assume the results listed in *Exhibit 5-6* were achieved.

How does the administrator evaluate the $1,400 variance? Who is responsible for the overspending? Is it the result of a change in cost of the materials or were more materials used than planned? Answers to these questions must be obtained if the administrator is to take effective action.

In order to develop answers to these questions, a general framework for analysis can be developed which can be used for all variable costs such as materials, labor and variable overhead. This model separates the total variance into price and quantity components, thereby providing more information to the administrator. *Exhibit 5-7* depicts this general framework for the price variance. Basically the price variance represents the actual quantity purchased times the difference between the actual price and the standard price.

Using the data from *Exhibit 5-6* for Department A, the analysis in *Exhibit 5-8* illustrates the computation of Department A's price variance for materials.

The computations in *Exhibit 5-8* indicate that about $400 of the total variance of $1,400 can be explained by the increase in prices. If the Department A supervisor had no control over the prices paid for the

Exhibit 5-8
Price variance for Department A (materials)

$(AQ \times AP) - (AQ \times SP) =$
$(2,000 \times \$2.20) - (2,000 \times \$2.00) = \$4,400 - \$4,000$ or $2,000 \times \$0.20 =$
$\$400$ unfavorable price variance

Exhibit 5-9
A general framework for quantity variances

Key definitions
Actual quantity of materials used (AQ) times standard price (SP) = SA =
$AQ \times SP$

Standard quantity of materials allowed (SQ) for actual output times standard
price (SP) = $SQ \times SP$ = SC

$SA - SC = (AQ \times SP) - (SQ \times SP) =$ quantity variance*

*This is typically called a usage variance for materials, and an efficiency variance for
labor and variable overhead.

Exhibit 5-10
Quantity variance for Department A (materials)

$(AQ \times SP) - (SQ \times SP) =$
$(2,000 \times \$2) - (1,500 \times \$2) = \$4,000 - \$3,000 = \$1,000$ unfavorable usage
variance or $500 \times \$2 = \$1,000$

materials, then he/she should not be held responsible for this variance.
The remaining $1,000 unfavorable variance also needs to be explained.
Exhibit 5-9 explains the development of the quantity or usage variance.
The quantity variance represents the difference between the quantity
actually used and what should have been used.

Using the data from *Exhibit 5-6* for Department A, *Exhibit 5-10*
indicates how an analysis of the quantity variance can be made.

The analysis in *Exhibit 5-10* indicates that the supervisor in
Department A used $1,000 more in materials than the standard allowed.
It should be stressed at this time that variance analysis does not give a
definitive indication that the supervisor of Department A was in error
because of either the price or usage variances. For example, the standards
may have been in error, the materials may have been of an inferior quality
or the procedure may have been changed. It does, however, point to
possible causes of the variances, and the administrator can decide whether
to investigate further. Variance analysis gives some indication of which

variance should be investigated. In this case, the quantity variance is certainly more important than the price variance. The manager must decide, as a result of subsequent investigation, whether a variance is controllable or not.

To summarize the variances detailed so far:

1. The price variance represents the difference between the actual price paid and the standard price allowed times the actual quantity used, or AQ (AP-SP).
2. The quantity variance represents the difference between the actual quantity used and the standard quantity that should have been used for the actual output obtained times the standard price, or SP(AQ minus SQ).
3. Separating the total variance into its price and quantity components provides more information to help the administrator decide which variances to investigate further. Breaking the variances into components allows the manager to evaluate the relative importance of each variance.

Exhibit 5-11
Labor costs for Department A

Actual labor hours used	11,000 hours
Actual wage rate	$7.00 per hour
Total labor costs	$77,000
Standard hours allowed for 20,000 procedures accomplished, based on 30 minutes per procedure = 20,000 (.5 hrs. per procedure) =	10,000 hours allowed
Standard wage rate	× $6.50 per hour
Total standard labor costs	$65,000

Actual labor costs minus standard costs = $77,000 − $65,000 =
$12,000 unfavorable labor variance

Exhibit 5-12
Labor rate and labor efficiency variances for Department A

Labor rate variance	= AQ (SP − AP)
	= (11,000 hours) ($6.50 − $7.00) =
	(11,000 hours) (−$ .50 per hour) = $5,500 U
Labor efficiency variance	= SP (SQ − AQ)
	= ($6.50 per hour) (10,000 − 11,000) =
	($6.50 per hour) (−1,000 hours) = $6,500 U
Total labor cost variance	= (−$5,500) + (−$6,500) = −$12,000 or
	$12,000 unfavorable labor variance

The labor variance

The variance for labor can be explained using the framework developed for materials. For example, assume the operating results for labor costs in Department A were as indicated in *Exhibit 5-11*.

The total labor cost variance (*Exhibit 5-12*) can be analyzed using the formulas in *Exhibits 5-7* and *5-9*.

Some of the questions that could be asked of the Department A supervisor are: Why did the average wage rates change from $6.50 to $7.00, and why were 11,000 hours used instead of the 10,000 that should have been used? Answers to these questions can determine if corrective action is needed to prevent future problems in this area.

Although the labor variances in the examples above were both unfavorable, it is also important to examine situations where one favorable variance offsets an unfavorable variance, especially when different supervisors are responsible for each component. For example, in Department A, let us assume that the wages to be paid are negotiated by the hospital personnel specialists while the supervisor of Department A is only responsible for the hours worked. Let us assume that the same actual conditions prevailed as in *Exhibit 5-11* for the wage rates but the actual number of hours used changed. The new condition is presented in *Exhibit 5-13*.

Exhibit 5-13
Revised labor costs for Department A

Actual labor hours used	9,300
Actual wage rate	$ 7.00
Total labor costs	$65,100
Standard hours allowed for 20,000 procedures accomplished, based on 30 minutes per procedure (20,000 × .5) =	10,000 hours
Standard wage rate	$ 6.50
Total standard labor costs	$65,000
Unfavorable labor variance ($65,000 −$65,100)	$ '100

Revised labor rate and labor efficiency variances
Labor rate variance = AQ (SP − AP)
= 9,300 ($6.50 − $7.00)
= $4,650 U
Labor efficiency variance = SP (SQ − AQ)
= $6.50 (10,000 − 9,300)
= $4,550 F
Total labor cost variance = $4,650 U − $4,550 F = $100 U

In the example in *Exhibit 5-13*, the Department A supervisor was actually doing a superior job of meeting the standard hours, but the total variance approach would have hidden the full impact of his/her efforts. Questions as to why the average salary costs were higher should be directed to the personnel section. On the other hand, perhaps a more costly mix of RNs was used. Answers to these questions can result in more effective control of future costs.

Standard costs and the accounting system

In the healthcare environment, costs are allocated for two primary reasons: first, to measure departmental or supervisory effectiveness and efficiency (the management control problem identified in Chapter 1), and second, to determine the costs of providing specific services for reimbursement purposes and for income determination. This is analogous to product costing in manufacturing firms.

Accounting systems should be designed to collect both types of information. Generally, accounting systems in healthcare organizations provide satisfactory data for control purposes, but they are basically weak in product costing, especially for prospective reimbursement. In the next section, we will develop the product costing concepts and how they can be applied to health care organizations. But first the overhead costs must be discussed.

Overhead costs

The direct labor and direct material costs can usually be collected through payroll records and supply requisition sheets. These are the actual costs which are necessary for both retrospective reimbursement and budgetary control purposes. On the other hand, overhead costs are more difficult to trace to specific products or services because, by their very nature, they cannot be specifically identified with the particular output. For example, both department supervisors and administrative clerks are necessary inputs to a laboratory, and their salary costs are part of the cost of providing lab tests. Yet, how much of each person's salary "belongs" to each test? In the current retrospective reimbursement environment, this allocation is done by cost finding techniques at the end of an operating period using aggregate data by cost centers. It is difficult to control spending without sufficient detailed information, and it is clearly impossible to do so after the funds have been expended.

In order to allocate overhead costs before the spending period, as is the case with prospective reimbursement, an overhead allocation rate is developed. This will be illustrated more thoroughly in Chapter 6. However, the basic concept is to divide the total overhead costs of the department or cost center by the estimated output of the department.

For example, with total budgeted overhead of $2,000,000 and an estimated volume of 1,000,000 tests, the overhead allocation rate would be $2 ($2,000,000 ÷ 1,000,000 tests) per test. This is the same as the method used in *Exhibit 5-2* for indirect expenses.

Clearly, if the actual volume of output achieved is different from the estimated amount, a different overhead rate would be required to meet the total overhead dollar amount. For variable costs this does not present a problem, because total variable costs are a function of changes in output or volume. However, fixed overhead costs per unit (of volume) would change, creating the volume variance explained in detail in the next chapter.

One way to alleviate the problems caused by fluctuating actual expenses is to credit the department with the standard costs of providing the service. Each unit of output accomplished by the department would be credited with the standard costs for labor, material and overhead. The actual costs would still be collected but they would not be identified with specific products. The amounts in the standard cost accounts would be reconciled with the actual costs each month at the end of the accounting period. Variances could be calculated and explained as illustrated earlier in this chapter. In this case, standard costs would be used for performance evaluation and for interim financial statements.

The basic reason for using the standard costs for entries in this manner, within the department, is to remove seasonal variations, unusual expenses and volume effects from the cost calculations used for management control. If the department is performing at standard, this should be an acceptable goal for both the supervisor and the hospital.

As mentioned earlier in this chapter, the determination of standards for various services and procedures is a vital input into the flexible budgeting process explained in Chapter 4. Using the predetermined individual standards, aggregate standards can be developed for each department to determine the budget for the given volume and mix of services or procedures to be performed during the budget period. The flexible budget adjusted for the actual volume achieved can be compared with the actual costs incurred, and suitable variance analyses can be completed.

Cost accounting techniques and product lines

Cost Accounting Systems are designed to facilitate the determination of the cost per unit of output. To accomplish this objective, the hospital output or product line must be specified. However, there is not universal agreement on what the output of a healthcare provider should be. Is it a service such as a test, procedure, or inpatient day? Or should it be a function of a positive change in health status? Rather than enter this argument, assume that the output and resulting product line is a measurable activity. Rather than focus on the test, procedure, or inpatient day approach, consider them as sub-activity measures which will be costed in order to determine the cost of the hospital product. This is in general agreement with the standard cost models developed earlier in this chapter.

Based on this simplification, the hospital product line is defined as one of three possible choices: per diem, case/discharge, or case/diagnosis. To select the most appropriate basis, we need to determine a set of criteria to evaluate each of these approaches. *Exhibit 5-14* presents a set of criteria which could be used.

Exhibit 5-14
Product line selection criteria

- Does it measure services provided?

- Can profitability be determined for individual cases?

- Does it facilitate cost monitoring and control?

- Does it facilitate resource use monitoring and control?

- Does it facilitate comparison with competitors?

- Does it facilitate budgeting and forecasting capabilities?

Exhibit 5-15 demonstrates how each of the proposed product lines meets the criteria established in *Exhibit 5-14*.

Exhibit 5-15
Evaluation of proposed product lines

Measure services provided	Average of all services	Average by discharges	Average by diagnosis
Profitability determination	Average revenue−average cost	Departmental profit	Departmental profit
Cost control and monitoring	Cost control by average. Cost shifting occurs	Departmental costs	Departmental costs
Monitoring resource use	Resource consumption based on average	Average use by number of discharge	Resources use by diagnosis
Competitive comparison	No allowance for case mix	No allowance for case mix	Comparison by specific diagnosis
Budget/forecasting	Macro approach only (number of patient days)	Some micro potential	Micro potential

The analysis in *Exhibit 5-15* indicates that a case approach to product line offers the best potential to provide information for managerial decision-making, and using a qualifier such as diagnosis permits collection of data which relates more effectively the consumption of resources to the specific product. For example, DRGs are currently used by many payers and providers as an output surrogate. The use of DRGs as a product has certain advantages. First, it provides a limited number of products as compared to the ICD9-CM approach (470 to 10,000). They are clinically-based and provide a reasonably understood format. It is possible to compare your DRG costs and resource consumption with other healthcare providers. Finally, it appears that more and more payers recognize the DRGs as a basis for payment.

DRGs also have several disadvantages. Perhaps most importantly, the data from which DRGs were developed were averages based on Medicare cost reports from a time frame when the data could be considered suspect at best. Resource use by DRG was based on past medical practice and service patterns; cost data depended on the ratio of costs to charges when revenue reimbursement maximization was the primary goal. Finally DRGs do not adequately reflect severity of illness within the DRG.

Cost accounting techniques

Two types of cost accounting techniques are presently used in cost accounting systems. They are:

— Process Costing
— Job Order Costing

Process costing is used when a department produces a series of homogeneous products: laboratory, radiology, housekeeping, laundry, and nursing services are representative departments. Costing of units of output is done on an averaging basis as illustrated in *Exhibit 5-16*.

Exhibit 5-16
Process costing

Total Costs	$20,000,000
Units of Outputs	5,000,000
Average Cost	$4.00

Job order costing depends on accumulating individual costs by specific job. For example, the cost per DRG is a classic example of job order costing. Costs are collected by services received. An example of a job order system is illustrated in *Exhibit 5-17*.

Most healthcare providers have both types of systems in use in their patient billing system. It is important to recognize when averages are involved. *Exhibit 5-18* presents an overview of the hybrid cost system in use in a typical healthcare provider.

Exhibit 5-17
Job order costing
DRG 101

Inpatient Service Charge (days × rate) = Amt.

Radiology (procedure × rate)   = Amt.

Laboratory (test × rate)   = Amt.

Total Cost

Exhibit 5-18
The hybrid cost accounting system

PER DIEM/DISCHARGE/DIAGNOSIS   Requires
                                           Job Order
                                           Costing

Hospital Departments

NURSING   LAB   X-RAY   DRUGS   etc.   Requires
                                           Process
                                           Costing

Since process costing is primarily an averaging technique, close monitoring of management and understanding of cost behavior is vital to controlling costs and quality parameters.

Output measurement and standard cost

In the past, sufficient attention has not been paid to the difficult task of measuring hospital output, especially at the department level. This output measurement problem is closely identified with the setting of standards, both in terms of input costs and output costs. Measuring output is also an important part of the rate-setting process for specific services. Finally, the use of standards can aid in the measurement of individual performance for merit increases and promotions. One of the more difficult aspects of output measurement is the determination of the physical unit to be used for each department. This unit should be a factor that accurately reflects the procedure or service being produced by the department. It should be subject to objective identification and should have identifiable cost elements. Fortunately, the increasing use of computers by most large- and medium-size hospitals can alleviate many of the problems that may be encountered in establishing micromeasures of output for individual procedures and services. In smaller hospitals with minimal access to computers, the use of macromeasures of output is preferred to the absence of any attempt to measure output. Since the volume of output is low and the mix of patients fairly constant, the use of macromeasures of output still provides sufficient information for managers to take appropriate corrective actions.

Herkimer identifies the output of healthcare organizations as falling into two types: 1) gross or macro units of measurement and 2) weighted or micro units of measurement (see *Exhibit 5-19*).[1]

Exhibit 5-19
Comparative study of healthcare departmental gross service units and weighted production units*

Department	Gross production unit (Macro)	Weighted production unit (Micro)
Operating room	Surgical case	Person-minutes
Anesthesiology	Anesthesia case	Person-minutes
Postoperative rooms	Postoperative case	Person-minutes
Radiology	Examinations	RVU's
Laboratory	Tests	RVU's
Physical therapy	Modalities	Person-minutes
Isotopes	Treatments	RVU's
Blood bank	Transfusions	RVU's
Delivery room	Deliveries	Person-minutes
Social service	Visits	Person-hours
Emergency room	Visits	Person-minutes
Nursing	Patient days	Hours of care
Nursery	Patient days	Hours of care

*Reprinted from *Understanding Hospital Financial Management* by Allen G. Herkimer, Jr., by permission of Aspen Systems Corporation: Germantown, MD, ©1978, p. 78.

Most hospitals have developed macromeasures of output. Unfortunately, they typically do not reflect the complexity or mix of the micro outputs for various departments. Weighted units of measurement are designed to allow for different complexities and mixes of procedures. They take into account the different amounts of labor, materials and overhead required for the different procedures. Many professional societies have developed weighted units of measurement for their professional disciplines; these are called relative value units. This term is becoming a synonym for the weighted average unit. Herkimer presents detailed information on the methodology used by the College of American Pathologists and the Connecticut Hospital Association's Laboratory Cost Distribution Statistics.[2]

[1]Herkimer, Allen G., Jr., *Understanding Hospital Financial Management,* Germantown, MD: Aspen Systems Corporation, 1978, pp. 77-99.
[2]Ibid, pp. 285-329.

The calculation of standard costs requires the use of weighted or micromeasures of output in the management control process. Standard costs based on gross or macromeasures do not have sufficient precision to permit the identification of price and quantity variances. They do not allow managers to assess the causes of the variances. In the management control process, this type of gross (macro) measure is acceptable at the total hospital level, but not at the departmental level.

Summary

The establishment of standard costs is not an exact science. It requires input from several knowledgeable sources, including the department manager. In addition, several professional associations and independent groups publish averages on such items as costs, labor and materials, which afford an opportunity to compare individual hospital standards with those from similar institutions. These comparisons and past experiences can be helpful; however, these data must be used with caution, as they probably contain inefficiencies and other undesirable characteristics. The data must be modified to adjust for changing economic conditions, volume requirements and technology. Effective standards must reflect what a procedure should cost, *not what it cost in the past. Exhibit 5-20* summarizes some of the key factors in developing standards.

Exhibit 5-20
Key factors in developing standards

- Standards must correspond to department's primary patient care activity.

- They must consider mix of controllable and uncontrollable costs.

- They should be precise enough to meet management needs but not require extensive accounting systems.

- Standards should consider quality as well as time and quantity.

- Department personnel and management must accept standards.

- Standards must be periodically reevaluated with respect to operational and organizational changes in department.

Questions and problems

1. Define the concept of "standard cost."

2. What advantages can be gained from using a "standard cost system?"

3. What factors should be considered in developing a standard cost for an X-ray procedure?

4. Define three types of standard costs.

5. Define the term "variance" as it pertains to a standard cost system.

6. Why are "overhead rates" developed for procedure/service costing purposes?

7. Explain two types of output measurement for healthcare organizations.

8. Why are output measurements necessary for management control in healthcare organizations?

9. Explain the differences between process and job order costing systems, the need for each in a healthcare provider, and potential problems in using both.

10. University Hospital management personnel collected the following information to be used in establishing a standard cost for DRG 101:

Resources Required	
Inpatient Care	4 days
Radiology	5 diagnoses
Laboratory	4 tests
Surgical	2 procedures

Cost Information

Routine Care
Direct Costs $2,000,000
Indirect Costs $4,000,000
Total Estimated Days of Care 20,000 days

Radiology
Direct Costs
    Fixed $2,000,000
    Variable $10 per diagnosis
Indirect Costs $400,000
Estimated number of diagnoses 10,000

Laboratory
Direct Costs
    Fixed $400,000
    Variable $1 per test

Indirect Costs
    Fixed $600,000
    Variable $.50 per test
Estimated number of tests 20,000

Surgical
Direct Costs $500,000
Indirect Costs $5,000,000
Estimated number of procedures 5,000

Required:
Develop a standard cost model for DRG 101. Make any assumptions you need and identify them in your answer.

11. Department A of a nonprofit clinic has a standard materials usage of three units per procedure. The standard cost of the materials is $4 per unit. Last month this department completed 1,500 procedures at a cost of $27,000. Assuming the actual cost of materials was $4.50 per unit, calculate 1) the total variance, 2) the price variance and 3) the quantity variance.

12. A specialized hospital treats only one type of patient, with these planned results:

Services (10,000 units)	$80,000
Variable costs	32,000
Contribution margin	$48,000
Fixed costs	40,000
Net income	$ 8,000

Actual results were:

Services	$84,000
Variable costs	38,400
Contribution margin	$45,600
Fixed costs	40,000
Net income	$ 5,600

Required:

If 12,000 patients were served at a price of $7.00 per unit, what quantity and price variances would explain the change in net income?

13. The pharmacy department of Community Hospital developed the following standards for manufacturing one unit of Solution X:

Direct chemicals	7.5 ounces at $1.50 per ounce
Direct labor	0.5 hours at $6 per hour

During a recent period, 1,760 units were produced, 15,000 ounces of chemicals were purchased at a cost of $1.25 per ounce and 835 hours of direct labor time were used at a total labor cost of $5,177.

Required:

Compute the materials and labor variances for the period.

14. The radiology department at Suburban Hospital computed the following standard times for completing diagnostic treatments on the CAT scanner:

Direct technician time	15 minutes per test
Direct technician rate per hour	$24.00

During 1970, the department worked 7,750 hours to produce 30,000 treatments. The technician cost was $175,000.

Required:
a. Determine the total labor cost variance for the department.
b. Separate the total labor cost variance into rate and efficiency variances.

15. During 198X, the nursing department at Community Hospital completed 300,000 paid nursing hours for 75,000 actual patient days. During the budgeting process, the nursing supervisor had estimated that the nursing salary budget would be $2,500,000 and that 275,000 nursing hours would be needed for 80,000 planned patient days. Actual nursing salary costs were $2,700,000. Assuming the nursing hours in excess of 200,000 are considered variable, what are some possible reasons for the budget overrun?

16. The Wild West County Clinic provides a single service to its clients. The following data were available from the clinic records:

	Test material	Test labor
Standard quantity per test	3 lbs.	?
Standard input price	$5 per lb.	?

During a recent month, the clinic paid $55,650 for test materials, all of which were used in the completion of 3,200 tests, and worked 4,900 labor hours at a cost of $36,750. The following variance data are available:

Test material quantity variance	$4,500 U
Total test labor variance	1,650 F
Test labor efficiency variance	800 U

Required:
a. Compute the actual cost paid per pound for test material.
b. Compute the test materials price variance.
c. Compute the standard direct test labor rate per direct labor hour.
d. Compute the standard hours allowed for the tests completed during the period and the standard labor hour per test.

17. Assume the following types of services offered by the Mary Grace Gans Speech and Hearing Center for the next planning period:

	Percentage of total
Audiological examination	30
Pediatric audiological examination	20
Pure tone—air and bone	10
Speech evaluation	10
Speech therapy	15
Hearing therapy	10
Hearing and evaluation	5
Total number of procedures	100%

Also assume the following cost structure for the center:

	Fee	Variable *costs*	Contribution *margin*
Audiological examination	$25	$ 5	$20
Pediatric audiological examination	20	5	15
Pure tone—air and bone	15	5	10
Speech evaluation	30	5	25
Speech therapy	15	3	12
Hearing therapy	30	10	20
Hearing and evaluation	24	10	14

Using the above data, construct a composite or weighted average contribution margin for the center based on 20,000 planned procedures.

18. Given the contribution margin developed in Question 17, determine the volume of procedures the speech and hearing center needs to meet its profit goals for the next budget year.

Estimated fixed costs	$240,000
Desired additional income	$100,000

19. Develop the departmental budget based on a contribution margin concept for the speech and hearing center based on the information contained in Questions 17 and 18. Assume that $140,000 of the estimated fixed costs are direct costs of the program and $100,000 are indirect.

20. The Mary Grace Gans Speech and Hearing Center reported the actual results on page 104 for the year 198X. Explain why the reported income was less than the desired objective. (Use data from Questions 17, 18, and 19 if needed.)

21. Saint Mary Hospital has an estimated patient mix and reimbursement basis as follows:

	Mix	*Reimbursement*
Self-pay	25%	$140 per patient day
Private insurance	40	140 per patient day
Medicare	15	120 per patient day
Medicaid	20	130 per patient day

Fixed costs = $85,000
Variable costs = $20 per patient day

a. Calculate the breakeven point in terms of revenue.
b. Calculate the required patient days.
c. Calculate the mix variance assuming the following actual mix of patient days (Note: No other variances can be computed from the data given).

Self-pay	187
Private insurance	301
Medicare	108
Medicaid	150
	746 days

Actual results for the year 198X
for the Mary Grace Gans Speech and Hearing Center

	Total	Audio- logical examination	Pediatric audio. exam.	Pure tone	Speech eval.	Speech therapy	Hearing therapy	Hearing and evaluation
Number of procedures	19,500	5,500	4,200	2,100	2,300	2,700	1,500	1,200
Revenues (assume fees were as planned)	$436,300	$137,500	$84,000	$31,500	$69,000	$40,500	$45,000	$28,800
Variable costs	117,500	32,000	20,000	11,000	15,000	9,500	18,000	12,000
Contribution margin	318,800	105,500	64,000	20,500	54,000	31,000	27,000	16,800
Direct fixed costs	140,000	30,000	40,000	5,000	10,000	18,000	27,000	10,000
Program contribution	178,800	75,500	24,000	15,500	44,000	13,000	-0-	6,800
Indirect fixed costs	110,000							
Net income	$ 68,800							

22. The Lakeview Memorial Hospital has the following projected patient mix:

Self-pay	15%
Private insurance	30
Medicare	20
Medicaid	35

The reimbursement basis is $180 per patient day for both Medicare and Medicaid, and $190 for self-pay and private insurance.

Fixed costs = $840,000
Daily charges = $190 per patient day
Variable costs = $30 per patient day

a. Find the total revenue needed to operate at breakeven.
b. Find the patient days required to operate at breakeven.

Assume actual results were:

	Patient days	Contribution margin
Self-pay	910	$157
Private insurance	1,610	163
Medicare	1,050	148
Medicaid	1,720	145

c. Find the price, quantity and mix variances.

23. A nonprofit clinic provides four types of services in the following proportions:

Service A	25%
Service B	40
Service C	25
Service D	10

It is estimated that the clinic will service 2,540 people next month. Planned charges are $55 per person, with variable costs of $5 per person and fixed costs of $90,000. Actual results are:

Service A	658 people
Service B	1,024 people
Service C	605 people
Service D	348 people
	2,635 people

Actual contribution margin rate = $45

Calculate the contribution margin variances.

24. Assume the same facts as in Question 23 except that the planned contribution margin (CM) and actual results are as follows:

Planned		CM	Actual people served
	Service A	50	607
	Service B	45	1,072
	Service C	40	612
	Service D	50	246

Calculate the variance(s) in the contribution margin.

25. The Sun Valley Health Care Center offers three services with the following projected patient mix:

Nursing care	120 patients per week
X-ray and lab tests	1,350 patients per week
First aid classes	530 patients per week

Nursing care charges are $70 per patient week with variable costs of $15 per patient week. Lab fees are $25 per patient with variable costs of $10 per patient. Class charges are $10 per patient with variable costs of $2 per patient. Fixed costs = $1,310 per week.
   What is the mix variance if the actual patient mix is:

Nursing care	109 patients per week
X-ray and lab tests	1,431 patients per week
First aid classes	460 patients per week

26. Valley Center Hospital has reimbursed rates of $210 per patient day from Medicare, $195 per patient day from Medicaid and $225 per patient day from self-pay or private insurance patients. Fixed costs are estimated at $884,000 with variable costs of $25 per patient day.
   a. Calculate the patient days required to operate at breakeven if projected patient mix is 20 percent for self-pay, 40 percent for private insurance, 15 percent for Medicare and 25 percent for Medicaid.
   b. Find the price, quantity and mix variances with actual results as follows:

Self-pay	901 patient days	$197 contribution margin
Private		
insurance	1,842 patient days	201 contribution margin
Medicare	688 patient days	200 contribution margin
Medicaid	1,165 patient days	208 contribution margin

27. Hillside Hospital estimated its patient mix to be:

	Planned mix	Actual mix	Planned contribution margin	Actual contribution margin
Self-pay	3,150	3,000	$203	$200
Private				
insurance	2,625	2,500	197	200
Medicare	1,575	1,500	181	180
Medicaid	3,150	3,000	163	170

Calculate the price and quantity variance.

28. Harborside Clinic estimated its volume for the next month at 5,150 units of activity. Harborside expects a mix of 30 percent inpatient, 25 percent outpatient and 45 percent emergency services. Charges are $140 per patient day to inpatient, $110 for outpatient services and $80 per unit for emergency. Actual results are:

	Mix	Contribution margin
Inpatient	1,530	$112
Outpatient	1,275	93
Emergency	2,295	57

Assume variable costs of $20. Calculate the price and quantity variances.

29. Saint George Hospital projected its patient mix for the next month:

	Mix	Charges
Inpatient	25%	$170
Outpatient	20	145
Ambulatory	25	70
X-ray	30	80

Fixed costs are estimated at $73,000 with variable costs of $30.
a. Compute the breakeven volume and the planned number of patients in each category.
b. Compute the mix variance from the actual patient mix given below.

	Mix
Inpatient	212 patient days
Outpatient	169 patient days
Ambulatory	228 patient days
X-ray	259 patient days

30. Select operating information on four different ambulatory care centers for the year 19XX is given below:

	A	B	C	D
Full capacity direct labor-hours	9,000	16,000	14,000	11,500
Budgeted direct labor-hours*	6,000	15,000	14,000	9,000
Actual direct labor-hours	6,000	15,500	13,500	9,250
Based on actual output	6,500	14,000	14,000	8,600
*Planned activity level				

Required:

In each case, state whether the company would have:
a. No volume variance.
b. A favorable volume variance.
c. An unfavorable variance.

Substantiate your answer.

31. Calculate cost variances for an ancillary department for one period[1]

Standards & Budgets
- The standard labor hours for all procedures is ½ hour each.
- The standard labor rate is $10 per hour.
- The standard labor cost is $5 per procedure (½ hr. @ $10/hr.).

- Budgeted number of procedures are 1,000 this period.
- Budgeted *standard* labor hours are 500 (1,000 procedures @ ½ hr. each).

----

[1]Price Waterhouse and Co. (St. Louis).

- Budgeted *standard* labor cost is $5,000 (500 hrs. @ $10/hr.).
- Budgeted *actual* labor hours are 528 (3 technicians @ 8 hrs./day @ 22 working days).
- Budgeted *actual* labor cost is $5,280 (528 hrs. @ $10/hr.).
- Budgeted labor spending variance is $280 ($5,280-$5,000).

Actual Results
- Total hours worked were 540 hrs.
- Hourly rate paid averaged $10.50/hr.
- Total actual labor cost was $5,670 (540 hrs. @ $10.50/hr.).

- Total procedures performed were 950.
- Actual hours spent *performing procedures* were 450 hrs.

a. Calculate the following standard cost and variance information:
   Standard cost of procedures performed
   Labor efficiency variance
   Labor rate variance
   Labor volume variance
   Labor spending variance (net of
   labor volume component)
      Total actual labor cost $5,670
b. Calculate and categorize cost variances.
c. Discuss the implications.

32. The finance department at Memorial Hospital has devoted all its efforts to compiling the data needed for Blue Cross and Medicare reports, reports which were not particularly useful for management decisions because of the cost allocations made to satisfy the reporting requirements of these two agencies.

You would like to change the emphasis in the accounting department from developing information for external reports to developing information for internal reports that lead to sound management decisions. If a good reporting system for internal purposes can be developed, Blue Cross and Medicare reports could be prepared from information in the accounting records. In this way both external reporting information and internal accounting information that helps in planning and controlling the hospital's operations can be developed by the accounting system. You would like to establish a flexible budget system but before you can even consider making the change, you must first analyze some of the expenses to determine which are fixed and which are variable.

You have discovered that there has been no analysis of fixed and variable costs for any of the departments of the hospital. Such a classification of expenses is useful if costs are to be controlled—

primarily because variable costs are controllable in the short run, and fixed costs are controllable over a longer time period. By separating expenses into fixed and variable, the use of the flexible budget and standard costs becomes feasible.

In addition to determining cost behavior patterns, you want to get a standard cost system installed as soon as possible because it is essential for pinpointing costs that are out of control. An effective standard cost system will enable the hospital managers to determine more quickly which costs are not in line with planned amounts. Standard costs can also be used to introduce the flexible budget process to the hospital.

Standard cost determination

The accounting department has collected the information below for the dietary department. From the information, you plan to develop a standard cost for the noon meal #16.

Cost elements for the dietary department		

Standard prices for ingredients used in noon meal #16 (200 portions):

	Price	Unit	Quantities per meal
Meat	$2.40	Pound	4 oz.
Vegetable #1	1.92	Two-pound package	1 oz.
Vegetable #2	1.60	Five-pound package	4 oz.
Salad	.64	Pound	2 oz.
Dessert	.96	Pound	2 oz.
Coffee	8.00	Five-pound can	2 oz.
Bread	6.40	Twenty 1-pound loaves	2 oz.

Additional direct expenses incurred in preparing meal #16:

	Estimated cost per individual meal prepared
Electricity, steam, etc.	$.075
Supplies	.010
Maintenance expense	.025

Two cooks spend four hours each to prepare meal #16. These two cooks work overlapping shifts, so half of each cook's shift is devoted to this meal. In addition, a cook's helper spends one and one-half hours preparing the salad: another cook's helper spends two hours helping to prepare the meal. Two cooks and two cook's helpers are on duty every day to prepare the necessary meals each day.

The hourly wages of these employees are:

Cook	$8.00
Cook's helper	4.00

Patient mix and variance analysis

Introduction

In Chapter 4, the authors discuss how to use the well-known management accounting technique of "breakeven analysis" to help accomplish better planning and budgeting for hospitals and other healthcare organizations. This appendix extends the concepts of cost behavior analysis to the management control process of determining why actual results differ from the planned budget.

Background and description of the problem

Breakeven analysis, or cost-volume-profit analysis as it is commonly called, depends on the ability to determine cost behavior patterns and to segregate costs that vary with some index of activity, such as volume. For an entire hospital, the contribution margin is the difference between patient revenues and the variable cost of treating the patient. For example, assume that a patient's daily charge is $120 and variable costs of treating that patient are $40. In this case, the contribution margin is $80. The contribution margin is available to cover fixed costs (including nonreimbursable costs) and to provide funds needed for future expansion.

In the following analyses, the concept of contribution margin will be used because the difference between reimbursement rates and variable costs seems to clearly indicate the effects of important decision variables. However, the same type of variance analysis could be done based on total reimbursement rates and total costs (fixed and variable).

Given the relationship between revenues and variable costs, the role of breakeven analysis can be clearly shown. The breakeven point in a hospital is assumed to be that level of charges or patient days that allows the hospital to cover all fixed costs and all nonreimbursable costs, provide funds for the future and, in a proprietary hospital, earn a return on investment. The hospital will break even at the level of activity where the contribution margin equals the total of these committed costs.

For example, consider a hospital with the following data:

Patient mix		Reimbursement basis per patient day
Self-pay	20%	$120 (total charges)
Private insurance	25%	120 (total charges)
Medicare	30%	110 (cost or charges whichever is lower)
Medicaid	25%	100 (reimbursable costs only)

Fixed costs =	$800,000
Other necessary costs =	$200,000
Daily charges =	$120 per patient day
Variable costs =	$ 40 per patient day (these costs are assumed to be the same for each patient, regardless of the method of payment)

Given the above data, what level of total revenue must be achieved to operate at breakeven? In order to determine this point, a composite contribution margin is developed in *Exhibit 1*.

Exhibit 1
Composite contribution margin

Method of payment	Patient mix	× Contribution margin	= Weighted contribution margin	Reimbursement rate	Weighted reimbursement rate
Self-pay	20%	(120 − 40) = $80	$16	$120	$24
Private insurance	25%	(120 − 40) = $80	20	120	30
Medicare	30%	(110 − 40) = $70	21	110	33
Medicaid	25%	(100 − 40) = $60	15	100	25
Composite contribution margin =			$72		
Composite average daily adjusted rate =					$112

The composite contribution margin ratio is .64 ($72/$112). Therefore, the composite average variable cost ratio is 36 percent because the variable cost ratio plus the contribution margin must equal unity.

As shown in Chapter 4, the breakeven level of revenue is projected to be $1,562,500. The total revenue can be used to determine the number of each category of patient days needed from each reimbursement source by first multiplying the projected level of breakeven revenue ($1,562,500) by the patient mix stated in percentage terms:

Method of payment	Patient mix	Adjusted revenue
Self-pay	20%	$ 312,500
Private insurance	25%	390,625
Medicare	30%	468,750
Medicaid	25%	390,625
Total revenue at breakeven =		$1,562,500

The average number of patient days in each category is obtained by first determining the total number of expected patient days ($1,562,500 ÷ $112 = 13,951 patient days). The quantity of expected patient days indicates an expected level of volume that is necessary to operate at breakeven and cover all identified costs. The number of patient days in each patient category is determined by multiplying the projected volume (13,951) by the patient mix.

Method of payment	Patient mix	Patient days
Self-pay	20%	2,790
Private insurance	25%	3,488
Medicare	30%	4,185
Medicaid	25%	3,488
Total patient days =		13,951

The analysis above indicates that 13,951 patient days would be required to operate at the breakeven point if costs and patient mix are at the planned levels. A budget could be developed for the coming operating period which would incorporate these assumptions regarding patient mix and expected cost behavior patterns. If these assumptions hold, there would be no differences between the planned level of operation and the actual results achieved, and, therefore, no need for variance analysis. However, under most actual conditions, some variances could be expected.

In order to take corrective action and to allow for better planning in future periods, hospital administrators and managers need to be able to determine what caused the actual results to differ from the plan.

Applications

A. In the example discussed above, a composite contribution margin was developed from a planned patient mix and a planned cost behavior. With the composite contribution margin and planned fixed costs, the number of patient days was determined. Assume that during the period of operation the planned number of patient days (13, 951) was achieved (this assumption is relaxed later), yet the hospital had a deficit contribution margin of $16,693. What caused this deficit? Two reasons typically are responsible—the mix of patients may have varied from the plan and/or the contribution margin may have differed from the plan.

For ease in following the analysis, the data from the planning phase are recapitulated:

	Planned mix (Patient days)		*Planned contribution margin*	*Weighted contribution margin*
Self-pay	20%	2,790	$80	$16
Private insurance	25%	3,488	80	20
Medicare	30%	4,185	70	21
Medicaid	25%	3,488	60	15
Total patient days		13,951		
Composite average contribution margin				*$72*

Planned total contribution margin = $1,004,470 =
(patient days) (planned contribution margin)

Assume the actual results were:

	%	*Actual mix Patient days*	*Actual contribution margin rate*	*Actual contribution margin*
Self-pay	18.6%	2,600	$78	$202,800
Private insurance	24.7%	3,450	82	282,900
Medicare	30.9%	4,310	69	297,390
Medicaid	25.8%	3,591	57	204,687
Total days		13,951		$987,777

Total variance in contribution margin = $987,777 − $1,004,470 = $16,693.

Hospital managers need to be able to identify why the variance ($16,693) in contribution occurred. What controllable or uncontrollable variables produced this unfavorable variance? A patient mix variance and a contribution margin rate variance can be developed from the above data.

The patient mix variances and the contribution margin rate variances (*Exhibits 2* and *3*) indicate that the deficit contribution margin was caused both by a change in patient mix and by a difference in the contribution margin rates per patient day. However, it highlights the fact that a significant portion of the total variance ($16,693) was caused by a reduction in the contribution margin rates. Further analysis should be made to find out why either the reimbursement rate and charges or variable costs (or both) differ from the planned amounts. In addition, the patient mix variance indicates that contribution margins have decreased in all (four) patient classes. Decreases in contribution margins from self-pay and private insurance patients resulted from a decrease in the number of patient days in those classes. Patient days increased in both Medicare and Medicaid classes; however, this had a negative effect on contribution margin because of the shift from patients with above-average contribution margins to patients providing below-average margins.

Exhibit 2
Variance due to patient mix differences

	Difference in patient days (actual-planned)	×	Expected contribution margin rate difference	=	Variance in contribution margins due to patient mix
Self-pay	(2,600 − 2,790) = −190		(80 − 72) = 8		$1,520 U
Private insurance	(3,450 − 3,488) = −38		(80 − 72) = 8		304 U
Medicare	(4,310 − 4,185) = 125		(70 − 72) = −2		250 U
Medicaid	(3,591 − 3,488) = 103		(60 − 72) = −12		1,236 U
Total mix variance					$3,310 U

Exhibit 3
Variance due to contribution margin rate differences

	Actual patient days	×	Difference in contribution margins (actual-budget)	=	Variance in contribution margin rates
Self-pay	2,600		(78 − 80) = −2		$5,200 U
Private insurance	3,450		(82 − 80) = 2		6,900 F
Medicare	4,310		(69 − 70) = −1		4,310 U
Medicaid	3,591		(57 − 60) = −3		10,773 U
Total contribution margin rate allowance					$13,383 U

B. The earlier constraint that the actual patient days were equal to planned patient days can now be relaxed. If, for example, the hospital achieved only 13,551 days, with a total contribution margin of $959,177 instead of the planned 13,951 patient days and $1,004,470 of contribution margin, the deficit contribution margin is now $45,293. A quantity variance (400 days) ($72.00 per day) = $28,800 is added to the analysis indicated above. All three variances are recalculated in *Exhibits 4, 5* and *6*. Given that the actual distribution of patient days is:

		Actual patient days
Self-pay		2,500
Private insurance		3,350
Medicare		4,210
Medicaid		3,491
	Total patient days	13,551

the total variance would consist of the following components:

Total quantity variance (Exhibit 4)	$28,800 U
Total mix variance (Exhibit 5)	3,510 U
Total rate variance (Exhibit 6)	12,983 U
Total contribution margin variance	$45,293 U

It is important to note that other quantity and mix variances can also be calculated. There is no unanimity regarding the theoretical, correct calculation of mix variances. The authors feel that the quantity and mix variance illustrated above will provide the most useful information to hospital managers regarding shifts in types of patients.

The analyses of variance presented above permit hospital administrators to determine which areas of operation need further attention. These analyses direct him/her to analyze further why the variances in rate and quantity occurred. The unfavorable variances, by themselves, are only an indicator that some change may need to be made. On the other hand, the administrator may find that certain exogenous effects may be resulting in the identified variances. The hospital may have little control over some of these variables. In any event, isolating the effects of both controllable and uncontrollable variables will permit the manager of healthcare organizations to devote his/her attention and energy in areas where significant positive changes in contribution margin may be attained. Furthermore, the analyses outlined above do provide additional data for planning and for improving budgeting and motivation within the organization.

Exhibit 4
Variance due to patient quantity differences

	Difference in patient days (actual-planned)	×	Budgeted composite-contribution margin	=	Variance in contribution margins due to quantity differences
Self-pay	2,500 − 2,790 = −290		72		$20,880 U
Private insurance	3,350 − 3,488 = −138		72		9,936 U
Medicare	4,210 − 4,185 = 25		72		1,800 F
Medicaid	3,491 − 3,488 = 3		72		216 F
∎Total quantity variance					$28,800 U

Exhibit 5
Variance due to patient mix differences

	Difference in patient days	×	Expected contribution margin rate difference	=	Variance in contribution margins due to patient mix
Self-pay	−290		8		$2,320 U
Private insurance	−138		8		1,104 U
Medicare	25		−2		50 U
Medicaid	3		−12		36 U
Total mix variance					$3,510 U

Exhibit 6
Variance due to contribution margin rate differences

	Actual patient days	×	Difference in contribution margins (actual-budget)	=	Variance in contribution margin rates
Self-pay	2,500		(78 − 80) = −2		$ 5,000 U
Private insurance	3,350		(82 − 80) = 2		6,700 F
Medicare	4,210		(69 − 70) = −1		4,210 U
Medicaid	3,491		(57 − 60) = −3		10,473 U
Total contribution margin rate variance					$12,983 U

Variance analysis for a state Medicaid program

This section summarizes the variance analyses used by a state agency to monitor the effects of patient mix changes on total program costs. The actual FY76 data are a "standard," and variance analysis techniques are used to analyze the changes in costs of inpatient services from one year to the next. Realistically, this type of analysis is believed to be useful for monitoring components of the Medicaid program. Linear regression techniques are used to develop estimates for the budget request to the legislature, but are not used to analyze cost changes from year to year.

The variance analysis performed is based on the data in *Exhibit 7* on the following assumptions:

Exhibit 7
Inpatient hospital service

	FY74	FY75	FY76	Projected FY77	Actual FY77
Recipients	8,604	9,727	8,323	8,756	7,546
Units of service	49,267	56,108	49,022	52,064	58,236
Total cost	$4,328,962	$5,757,866	$6,139,005	$7,305,968	$7,651,229
Units/ recipient*	5.73	5.77	5.89	5.95	7.72
Price/unit*	$87.87	$102.62	$125.22	$140.33	$131.38

*Averages derived from the first lines of data.

$TC = RUP$
R = Number of unduplicated Medicaid recipients.
U = Units of service (days) per recipient (average) and
P = Price per unit of service (average).

Thus, the change in the total cost of a specific component of the Medicaid program, such as inpatient hospital care, is a function of the change in the utilization of services by each recipient and the change in the price of each unit of service.

The variance analysis for inpatient hospital services is shown in *Exhibit 8*. The total variance in hospital inpatient costs in 1977 is an increase of $1,512,224, noted as an unfavorable (U) variance. This total is broken down first into a price and a quantity variance, and the quantity variance is further broken down into a utilization rate variance (services per recipient) and a usage variance (recipients). Thus, the net increase in cost of $1,512,224 is explained by: 1) an increase in price per unit of service that accounted for a $358,917 increase in total cost; 2) an increase in the number of services consumed by each recipient which accounted for a $1,726,784 increase in total cost; and 3) a decrease in the number of recipients which accounted for a $573,006 decrease in total cost.

Exhibit 8
Inpatient hospital variance analysis

$7,651,229	TC - FY77	
6,139,005	TC - FY76	
$1,512,224	Total variance to be explained*	

AQ × AP	AQ × SP	SQ × SP
(58,236 × $131.38)	(58,236 × $125.22)	(49,022 × $125.22)
= $7,651,229	= $7,292,312	= $6,139,005

Price	Quantity	Total
$358,917 U	₁ $1,153,307 U	$1,512,224 U

AQ × AU	AQ × SU	SQ × SU
(7,546 × 7.72) = 58,236	(7,546 × 5.89) = 44,446	(8,323 × 5.89) = 49,022

Utilization rate	Usage	Total
13,790 U	4,576 F	9,214 U

13,790 × $125.22 = $1,726,784 U= Utilization rate variance
(4,576) × 125.22 = (573,006) F= Usage variance
358,917 U= Price variance
$1,512,695 = Total variance explained*

*Differences due to rounding.

Once the variances are isolated, the next and most important step is to analyze the reason(s) for the variances. In the case of the price variance, the most obvious reason for an increase is inflation. The rate of increase observed between FY76 and FY77 was 4.9 percent. Nationally, the rate of increase in the medical care component of the CPI (1975-1976) was 9.5 percent. Due to the rural nature of the state and the number of small hospitals in it, the absolute increases in costs that show up in the Medicaid program reimbursement statistics are probably less than the national average. However, in any given year, the percentage increase may be greater.

The usage variance is difficult to explain. Why did fewer people utilize hospital services in FY77? One possibility is that the number of people on AFDC (welfare) decreased in FY77, as it did in FY76. This seems to correlate with the historical data for recipients presented in *Exhibit 7.* Another possibility is the increased usage of outpatient and clinic services (data not presented here).

Because the utilization rate variance is the most significant factor in the increase in total costs, it demands the most attention. It is also the most difficult to analyze. Possible explanations are that Medicaid patients with multiple diagnoses must have a longer hospital stay and private pay patients have become more cost conscious, opting for shorter stays. It is also possible that persons eligible for Medicaid are becoming more aware of the program and of their right to use it, and are therefore using it more fully. Still another possibility is that there is no real incentive to control utilization, despite the Professional Standards Review Organization.

Essentially, the total contribution margin variance can be divided into several variances. With this type of information, the administrator is better able to fix responsibility, ask relevant questions and take corrective action if needed.

Although this appendix focused on the variances associated with method of payment, the same analyses could easily be applied to patient care categories. The underlying objective of any variance analysis should be to obtain better information for decision-making. These techniques can be adapted to a wide variety of managerial decisions.

Summary

In most organizations, actual results will differ from the planned budget. The hospital administrator needs to know not only what the amount of differences were, but, perhaps more importantly, why these differences occurred. Analytical techniques, such as variance analysis, are helpful in identifying the causes of these differences.

References

Bennington, James L., George E. Westlake and Gordon E. Louvau, *Financial Management of the Clinical Laboratory,* Baltimore, MD: University Park Press, 1974.

Boer, Germain, "Management Accounting Belongs in the Clinical Laboratory," *Hospital Financial Management,* May, 1972, pp. 10, 12, 14, 39, 41.

Burek, David and Thomas J. Duvall, "Hospital Cost Accounting: Strategic Considerations" *Healthcare Financial Management,* Feb. 1985, pp. 18-28.

de Mars Martin, Pamela and Frank J. Boyer, "Developing a Consistent Method for Costing Hospital Services" *Healthcare Financial Management,* Feb. 1985, pp. 30-37.

Griffith, John R., *Measuring Hospital Performance,* Chicago: Blue Cross Association, 1978.

Herkimer, Allen G., Jr., *Understanding Hospital Financial Management,* Germantown, MD: Aspen Systems Corporation, 1978.

Holder, William W. and Jan Williams, "Better Cost Control With Flexible Budgets and Variance Analysis," *Hospital Financial Management,* January, 1976, pp. 12-20.

Messmer, Victor C., "Standard Cost Accounting: Methods that can be Applied to DRG Classificatons" *Healthcare Financial Management,* Jan. 1984, pp. 44-48.

Suver, James D., Edward B. Opperman, and Theodore Helmer, "Variance Analysis: Using Standards to predict recognized Nurse Staffing Patterns" *Healthcare Financial Management,* Sept. 1984, pp. 48-50.

CHAPTER 6

Indirect costs, overhead rates and variance analysis

Introduction

In Chapter 5, the discussion of standard costs focused on direct labor and direct materials costs. Direct costs, costs that can be directly traced to a specific service or procedure, are usually the easiest to control because they occur at the departmental level. They also pose fewer problems in determining the full cost of a service or procedure. However, in most health services organizations, there is another major category of overhead costs. These costs include the indirect administrative costs of patient care departments and other administrative and support services of the hospital such as information services, maintenance, housekeeping, etc. They cannot be traced directly to a service or procedure because 1) no clear relationship exists between the incurrence of the cost and the providing of the service or 2) it is not cost effective to do so. An example of costs in the latter category are utility costs. Every use of electricity could be monitored by putting meters on each receptacle. This would transform the indirect cost of utilities into a direct cost. However, the additional cost of installing meters would probably not be cost effective in terms of the additional management information obtained. Therefore, it is a management decision not to treat certain overhead costs as direct costs, even though such treatment would facilitate both management control and cost determination.

Types of overhead costs

Many hospital overhead costs fall into the indirect category for cost determination purposes, yet they can be considered direct costs for management control. For example, the costs of housekeeping, laundry, dietary, maintenance, administration, etc., must be allocated to procedures or services in order to obtain the full cost of providing a given service or procedure. However, in terms of responsibility accounting, there is a supervisor of each of those sections who is responsible for the direct costs incurred in those departments. It is important to stress again that the direct and indirect cost categories are determined by the cost objective being pursued. Costs may be direct or indirect depending upon the level of responsibility. In summary, overhead costs can be designated as either direct or indirect. It depends upon the purpose for which the cost information is being collected: a direct cost in a department for control purposes may be treated as an indirect cost for some other cost determination purpose, such as rate setting.

Allocation of overhead costs

If a hospital is to remain financially viable, it must receive the full cost of maintaining the institution. Full costs should be defined as the total financial requirements of the hospital as identified in Chapter 1. These total financial requirements include both the direct and indirect costs of the hospital. The direct costs, whch are variable (such as labor and materials), are generally easy to trace to individual procedures. However, the full cost of providing a service must also include the overhead costs, which are not directly traceable to the specific service.

Overhead costs must be allocated to the individual service in order to determine the full costs of providing that service. The allocation process requires two inputs: the set of costs to be allocated and the selection of a volume base on which to allocate those costs. The accumulation of costs to be allocated is a function of the accounting system and the chart of accounts. The choice of the allocation base is much more difficult and subjective. For example, an allocation base could be patient days, square feet of space, pounds of laundry, number of personnel, etc. However, it is generally agreed that the allocation process should be accomplished on a logical and rational basis.

The choice of the allocation base should depend on some clear relationship between the activity and the incurrence of the cost. The relationship may be causal, that is, the particular activity causes the costs to change. Alternatively, the relationship may be correlational; the costs and activities may change in a known direction and in a known relationship. The base should be simple and easily understood whenever possible. Although the criteria for selecting the bases are well known, it is also true in many cases the choice is made on a purely subjective basis; whatever is most apparent, convenient and/or feasible is selected. The allocation procedures discussed above typically fall into the area of cost finding, which will be discussed in greater detail in Chapter 9. However, the impact of the allocation base on full cost determination has forced many cost-based reimbursers to establish very detailed and restrictive policies for deciding what bases can be selected for allocating specific costs. When these external reimbursement policies are used for internal decision-making, major inconsistencies and improper decisions can result. For example, an allocation of social service department costs to outpatient care may be proper to maximize reimbursement. However, in deciding whether to expand the outpatient clinic, this cost allocation could distort the incremental costs of that decision.

For management control, there is no need to allocate direct overhead costs because, by definition, these costs are traced directly to the department responsible for incurring the costs. For example, the direct cost associated with the plant maintenance department is the responsibility of the supervisor of that department. There can be both fixed and variable overhead costs in the plant maintenance department, but the determination of fixed and variable is usually related to the volume base selected. For example, the variable expenses of running emergency generators would be the gas and oil used. This would probably be a function of utilization (number of hours). The fixed expenses would be the cost of buying the generator and related equipment, prorated over the life of the generator through the use of depreciation formulas. Depreciation is the accounting process of allocating acquisition costs over a period of time. When the cost objective becomes the full cost determination of providing a specific service or procedure, a fair share of the full cost of the plant maintenance department must be allocated to the department that provides the service. *Exhibit 6-1* illustrates some typical allocation bases.

Exhibit 6-1
Typical allocation bases*

Cost element	Allocation bases
Depreciation	Square footage
Employee benefits	Payroll dollars
Fiscal services	Accumulated costs
Administrative services	Accumulated costs
Plant operations	Square footage
Plant maintenance	Square footage
Central purchasing department	Cost of supplies used
Laundry and linen	Pounds of soiled (or clean) laundry
Housekeeping	Hours of service
Dietary–cafeteria	Payroll dollars
inpatients	Number of meals served
Nursing administration	Hours of nursing service
Central services and supply	Amount of priced requisitions
Pharmacy	Amount of priced requisitions
Medical records	Patient days or admissions and outpatients
Social services	Time estimate

*From *Cost Finding and Rate Setting for Hospitals*, Chicago: American Hospital Association, 1968, p. 87.

Exhibit 6-2
Development of overhead rates

Macro-Level (Average Basis)

$$\frac{\text{Total Overhead Costs}}{\text{Activity Measures}} \quad = \quad \text{Overhead Rate}$$

Total Overhead Costs = All Indirect Fixed Costs of Provider

Micro-Level (Dept. Specific Basis)

$$\frac{\text{Dept. Overhead Costs}}{\text{Activity Measures}} \quad = \quad \text{Dept. Overhead Rate}$$

Possible Activity Measures

- Units of Service (i.e. Patient Days, Procedures, Tests)
- Surrogate Measures (Revenues, Costs)

Overhead rates

Most pricing decisions are based on the concept of full cost recovery. This would include the variable costs and a fair share of the overhead costs. It is generally expressed as follows:

$$\text{per unit cost} = \frac{\text{overhead costs}}{\text{activity measure}} + \text{variable costs per unit}$$

Notice the similarity to the flexible budget formula in Chapter 4. Since most prices or charges need to be determined before the services are provided, the per unit costs need to be estimated when costs serve as the basis for rate setting. The change from a retrospective to a prospective pricing system by many third-party reimbursers has put added emphasis on better cost information in establishing or reviewing existing charges, since the healthcare provider is now at economic risk for inadequate rates. The assignment or allocation of overhead to specific products to determine a full per unit cost can be facilitated by the development of overhead rates.

A key decision in the development of overhead rates is the choice of an activity measure. The base or activity measure for developing overhead rates is typically more closely identified to the patient care activity than the allocation bases listed in *Exhibit 6-1*. The most common bases would be the number of procedures, services, or tests provided, the amount of labor or machine time used for the service, the amount of drugs, supplies, etc. used, or a weighted average approach such as relative value units. A key determinant in the decision on what base to use would be the availability of data. Rather than create a new data requirement, many providers use existing data such as labor hours, dollar amount of supplies, or equipment time. *Exhibit 6-2* summarizes the major steps in developing an overhead rate for a healthcare provider. *Exhibit 6-3* illustrates how the actual overhead rate would be determined.

The rates determined in *Exhibit 6-3* will be correct or the total overhead costs will be recovered only if the total overhead budget was correct and if the estimated units of service were provided. However, variances from the plan usually occur. The reasons for the variances need to be investigated the same as for the variable cost factors discussed in Chapter 5.

Exhibit 6-3
Determination of overhead rates

Data

Total Overhead Costs	=	$10,000,000
Total Revenues	=	$20,000,000
Patient Days	=	50,000
Routine Service Overhead Costs	=	$ 4,000,000
Routine Service Revenues	=	$16,000,000

Macro Level (Average Basis)

$$\frac{\text{Total Overhead Costs}}{\text{Patient Days}} = \frac{\$10{,}000{,}000}{50{,}000} = \$200 \text{ per patient day}$$

$$\frac{\text{Total Overhead Costs}}{\text{Total Revenues}} = \frac{\$10{,}000{,}000}{\$20{,}000{,}000} = .50 \text{ per revenue dollar}$$

Micro Level (Dept. of Specific Basis)

$$\frac{\text{Routine Service Overhead Costs}}{\text{Patient Days}} = \frac{\$ 4{,}000{,}000}{50{,}000} = \$80 \text{ per patient day}$$

$$\frac{\text{Routine Service Overhead Costs}}{\text{Routine Service Revenue}} = \frac{\$ 4{,}000{,}000}{\$16{,}000{,}000} = .25 \text{ per routine service dollar of revenues}$$

Overhead costs, flexible budgeting and the management control process

Overhead costs must be budgeted in the same manner as other costs in the institution. Although most overhead costs fall into the fixed cost category, the total amount to be spent must be determined and included in the approved budget. The amount budgeted for the variable overhead costs is, of course, dependent on the volume of services to be offered.

As discussed in Chapter 4, flexible budgeting offers a considerable improvement over a static budget because 1) it is geared to a range of activities rather than to a single level of activity and 2) a budget can be constructed for the actual level of activity accomplished. That is, the supervisor can look at the actual level of activity and construct a flexible budget to determine what costs should have been incurred at each activity level.

In terms of management control, we now have the two facts necessary to evaluate the operating results of the period—the actual cost incurred and what the cost should have been from the flexible budget. The analysis of this variance, or difference between these two costs, can provide the administrator with the information necessary to take corrective action. The remainder of this chapter concentrates on these concepts.

Overhead variance analysis

Overhead costs have both fixed and variable components. The variable overhead costs are similar to the labor and material components discussed earlier except they cannot be traced directly to the services provided. Even though they are variable, they are also indirect because the cost to trace them to a specific service is not cost effective. Small medical supplies typically fall into this category.

The basic framework for overhead variance analysis is similar to the techniques developed in Chapter 5 for labor and materials. The difficulty occurs when fixed overhead is analyzed. As a review, let's look at the following variable overhead problem. The standards established for the

Exhibit 6-4
Variable overhead costs* for X-ray Department B

Indirect labor	$.10 per film
Maintenance	.05 per film
Misc. supplies	.12 per film
Total variable overhead per film	$.27 per film

*Based on number of films.
(Variable overhead costs are those costs that vary with volume changes in the base selected; in this example, the amount of film used.)

variable overhead terms are as shown in *Exhibit 6-4*. Determination of these costs would be part of the flexible budgeting process.

The allocation base selected for X-ray Department B is the number of X-ray films processed. Let's assume 5,800 films were processed last month. The actual variable overhead costs incurred were $1,740. What should the costs of processing 5,800 films have been? This can be determined by using the flexible budget data in *Exhibit 6-4* and multiplying the number of films by the cost per film (5,800 × $.27) = $1,566.

The variance of $1,740 − $1,566, or $174, needs to be explained. If all the films were good, we could explain the $174 as a spending variance; the department spent more than it should have. However, let's introduce the concept of efficiency into X-ray Department B. For example, assume out of the 5,800 films processed, only 5,000 were usable for diagnostic purposes. The standard costs are now 5,000 × $.27 = $1,350 and the total variance is $390. We now can complete the variance framework introduced in Chapter 5. Remember how the two variances are calculated: spending variance = actual cost (AQ × AP) − budgeted costs (AQ × SP), and efficiency or quantity variance = budgeted costs (AQ × SP) − standard costs (SQ × SP).[1] In terms of X-ray Department B, the variance components are:

Spending variance = 5,800 (.30 − .27)	= $174 U
Efficiency variance = .27 (5,800 − 5,000)	216 U
Total	$390 U

The total variance achieved by X-ray Department B would be $390, composed of a price variance and a quantity variance as determined above.

This example stresses the similarity between variable overhead variances and the variance for materials and labor. Variable overhead variances are calculated in the same manner for any variable costs. The most meaningful variances are price and quantity/efficiency variances.

The inclusion of fixed costs into the analysis poses different types of problems. Fixed overhead costs include depreciation on equipment, supervisors' salaries and clerical costs. Fixed costs by definition do not vary with volume levels. In the flexible budgeting process, fixed costs were shown as a static amount and variable costs as a function of volume. This can be expressed as a linear equation ($y = a + bx$), where a = fixed costs, b = variable cost per unit basis and x = volume (units). If we assume the fixed costs in X-ray Department B were $6,000 for one month, the flexible

---

[1]The variances could also be expressed as AQ(AP − SP) and SP(AQ − SQ).

budget total for this department would be $7,566 = $6,000 + .27 (5,800). Let's assume the actual overhead costs for X-ray Department B were $8,000 ($6,260 fixed and $1,740 variable).

The administrator would like to have more information to evaluate the operating results since the budget was only $7,620, or 6,000 + $.27 (6,000) = $7,620, based on an estimated 6,000 films to be processed. In X-ray Department B the actual fixed costs were $6,260. Because by definition fixed costs do not vary with volume, and the fixed overhead budget for the department was $6,000, the spending variance for fixed overhead was $260 ($6,000 − $6,260) unfavorable.[2] When the fixed overhead spending variance is combined with the variable overhead variances computed earlier, the report in *Exhibit 6-5* could be made to the administrator. Note that the flexible budget total of $7,566 is irrelevant to this comparison because it is based on 5,800 total films. Of these, 800 films were deemed unacceptable, and only the 5,000 acceptable films should be used for evaluating management control. Of course, the waste and scrap must be separately evaluated.

In most hospitals, the variance information presented in *Exhibit 6-5* would be sufficient for the administrator to evaluate the performance of the supervisor of X-ray Department B. In terms of evaluating the rates or charges established for X-ray Department B, the analysis of variance must be carried one step further. Let's assume that the output of X-ray Department B (number of good films processed) was used to determine the fee that was to be charged for each film. The fee was established in advance, based on costs of the department. The overhead cost calculations follow:

Variable overhead costs	$ .27 per film
Fixed overhead rate	1.00 per film*
	$1.27 overhead cost/film†

$$\frac{\text{*\$6,000 (total fixed overhead cost)}}{\text{6,000 (number of films to be processed)}} = \$1.00 \text{ fixed overhead rate per film}$$

†This would be considered the standard overhead cost per film or the standard overhead rate per film. The direct labor and materials plus other allocated costs would be added to this amount to develop total standard costs.

Therefore, each time an acceptable film was processed, X-ray Department B would be credited with $1.27 for overhead costs. Given the actual results for the month of March, X-ray Department B would be credited with the overhead rate per film ($1.27) × the number of good films (5,000), or $6,350. The actual costs were $8,000; therefore, X-ray

---

[2]In some textbooks this would be called the fixed overhead budget variance.

Department B would show an unfavorable variance of $1,650 ($8,000 − $6,350). What caused the difference between the variance computed in *Exhibit 6-5* and the $1,650 unfavorable variance computed above? The additonal $1,000 of variance ($1,650 − $650 in *Exhibit 6-5* can be explained by reviewing how the $1.27 rate was determined.

Exhibit 6-5
Analysis of spending and efficiency variances for X-ray Department B

Actual costs: $8,000	Budgeted costs based on good films achieved: $7,350*	Total variance to be explained: $650 unfavorable
Spending variance (variable overhead)	$174 U	5800 (. 27 −. 30)
Spending variance (fixed overhead)	260 U	(6000−6260)
Efficiency variance (variable overhead)	216 U	. 27 (5000−5800)
Net variance	$650 U	

*$7,350 = 6,000 + $.27 (5,000)

	Summary of overhead variances for X-ray Department B	
(1) *Actual Costs* *$ incurred*	*(2)* *Flexible Budget* *(Based on 5000 films)*	*(3)* *Amount Recovered* *Through Overhead Rate* *(5000 × $1.27)*
$8,000	$7,350	$6,350

$$\begin{array}{cc} (1) & (3) \end{array}$$
Total variance to be explained = Actual Costs − Amount Recovered
$8,000 − $6,350 = $1,650

Detailed Variances* (See footnote for computations)

Variable overhead spending variance	=	174U
Variable overhead efficiency variance	=	216U
Fixed overhead spending variance	=	260U
Fixed overhead volume variance	=	1000U
		$1650U

---

*Variable overhead spending variance = AQ (AP − SP) = 5,800 × (.30 − .27) = 174U

Variable overhead efficiency variance = SP (AQ − SQ) = .27 × (5,800 − 5,000) = 216U

Fixed overhead spending variance = actual fixed overhead − budgeted fixed overhead, or 6,260 − 6,000 = 260U

Fixed overhead volume variance = standard fixed overhead rate × (planned volume − actual "good" volume or output) = $1.00 per unit (6,000 − 5,000) = $1,000U. The volume variance also may be computed as the fixed overhead budget minus the standard fixed overhead allowed = $6,000 − (5,000 × $1.00) = $1,000U.

It was initially estimated that 6,000 films would be processed by X-ray Department B. Dividing the fixed overhead costs ($6,000) by the 6,000 estimated volume resulted in a fixed overhead rate of $1.00 per film. However, only 5,000 films were processed. The difference (1,000) between the 6,000 estimated and the 5,000 obtained times the $1.00 fee equals the $1,000 unfavorable variance achieved. This variance, typically called the volume variance, is caused by calculating and establishing rates at an estimated volume. Unless the actual volume is the same as the estimated volume, there will always be a volume variance. The volume variance may not be controllable by the department manager and should rarely enter the performance evaluation process. The volume variance can be used to explain why charges may be insufficient to cover all costs. The volume variance may also be called the denominator activity variance.

Management control and performance measurement using variance analysis

An effective management control system depends primarily on two factors: 1) a system that informs people of what is expected of them, i.e., a set of standards or budgets and 2) a feedback mechanism which lets them know how they are doing. The feedback mechanism consists primarily of performance reports which compare the actual performance with the planned performance. This management control process was discussed in detail in Chapter 1. Therefore, this chapter will primarily focus on the performance measurement aspects of variance analysis. *Exhibit 6-6* describes the relationship of performance reporting to managerial decisions.

Exhibit 6-6
Performance reporting and evaluation

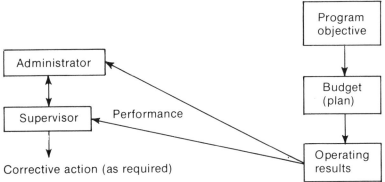

Any effective performance measurement system consists of timely reports that are considered fair by the person being evaluated.

The ideal performance report would be structured so as to motivate the supervisor to take corrective action when it is required. Timely informative reports can play a vital role in developing the manager's own initiative to take such action.

The concept of variance analysis was discussed in some detail earlier in this chapter. This section describes how variance analysis can be integrated into the planning and control process. The variance analysis, although typically supervised by the controller or vice president for finance, should be understandable to each supervisor. A useful way of accomplishing this is to develop a series of reports based on the flexible budget concept using our framework for analysis.

Before the operating period starts, the supervisor and the budget personnel should develop the necessary inputs to complete the flexible budget. A flexible budget for lab services is shown in *Exhibit 6-7*.

Exhibit 6-7
Flexible budget for laboratory services

	Standard variable costs	Fixed costs	Budget*
Direct labor (per test)	$2.00	-0-	$60,000
Direct materials (per test)	.60	-0-	18,000
Variable overhead (per test)			
Indirect labor	.05	$ 1,500	3,000
Miscellaneous supplies	.09	1,800	4,500
Fixed overhead			
Department supervisor	-0-	3,000	3,000
Automatic equipment			
lease costs	-0-	6,000	6,000
	$2.74	$12,300	$94,500

Flexible budget formula = (2.74) (number of tests) + 12,300 =

2.74 (30,000) + 12,300 = $94,500

Variable overhead rate	$.14 per test
Fixed overhead rate	
(12,300/30,000)*	.41 per test
Total overhead rate	$.55 per test

*Estimated volume of tests = 30,000 per month.

The supervisor can use the information contained in *Exhibit 6-7* to monitor the costs as they are incurred relative to the volume of tests completed. He/she does not have to wait until the end of the budget period to take corrective action. Periodic performance reports can be used to describe the actual costs and budgeting cost using the flexible budget. These performance reports, provided to both the supervisor and administrator, can be based on the variance analysis framework developed earlier in this chapter. For example, assume the actual costs for the laboratory for one month are as shown in *Exhibit 6-8*.

Exhibit 6-8
Actual laboratory costs

Number of tests completed	29,000
Number of satisfactory tests	28,500
Actual direct labor	$ 65,291
Actual direct materials	19,591
Actual variable overhead	7,100
Actual fixed overhead	12,500
Total actual costs	$104,482
Budget from Exhibit 7-6 (based on 30,000 tests)	94,500
Total variance from original budget	$ 9,982 U

Exhibit 6-9
Variances for laboratory department

Rate variance	65,291	− (29,000 × 2.00)	=	$ 7,291 U
Efficiency variance	(29,000 × 2.00)	− (28,500 × 2.00)	=	1,000 U
Price variance	19,591	− (29,000 × .60)	=	2,191 U
Usage variance	(29,000 × .60)	− (28,500 × .60)	=	300 U
Variable overhead spending variance	7,100	− (29,000 × .14)	=	3,040 U
Variable overhead efficiency variance	(29,000 × .14)	− (28,500 × .14)	=	70 U
Fixed overhead variance	12,500	− 12,300	=	200 U
	Total variance*			$14,092 U

*Total variance = $104,482 − [12,300 + 2.74(28,500)].

Exhibit 6-10
A standard cost system for
laboratory department

	Standards derived from Exhibit 7-6
Direct labor	$2.00
Direct materials	.60
Variable overhead	.14
Fixed overhead	.41
Total standard cost per satisfactory test	$3.15

Standard costs for 28,500 satisfactory tests would be $89,775 = (28,500 × $3.15).

Comparing the actual costs with the budgeted totals would indicate an unfavorable variance of $9,982, which should be investigated. But is this the most relevant variance that could be calculated? In the analysis of

Exhibit 6-8, the manager is being evaluated on the basis of a budget for 30,000 good tests. However, the manager should have incurred costs for only 29,000 tests. Of these, only 28,500 were acceptable tests. Under these conditions, a flexible budget can perform an important role in performance measurement.

Using the flexible budget formula developed in *Exhibit 6-7,* flexible budgeted cost = ($12,300 + 2.74x), where x = number of tests. The clinical laboratory costs should have been $90,390, or $12,300 + 2.74 (28,500). Comparing the actual costs of $104,482 with the flexible budget costs of $90,390 gives an unfavorable variance of $14,092, a sizable increase over the $9,982 variance that would normally be reported.

Based on the information in *Exhibits 6-7* and *6-8,* the analysis in *Exhibit 6-9* summarizes all the potentially relevant variances.

The variances in *Exhibit 6-9* should be evaluated to see which are considered significant. They should then be investigated to determine what can be done to eliminate or reduce the significant unfavorable variances. Perhaps some of these variances are uncontrollable. If so, the total variance of over $14,000 cannot be eliminated, and managerial attention should be concentrated on only the controllable portion.

The variances contained in *Exhibit 6-9* could be further refined if a standard cost system were used. If the department were credited with a standard cost for each good completed test, it would be possible to further refine overhead variances. For example, the standards shown in *Exhibit 6-10* are based on the data originally developed in *Exhibit 6-7.*

A new variance would then be calculated based on the standard cost in *Exhibit 6-10.* This new variance would be $14,707U, or $104,482 actual costs − $89,775 standard costs. The difference between the unfavorable variance of $14,092 developed in *Exhibit 6-9* and the $14,707 is $615. This can be explained by calculating the volume variance developed earlier. The volume variance is caused by the fact that the fixed overhead rate of $.41 was computed by dividing the fixed costs of $12,300 by 30,000 tests. When only 28,500 good tests were completed, the volume variance is computed as shown in *Exhibit 6-11.*

Exhibit 6-11
Computation of volume variance
for laboratory department

Budget for fixed overhead (does not change with volume)	$12,300
Standard costs allowed (28,500 × $.41)	11,685
Volume variance	$ 615 U

It seems clear that the different variances shown in *Exhibits 6-9* and *6-11* provide a clearer picture of why the actual costs differed from the budgeted costs. Whether correction is needed depends on the reasons for the variances. However, the supervisor and the administration now have a better idea of what questions to ask or what areas to explore in greater detail.

Summary

Indirect costs pose a special challenge to the hospital management. Because of the difficulty in relating this type of cost to specific outputs, an allocation process must be designed to arrive at the full cost of providing a service. The allocation is a function of the total costs incurred and the volume of output achieved. Variances can be caused by changes in many different factors. In order for hospital managers to take corrective action, they need the type of information contained in the variance analyses described in this chapter. Performance reports must be timely and fair if they are to lead to corrective action which is in the best interests of the hospital. Variance analysis can help in insuring that the reports reflect what has actually happened.

Questions and problems

1. Define indirect costs for a hospital.

2. Define overhead costs for a hospital.

3. Why must indirect costs be allocated in a healthcare organization?

4. Name the two inputs necessary for the allocation process in a healthcare organization.

5. Name the criteria for selecting a proper base for allocating indirect costs in a healthcare organization.

6. For the following cost elements, select the proper allocation base and state your reasons for selecting that base.

Depreciation	Dietary—cafeteria
Employee benefits	Inpatient—cafeteria
Fiscal services	Nursing administration
Administrative services	Central services
Plant operations	Pharmacy
Plant maintenance	Medical records
Laundry and linen	Social services
Housekeeping	Central purchasing dept.

7. Explain the difference between variable and fixed overhead costs.

8. Define the volume variance for a healthcare organization.

9. Name the three variances that can be computed from overhead costs.

10. Given the data on nursing administration indirect costs, develop the overhead rates for the hospital as required based on a planned volume of 4,880 patient days. You should develop a fixed and variable component if possible.
    a. The overhead rate per patient day at the planned level of activity (4,880 patient days).
    b. An overhead rate based on the entire range of activity (0-6100).
    c. An overhead rate based on the relevant range of activity (3660-6100).

Nursing Administration Indirect Costs

Patient Days	0	1,220	2,440	3,660	4,880	6,100
Occupancy	0	.20	.40	.60	.80	100%
Supervision	$2,000	3,000	3,000	3,500	3,500	3,500
Clerical	300	400	500	600	700	800
Supplies	60	120	180	240	300	360
Education	200	200	200	200	200	200
	$2,560	3,720	3,880	4,540	4,700	4,860

11. The radiology department of St. Louis Hospital has requested that an analysis be made of their overhead costs for the month of May.

    The standards as developed by the controller, Paul Tollison, are:
    Standard cost per test:

Variable overhead	$5.00
Fixed overhead	2.00
Total overhead per test	$7.00

    The flexible monthly overhead cost budget on a direct labor basis is:

Standard direct labor hours	Budgeted overhead
1,000	$ 5,500
2,000	8,000
3,000 (normal capacity)	10,500
4,000	13,000
5,000	15,550

It takes two direct labor hours at standard to complete one test. In May, 1,600 tests were made, and actual total overhead was $12,000.

Required:
a. Calculate the flexible budget formula.
b. Calculate the overhead variances.
c. Calculate the overhead variances assuming actual fixed overhead was $3,000.

12. The dietary service of Memorial Hospital established the following standard cost per breakfast served:

Raw food costs	6 ounces at $.08 per oz. =	$ .48
Labor	12 minutes at $.06 per min. =	.72
Variable overhead		.18
Fixed overhead		.25
	Total standard costs	$1.63

During January, 7,000 ounces of raw food was purchased at a cost of $563.50, and total labor costs were $712.48. One thousand breakfasts were served during the month, which required 6,220 ounces of food and 11,680 minutes of labor. Normally they expect to serve 1,100 breakfasts. Actual total overhead for the month was $450.

Required:

Compute all possible variances.

13. Ellen Townsend, associate administrator of St. Joseph's Hospital, was concerned about the overhead costs for her billing department. The total variable-overhead budget variance was $4,000 unfavorable, while the fixed overhead spending variance was computed to be $2,000, also unfavorable. Actual overhead costs were $168,500, with $110,000 being fixed. Other available information indicates the standard variable cost per billing was $.05, and the standard productivity per clerk was 10 billings per hour.
   If the variable overhead spending variance was determined to be $2,000 favorable, compute the:
a. actual hours of output
b. standard hours allowed for output achieved
c. variable overhead efficiency variance

14. Beth Butler, controller of Total Health Center, was reviewing the results of that year's operation to prepare the operations performance report for the administrator, Jeff Elland. The Total Health Center provides medical and psychiatric services to persons recovering from drug and alcohol abuse. A standard cost system had been derived and used by the center in budgeting and controlling costs. For example, the standard costs per unit based on 60,000 patient days were:

Materials—1 pound at	$ 2.00
Direct nursing labor	
(1.6 hours at $4 per hour)	6.40
Variable overhead cost	3.00
Fixed cost per patient day	2.00
Total standard costs	$13.40

The variable overhead cost per unit was calculated from the following annual overhead cost budget for the 60,000 patient days volume.

Indirect labor	
30,000 hours at $4 per hour	$120,000
Supplies—medical	
60,000 units at $.50 per hour	30,000
Allocated variable service costs	30,000
Total variable overhead costs	$180,000

The actual costs for the Total Health Center for March, when 5,000 patient days were achieved, were:

Materials	5,300 lbs. at $2.00 per lb.	$10,600
Direct nursing labor	8,200 hrs. at $4.10 per hr.	33,620
Indirect labor	2,400 hrs. at $4.10 per hr.	9,840
Supplies—medical	6,000 units at $.55 per unit	3,300
Allocated variable		
service department costs		3,200
Fixed costs		11,000
		$71,560

Required:
a. Calculate all possible variances from the data presented.
b. Prepare a report to the administrator which highlights the information in ways that will be useful in evaluating the performance of the Total Health Center.

15. The Free Standing Laboratory prepares pharmaceutical supplies for several private practices in Central City. These tests are usually accomplished in standard batches of 5,000 units. The standard cost for a batch is:

Raw materials	200 lbs. at $.04 per lb.	$ 8.00
Direct labor	4 hrs. at $5.15 per hr.	20.60
Overhead (including variable overhead of $4.50)		10.00
	Total standard cost per batch	$38.60

Data for December are:

Planned production	240 batches
Actual production	250 batches
Cost of raw materials purchased (55,000 lbs.)	$2,310.50
Cost of raw materials used (51,250 lbs.)	2,152.50
Direct labor cost (988 hours)	5,189.60
Actual overhead cost	2,560.00
Budgeted fixed overhead cost	1,320.00

Required:

Compute all possible variances.

16. Memorial Hospital would like to evaluate DRG 101 and institute a standard cost approach for budgeting and planning purposes. The following data were collected for the DRG from hospital operations:

Costs
— Operating room direct costs = $13,000 fixed costs plus $3.00 per operating room minute
— Radiology direct costs = $4,000,000 fixed costs plus $1.00 per relative value unit (RVU)
— Laboratory direct costs = $2,000,000 fixed costs plus $.50 per lab test
— Pharmacy direct costs = $800,000 fixed costs plus $3.00 per prescription
— In-patient routine costs = $25,000,000 fixed costs plus $2.00 per patient day

—Indirect costs = $50,000,000 fixed costs plus $.25 per DRG
—Medical procedures costs = $1,000,000 plus $25 per medical procedure
—All other direct costs = $5,000,000 plus $3 per DRG

Resources Required for DRG 101

4 medical procedures	4 pharmacy prescriptions
10 in-patient days	2 radiology procedures
3 lab test	

Miscellaneous Data

Total DRGs for year	= 100,000
Total medical procedures	= 10,000
Total operating room minjtes	= 351,000
Total lab tests	= 20,000
Total radiology relative value units	= 20,000
Total patient days	= 116,800
Total pharmacy prescriptions	= 20,000

Make any assumptions you need to complete the standard cost computation.

Required:
a. Develop a standard cost for DRG 101 using a direct cost format.
b. Develop a standard cost for DRG 101 using a full cost format.

17. Dietary costs at Memorial Hospital can be divided into two categories: labor costs and supply costs. Labor costs are considered 100 percent variable and are related to the number of meals served. Analysis of labor costs identifies two factors: the average hourly rate paid per manhour and the number of manhours per meal served. The following labor budget formula is used: dietary labor costs = meals served × (manhours per meal) (rate per manhour).

Supply costs are divided into two groups: food and all other. Food costs are 100 percent variable relative to the number of meals served. All other costs are considered fixed. Therefore the following budget formula is used for supply costs: supply costs = (meals served × food cost per meal) + fixed costs.

The dietary worksheet (shown below) identifies all the factors used to analyze the budget variances for April.

The following narrative was provided by the department manager:

April	Actual	Budget
Volume of meals served	19,476	21,250
Manhours per meal served	.28	.26
Rate of pay per manhour	$3.60	$3.79
Meals wasted	0	0
Food costs per meal	$0.96	$0.73
Fixed costs	$2,191	$3,425

A general summary indicates that productivity is not as high as was anticipated; however, this is more than offset by the lower pay rates and lesser volumes than were expected. This creates an overall favorable labor cost variance. Food costs, although partially offset by lower volumes are so much higher than planned that there is an overall unfavorable variance in this department.

Required:
a. Evaluate the variance analysis used in the dietary department.
b. Revise the analysis as appropriate.

18. The following information is available on the single service offered by Emergency Medical Supplies Company for the month of March:

	Materials used	Direct labor	Variable overhead
Total standard cost*	$260	$1,900	$950
Actual costs incurred	276	?	985
Materials price variance	?		
Materials quantity variance	20F		
Labor rate varience		?	
Labor efficiency variance		?	
Overhead spending variance			?
Overhead efficiency variance			?

*For the month's production.

The following additional information is available for March production:

Number of units produced	100
Actual direct labor-hours	410

Standard overhead rate per hour	$2.50
Standard price of one pound of materials	$0.40
Overhead is based on	Direct labor-hours
Difference between standard and actual cost per unit produced during March	$1.19 U

Required:

a. What is the standard cost of a single unit of service?
b. What was the actual cost of a unit service produced during March?
c. How many pounds of material are required at standard per unit of service?
d. What was the materials price variance for March?
e. What was the labor rate variance? The labor efficiency variance?
f. What was the overhead spending variance? The overhead efficiency variance?

19. Fair Weight, Inc., produces testing instruments for laboratories. The company uses standards to control its costs. The labor standards which have been set for one very popular instrument are:

Direct labor time per instrument	15 minutes
Direct labor rate per hour	$5.20

During 19X5, the company worked 7,750 hours in order to produce 30,000 of these instruments. The direct labor cost amounted to $39,525.

Required:

a. What direct labor cost should have been incurred in the manufacture of the 30,000 instruments? By how much does this cost differ from the cost that was incurred?
b. Break down the difference in cost from (1) above in terms of a labor rate variance and a labor efficiency variance.
c. For each direct labor-hour worked, the company expects to incur $5 in variable overhead cost. This rate was experienced in 19X5. What effect did the efficiency (or inefficiency) of labor have on variable overhead cost in 19X5?

Memorial Hospital variance analysis — dietary costs — April

( ) = favorable variance

Labor costs:

Actual: 19,476 actual meals × (.28 hrs./meal)
($3.60/hr.) = $19,632

Budget: 19,476 actual meals × (.28 hrs./meal)
($3.79/hr. @ std.) =   20,668

Pay rate variance   ($1,036)

Actual: 19,476 actual meals × (.28 hrs./meal)
($3.79/hr. @ std.) =   20,668

Budget: 19,476 actual meals × (.26 hrs./meal @ std.)
($3.79/hr. @ std.) =   19,192

Efficiency variance   1,476

Labor price variance $ 440

Actual: 19,476 actual meals × (.26 hrs./meal)
($3.79/hr. @ std.) =   19,192

Budget: 21,250 budgeted meals × (.26 hrs./meal)
($3.79 per hr. @ std.) =   20,940

Labor budget variance   (1,748)

Total labor cost variance   ($1,308)

Supply costs:

Actual: 19,476 actual meals × $.96/meal =	18,697		
Budget: 19,476 actual meals × $.73/meal @ std. =	14,217		
Variable supply price variance		4,480	
Actual: 19,476 actual meals × $.73/meal @ std. =	14,217		
Budget: 21,250 budgeted meals × $.73/meal @ std. =	15,513		
Variable supply budget variance		(1,296)	3,184
Fixed supply cost – actual	2,191		
Fixed supply cost – budget	3,425		
Fixed supply cost variance			(1,234)
Total supply cost variance			1,950
			$ 642

Total dietary cost variance

Total actual costs	40,520
Total budgeted costs	39,878
Total dietary cost variance	$ 642

20. General Laboratory flexible budget (in condensed form) is given below.

| | Cost Formula (per DLH) | Direct Labor-hours | | |
		8,000	9,000	10,000
Variable overhead costs	$1.05	$ 8,400	$ 9,450	$10,500
Fixed overhead costs		24,800	24,800	24,800
Total overhead costs		$33,200	$34,250	$35,300

The following information is available:

a. For 19X1, a standard activity of 8,000 direct labor-hours was chosen to compute the predetermined overhead rate:
   Overall rate: $33,200 ÷ 8,000 DLH = $4.15
   Variable element: $8,400 ÷ 8,000 DLH = $1.05
   Fixed element: $24,800 ÷ 8,000 DLH = $3.10

b. In working 8,000 standard direct labor-hours, the company should produce 3,200 units of output.

c. During 19X1, the company's actual operating results were:

Number of output units	3,500
Actual direct labor-hours	8,500
Actual variable overhead costs	9,860
Actual fixed overhead costs	25,100

Required:

a. What were the standard hours allowed for the output of 19X1?

b. Compute the variable overhead spending and efficiency variances, and the fixed overhead budget and volume variances for 19X1.

21. Select operating information on four different ambulatory care centers for the year 19XX is given below:

	A	B	C	D
Full capacity direct labor-hours	9,000	16,000	14,000	11,500
Budgeted direct labor-hours*	6,000	15,000	14,000	9,000
Actual direct labor-hours	6,000	15,500	13,500	9,250
Standard direct labor-hours based on actual output	6,500	14,000	14,000	8,600

*Planned activity level

Required:

In each case, state whether the company would have:
a. No volume variance.
b. A favorable volume variance.
c. An unfavorable volume variance.

Substantiate your answer.

22. Paradise Hospital's flexible budget is given below:

	Cost formula patient day	*Number of patient days*		
Overhead costs		*10,000*	*11,000*	*12,000*
Maintenance	$1.15	11,500	12,650	$13,800
Indirect material	0.80	8,000	8,800	9,600
Rework time	0.50	5,000	5,500	6,000
Total	$2.45	$24,500	$26,950	$29,400

During a recent period the company provided 11,400 patient days. The overhead costs incurred were:

Maintenance	$11,200
Indirect materials	9,750
Rework time	7,300

The patient days budgeted for the period had been 12,000 units.

Required:
a. Prepare a performance report for the period. Indicate whether variances are favorable (F) or unfavorable (U).
b. Discuss the significance of the variances. Might some variances be the result of others? Explain.

23. Performance reports and variance analysis
The laboratory manager, Tobie Adler, has been consulting with you periodically for help in installing standard costs in the laboratory. She eventually developed a standard cost system, but she now wants you to help her analyze why the laboratory contribution margin for January is so much higher than originally forecast. The forecast data and actual results are shown below.
  Adler would like to have a contribution report which she could use to train her personnel and to take corrective action.

Clinical laboratory data for January

I. Forecast budget

	Planned volume	Standard charge	Total
Serum chemistry	2,000	$15	$30,000
Urinalysis	1,500	10	15,000
Complete blood count	1,500	10	15,000
	5,000		$60,000

Labor costs	Planned volume	Standard cost	
Serum chemistry	2,000	$1.00	$ 2,000
Urinalysis	1,500	.50	750
Complete blood count	1,500	.20	300
	5,000		
	Total labor costs		$ 3,050
	Planned contribution margin		$56,950

Fixed costs

Lab supervisor		$20,000
Maintenance		3,000
Depreciation		5,000
Total fixed costs		$28,000
Planned profit		$28,950

II. Standard cost data

Average hourly rate:	$10
Standard time allowed:	
Serum chemistry	6 minutes
Urinalysis	3 minutes
Complete blood count	1.2 minutes

III. Actual data

Tests completed		Actual charge
Serum chemistry	2,300	$16
Urinalysis	2,000	12
Complete blood count	2,100	12
	6,400	

Actual labor costs	
Serum chemistry	$ 2,400
Urinalysis	1,200
Complete blood count	840
The average hourly wage was $12	
Actual fixed costs	$29,000

References

Anthony, Robert N. and David W. Young, *Management Control in Nonprofit Organizations,* Homewood, IL: Richard D. Irwin, 1984.

Anthony, Robert N., Glenn A. Welsch, and James S. Reece, *Fundamentals of Management Accounting,* Homewood, IL: Richard D. Irwin, 1985.

Bennington, James L., George E. Westlake, and Gordon E. Louvau, *Financial Management of the Clinical Laboratory,* Baltimore, MD: University Park Press, 1974.

Berman, Howard J. and Lewis E. Weeks, *The Financial Management of Hospitals* 5th ed., Ann Arbor, MI: Health Administration Press, 1982.

Boer, Germain, "Management Accounting Belongs in the Clinical Laboratory," *Hospital Financial Management,* May, 1972, pp. 10, 12, 14, 39, 41.

Buckley, Adrian and Eugene McKenna, "Budgetary Control and Business Behavior," *Accounting and Business Research,* Spring, 1972, pp. 137-150.

Chart of Accounts for Hospitals, Chicago: American Hospital Association, 1966.

Cleverley, William O., *Essentials of Hospital Finance,* Germantown, MD: Aspen Systems Corporation, 1978, Chapter 6.

Conrad, Douglas A., "Returns on Equity to Not-for-Profit Hospitals: Theory and Implementation" *Health Services Research* Vol. 19, No. 1, Apr. 1984, pp. 41-63.

Esmond, Truman H. *Budgeting Procedures for Hospitals,* Chicago: American Hospital Association, 1982.

Griffith, John R., "Budgeting Process Integral to Effective Cost Control Systems, *Hospital Financial Management,* July, 1974, pp. 12-28.

Hancock, Walton M. and Paul A. Fuhs, "The Relationship Between Nurse Staffing Policies and Nursing Budgets" *Healthcare Management Review,* Vol. 9, Number 4, Fall, 1984, pp. 21-25.

Herkimer, Allen G., Jr., *Understanding Hospital Financial Management,* Germantown, MD: Aspen Systems Corporation, 1978, Chapter 7.

Holder, William W. and Jan Williams, "Better Cost Control with Flexible Budgets and Variance Analysis," *Hospital Financial Management,* January, 1976, pp. 12-20.

Horngren, Charles T., *Cost Accounting: A Managerial Emphasis,* 4th ed., New York: Prentice Hall, 1982.

Howard, Patrick, Dur N. Voetberg, and Allwyn J. Baptist, "Measurement, Feed Back, and Control: A Framework for Hospital Cost Management" *Healthcare Management Review* Oct. 1984, pp. 20-23.

Plomann, Marilyn P. and Truman Esmond, "Using Case Mix Information for Budgeting" *Healthcare Management Review* Oct. 1984, pp. 38-42.

Rakich, Jonathan S., Beufort B. Longest, Jr., and Thomas R. O'Donovan, *Managing Health Care Organizations,* Philadelphia: W.B. Saunders Company, 1977.

Ramsay, Louis P. and R. Stephen Cantrell, "Investigating Cost Variances Using Control Charts" *Healthcare Financial Management,* Jan. 1985, pp. 61-62.

Ridgeway, V. F., "Dysfunctional Consequences of Performance Measurements," *Administrative Science Quarterly,* September, 1965, pp. 240-247.

Schafer, Eldon L., Frank L. McCarthy, Dwight Z. Zulauf, and Bruce R. Neumann, *Practical Financial Management for Medical Groups,* Vol. 2: *Data Accumulation Systems,* Denver, CO: Center for Research in Ambulatory Health Care Administration, Medical Group Management Association, 1978.

Stairs, John D. and John R. Coleman, "Study Shows Budgeting Art Improved in Hospitals," *Hospital Financial Management,* October, 1979, pp. 52-61.

CHAPTER 7

Budgeting, performance measurement, and responsibility accounting

Introduction

In previous chapters, we developed a foundation for understanding the behavior of costs. In this chapter we will develop the technical and behavioral aspects of the budgeting process and its relationship to the planning function. It is generally recognized by most experienced managers that a properly prepared budget can be a vital tool in the effective control of hospital operations. Because of the service orientation of most hospitals and the lack of an overall output measurement similar to a profit margin, the budget may be one of the most valuable tools the administrator has to monitor costs. Therefore, a detailed understanding of what it is and how it works is vital. Since the planning function should establish the foundation for the preparation of the budget, it will be discussed first.

The planning function

Planning for the future is a vital aspect of the administrator's job. Typically he/she will be helped by several committees composed of members of the hospital staff and the trustees. Regardless of the organization entities involved, the planning function should consider two major areas: 1) environmental factors and 2) decision factors.

Environmental factors cannot usually be changed by the hospital in the short run; therefore, the hospital must base its strategies on these factors as they are. This should include consideration of the economic, social and political forces which will affect the future of the hospital. Examples of such forces are future population mix (both in absolute numbers and composition), age factors, mobility, special health risk categories, etc. The number of competitive hospitals in the area, the types of equipment available and community support are also vitally important in planning future operations. Finally, relationships with local health planning agencies and political leaders should be clearly assessed and analyzed in preparing plans for the future.

The decision factors are those specific goals, objectives and programs that are directly decided by management. For example, decisions may be made on quality of care, type of services to be offered, emergency room hours of service and the composition of the medical staff.

Generally, the planning function can be separated into two related aspects: strategic and operational. The strategic aspect includes the process of deciding the future direction of the hospital. It involves:

1. identifying the healthcare organization's mission,
2. setting goals and objectives,
3. identifying the resources available to the hospital in the future and
4. defining programs to accomplish the goals and objectives within the constraints of available resources.

The operational aspect of the planning function primarily deals with the preparation of the budget. It consists of organizing the hospital resources to accomplish the programs identified in the strategic planning process. Operational planning involves projecting financial resources needed for up to three years in the future. The first year of the projection would be the detailed operating budget, which will be discussed in the next section. The next two years would be summarized to capture the major aspects of the long-range plan. The budgeting and planning process will be repeated each year to maintain a multiyear approach at all times. Typically, the operational planning process can be developed from the bottom up. However, the strategic function must be accomplished from the top down because it requires the special expertise and judgment of top managers and medical personnel.

A diagram of the budget and planning process is shown in *Exhibit 7-1*.

What is a budget?

A completed budget is usually defined as the plan of operations for the coming year expressed in quantitative terms. The budget, if properly accomplished, combines and coordinates all the individual activities of the hospital into an approved statement of revenues and expenses for the coming year. In a sense, the preparation of the budget becomes the process of planning for the next fiscal period. When completed, the budget communicates the approved plans to supervisors responsible for carrying out specific functions. It can motivate managers and personnel at all

Exhibit 7-1
The planning and budgeting process

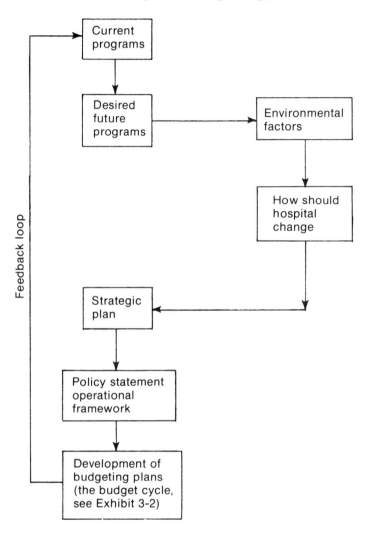

levels, and finally it offers a measurement device against which actual performance subsequently can be compared. In states with hospital commissions which are charged with approving rate structures, the negotiated budget becomes the focal point for the review and approval process.

In all cases, budgeting is a top management responsibility, and the effective preparation and utilization of the data should be a continuing concern.

Checklist for an effective budgeting process

For a budget to be an effective management tool, several key factors are necessary:

1. Top management must support and be involved with the budget process.
2. The hospital must be divided into responsibility centers with individuals who have the necessary training and authority to make daily operating decisions assigned to those centers.
3. These responsibility center supervisors should participate in the preparation of the budget.
4. There must be a management information system (MIS) which provides accurate and detailed information by responsibility centers. Since the accounting system is usually the major part of the MIS, the chart of accounts for the organization must be current and aligned with the responsibility centers.

If any of these factors are weak or missing, it will be exceedingly difficult to achieve the positive results of the budget process. Administrators can and should concentrate on correcting deficiencies.

The total budget concept

Although we have used the term budget in a unitary sense, a completed budget actually has several components. This master budget should consist of the following principal parts:

1. A statistical budget showing planned levels of patient days, ancillary services and related activities.
2. An operating budget combining the statistical budget and the resources needed to accomplish the activities. The operating budget should be expressed in terms of responsibility centers and the personnel responsible for accomplishing the objectives. A pro forma or projected statement of revenues and expenses should be the natural outgrowth of the operating budget.
3. A capital expenditure budget for the acquisition of fixed assets for the fiscal period.
4. A cash budget which shows the anticipated sources and uses of funds to meet the requirements of the operating budget and the capital expenditure budget. A pro forma balance sheet and source and uses of funds would be prepared at this time. The entire budget cycle is shown in *Exhibit 7-2.*

Exhibit 7-2
The budget cycle

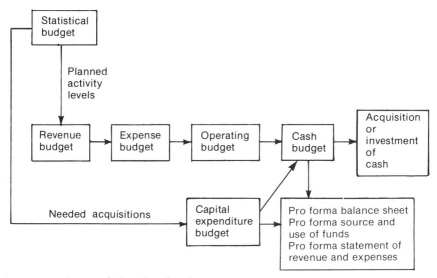

An overview of the budget process

In most large hospitals, an effective budget process requires input and coordination between several departments in the hospital. One way to achieve this is to establish a budget committee composed of the associate administrator, the controller and the major department heads. This committee recommends to the administrator the general planning factors for the next fiscal period, reviews the submitted budgets and resolves differences whenever possible.

The controller takes the guidelines and activity levels approved by the administrator and disseminates them to the operating supervisors responsible for individual budget preparation. This information should include the planned level of operations for the coming year, this year's actual expenses and any known increases in costs for salary, supplies, etc. In addition, it is useful to hold training sessions before actual budget preparation starts to clear up any misunderstanding of the formal budget documents and due dates.

In most cases a formal budget manual should be provided to the supervisors responsible for preparing departmental budgets. It should be recognized that many operating supervisors will have had little formal training in budget preparation. A budget manual should explain in considerable detail how the budgeting system works in the hospital. It should include deadlines for completion of individual steps, the approval process, samples and instructions for completing the required forms and the glossary of definitions. Many finance and accounting terms are foreign to personnel trained to provide healthcare. Thus, a ready reference source can prove to be invaluable during the budget preparation period.

The meetings and the budget manual can do much to minimize the frustrating budgeting experiences for many operating supervisors. The manual should be prepared with their needs in mind—above all, the controller and his/her staff should be available to assist the supervisors at all times.

The budget timetable

To be effective, budget preparation should start well in advance of the implementation date. At least six months should be allowed in those states which require regulatory approval of the budgets for rate-setting. In other cases, a minimum of at least three months should be established. This time constraint means that the most recent or current year figures can not always be incorporated into the budget. The decision to wait as long as possible before preparing the budget in the hope of including the most up-to-date figures will depend on the current healthcare environment, the budgetary experience of the supervisors, and the preference of top management. Generally, the need for sufficient time to prepare and review the budgets should outweigh the disadvantage of not having the last few months of actual data. The controller and his/her staff and the supervisors should be able to estimate sufficiently accurate cost data for budget preparation to begin. Statistical techniques similar to those discussed in Chapter 13 can help in estimating. An example of a budget timetable is shown in *Exhibit 7-3*. This timetable should and will vary by hospital. However, it is usually better to err on the side of too much time

Exhibit 7-3
The budget preparation timetable

Implementation date plus	Activity
+ 7 months	Budget committee meets
+ 6 months	Guidelines and instructions to operating supervisors
+ 5 months	Initial budgets from operating departments
+ 4 months	Controller review of initial budgets
+ 3 months	Budget committee review with operating supervisors. Submission to regulatory agencies
+ 2 months	Integration and review of final budgets
+ 1 month	Final budget approval. Submission to operating department
0	Operations started

rather than not enough time to resolve differences and make a proper review.

Preparing the operating budget

The controller's organization and the responsibility center supervisors must work together to estimate the level of activity for the budget period. Generally, the hospital management will provide an estimate of the level of occupancy to be anticipated. This occupancy level can then be used by the individual supervisors to project the activity levels for their departments based on the most appropriate measurement. For example, nursing wards can use patient days and acuity levels to estimate required nursing hours. Ancillary departments can use tests, procedures, visits, etc. The important factor is to pick the statistical measure which most nearly approximates the factors which cause the incurrence of costs.

Exhibit 7-4
Statistical worksheet

Ancillary revenue departments only

Description of statistical activity which is your basic revenue-producing statistic, e.g., exams, tests, procedures, visits, etc.

_____

Outpatient statistical activity
6-month outpatient
statistical activity   × 2   =   Your department's 1985-86 budget outpatient statistical activity base
(1) _____   (2) _____

Additions (decreases) to the   Adjusted outpatient statistical
base statistical activity*   =   activity 1985-86 budget
(3) _____ (4) (_____)   (5) _____

*Explain in detail any additions (or decreases) noted in Items 3 and 4. If additional space is required, please use the back of this form.

NOTE: *Please submit only the method for outpatient activity you wish to use for your 1985-86 budget.*

Dept. director _____   Vice president _____

Date _____   Date _____

                                      Finan. Serv. _____

                                      Date _____

For example, some ancillary department supervisors may base their projections on an average number of tests per patient day. However, this type of projection may ignore a change in the patient mix or the addition of a new service. Care should be taken that projections reflect the new budget period, not just what happened in the past.

After statistical worksheets are prepared and approved, revenue and expense worksheets can be prepared. Statistical projections must be reviewed to insure that the hospital departments are coordinated. Difficult adjustments could be required if, for example, one department was planning on implementing a new test which required participation by another department. An example of a statistical computation worksheet is shown in *Exhibit 7-4*.

Preparing the revenue budget

The revenue projections for a healthcare provider must reflect the type of services provided for each patient payment category. For example, some patients will pay full charges, others will pay a negotiated charge, and the remainder may pay on a DRG basis. The use of DRGs for reimbursement for Medicare patients, and in many states for Medicaid, makes the estimating of the type and volume of DRGs crucial to the revenue budget. Since payments for each DRG are now determined prospectively by the federal and state government, this has taken out some of the uncertainty on how much will be paid; however, the estimating of volume for each DRG by type of patient is not a minor task for most healthcare providers.

Outpatient reimbursement for government patients is primarily a function of reasonable costs. There has been some shifting in outpatient charges for non-government patients to reflect the intensity of services provided. This refinement will add to the complexity of estimating revenue for the outpatient department, but it should be done as accurately as possible. The outpatient revenue may be a function of patient visits or it may be based on a categorization of visits by intensity of care received.

Finally, many healthcare providers are entering into capitation rates with HMO's or other alternative health providers. This revenue can be considered fixed for the budget period as contrasted to the payment by DRG which will vary by the volume and type of DRG.

For other patients, the rate to be charged for each type of service will be determined by the previous year's charges, the state regulatory agencies, federal reimbursement regulations and competitive conditions; i.e., what other hospitals in the area are charging. Many hospitals typically estimate their expenses for the budget year first, then establish rates to cover these expenses. Before cost containment became an issue, this may have been acceptable, but in today's environment, it is not realistic or appropriate.

Some hospitals prepare the revenue and expense budgets at the same time. The revenue budget is projected first at last year's charges. These revenue projections are compared with the expense projections for the same volume of activity and adjustments are made in both rates and expenses to meet cost containment objectives.

In some hospitals, revenues are projected first, and guidelines are then given to the department supervisors to help them establish their expenses. Under prospective reimbursement concepts, this may be the most logical manner in which to proceed if caps are to be placed on total authorized revenues. To summarize, revenue projections should be done at the departmental level based on: 1) type of service to be provided and 2) amount of payment to be received.

An example of a worksheet that can be used for revenue budgeting is shown in *Exhibit 7-5.*

Exhibit 7-5
Radiology department
Memorial Hospital
For the month of January 198X

Payment categories	Number of procedures to be accomplished	Planned rate*	Contractual allowance/ bad debt	Revenue to be received
Blue Cross Medicare** Medicaid** Comm. insur. Self-pay	Relative value units or other type of unit measurements			

*This can be computed for existing and revised rates.

**Under prospective reimbursement, this service will probably be included in the DRG rate.

Preparing the expense budget

The labor hours worksheet and full-time equivalent (FTE) projections are very significant cost projections, as most hospital departments are labor-intensive. The division between productive and nonproductive labor hours is an important management decision. Small changes can lead to significant labor cost-savings, but they can also create considerable employee unrest. An example of the labor hours computation worksheet is shown in *Exhibits 7-6* and *7-7.*

Exhibit 7-6
Labor hours worksheet

Departments with statistical units of service

Total statistical units of
service budget 1985-86
(1) _____

1985-86 budgeted productive
× labor hour performance unit
(2) _____

Total productive labor hours
budget 1985-86
(3) _____

Nonproductive labor hour
factor
(4) _____

Total nonproductive labor
hours budget 1985-86
(5) _____

Total productive labor hours
Item (3) plus total nonproductive
labor hours, Item (5)

Total 1985-86 budget labor hours
(6) _____

÷ 2,080 labor hours

Total 1985-86 budgeted FTEs
(7) _____

NOTE: Total nonproductive labor hours budget (#5) uses the following formula:

$$\frac{\#3 \text{ productive labor hours}}{100\% - \#4 \text{ nonproductive factor}} \times \#4 = \#5$$

Once the total labor hour and FTE budgets are prepared, salary dollars can be computed on the basis of planned cost of living increases, merit raises and implementation dates *(Exhibit 7-8)*.

Other expense items such as supplies, maintenance, service contracts, etc., would be estimated to prepare the total department budget, which would be submitted to the reviewing authority.

Preparing the capital expenditure budget

Because of the large amounts of money involved and the long-term commitment aspect of the decision, the capital expenditure budget is usually considered separately from the operating budget. However, the same information on planned activity levels is also required to make judgments about the capital expenditures. Capital expenditure decisions can be grouped according to their purpose, such as:

1. health and safety requirements,
2. cost reduction and replacement equipment,
3. expansion and improvement of existing services,
4. new services and
5. special requirements.

Exhibit 7-7
Labor hours worksheet
Budget year June 1, 1986 through May 31, 1986

		Labor hours				
	FTEs	*Total*	*Productive*	*Overtime*	*Total productive hours*	*Nonproductive*
100 Management						
105 Supervisory						
110 Professionals						
120 Residents						
130 LPNs						
140 Aides						
150 Clerical/ secretarial						
160 Technicians						
170 Other						
200 Contract						
Totals						
	(7)	(6)	(A)	(B)	(3)	(5)

Note: Columns A and B should equal Column 3, and Columns 3 and 5 should equal Column 6.
Note: One FTE (full-time equivalent) equals 2,080 hours.

Exhibit 7-8
Departmental staffing summary

Department _____ Department no._____ Page_____ of _____pages

Effective date _____

Occupational title (1)	Salary grade	Salary range	Position control number	Regular (2) FTE positions			Relief FTE positions (if part-time, show hours worked for each position)	Total FTE positions
				day	evening	night		
			Totals					

(1) Occupational title must conform to existing personnel salary structures.

(2) Unless otherwise indicated, regular FTE positions indicate normal staffing pattern 7 days per week. (number of employees on duty on a typical day)

Approvals:

_____	_____	_____	_____
Department head	Date	Personnel director	Date
Division assistant administrator	Date	Administrator	Date

Exhibit 7-9
Capital investment proposal

Date _____

Hospital _____ Group _____

Project title _____

Classification:

_____ improved profit   Budgeted project cost: _____

_____ improved patient care   Amount requested: _____

_____ improved doctor relations   capital _____

_____ replacement   expense _____

_____ other   Total to be approved _____

                                           less: trade-in (_____)

Disposition: Total requested _____

Book value _____   plus: working cap. _____

Current market value _____   Total project cost _____

Capital expenditure request summary

	under $7,500	$7,500 to $25,000	over $25,000
Current year budget	$ _____	$ _____	$ _____
Total requested to date	_____	_____	_____
Remainder	$ _____	$ _____	$ _____

Brief description of project:

Estimated annual increase (decrease) in pretax profit ..... $ _____

Profitability indices:
  DCF rate-of-return   _____ %
  Average pretax return
    on original investment   _____ %
  Cash payback period   _____ years

Hospital:
Requested by: _____   Date: _____
Controller _____   Date: _____
Administrator _____   Date: _____

Capital budgeting requirements should include an economic analysis whenever possible in order to help in the evaluation of the project. It is recognized that political and nonquantifiable aspects of the project may overwhelm the economic aspects. However, it is always useful to obtain the best possible estimates of the economic impact of the project. Techniques for evaluating capital expenditure proposals will be discussed in greater detail in Chapter 10. One example of a capital investment request form is shown in *Exhibit 7-9.*

Preparing the cash flow budget

After the operating and capital expenditure budgets have been completed and approved, the financial staff can review the cash position of the organization for the budget period. This usually can be done on a macro level by comparing total cash requirements and total cash receipts for the year. This macro review tests the overall feasibility of the master budget. However, it will not indicate when cash shortages may occur during the budget period. This is accomplished by preparing monthly cash inflow and outflow projections. Shortages can either be met by short-term borrowing or delaying certain capital expenditures.

For example, the total cash budget for the period could be projected as shown in *Exhibit 7-10.*

Exhibit 7-10
Determination of financial feasibility
of budget planning

Cash requirements		
Capital investments	$500,000	
Repayment of debt	300,000	
Third–party audit	50,000	
Depreciation fund	200,000	
Expansion reserve	100,000	
Total requirements		$1,150,000
Cash available		
Excess of revenues over expenses (loss)	(100,000)	
Add noncash expenses:		
Depreciation	300,000	
Total cash from operations		$ 200,000
Endowment income		300,000
Donations		500,000
Misc. income		50,000
Total cash available		$1,050,000
Anticipated cash shortage		$ 100,000

Hospital management would have to decide on actions that could be taken to make up the estimated shortage indicated in *Exhibit 7-10*. This could involve postponing capital investments, reducing the deficit from operations by increasing rates or reducing expenses or delaying other cash outflows. For the short-term cash budget, the financial staff would prepare a more detailed statement as shown in *Exhibit 7-11*.

Exhibit 7-11
Monthly cash flow budget

	*August**
Beginning cash balance	$ 50,000 †
Cash receipts	
Patient service income	1,050,000
Misc. cash income	20,000
Other cash receipts	30,000
Total cash available	$1,150,000
Cash outflows	
Cash operating expenses	80,000
Accounts payable	850,000
Salaries	20,000
Other cash expenses	20,000
Debt repayment	100,000
Capital investment purchase	50,000
Total cash outflow	$1,120,000
Ending cash balance	$ 30,000 †

*This format would be used for each month of the year.
†The ending balance becomes the beginning balance for the next month.

The completed cash budget becomes an integral part of the total budget process and can lead to revisions in the operating and capital budgets in order to meet overall hospital objectives.

Summary of the budget process

1. The trustees establish goals and objectives for the institution for the coming budget period.
2. The budget committee establishes and the administrator approves budget guidelines for the budget period, including such factors as planned activity levels and salary guidelines.
3. The revenue budget is prepared by the controller's department and involved supervisors.
4. The initial expense budgets are prepared by the operating departments.

5. Initial review and negotiation take place between the controller and the operating staff.
6. The capital budget is prepared.
7. The cash budget is completed and coordinated with the operating and capital budgets.
8. The budget committee coordinates and reviews the budgets.
9. Final approval is given by the administrator, trustees and the regulatory agencies (if required).
10. The approved budget is distributed to all department heads.

Appendix 7-1 is an example of the budget process in one hospital. Students are encouraged to review these documents and decide whether the forms provided meet the required steps for an effective budget process.

Types of budgeting systems

The preceding discussion focused on the budget process and did not explore how the guidelines were prepared. In some hospitals the guidelines for expenditures for next year are based on last year's costs plus an inflation factor. This type of budgeting, called incremental budgeting, is common in many organizations. Its major weakness is that it assumes that last year's spending was correct. This may not be true because conditions may have changed—some existing programs may not be needed, and "slack" can creep into the budget over a period of time.

One alternative to the incremental budgeting concept is called zero base budgeting (ZBB). It requires each supervisor to review each of the discrete activities performed by his/her department in terms of resources required and outputs achieved. This review is usually based on several funding levels. Although the name may indicate there should be a review at a zero level of funding, this is seldom required. Instead, a minimum level of spending is defined below which an activity would cease to be effectively accomplished. This typically is defined as 70-80 percent of existing levels. In addition to the minimum level, the existing level and an increased level of spending are also reviewed.

The major components of the zero base budgeting process are the preparation of decision packages and the ranking process. The decision packages are analyses of the activities to be performed at various levels of funding and involve the operating supervisors to a great extent. The ranking process consists of review and establishment of priorities for the decision packages by successive levels of management. The end result is a ranking of all the activities performed by the organization. Activities would be funded from this ranking until the available budgeted amounts are exhausted. The preparation of a zero base budget is discussed in greater detail in *Appendix 7-1*.

Performance measurement

Performance measurement is a vital part of the management function. It requires an information system which provides data by departments, by product lines, and by physician. Much of this information flows from the patient medical record, the charge sheets, and the accounting system. *Exhibit 7-12* illustrates the flow of information necessary to accomplish the performance measurement function in an organization.

An effective Performance Measurement System requires a responsibility accounting system, standards for performance, and variance analysis.

Exhibit 7-12
Performance measurement

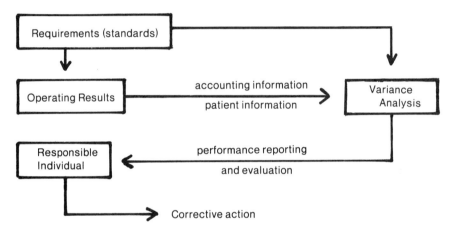

Responsibility accounting

The preceding section focused on some of the techniques that can be used to plan and control costs in a healthcare organization. However, it must be recognized that people, not methods or systems, actually make the decisions that achieve the desired results. In this section we will concentrate on fixing responsibility for each cost. This fixing of responsibility generally falls under the heading of responsibility accounting.

Accounting information

Anthony and Welsh characterize management accounting information as:

1. full cost accounting
2. differential accounting

3. responsibility accounting[1]

Each of these categories is, of course, related to the others, but each is used for a different purpose. For example, the full cost of an item is usually identified as direct costs plus an allocated share of any indirect costs. In healthcare organizations indirect costs may comprise 50 percent or more of the full cost of services, and the allocation process is vital to rate-setting and reimbursement decisions. In this case, full costs include elements from many different responsibility centers.

Differential accounting, also called incremental analysis, focuses on those costs that would be different if one alternative were selected over another. Costs that would not change under different alternatives are clearly not relevant to the decision process. In most cases, indirect costs do not change under different alternatives. Most capital investment decisions require differential accounting information. Examples would include such decisions as whether to add a service to an existing department or whether to offer a reduced rate for a short-run increase in volume.

The third type, responsibility accounting, collects and reports costs for various organization entities or levels. It is used to motivate, direct and control the actions of managers. Behavioral considerations are much more important in responsibility accounting, where people's motivations and objectives are an important component of management control. The ability to affect future decisions is an important component of responsibility accounting.

Responsibility accounting requirements

Responsibility accounting is a vital part of the management control process in every organization. Anthony and Herzlinger define management control as the process by which managers insure that resources are obtained and used effectively and efficiently in the accomplishment of an organization's objectives.[2]

Effectiveness is the relationship between a department's outputs and its objectives. For example, an objective in a radioligy department may be to report on the results of all "stat" tests in six hours. Accomplishing this objective would indicate effective behavior or effective results. A nursing station may establish an objective of completing all patient records within

[1]Anthony, Robert N., Glenn A. Welsh, and James S. Reece, *Fundamentals of Management Accounting,* Homewood, IL: Richard D. Irwin, Inc., 1985, pp. 13-17.

[2]Anthony, Robert W. and David Young, *Management Control in Nonprofit Organizations,* Homewood, IL: Richard D. Irwin, Inc., 1984.

two hours after discharge. The degree to which this is accomplished could also be measured.

Efficiency, on the other hand, is defined as the relationship between inputs and outputs. In the radiology and nursing examples above, the amount of resources required to accomplish each objective would be a measure of efficiency. If three X-ray technicians are normally required to meet the objective, the budget would logically include resource costs for three (FTE) technicians. However, the number of FTEs also depends upon the volume of procedures completed. The relationship between resources consumed and number of procedures completed would be a measure of efficiency.

A properly designed management control system will motivate managers to control their operations in such a manner as to satisfy both efficiency and effectiveness requirements. Managers must be able to balance both efficient and effective behaviors so that neither is neglected.

Responsibility centers

A key aspect of a management control system is the concept of a responsibility center. A respnsibility center is an organizational unit in which the manager has clearly defined areas of responsibility or activities over which he/she exercises some measure of control. A department supervisor or chief nurse who has both supervisory and budgetary control fits this definition. Responsibility centers are typically one of three types:

1. Cost center: A cost center is an organizational entity in which the supervisor is responsible for the expenses that have been measured. The output, however, is not measured because it is not feasible or practical from a cost viewpoint. Examples would be the accounting department or the maintenance department.
2. Revenue center: In this type of center, the supervisor is held responsible for both expenses and revenues. Examples may include any department through which patient care is provided, e.g., laboratories, nursing wards and pharmacies.
3. Investment center: This center is considered the final evolution in the responsibility center concept. The supervisor is held accountable for revenues, expenses and the capital assets utilized to provide the services. Examples might include radiology departments and laboratories. From a theoretical point of view, any revenue center could easily be made into an investment center; however, from a practical point of view, only departments with a clearly defined asset base are feasible investment centers.

Establishing responsibility centers

A hospital that wants to implement the responsibility center concept must meet two major requirements: a sound organizational structure that assigns responsibility clearly to specific individuals and an accounting system that supports the organization structure. Without these two factors, it is impossible to establish an effective responsibility center concept.

Organization

As stated above, individuals must be responsible for achieving the goals and objectives of the hospital if they are to be accomplished. These individuals need clearly defined areas of responsibility and authority. The hospital organizational structure plays a vital role in establishing responsibilities and duties. If properly designed, the organizational structure becomes the basis for reporting operating data and evaluating results. At a minimum, the hospital must be divided into manageable units designed to foster a coordinated effort to accomplish these objectives. There is no type of structure that is better than others. Berman and Weeks illustrate several possible arrangements in their text on hospital financial management.[3]

Some hospitals perform well with poor organizational structures while others do poorly with sound organizational structures. The key features are and will continue to be the motivation of the personnel. Needless to say, it is a highly important area, and the reader is encouraged to review some of the suggested reference books in this area.

One important behavioral aspect of responsibility accounting must be recognized by managers in healthcare organizations. This is the concept of goal congruence. People have their own individual objectives. They also have professional objectives that are a function of their educational background and experience. Healthcare organizations certainly have objectives that encompass both professional objectives and patient care objectives. They also have a responsibility to evaluate and maintain fiscal solvency, financial viability and long-run survival. Many of these objectives require a healthcare organization to be concerned about the control of both internal and external (societal) costs. In some cases, a conflict between an individual's personal and professional objectives and the organization's objectives may arise.

The goal congruence concept attempts to identify and minimize such conflicts. The basic idea is that accounting reports should show how an

---

[3]Berman, Howard J. and Lewis E. Weeks, *The Financial Management of Hospitals,* 5th ed., Ann Arbor, MI: Health Administration Press. 1982, Chapter 3.

individual's objectives and the organization's objectives can be simultaneously accomplished. Goal congruence suggests that such conflicts need not occur and that changes in accounting data and accounting reports can help to achieve additional congruence between organizational and individual objectives. If an individual can satisfy both his/her own objectives and those of the organization, there is a much higher probability that both will be better off in the long run. The concepts of responsibility accounting discussed in this chapter will lead to higher degrees of goal congruence.

The chart of accounts

The second major element in the design of a responsibility accounting system is the chart of accounts. The chart of accounts is the primary vehicle for collecting and compiling accounting information. Basically, it consists of a group of accounts appropriately coded to organizational elements and expense categories which permits systematic reporting of information. An example of a typical coding system is shown in *Exhibit 7-13*.

The seven-digit number was designed to accommodate all sizes of hospitals, from the very small (under 50 beds) to the very large. This system provides considerable flexibility in collecting accounting information. For example, the basic account number sequence consists of seven digits—a four-digit prefix and a three-digit suffix (XXXX.XXX). The first digit represents major balance sheet categories as shown in *Exhibit 7-13* (1 for assets, 2 for liabilities, etc.). The second, third and fourth digits are used to further identify specific accounts and departments. For example, the prefix 1114 would represent a dietary cash account in the general fund. The suffix digits could be added to provide more information. The bakery goods inventory in the dietary department would be identified by the accounting code 1114.401. Management can monitor costs in as much detail as necessary for performance evaluation and financial reporting. In the past, the focus was solely on the recording of information for financial reporting. Accounts were grouped into revenue and expense categories for determining the financial condition of the hospital. Charts of accounts were not typically designed to facilitate management control or responsibility accounting. Although financial reporting is still important, there has been a shift into collecting and reporting the information by organizational elements. The section on cost definition in the latter part of the chapter focuses on this concept. However, this shift has been hampered to some degree by the current emphasis on the design of a uniform accounting system for reporting to regulatory and reimbursing agencies. Although this may be effective external financial reporting, it has a negative impact on the internal reporting requirements of a hospital. All hospitals are not organized in a

Exhibit 7-13
Sample coding system for chart of accounts

Balance sheet

Assets:	1xxx.xxx
Liabilities and equity:	2xxx.xxx

Operations—sequence designed to follow basic format for reporting the results of operations.

Prefixes

Revenue—daily patient care	3xxx.xxx
Revenue—ancillary services	4xxx.xxx
Deductions from revenue	5xxx.xxx
Expenses—daily patient care	6xxx.xxx
Expenses—ancillary services	7xxx.xxx
Expenses—general services, administrative, and other operations	8xxx.xxx
Nonoperating revenue and expense	9xxx.xxx

Unique departmental codes

Daily patient care	3 or 6	000.xxx to 199.xxx
Ancillary services	4 or 7	200.xxx to 499.xxx
General services	8	3xx.xxx
Administrative—		
Nursing and medical	8	6xx.xxx
Business	8	7xx.xxx
Deductions from revenue	5	8xx.000
Other services and expenses	8	900.xxx to 959.000
Nonoperating revenue and expense		960.xxx to 999.xxx

Revenue suffixes

Charges for patient care	3 or 6	xxx.000 to xxx.099
Investment income		9xxx.1xx
Tax revenue		9xxx.2xx

Exhibit 7-13 (cont.)
Sample coding system for chart of accounts

Expense suffixes	(any may be preceded by 6xxx., 7xxx. or 8xxx.)
Labor/personnel expenses	.000 to .299
Supplies and materials—medical	.300 to .399
Supplies and materials—special	.400 to .499
Supplies and materials—general	.500 to .599
Other direct expenses	.600 to .799
Depreciation/leases/rental	.800 to .899

Source: *Chart of Accounts for Hospitals*, American Hospital Association, 1976, and *Colorado Hospital Association Exposure Draft on Uniform Accounting*, 1977.

similar manner, and there must be sufficient flexibility in the accounting system and the chart of accounts to allow for such flexibility.

In the revenue accounts, the code 3011.010 would represent the charges for medical surgical acute care units. In a similar manner, the accounting code 6010.010 could represent the salaries for management and supervision for the medical surgical acute care units.

The Medical Group Management Association (MGMA) has published a chart of accounts for medical groups (Schafer, McCarthy, Zulauf and Neumann, 1978). This chart of accounts is based on four basic data fields within a nine-digit account code. The four fields are:

Field	Description	Number of digits
1	Entity	1
2	Basic financial reporting	4
3	Responsibility center	2
4	Provider	2

Exhibit 7-14 summarizes the numerical coding system of the MGMA's suggested chart of accounts. The healthcare organization can use or ignore any of the last two fields (responsibility center and provider fields).

Managers can decide how to most effectively implement the entire chart of accounts or only the primary account groups.

Managers in healthcare organizations must be cognizant of the flexibility that is usually inherent in most recommended (uniform) charts of accounts. However, they should be more aware of the need to establish an organization structure that permits and encourages managers to operate effectively and efficiently. The assignment of responsibility and the evaluation of performance are fundamental managerial activities that are directly affected by both formal and informal organization structures. Once managerial responsibilities are sufficiently delineated, managers in healthcare organizations should verify that the chart of accounts is consistent with the organization structure. A lack of consistency will lead to incorrect or biased performance evaluation. It can result in chaotic and confusing performance reports. The correlation between organization charts and account structures is an important, but often ignored, facet of the management control process.

An effective accounting system must satisfy the requirements of all three uses of accounting information. A full cost determination requires the collection of direct and indirect expenses by major services offered. The indirect costs are typically allocated to the service. Conversely, responsibility accounting requires the collection of all direct and indirect costs by organization unit and is only secondarily concerned with the allocation process. Differential accounting, on which capital investment decisions are based, typically calls for special grouping and classification, and the accounting system must be flexible enough to accommodate these needs. *Exhibit 7-15* summarizes the requirements of three different types of accounting information.

The reporting process

In order to effectively monitor progress toward objectives, periodic financial statements must be furnished to both operating supervisors and management. These reports would typically be presented as shown in *Exhibit 7-16.*

The difficulty in measuring and motivating the responsible supervisor is that some of the costs reported in this type of report are not fully controlled by him/her. In this case, indirect expenses equalled more than 35 percent of the total costs ($15,000/$42,300) and were allocated on the basis of reimbursement maximization. They included a share of the hospital administration, housekeeping and other support areas. Clearly, the emergency room supervisor had little control over the amount of these expenses. A more effective reporting format would require dividing the expenses into controllable and noncontrollable expenses. In this case,

Exhibit 7-14
Chart of accounts numerical coding system

Entity field		Basic field			—	Responsibility center field	Provider field
First digit	*Second*	*Third*	*Fourth*	*Fifth*		*Sixth Seventh*	*Eighth Ninth*
		Statement of financial position (balance sheet)			Dash		
Entity	Financial statement section	Primary classification	Control account				
0	0 Not used	0	0 (Minimum breakdown of items in primary classifi-cation)	0 (Optional maximum breakdown of items in primary classification)		0 (Responsibility centers)	0 (Physicians)
1	1 Assets	1	1	1		1	1
2		2 Current assets	2	2		2	2
3		3	3	3		3	3
4		4 Investments	4	4		4	4
5		5	5	5		5	5
6		6 Noncurrent tangible assets	6	6		6	6
7		7	7	7		7	7
8		8 Intangible and other assets	8	8		8	8
9		9	9	9		9	9
	2 Liabilities and owners' equity	0	0	0		0	0
		1 Current liabilities	1	1		1	1
		2	2	2		2	2
			3	3		3	3

		Dash		(Responsibility centers)	(Physicians)

Chart of accounts coding structure

3 Long-term liabilities
4 Partners' equity
5 Stockholders' equity
6 Not-for-profit equity
7 Revenue and expense summary

Dash

Income statement

3 Revenues
  1 Gross charges
  2 Adjusted gross charges
  3 Net revenue
  4 Cash collected
  5–7 Gross charges—contract
  8 Contract revenue
  9 Gross charges—other

4 Adjustments and allowances
  1–9 Type of adjustment and write-off

1–9 Location of billed patient

1–9 Patient pay type

(Optional maximum break-down of expenses in primary classification)

0 1 (Responsibility centers)
2 3 4 5 6 7 8 9

0 1 (Physicians)
2 3 4 5 6 7 8 9

Exhibit 7-14 (cont.)
Chart of accounts numerical coding system

Entity field	Basic field					Responsibility center field		Provider field	
First digit	*Second*	*Third*	*Fourth*	*Fifth*		*Sixth*	*Seventh*	*Eighth*	*Ninth*
	5 Expenses—human resources	0 1 Physician salaries 2 Physician benefits 3 Physician extender salaries, etc.	0 1 Physician salary—owner 2 Physician bonus—owner 3 Physician salary —employee 4 Physician bonus— employee (Minimum breakdown of expenses in primary classification)	(Optional maximum breakdown of expenses in primary classification)	—				
	6 Expenses—physical resources	0 1 Supplies 2 Ancillary department supplies 3 Cost of goods sold—ancillary 4 Occupancy and use—buildings and ground, etc.			Dash				

Dash

7 Expenses—purchased services and general and administrative expenses (G&A)
  0 Purchased services—professional and medical
  1 Purchased services
  2 Purchased services
  3 G & A purchased services
  4
  5 } G & A
  6
  7
  8 Interest and taxes
  9 Other

8 Nonoperating revenues and expenses
  0
  1 Nonoperating revenue
  2 Nonoperating expense

Other reports

9 Nonfinancial data

Source: *Practical Financial Management for Medical Groups*, vol. 2: *Data Accumulation Systems*, Center for Research in Ambulatory Health Care Administration, Medical Group Management Association, 1978.

Exhibit 7-15
Summary of accounting system requirements

1. Full cost determination = direct costs of providing a service + share of indirect costs;
   or total costs for providing a service
2. Responsibility accounting = direct and indirect costs controlled by the supervisor;
   or total costs controlled by the supervisor
3. Differential accounting = all costs that will change with a particular decision

Exhibit 7-16
Statement of income and expense
for the month of May 1978
Emergency room

Operating revenues			
Emergency room nursing services			
Inpatient revenues		$ 7,000	
Outpatient revenues		23,000	
			$30,000
Direct Expenses			
Salaries		$17,000	
Employee benefits; professional fees		5,000	
Supplies			
Drugs	$1,000		
General supplies	4,000		
Total supplies		$ 5,000	
Minor equipment		100	
Utilities		25	
Education		150	
Miscellaneous equipment		25	
Total direct expenses			$27,300
Net after direct expenses			2,700
Indirect expenses (from cost finding report)			15,000
Net after indirect expenses			($12,300)
Statistics:			
Admissions	3,000		
Emergency visits	1,100		
Outpatient visits	400		

controllable expenses would be those over which the supervisor had some measure of responsibility and direct control. Using this concept, a report similar to *Exhibit 7-17* could be presented.

This report highlights the costs the supervisor can control. Comparing the two reports indicates a considerable difference in the reported results. *Exhibit 7-16* the department shows a loss of $12,300 (more than 40

Exhibit 7-17
Responsibility center reporting:
ambulatory care unit
for the month of May 1978
Emergency room

		%
Gross operating revenues	$33,000	110
Deduct allowances	3,000	.10
Net revenues	$30,000	100
Controllable operating expenses		
Variable costs	4,500	.15
Contribution margin	$25,500	.85
Controllable fixed costs	22,800	.76
Controllable operating margin	$ 2,700	.09
Allocated costs	15,000	.50
Net operating margin (loss)	($12,300)	(.41)

percent of net revenues). *Exhibit 7-17* where costs are segregated by responsibility, indicates a contribution margin of $2,700 or nine percent. It seems clear that *Exhibit 7-17* presents more useful information than the typical format *(Exhibit 7-16).* The recommended approach clearly differentiates between controllable and noncontrollable costs.

A typical approach to reporting for performance measurement is illustrated in *Exhibit 7-18.* This report focuses on a comparison with budget and the relationship of costs to volume. However, it does not highlight which of the costs are controllable. In the next section, a series of reports which can be used for performance measurement will be presented. Each of them is designed to stress certain performance measurement aspects. The responsible manager will use several of them to properly evaluate the performance of key individuals.

Alternative reporting formats

Basic reporting format is illustrated in *Exhibit 7-19.* Its strength lies in its summary approach to presenting data by specific cost categories. Specific tests may be reviewed in greater detail. *Exhibit 7-20* illustrates this type of measurement with an emphasis on labor efficiency.

It is also possible to focus on the contribution margin for various cases, product/diagnosis output. *Exhibit 7-21* is an example of this approach.

A more macro approach to contribution margin is illustrated in *Exhibit 7-22.* The focus on averages can be useful as long as the basis for computing the average costs and revenues is known.

Exhibit 7-18
Performance measurement

Emergency Room Department 3A

Date: July 31, 198X

	ACTUALS		BUDGET		VARIANCE	
	Current Month	Year To Date	Current Month	Year To Date	Current Month	Year To Date
Salaries	$111,000	$803,000	$105,000	$750,000	6000 U (5.7%)	53,000 U (4.7%)
Supplies	86,750	600,000	90,000	630,000	3250 F (3.6%)	30,000 F (4.8%)

Statistics	ACTUALS		BUDGET		VARIANCE	
	Current Month	Year To Date	Current Month	Year To Date	Current Month	Year To Date
Patient Visits	10,000	80,000	9,500	105,000	5000 F	25,000 U

Exhibit 7-19
Departmental performance area: clinical laboratory

Department	Current Month			YTD		
	Standard	Actual	Variance (U or F)	Standard	Actual	Variance (U or F)
Chemistry:						
Volume	813,409	807,320	6,089 U	2,400,000	2,400,000	-0-
Labor	137,354	114,263	23,091 F	528,145	518,145	10,000 F
Materials	84,300	70,093	14,207 F	322,100	328,100	?00 U
Indirect	14,033	16,033	2,000 U	60,000	56,000	4,000 F
Total	235,607	200,389	35,298 F	910,245	902,245	8,000 F

Adapted from Peat, Marwick, and Mitchell presentation, Boulder, Colorado, June, 1984.

Exhibit 7-20
Body scanning
(cost center)
Labor efficiency report
(period)

Number	Procedure Description	Volume Total	Labor Standard (Minutes)	Applied Hours
	Body Scanning	3	20.00	1
0650	Head scan, ltd. (0-5 cuts)	228	30.00	114
0655	Head scan, comple. (6-12 cuts)	41	45.00	30.75
0660	Head scan, rutn. (13-19 cuts)	4	60.00	4
0665	Head scan, exten. (20-29 cuts)	3	35.00	1.75
0670	Head scan, ltd. (0-5 cuts)	157	45.00	117.75
0675	Head scan, comple. (6-12 cuts)	207	60.00	207
0680	Head scan, rutn. (13-19 cuts)	3	75.00	3.75
0685	Head scan, exten. (20-29 cuts)	37	30.00	18.5
6200	Body scan, ltd. (0-9 cuts)	296	60.00	296
6205	Body scan, comple. (10-19 cuts)	406	90.00	609
6210	Body scan, rutn. (20-41 cuts)	53	120.00	106
6215	Body scan, exten. (42-70 cuts)	18	45.00	13.5
6250	Body scan, ltd. (0-9 cuts)	220	75.00	275
6255	Body scan, comple. (10-19 cuts)	357	105.00	624.75
6260	Body scan, rutn. (20-41 cuts)	1	135.00	2.25
6265	Body scan, exten. (42-70 cuts)	2034		2425

Total 450

Other Hours:	
Supervision	1768
Total Required Worked Hours	4193
Total Worked Hours	5304
Total Paid Hours	6240
Labor Efficiency Index	79.1%

Adapted from Peat, Marwick, and Mitchell presentation, Boulder, Colorado, June, 1984.

Exhibit 7-21
Case performance

Description	DRG/MDC	Revenue	Cost	Contribution
Hernia	D379			
Expected		239,427	214,881	24,546
Actual		287,337	273,439	13,898
Variance		-47,910 F	-58,558 U	
G.I. Disease	M7			
Expected		2,877,993	2,497,897	380,096
Actual		3,667,000	2,937,901	729,099
Variance		-789,007 F	-440,005 U	
Hospital	All DRG/MDC			
Expected		189,789,040	189,697,088	6,226,974
Actual		184,066,322	179,239,113	4,827,209
Variance		5,722,718 U	10,457,975 F	

Adapted from Peat, Marwick, and Mitchell presentation, Boulder, Colorado, June, 1984.

It is also possible to focus on the mix of services by DRGs, according to HFCA Weighting Factor ranking. This can be useful in evaluating potential changes in services offered. *Exhibit 7-23* presents an example of this report.

Finally, it is important to be able to monitor performance of specific physicians. *Exhibit 7-24* illustrates this type of report.

The reports in this chapter illustrate some of the variations possible to monitor performance measurement either by department, service, or individual. They should be customized to fit the needs of decision makers in a particular institution. If they are considered rigid formats, they probably will be less effective.

Cost definitions

Responsibility center procedures require further refinement of cost terminology. The fixed and variable cost definitions of Chapter 2 take on another dimension, this time in terms of controllability. An item of cost can be considered controllable if its amount is significantly influenced by the actions of the supervisor. As one moves upward in the hospital management structure, costs become more and more controllable. When the hospital is viewed as a single entity, all costs must be considered controllable by the hospital administrator. Whether this is true will depend upon the range of authority and responsibility given to the administrator. It should be stressed that the concept of controllability does not mean absolute control. Few managers have absolute control of

Exhibit 7-22
Clinical service contribution

Clinical Service	Discharges	Average Cost	Average Revenue	Average Contribution	Net Contribution
Gynecology	429	2918	2944	26	11154
Medicine/General	1047	3142	3313	171	179037
Surgery/General	1353	4652	4906	254	343662
Cardiology	1233	2932	3492	560	690480
Hematology	410	4014	4340	326	133660
Hemodialysis	34	4084	4177	93	3162
Neurology	287	2616	2596	-20	-5740
Pulmonary Chest	97	2790	3167	377	36569
Trauma/General	140	6754	7133	379	53060
Ear/Nose/Throat	376	2764	2755	-9	-3384
Opthalmology	2	2561	2118	443	-886
Orthopedics	594	3375	3443	68	40392
Plastic Surgery	259	3387	3357	-30	-7770
Urology	306	3542	3628	86	26316
Vascular Surgery	810	8660	10845	2185	1769050
Psychiatry	317	3117	2488	-629	-199393
	7694				3069369

Exhibit 7-23
Cases by HCFA weight

Order	DRG	DRG Description	HFCA Wt.	Jan-Aug Number Dischg.
Top 5 cases by HCFA Weight:				
1	104	Cardiac Valve Procedure w/Pump & Cardiac Cath.	6.8527	3
2	302	Kidney Transplant	6.6322	2
3	106	Coronary Bypass w/Cardiac Cath.	5.2624	22
4	105	Cardiac Valve Procedure w/Pump & Cardiac Cath.	5.2308	13
5	108	Cardiothor. Procedure, except Valve & Coronary Bypass, w/Pump	4.3756	2
Median 5 cases by HCFA Weight:				
164	90	Simple Pneumonia & Pleurisy Age 18-68 w/o C.C.	0.9849	3
165	83	Major Chest Trauma Age = 70 and/or C.C.	0.9809	3
166	467	Other Factors Influencing Health Status	0.9799	12
167	300	Endocrine Disorders Age = 70 and/or C.C.	0.9731	12
168	93	Interstitial Lung Disease Age = 70 w/o C.C.	0.9724	5
Last 5 cases by HCFA Weight:				
328	40	Extraocular Procedures Except Orbit Age = 18	0.3977	3
329	410	Chemotherapy	0.3527	86
330	412	History of Malignancy with Endoscopy	0.3400	3
331	351	Sterilization, Male	0.2655	1
332	465	Aftercare with History of Malignancy as Secondary Dx.	0.2071	20

Adapted from MGMA presentation, March, 1984, Denver, Colorado.

Exhibit 7-24
DRGs by physician

MD XXX

DRG 1 Craniotomy
Age Less than 18
Except Trauma:
National Los _____

	Discharge Date	Length of Stay DRG[1]	Length of Stay Actual[2]	Mean Chgs. VMH DRG[3]	Medicare Payment[4]	Actual Total Chgs.[5]	Difference Chgs. Payment
Patient # XX-XX-XX	7/15/83	35.0	30.0	21,500	17,500	18,500	-1,000
Patient # XX-XX-XX	8/01/83	35.0	32.0	21,500	17,500	19,100	-1,600
Patient # XX-XX-XX	8/04/83	35.0	34.0	21,500	17,500	22,700	-5,200
Total DRG 1		105.00	96.0	64,500	52,500	60,300	-7,800
Mean DRG 1		35.0	32.0	21,500	17,500	20,100	-2,600
Total MD XXX			32.0	64,500	60,300	60,300	

[1] Average length of stay for all Patients w/specified DRG
[2] Actual length of stay for Patient
[3] Average charge for all Patients w/specified DRG
[4] Medicare Case Mix WDEX multiplied by standard base reimbursement per Case Mix Unit
[5] Actual charges for Patient

Adapted from MGMA presentation, March, 1984, Denver, Colorado.

their costs; rather, controllability is a measure of significant influence over their incurrence.

In Chapter 2, we classified costs as either direct or indirect. Indirect costs are usually allocated to the responsibility center; therefore, they cannot be considered controllable by the supervisor. For example, the allocated share of hospital administration is an indirect and noncontrollable cost. On the other hand, all controllable costs are direct costs; however, not all direct costs are controllable, at least in the short run. For example, the depreciation on X-ray equipment is a direct cost to the radiology department; however, it is not a controllable cost. There is no way the supervisor can undo the decision to buy the equipment after it has been purchased. The preceding discussion highlights the "committed" cost concept. Committed costs are for decisions previously made. The depreciation referred to above, or a long-term contract with a radiologist, are committed costs in that the supervisor has little influence on their amounts after the decision to incur them has been made.

Variable costs can also be compared with controllable costs. Usually all variable costs are controllable. However, the amount of medicine or medical supplies used by a department may not be a cost controllable by the supervisor. Typically, the medical staff and health standards require certain usage rates. In such cases, variable costs are not necessarily controllable.

Given the responsibility accounting associated with controllable costs, some supervisors may try to put as many costs into the noncontrollable area as possible. Hospital administrators must be aware of this possibility. Effective management control requires identifying controllable costs at the lowest possible level in the organization hierarchy. In most cases, all costs can be made controllable by assigning different levels of responsibility and by turning indirect costs into direct costs. For example, utility expense is usually allocated to each department. The installation of meters could change the cost from indirect to direct and increase the controllability of some utility costs. This type of change requires a detailed analysis of the costs versus the benefits to be gained from the conversion program.

Quantitative aspects of performance measurement

Although the material in this chapter emphasizes the cost aspect of management control and the reporting of cost information, it is equally important to define qualitative goals for performance measurement. At higher levels in the organization, qualitative goals become even more important in assessing performance because few cost items are directly controlled at this level. For example, the vice president for fiscal affairs is clearly responsible for many of the day-to-day financial operations of the hospital but he/she does not actually control the operations. Rather, he/she has delegated that authority to lower-level supervisors. Yet, the requirement to measure performance still exists. Therefore, performance measurement standards need to be developed for the key areas of responsibility such as cash management, budgeting and financial reporting. An example of a performance standard is shown in *Appendix 7-2.*

Behavioral aspects of budgeting

No chapter on budgeting would be complete without considering the behavioral aspects of the budgeting process. People, not systems, incur costs. A manager would like the budget process to influence the responsible persons to take actions which are consistent with the goals of the hospital administration and to refrain from those actions which are not. To do this, the budget system must recognize the needs of the human beings involved. These needs can be grouped into material needs (monetary) and psychological (recognition and involvement). In most cases, material needs can be quickly identified and met to a large extent through the personnel policy. However, psychological needs are much more difficult to identify and satisfy. They can vary from person to person and within the same person at different times.

The budgeting system must be aware of and take into account the human elements. Otherwise, even the best designed system is doomed to failure.

Summary

The preparation and proper utilization of the budget can be an extremely effective management control tool for the administrator. It can communicate to all levels of supervision the goals and objectives of top hospital management and the resources that should be used to achieve these objectives. It also provides a yardstick for measuring performance in accomplishing these goals and objectives. The hospital administrator must take an active role in the budget process if the maximum benefits are to be obtained.

Responsibility accounting offers an important advantage to the hospital administrator. By classifying costs as controllable or noncontrollable, he/she can motivate the department supervisor to take action on those costs he/she can control. In the total hospital picture, all costs should be the responsibility of an individual who can influence their incurrence. If a cost is not the responsibility of an individual, in most cases, it will not be controlled effectively. The responsibility center reporting format offers a significant improvement in the potential to control costs.

Questions and problems

1. Define the planning function for a healthcare organization.

2. Define the budgeting function for a healthcare organization.

3. What are the differences between the strategic and operational planning functions in a healthcare organization?

4. What environmental factors should be considered in designing a strategic plan for a healthcare organization?

5. Name the major budget components of the hospital master budget.

6. In most hospitals the expense budget is prepared before the revenue budget. Discuss the impact of this policy.

7. Discuss the budget timetable. Why is such a long time frame involved?

8. What are the major requirements of an effective budget process?

9. Explain the three types of management accounting information.

10. What is the management control process in a healthcare organization?

11. Define effectiveness and efficiency in a healthcare organization as it pertains to the management control process.

12. Explain the three types of responsibility centers.

13. What are the two major requirements for establishing a responsibility center concept in a hospital?

14. What is a "chart of accounts"?

15. Explain the major differences between the normal revenue and expense statement for a revenue department and the responsibility center report.

16. It has been stated that all variable costs are usually direct costs but that all direct costs are not variable. Explain this concept.

17. Define a controllable fixed cost and a committed fixed cost.

18. What are the benefits of a uniform chart of accounts to:
    a. the institution,
    b. regulatory agencies and
    c. professional associations?
    Under what conditions would you recommend the adoption of a uniform chart of accounts?

19. Why would a healthcare organization prefer a revenue center to an investment center? When would a cost center be preferable?

20. Define goal congruence. How is it related to responsibility center accounting?

21. Give some examples of direct and indirect costs. Indicate the level in the organization where such costs are controllable.

22. Explain the type of reports required to evaluate an outpatient clinic with salaried physicians and minor surgical procedures, being performed.

23. You have been employed as the budget officer of Memorial Hospital. In outline form, list the steps you would take in fulfilling this responsibility. Give particular emphasis to the manner in which the accounting office may be of assistance to you.

24. You are discussing with your administrator the advantages of a budgeting program for your hospital. The administrator asks, "Why can't we just continue to compare our monthly figures with last year's monthly figures instead of going through all this trouble to set up a budget?" In addition to answering the administrator's specific question, present in outline form the benefits of a budgeting system.

25. Prepare an annual income and expense budget for the laboratory department of Community Hospital using the information supplied. The budget is for the period from July 1, 1987, through June 30, 1988. Indicate what you would do if, at the end of six months, the actual increase in the number of units of service for the department is only 50 percent of that anticipated in preparing the budget.
    a. Community Hospital establishes charges for services at an amount that will approximate costs as nearly as possible. Total budgeted income for a department should be within range of $1,000 of total budgeted expenses. A relative unit system is used in the laboratory department. During the fiscal year ended June of total budgeted expenses. A relative unit system is used

in the laboratory department. During the fiscal year ended June 30, 1987, the average charge per unit was $1.02.

b. Allowances, such as Blue Cross, Medicare and bad debts, should be assumed to be 10 percent of gross income.

c. In preparing the budget, assume that the laboratory department will continue to grow at the same rate, as far as the number of relative units of service is concerned, as it has in the past two years.

d. The two pathologists are guaranteed a base salary of $20,000 each, plus a pool of 10 percent of net revenue (gross charges less deductions) which is divided equally.

e. The budget committee of the hospital has instructed you to allow for a five percent salary increase for all eligible personnel except pathologists. These increases are to become effective for each employee on the first of the month following the anniversary of his/her employment date.

f. Because of an increased workload, the budget committee has approved the addition of one new technologist to begin at the approved starting rate.

g. Overtime, vacation and holiday relief, and on-call pay should be computed at 15 percent of the technologists' and aides' salaries.

h. The indirect cost ratio for the laboratory department is 25 percent of direct expenses.

i. The nonsalary direct expenses for the laboratory department in the year ended June 30, 1987, amounted to $50,000. It is expected that the 1987-88 nonsalary direct expenses will continue at approximately $.25 per unit.

The Community Hospital	
Fiscal year	*Units of service Laboratory department*
7/1/84−6/30/85	165,300
7/1/85−6/30/86	181,820
7/1/86−6/30/87	200,000

The Community Hospital Laboratory department			
Fiscal year	*Gross charges*	*Deductions*	*Net charges*
7/1/84−6/30/85	$175,218	$17,500	$157,718
7/1/85−6/30/86	189,093	18,900	170,193
7/1/87−6/30/87	204,000	20,300	183,700

The Community Hospital
Schedule of selected wage range for
the fiscal year 7/1/87—6/30/88

Job code	Title	Range in dollars per month
23	Secretary	$325—450
44	Laboratory technologists	375—525
67	Aides	300—400

The Community Hospital
Analysis of personnel—laboratory department
as of July 1, 1987

Job code	Authorized position	Current annual rate	Monthly rate	Employment date
01	J. Brown, pathologist	$20,000	—	7/1/79
01	T. Smith pathologist	20,000	—	9/1/78
23	J. Rocket	4,800	$400	1/15/83
44	A. Dick	6,120	510	8/5/76
44	B. Searle	6,000	500	7/9/75
44	C. Noonan	5,520	460	9/14/80
44	O. White	4,680	390	12/13/83
67	N. Dupree	4,560	380	6/12/79
67	L. Jones	4,080	340	7/13/83

Exhibit "A"

The Valley Community Hospital
actual for 12 months 9/30/89
compared with
projection for 12 months—9/30/90
(before rate adjustments)

	9 mo. actual 3 mo. estimate 12 months 9/30/89	Projection 12 months 9/30/90	Variance increase amount
Patient days (excluding newborn)	66,029	69,000	2,971
Newborn days	3,870	3,870	—

Operating income			
Routine service			
—room and			
board	$3,152,616	$3,286,322	$ 133,706
Special			
professional			
service	2,970,628	3,012,600	41,972
Gross earnings			
from patients	$6,123,244	$6,298,922	$ 175,678
Deductions			
from earnings	622,136	—	622,136
Net earnings			
from patients	$5,501,108	$6,298,922	$ 797,814
Auxiliary			
services	98,286	114,359	16,073
Total operating			
income	$5,559,394	$6,413,281	$ 813,887
Total operating			
expense	$5,467,750	$6,655,623	$1,187,873
Operating gain	$ 131,644	$ (242,342)	$ (373,986)
Supplementary			
income	78,809	64,400	14,409
Net gain	210,453	$ (177,942)	$ (359,577)

26. The Valley Community Hospital has completed its budget of operations for the new fiscal year 10/1/89–9/30/90 as shown in the summary statement *Exhibit "A"* labeled "Before rate adjustments." The statement shows an operating (loss) of $242,342 and a net (loss) of $177,942.

Exhibit "B"

Cash objectives		
Capital budget		$173,974
Estimate due to Medicare		
for 9/30/87 & 9/30/88 audit		56,000
Estimate due to Blue Cross		
for 9/30/87 & 9/30/88 audit		20,000
Bond amortization:		
2/1/90	$43,000	
8/1/90	44,000	87,000
Property "A" note payment		15,603
Property "B" note payment		6,777
Cash tranfer to		
building fund		150,000
Total cash objectives		
for 1989–90		$509,354

The controller must make a recommendation to the Executive Committee in September 1989 regarding the hospital's cash objectives, *Exhibit "B."* He/she must also do a cash flow analysis to see if these cash objectives can be met. The analysis shows that cash flow is substantially under the cash objectives. Therefore, a recommendation for both routine service and special service rate adjustments must be made to the Executive Committee for implementation on 10/1/89.

Part A

Given below is information necessary for the controller to prepare the cash flow analysis:
a. Included in operating expenses for 9/30/90 is depreciation of $361,720.
b. The hospital was able to select an accelerated method of depreciation for non-government cost based patients. The amount for depreciation is $496,720 for the new fiscal year. Non-government cost-based patients account for one-third of the total patient days.
c. The HMO contract with the hospital provides a five percent plus factor superimposed over the basic reimbursable cost of $2,040,000 for the fiscal year ended 9/30/90.
d. Inpatient accounts receivable for patients not under a reimbursement program is expected to affect cash flow. The utilization of the hospital for the fiscal year ending 9/30/90 will increase patient days and cause an increase of five percent in receivables. Only 20 percent of such receivables are not under a cost reimbursement program. The inpatient accounts receivable total, as of 9/30/89, is $850,000.
e. Prepare a cash flow analysis and compare the results to the cash flow objectives (*Exhibit "B"*).

Part B

Since your analysis shows a substantial variance between cash flow and cash objectives, you must proceed with the recommendation for rate adjustments. Again, the controller is given certain information to prepare such an analysis.
a. Projected patient days for 9/30/90 is 72,870, of which 3,870 is applicable to newborn. The room rate adjustment per day is $6 for both categories. Additional income from patient days utilization can be obtained from *Exhibit "A."*
b. Special professional service rate adjustment is $5 per day.

Additional income from patient day utilization can be obtained from *Exhibit "A."*

c. The rate adjustments will have an effect on both inpatient and outpatient accounts receivable and will cause an increase of $50,000 and $20,000, respectively.

Requirement B1:

Prepare a projected statement of operations as of 9/30/90 (after the rate adjustments have been in effect for one year), comparing the 9/30/90 figures with the actual for 9/30/89 and showing variances in dollars.

Requirement B2:

a. Prepare a cash flow statement resulting from rate adjustments, and compare the statement to the cash objectives for the coming year.

b. Will the rate adjustment, as proposed, meet all objectives of the hospital? Do you have any comments regarding either the proposed rate adjustments or the cash objectives of the hospital?

27. Mulberry Memorial Hospital (MMH) is a 250 bed hospital providing the usual range of hospital services. As an outside consultant, you have been asked to provide consulting services for the year. The initial task is to help in the preparation of the client's budget.

Part A

Assume that for a department providing three services, management has given you the following information:

	Expected Volumes
Service	*Volumes*
A	100 units
B	200 units
C	300 units

Departmental Indirect (fixed) Costs	
Department head	$4200
Supplies	$ 325

Standard Cost Per Resource Requirement	
Resource	Unit Cost
Labor	
Level 1	$ 8.00 per hour
Level 2	$10.00 per hour
Level 3	$12.00 per hour
Supplies	
Supply 1	$ 6.00 per unit
Supply 2	$ 1.50 per unit

Standard Resource Requirements Per Unit of Service					
	Labor Hours by Skill Level			Supply Items in Units	
Service	Level 1	Level 2	Level 3	Supply 1	Supply 2
A	0	1.0	2.0	0	2.0
B	1.0	2.0	0	2.0	1.0
C	2.0	3.0	2.0	1.0	0

Using the preceeding information,

a. Prepare the budget for this department, itemizing by expense category and fixed and variable.

b. Assume that indirect costs are allocated to procedures on the basis of direct labor hours. Assume further that there is no overhead allocated to this department. What is the total cost for each service?

c. Determine the standard labor cost per unit of service.

d. Determine the supply cost per unit of service.

Part B

You have been notified by management that the hospital has been approached by Cottrell's, a local employer, to provide care to its employees at a flat rate of $1300 per discharge.
The following information is available.

Projected Patient Load	
Case Type	Volume
C1	1500
C2	3000
C3	6000
C4	4500

	Standard Resource Consumption Profiles				
	Ancillary Service (units)			*Nursing Services (days)*	
Case Type	*Lab*	*X-Ray*	*Pharm*	*Surgical*	*Medical*
C1	0	2	1	7	0
C2	3	4	0	0	6
C3	6	8	6	3	0
C4	0	2	3	0	5

Standard Cost Per Resource Requirement	
Resource	*Unit Cost*
Labor	
Level 1	$10.00 per hour
Level 2	$ 8.00 per hour
Level 3	$ 6.00 per hour
Supplies	
Supply 1	1.50 per unit
Supply 2	$ 2.00 per unit
Supply 3	$ 4.00 per unit

Standard Resource Requirement Per Unit of Service					
	Hours of Labor by Skill Level			*Supply of Items in Units*	
Service	*Level 1*	*Level 2*	*Level 3*	*Supply 1*	*Supply 2*	*Supply 3*
Lab	0	2.0	1.5	0	3.0	4.0
X-Ray	2.0	0	3.0	1.0	0	2.0
Pharm.	6.0	6.0	0	3.0	2.0	1.0
Surgical	8.0	0	2.0	1.0	0	0
Medical	0	4.0	3.0	2.0	0	1.0

Based on the relevant information, you have been asked to make a recommendation regarding acceptance or rejection of the proposal. Note any information which would be useful in making the recommendation. Regardless of your initial recommendation, what would be your recommendation if the projected patient load was adjusted as follows:

Case Type	*Volume*
C1	1,500
C2	3,000
C3	14,000
C4	4,500

Part C

Following your completion of the preceeding proposal from Cottrell, MMH provides you with the following budgets for its overhead departments, which consist of housekeeping, dietary and laundry.

Department	Cost	Basis	Sq. Ft.	Meals	Pounds
	Budgeted Allocation Statistics				
Housekeeping	30,000	Sq. Ft.	200	20	200
Dietary	70,000	Meals	300	40	800
Laundry	80,000	Pounds	500	10	20
Lab	—	—	400	18	30
X-Ray	—	—	230	12	22
Pharm.	—	—	170	15	28
Surgical	—	—	700	850	520
Medical	—	—	500	950	580
Total	—	—	3000	1915	2200

You have been told that the patient services and resources requirements used in calculating your recommendation for the Cottrell proposal comprise the hospital totals. In addition, you are to assume the following indirect (fixed) costs for the patient care departments.

Lab	$2300
X-Ray	$3850
Pharmacy	$1275
Surgical	$3300
Medical	$2950

Using the information available, determine the amount of overhead allocated to each patient case department, and develop the budget for the entire hospital.

Part D

It is the end of the year and management has noted actual results differ significantly from budget. The actual operating results are as follows:

Case Type	Volume
	Actual Patient load
C1	1700
C2	2850
C3	6400
C4	5800

| | *Actual Resource Consumption Profiles* | | | | |
| | *Ancillary Service (units)* | | | *Nursing Services (days)* | |
Case Type	*Lab*	*X-Ray*	*Pharm*	*Surgical*	*Medical*
C1	1	1.5	2	6	1
C2	2	6	0	0	8
C3	4	7	8	4	2
C4	1.5	1	2	2	6

	Actual Resource Usage Per Unit of Service					
	Hours of Labor					
	by Skill Level			*Supply of Items in Units*		
Service	*Level 1*	*Level 2*	*Level 3*	*Supply 1*	*Supply 2*	*Supply 3*
Lab	.5	2.5	1.0	0	2.0	4.0
X-Ray	3.0	0	2.0	2.0	1.0	3.0
Pharm.	5.0	7.0	1.0	2.5	1.0	0
Surgical	7.0	1.0	1.0	2.0	.5	1.5
Medical	0	2.0	4.0	3.0	1.0	0

| *Actual Cost Per Resource Requirement* | |
Resource	*Unit Cost*
Labor	
Level 1	$11.50 per hour
Level 2	$ 7.00 per hour
Level 3	$ 6.75 per hour
Supplies	
Supply 1	$ 2.30 per unit
Supply 2	$ 1.80 per unit
Supply 3	$ 4.40 per unit

Management has asked you to provide the following variances from budgeted costs:

Treatment
Labor (Lab. Dept.)
    Rate
Efficiency
Supplies (Surgical Dept.)
    Price
    Usage
Overhead (total only)

Note: Assume the following for overhead:

Std. OH case type unit costs are allocated based on total direct resource consumptions

Std. OH unit cost per case
C1 — $9.40 per case
C2 — $7.28 per case
C3 — $18.00 per case
C4 — $8.01 per case
Actual OH costs were $180,000 as budgeted

28. The director of the dietary department has been approached by a food preparation service that has offered to provide all patient meals at a price that seems attractive. However, careful evaluation of the offer is needed before a decision is made. If the offer is accepted, the food service department in the hospital will be eliminated, and the space now occupied by food service will be converted into additional working space for the laboratory. This conversion will entail additional costs, but the lab will also increase its contribution as a result of the modification.

You are asked to prepare the analysis of the proposal for the hospital administrator and the board of trustees.

Data for the food service contract

A. Food services department

The following personnel will remain with the hospital:

	Annual salary
Chief dietitian	$12,000
Food handlers (3)	15,000

The following personnel will be eliminated:

	Annual salary
One assistant dietitian	$10,000
Two cooks	14,000
One cook's helper	6,000

Stoves, refrigerators and other equipment can be sold for $10,000, and the purchaser of the equipment will remove it from the building. The remaining book value on the equipment amounts to $25,000.

Current costs of making each meal in the hospital are $0.50 per meal. This is the direct cost of each meal, and it is expected to remain at this level for the next 10 years.

All meals will be prepared for the hospital, and a price of $0.70 will be charged for each meal. The hospital currently serves 200,000 meals per year and is expected to serve the same annual quantity for the next 10 years.

If the meals are purchased from an outside firm, the following equipment will be purchased:

Three microwave ovens @ $500 ea.	$1,500
One freezer	500

This equipment will be used to store and prepare special meals. The outside firm will provide an initial inventory of special meals that are kept frozen until needed.

B. Clinical laboratory
The cost of converting the food services space into usable working area for the laboratory will be $40,000.

The laboratory will purchase a piece of equipment for $20,000 that will be installed in the added space. The equipment will generate an annual net cash inflow to the hospital of $20,000 for 10 years. Labor costs will not increase as a result of this new equipment because one of the current laboratory technicians will be reassigned to handle the equipment. This technician is paid $8,000 per year.

C. Other information
The treasurer has estimated that the hospital's cost for long-term debt is five percent. These bonds were obtained five years ago. The hospital has a line of credit with the local bank at 12 percent. Investments in the plant asset account are earning an effective hese bonds were obtained five years ago. The hospital has a line of credit with the local bank at 12 percent. Investments in the plant asset account are earning an effective rate of nine percent. No average cost of capital has been computed for the hospital.

If the decision is made to take the food service contract, it will be effective for at least 10 years.

29. Your goal is to develop a flexible budget for the nursing function and the laundry services department. This will be done for nursing services by developing a budget for only one nursing station.

    For laundry services a rate and amount budget will be developed which will be applied to the forecast level of operations to determine the expected level of expenses. Later, this same rate and amount budget will be used to prepare a control budget that will be used to pinpoint expenses that are out of line. The accounting department prepared the information in *Exhibits A* and *B* at your request.

    Using the information in *Exhibits A* and *B* develop budgets based on the planned volume of service for the laundry and nursing station 2N.

Exhibit A
Laundry service data

Laundry required by all departments except 2N for the coming week — 15,350 pounds.

Salaries for each of the following individuals are fixed expenses that remain constant each month regardless of the level of operation.

Manager	$1,030
Clean linen room manager	700
Sewing room seamstress	520
Line porter	450
Total	$2,700

The laundry is able to increase the size of the production work force as the number of pounds processed increases. As a result, production labor is a variable cost that varies directly with the number of pounds processed. Labor hourly rates and the times needed to process 100 pounds of laundry are shown in the table below.

Production labor	Hourly rate	Hours per 100 lbs.
Washroom	$4.30	.50
Flat department	4.30	1.50
Press department	4.00	.75

Maintenance on laundry equipment is made up of a fixed cost of $50 per month for preventive maintenance, and additional maintenance is required at the rate of one hour of maintenance for every 10,000 pounds processed. One hour of maintenance costs $40.

Soap and other supplies are estimated to be $.60 per 100 lbs. and are considered variable costs.

Exhibit B
Data for nursing station 2N

	Daily personnel costs
Head nurse	$55
Registered nurse	35
Licensed practical nurse	25
Aides	15

Exhibit B (cont.)
Data for nursing station 2N

Daily personnel requirements for each shift at three levels of occupancy:

	Below 70% occupancy	70-85% occupancy	86 - 100% occupancy
First shift			
Head nurse	1	1	1
Registered nurse	2	2	2
Licensed practical nurse	3	3	3
Aides	2	4	4
Second shift			
Registered nurse	3	3	3
Licensed practical nurse	2	3	3
Aides	2	3	4
Third shift			
Registered nurse	2	2	2
Licensed practical nurse	2	2	2
Aides	1	2	3

Supplies expense amounts to $0.25 per patient day with a fixed portion of $7 per week.

Laundry services are required at the rate of 10 pounds per patient day plus 150 pounds per week for items not related to the level of occupancy. The cost for laundry services is estimated to be $0.16 per pound. There are 46 beds in 2N.

Forecast occupancy levels for the coming week are as follows:

	Patient days
Sunday	45
Monday	44
Tuesday	43
Wednesday	40
Thursday	33
Friday	25
Saturday	20
Total	250

Percentage of patient days ordering meals on a specific day:

Breakfast	90%
Lunch	87%
Dinner	´99%

Standard cost for meals:

Breakfast	$1.40
Lunch	1.52
Dinner	1.53

APPENDIX 7-1

Zero base budgeting*

It is generally agreed upon by most practitioners and academicians that the proper design and use of the budget process is one of the most effective management tools. An effective budget process can be used to: 1. express the administrator's goals and objectives in a quantifiable manner; 2. serve as a communication and commitment device for the hospital staff; 3. act as a measurement tool and feedback loop for corrective action; 4. point out deficiencies in the current financial structure; and 5. forecast when shortages might occur.

For the budget to accomplish its function, there needs to be a well-designed process which can relate the resources committed to the outputs obtained. However, in most service organizations there are no clear input/output relationships similar to those found in manufacturing organizations. Most input resources fall in the category of managed costs. Many costs are discretionary and are set by management actions. It is uncertain how much costs will vary with changes in output. When this uncertainty is coupled directly with the difficulty in measuring both quantity and quality of outputs, a quandary exists. For example, if the number of nursing staff is reduced by 5%, will the quantity or quality also be reduced by 5%?

Despite these difficulties, hospital administrators do make decisions on the amount of resources to be committed to each area. Given the current emphasis on cost containment, better budgeting techniques are becoming more important to administrators and to hospital financial managers.

One tool is the zero base budgeting process. This concept requires that each activity be able to justify its budget request completely. It also requires that no level of expenditure be taken for granted. As President Carter, then governor of Georgia, explained zero base budgeting in his budget address on January 13, 1972: "Zero base budgeting requires every

---

*Adapted with permission from the quarterly journal of the American College of Hospital Administrators, *Hospital and Health Services Administration,* Vol. 24, #2, Spring, 1979, pp. 42-62.

agency in the state government to identify each function it performs and the personnel and cost to the taxpayers for performing that function."[1] Or, expressed in a more concise manner: "Perhaps the essence of zero base budgeting is simply that an agency provides a defense of its budget request that makes no reference to the level of previous appropriations."[2]

Whether zero base budgeting was successfully applied in Georgia can be debated; there are conflicting reports.[3] However, it is important to stress that the concept of zero base budgeting is not new. It has its roots in incremental budgeting, program budgeting and management by objectives. What is new is that it is recommended for all activities in an organization, particularly for the kinds of services that are usually found in hospitals.

Basically, zero base budgeting takes the program budgeting concept and applies it to a responsibility-oriented organizational structure. As such, program elements are transformed into organizational activities. The size of the program element (called decision package) depends upon which level in the organization structure is requested to participate in the zero base budgeting process. Basically, there are three key steps:

1. Develop decision packages.
2. Rank and prioritize them.
3. Allocate resources based on the priorities of the decision packages.

The design of the decision package is one of the most crucial elements in the budgeting process. Typically the first level of supervision in the hospital is responsible for preparing the decision package. This requires them to define their objectives and responsibilities and forces them to determine the costs of meeting objectives at various levels of effectiveness. The impact of this task can be traumatic, at best, or it can be totally dysfunctional if some guidelines are not formalized by top management. One approach would be to define specific levels of activity that should be calculated for each decision package. This could be some minimum budget level below the current budget figure at which the activity could not be reduced without ceasing to exist entirely, for example, 75% of the current budgeted amount. The next level of activity might indicate what could be achieved with the current budgeted amount. Another level would

[1]George S. Minmier and Roger H. Hermanson, "A Look at Zero Base Budgeting—The Georgia Experience," *Atlanta Economic Review* (July-August, 1976): 5-12.

[2]L. Merewitz and S. Sosnick, *The Budgets' New Clothes* (Markheim Series, Rand McNally), 1971, ch. 5.

[3]George S. Minmier, "An Evaluation of the Zero-Base Budgeting System in Government Institutions" *Research Monograph No. 68.* Publishing Services Division, School of Business Administration, Georgia State University, 1975.

be the amount of budget required to perform the current level of activity (adjusted for inflation). Finally, the highest level of activity should include a budget for any new activities to be performed. This might be limited to 125% of the current budgeted amount.

The preparation of this type of analysis requires considerable time, effort, and training. It is particularly difficult to identify relevant output measures. These are typically not identified in many hospital departments. Gross measurements, such as patient days, are not valid indicators of effectiveness or efficiency. Statistical indicators such as case mix, nurse experience or skill levels, or productivity norms, would probably be needed before realistic decision packages could be developed.

The ranking process

After the initial development of the decision packages, all of the supervisory levels must become involved in the ranking process. For example, the nursing supervisor would be required to give a priority ranking for all the decision packages submitted from team leaders or head nurses who have already assigned their priority rankings. In theory, each decision package should be ranked in order of decreasing benefits to the organization.

Peter Pyhrr describes the ranking process as an answer to the questions: How much should we spend? Where (or for what) should we spend it?[4] Each manager should rank the packages that he/she prepared, and each supervisor would rank the decision packages of all his/her subordinates. This process would continue, through each level of the organization, until a final list of prioritized decision packages is obtained. A tree diagram, such as *Figure 1,* would result.

Most large hospitals would have to rank a considerable number of decision packages. The state of Georgia had more than 10,000. If an effective review and prioritizing is to be accomplished, sufficient time must be spent at each review level. For example, assuming 500 decision packages and 6 minutes for each decision package, it would require 50 hours to review the entire budget. Clearly, most large hospitals would have more than 500 decision packages and it is doubtful a thorough analysis could be completed in 6 minutes.

There appears to be a great deal of benefit to be gained from minimizing the number of decision packages. One way of doing so would be to increase the size of the decision package. Yet there is a direct conflict between the size and the ability to complete and evaluate it. The larger the package, the more difficult it is to determine a direct input/output

---

[4]Peter Pyhrr, "Zero Base Budgeting" *Harvard Business Review* (November-December, 1970): 111-121.

Figure 1
Ranking the decision process

(Not all hospital activity shown—for illustrative purposes only.)

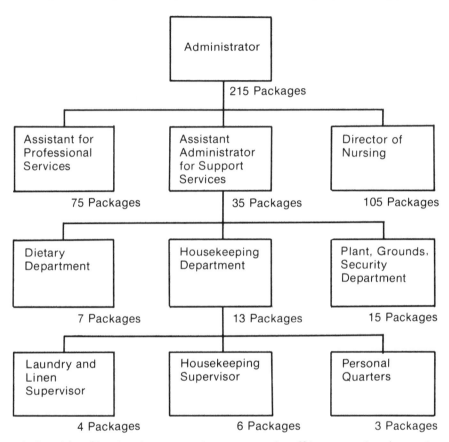

relationship. Clearly, there must be some trade-off between the size and the total number of packages.

To reduce the time required to rank decision packages, a hospital can establish specific cut-off points for review. Each level of supervision could be required to only review the lower 40% of the decision packages. The top ranking packages would be automatically approved. It should be stressed that detailed data on each decision package would be available to the administrator; but the zero base budgeting system should not require that the top-level administrator review every one; there simply is not enough time to do an effective job.

This brief introduction to the zero base budgeting concept should indicate that the implementation of a complete package in a hospital would be a monumental task. However, there are considerable advantages to be gained from its techniques. It forces supervisors to think of their activities and resources. They must determine what can be accomplished for marginal levels of resource expenditures. In addition, they must rank their activities in terms of importance to the hospital or, at least, to their department.

Recommendations

To minimize the costs (and frustration) associated with zero base budgeting, it is recommended that the techniques be applied selectively to a few departments. The process can be gradually expanded to the entire hospital. One local hospital selected their housekeeping and laundry departments as a first cut at zero base budgeting.

There are many benefits to a selective application. First, it minimizes the impact on the total hospital. Secondly, managers can develop a reservoir of experience. Finally, the hospital has the opportunity to gradually refine and improve its guidelines and instruction.

Regardless of which approach is used, there are several key steps which must precede implementation:

1. Top management must support it, especially in the initial steps and in the commitments to use of decision packages in allocating resources.
2. Adequate instructions must be developed so that each supervisor knows what information is required and how it should be prepared.
3. Sufficient time must be allowed both for the design of decision packages and for review of each set of decision packages.
4. The accounting system must be able to provide the data required for the decision package.

Conclusion

The zero base budgeting process offers a management technique for the administrator and for all levels of hospital management to get more fully involved in the budget process. It enables the administrator to make a more constructive allocation of resources. Zero base budgeting is not a panacea; it is a tool that requires careful preparation to be effective.

There are other alternatives that the administrator should consider. One is to adopt the "sunset law" concept and only review a department (or set of decision packages) in detail every few years. It is questionable that zero base budgeting must be an annual process to be utilized effectively and the basic similarities between the requirements of a sunset in-depth review and the zero base budgeting process make this a variable alternative.

Performance auditing is another alternative. It embodies an evaluation of managers in terms of visits achieved to improve the efficiency and effectiveness of an activity. Even though it does not include a ranking of activities, it does have the advantage of not requiring a change in the budget process or in the accounting system. Sunset reviews and performance auditing will offer many of the benefits of zero base budgeting at a lower cost and at a lower level of frustration.

Summary

The cost containment environment confronting most hospital administrators requires that all activities in a hospital be evaluated in a cost/benefit mode. Zero base budgeting is one way to accomplish this task. The administrator who desires to implement a zero base budget is encouraged to read the "Additional readings suggested by the authors" as the first step in implementing the process.

Additional readings suggested by the authors

Donald N. Anderson. "Zero-Base Budgeting—How to Get Rid of Corporate Crabgrass." *Management Review* 65 (October, 1976): 4-16.

Michael H. Carbutt and George S. Minmier. "Incremental, Planned, Programmed and Zero-Based Budgeting." *Public Finance and Accountancy* (November, 1974): 350-357.

Michael H. Granof and Dale A. Kinzel. "Zero-Based Budgeting: Modest Proposal for Reform." *Federal Accountant* 23 (December, 1974): 50-56.

Karla Miller, "Zero Budgeting Works in Yonkers, N.Y." *Government Executive* (January, 1977): 39-40.

T. J. Murray. "Tough Job of Zero Budgeting," *Duns* 104 (October, 1974): 70-72+.

Peter A. Pyhrr. "Zero Base Budgeting" MBA (April, 1977): 25-31.

Peter A. Pyhrr. *Zero Base Budgeting: A Practical Tool for Evaluating Expenses.* (Systems and Controls for Financial Management Series). New York: Wiley-Interscience, 1973.

Peter A. Pyhrr. "Zero Base Budgeting: Where to Use It and How to Begin." *Advanced Management Journal* 41 (Summer, 1976): 4-14.

David Singleton, Bruce A. Smith, and James R. Cleaveland. "Zero-Based Budgeting in Wilmington, Delaware." *Governmental Finance* (August, 1976): 20-29.

Paul J. Stonich and William H. St. Eeves. "Zero-Base Planning and Budgeting for Utilities." *Public Utilities Fortnightly* 98, no. 6 (September 9, 1976): 24-29.

James Suver and Ray Brown. "Where Does Zero-Base Budgeting Work?" *Harvard Business Review* (November-December, 1977): 76-84.

Sample Decision Packages

The following decision packages were developed by second-year MHA students. They are not intended to illustrate either effective or ineffective decision packages, but to show the diversity of approaches that can be used to design packages.

Sample Format

(MINIMUM) (BASE) (CURRENT WORK LEVEL) (ENHANCED)

Package Name ———————————————— Department————————

Management Review Level ———————————— (Organizational Level)

Prepared By ———————————————— Approved By————————

Purpose of Activity:	Resources Required:		
		Current Year	Budget Year	Change/%
	Personnel (FTE)			
Description of Activity:	Salary			
	Fringe			
	Equipment			
	Supplies			
	Travel			
	Other:			
	Total $			

Activity Measurements

Effectiveness:

Efficiency:

Benefits of Approval:

Consequences of Nonapproval

Incremental Packages:	Resources Required & Output Achieved
1.	
2.	
3.	

Ranking By Preparing Mgt. Level:	Ranking by Reviewing Mgt. Level:
No. ⎯⎯⎯ of ⎯⎯⎯ Packages	No. ⎯⎯⎯ of ⎯⎯⎯ Packages

Decision Package 1

(MINIMUM)(BASE)(CURRENT WORK LEVEL)(ENHANCED)

Package Name: Financial Analysis   Department: Finance

Management Review Level ——————————— (Organizational Level)

Prepared By ——————————   Approved By ———————————

Purpose of Activity:

To provide the necessary financial reporting and analytical functions for a large university medical center.

Description of Activity:

Responsible for the preparation and distribution of:
—Monthly financial statements
—Annual Financial reports
—Accounts receivable reconciliation
—Hospital administrative services
—Statistical charts

Performs accounts receivable analysis and correction.

Responsible for performing special financial analyses at the request of the state or administration.

Resources Required:

	Current Year	Budget Year	Change %
Personnel (FTE)	4	5	10.0
Salary	42,168	51,792	22.8
Fringe	4,428	5,438	22.8
Equipment			
Supplies	500	550	10.0
Travel			
Other:			
Total	$47,096	57,780	

Activity Measurements

Effectiveness:

Employees have been averaging 200 hours of overtime per year per employee, which is an indicator of inadequate staffing to fully assume assigned responsibilities. Effectiveness is impaired.

Efficiency:

Overall efficiency is decreased due to the heavy overtime schedule. Currently accountants are borrowed from other sections within Finance which interrupts daily activity and overall efficiency of the office.

Benefits of Approval:
—Provides the required manpower for effective timely financial reporting and analysis in a rapidly growing institution.
—Provides the required manpower to meet increased demands of state and federal governments as well as central administration.

Consequences of Nonapproval:
—Financial Statements would be late, Executive Budget Office Report would not meet the deadline, and there would be little reconciliation of Accounts Receivable. Overall effectiveness of the Finance Office would be curtailed because other sections are picking up part of the workload.

Incremental Packages: Resources Required and Output Achieved

1) 3 FTE's instead of 4 FTE's for entire Finance Ofc.	$28,872	75%
2) 2 FTE's instead of 4 FTE's for entire Finance Ofc.	$19,248	50%
3) 1 FTE instead of 4 FTE's for entire Finance Ofc.	$9,624	25%

Ranking By Preparing Mgt. Level:	Ranking By Reviewing Mgt. Level:
No. _____ of _____ Packages	No. _____ of _____ Packages

Decision Package 2

Consolidated Hospital Association

1. Program Area:
   Education and Training

2. Activity:
   Training the middle management personnel of member hospitals.

3. Objective:
   Insure hospital personnel are adequately trained to aid in managerial effectiveness and work center efficiency.

4. Activity Description:
   Provide, arrange for and/or coordinate continuing education sessions in the management sciences for mid-level managers.

5. Activity Result:
   Insure every mid-level manager receives 12 hours of high-quality continuing education credits in each two-year period. This training should enhance managerial development and improve organizational effectiveness and efficiency of operations as measured by lower operating costs for activities under their supervision and control.

   To accomplish an undertaking of this magnitude and to insure material is presented in a professional manner, a contractual arrangement with the University of Northern Colorado (which will serve as coordinator for this continuing education program) is considered the most desirable alternative. Education sessions will be conducted in various geographic regions of the state using both local and UNC faculty.

6. Resources:

CHA Man Years		Direct Expenses	
		Salaries	$ 6,000
Mgt.	0.1	Travel	$ 1,200
Clerical	0.5	UNC Contract	$45,000
	0.6		$52,200

7. Alternatives:
   No. 2: CHA use Annual Convention with additional guest speakers and workshops to reach mid-managers.

		Resource Requirements			
CHA Man Years		CHA Direct Expense		Additional Expense to Members	
Mgt.	0.1	Salaries	$ 2,400		
Clerical	0.2	Travel	$ 250	Travel	$33,000
	0.3	Facility	$ 1,000		
		Speaker Fees	$ 8,000		
			$11,650		

No. 3: CHA hire sufficient instructors and conduct training sessions in hospitals.

Resource Requirements

CHA Man Years		CHA Direct Expenses		Additional Expense to Members
Mgt.	0.1	Salaries	$ 70,000	0
Instr.	5.0	Travel	$ 25,000	
Clerical	2.0	Supplies	$ 5,000	
	7.1		$100,000	

8. Alternative Level of Effort:

No. 4: 100% of mid-managers receive training, but the 12 hours of CE credits are spread over 4 years.

Benefit/Result: Direct expenses reduced; hospital personnel will not be missing from their work centers as often; but only one-half of mangers will be reached in a two-year period with adverse effects on efforts to improve efficiency and effectiveness.

Resource Requirements

CHA Man Years		Direct Expenses	
Mgt.	0.1	Salaries	$ 2,500
Clerical	0.2	Travel	$ 600
	0.3	UNC Contract	$25,000
			$28,100

9. Ranking:

No.	Resource Requirements
1	$ 42,200
2	$ 44,650
3	$100,000
4	$ 28,100

Decision Package 3

Stripping, Sealing, Waxing of Floors

Program Area:
Housekeeping

Activity:
Stripping, sealing, waxing of floors

Objective:
To provide technically correct floor protection to all of the necessary square footage to increase the lifetime of the floor and to provide an aesthetically pleasing environment.

Activity-Description:
Specially trained floor care specialists, on year-round, regular basis, would strip, seal, and wax each appropriate square foot of floor in the institution at least once a year. High traffic areas would need more frequent attention.

Costs:

Personnel:	2 FTE's @ 6,760	$13,520
Supplies:	Stripper, sealer, wax for 90,000 sq. ft., scrub and buff pads	2,300
Equipment:	No New Purchases Necessary	N/C
Total:		$15,820

Benefits:
Effective floor protection and aesthetic environment without decreasing the present general cleaning standards presently adhered to. Shift to floor care specialists will not require more departmental FTE's, will provide other (fewer) sanitarians more time for general care, will place floor care responsibility on identifiable individuals, who will be responsible for use of floor care supplies and maintenance of expensive machinery. Presently 90,000 sq. ft. are waxed irregularly once a year. This program will allow 30,000 sq. ft. of high traffic area to be cared for twice yearly. 10,000 sq. ft. will be cared for 3 times yearly.

Alternatives: Same Result:
1. Contract to wax 30 + 30 + 10K = 130,000 sq. ft. yearly @15¢/sq. ft. = $19,500

Alternatives: Different Effort Levels:

Alternatives	Benefit	Resource	
2. Care for 120,000 sq. ft.	loss of 3rd waxing/yr.	salaries (1.75 FTE) supplies (.92 × 2300)	11,830 2,116
			13,946
3. Care for 90,000 sq. ft.	loss of 2nd & 3rd wax/yr.	salaries 1 FTE supplies (.69 = 2300)	6,760 1,587
			8,347
4. Do no floor care activity	loss of all floor protection & aesthetics		—0—

Decision Package 4

Program Area:

Materials Management

Activity:

Supplies and equipment management

Objective:

To manage the institution's inventory in an efficient and scientific manner to achieve the twin goals of cost reduction and stock out elimination.

Activity Description:

A trained inventory manger would, on an ongoing regular basis, establish and maintain supplies and equipment storerooms, a physical inventory record of all equipment and supplies on hand, optimum reorder points and quantities, and would monitor the actual flow and expense to user departments against the budgeted volume and dollar figures.

Costs:

Personnel:	2 FTEs	1 manager	$11,000
		1 assistant	7,000
			$18,000
Supplies:	Stock control forms, etc.		1,000
Total:			$19,000

Benefits:

Shift to full-time inventory manager would continue to provide all the services presently rendered (partial storeroom mgt., partial equipment mgt., shipping & receiving) and would substitute trained inventory mgt. hours for presently unskilled hours trying to do that job. Those unskilled hours would be used more efficiently on tasks appropriate to the skill level because that person would be supervised by the inventory manager. For the same amount of budgeted expense, this progam can expect to totally eliminate stock-out problems and reduce inventory carrying costs by 20% over the last year.

Alternative: Same Result:

1. Replace present shipping and receiving clerk and hire a new trained inventory manager. Cost = $11,000, plus present supplies manager at 11,000. Total, $22,000.

Alternatives: Varying Effort Level:

Alternatives	Benefit	Resource	
2. Maintain present system	loss of inventory cost reduction	1.5 FTE	$12,000
3. Eliminate part-time supplies mgt. function	loss of cost reduction & stock-out elimination benefits	1 FTE	7,000

Decision Package 5

Program Area:

Department of Pediatrics

Activity:

Pediatrics Day Treatment Program

Objective:

To provide medical, educational, and psychological services on a daytime outpatient basis to asthma pediatric patients. These patients require special services which cannot be provided in an ordinary school situation.

Activity Description:

This is a pilot program (14 mos.) which may be expanded into an ongoing activity of the hospital. The program would provide medical and psychological support services for 5-6 students in a classroom setting. The hospital would use psychiatrist, psychologist, nurse, social worker, and physician personnel to supply these support services.

Activity Benefit/Result:

This pilot program is intended to demonstrate the benefit of integrating psychological, medical and educational services in the treatment of the asthmatic pediatric patient.

Resources (Minimum Level):

		Direct Expenses (12 mos.)
Salaries:	1-half-time psychologist	$10,500
	1-1/4-time psychiatrist	9,000
	1-half-time R.N.	6,000
	1-half-time Psychiatric Social Worker II	14,000
Supplies:	School lunches for 5 children	1,500
	Supplies and expenses (includes desk, chair, typewriter)	2,500
		$43,500
Sub-total	Employee Benefits	$11,912
	Indirect expenese	16,142
Total (14 mos.)		$71,554

Alternative Way of Accomplishing the Same Result:

Alternative Levels of Effort:

A. Include a comprehensive evaluation for each student (one time activity/student)	
B. Complete psychological assessment	$400
Psychiatric evaluation	100
Parents psychological evaluation	90
Nursing evaluation	10
Physical evaluation	40
Total	640

Decision Package 6

Program Area:

Laboratory (Central)

Activity:

Microbiology Testing

Objective:

To perform complete microbiology testing procedures and provide accurate test results to the requesting physician in the minimum amount of time possible.

Activity Description:

Microbiology tests are ordered by Associated Permanente Medical Group (APMG) physicians in each of the region's four clinics. All cultures are drawn, plated, and incubated in the original clinic; only those cultures then exhibiting the possibility of positive identification of a suspected organism are sent to the Central Laboratory for complete testing. In addition to actual speciman testing, quality control testing should also be performed.

Activity Benefit/Result:

Currently the Central Laboratory averages 1,500 testing procedures per month, serving the health plan membership of 75,500. A 6% increase in membership is projected for 1977. This same 6% applied to the number of tests performed results in an increase of eventually 90 tests per month by year's end.

Resources:

Man Years

The following personnel are required to perform the function of Microbiology testing:

1 FTE Microbiologist

    Develop procedure manuals;
    Conduct inservice instruction for sample collections in each clinic;
    Investigate new products & techniques;
    Perform non-routine testing procedures.

1 FTE Microbiology Technician

    Perform routine and non-routine testing procedures.

1 FTE Clinical Lab Assistant

Perform routine testing procedures;
Perform quality control procedures.

Total   3 FTE

Direct Expense

Salaries	$29,533
Benefits (20% of salaries)	5,907
Supplies	43,232
Equipment (depreciation — no new equipment required)	1,500
Total	$80,172

Alternative Ways of Accomplishment:

1. All microbiology testing could be sent out to private laboratories in the area. This alternative would involve no personnel or direct expense as listed above, but would only recognize the price of the tests which are performed. Applying current test prices quoted by an outside laboratory to tests anticipated to be performed throughout the coming year, the annual price is projected to be $264,602.

2. All testing can be done internally as outlined above for an annual cost of $80,172.

3. Several alternatives exist at various degrees between A and B allowing some testing to be performed outside while some is done inside. These alternatives require resource amounts which would also vary between A and B.

   Due to the commitment of the Associated Permanente Medical Care Program to provide any and all laboratory services required by its membership, alternative levels of effort do not exist; only the one level which is dictated by the demand of the membership.

Ranking

No.		
1	Alt. A Internal testing procedures	$ 80,172
2	Alt. B External testing	$264,602
3	Alt. C Combination of A and B	varying

Note: Alternative C is the least desirable because of possible confusion over which tests shall be done where, as well as difference in quality and consistency of results which could not be monitored by any one person.

APPENDIX 7-2

Performance standards* Vice President, Fiscal Affairs

Financial solvency

1. Cash management

    a. Responsible for monitoring the implementation of aggressive cash management strategies to maximize investment income.

    Performance is acceptable when monthly bank statements support that the average bank balance does not exceed the balance required to service the account.

    b. Responsible for monitoring funding of depreciation consistent with corporate policies.

    Performance is acceptable when the hospital's accounting records support that annual depreciation has been funded.

    c. Responsible for monitoring deposits of cash receipts on a timely basis.

    Performance is acceptable when daily cash receipts are deposited within 24 hours. The vice president monitors compliance weekly.

    d. Responsible for monitoring funding of accounts payable on a timely basis.

    Performance is acceptable when all discounted payables are paid on the tenth of each month, when all other vendors are paid on the twenty-fifth day of each month, when all scheduled payments are paid when due and when payrolls are funded when due.

---

*Saint Joseph Hospital, Denver, Colorado. Performance Standards for 1979-80. Adapted and reprinted by permission.

e. Responsible for providing adequate working capital.

Performance is acceptable when the ratio of current assets to current liabilities is 1½ to 1 as documented by the hospital's interim financial statements.

f. Responsible for monitoring that inventory levels do not exceed needs.

Performance is acceptable when inventories are turned over at least eight times a year as documented by issue reports.

g. Responsible for monitoring accounts receivable on a regular and ongoing basis.

Performance is acceptable when gross accounts receivable represent not more than 45 days of revenues.

h. Responsible for negotiating and monitoring periodic interim payment mechanisms with KFHP of Colorado, Medicare and Blue Cross.

Performance is acceptable when PIP financing mechanisms are updated quarterly based upon volume and revenues.

i. Responsible for reviewing and approving annual cost reports for Medicare and Medicaid.

Performance is acceptable when annual cost reports for Medicare and Medicaid are filed on a timely basis, and when final settlements do not exceed $250,000.

j. Responsible for negotiating Medicaid per diems annually.

Performance is acceptable when Medicaid per diem rates have been negotiated at the highest level under existing reimbursement formulas.

k. Responsible for reviewing and monitoring quarterly construction cash flow updates.

Performance is acceptable when quarterly construction cash flow updates have been presented to and reviewed by the president and the board of directors.

2. Financial reports

a. Responsible for the review of interim financial statements and written interpretations.

Performance is acceptable when interim financial statements are released on the fifteenth working day of each calendar month accompanied by an executive summary highlighting major events.

b. Responsible for reviewing and monitoring all departmental operating statements.

Performance is acceptable when departmental operating statements have been reviewed on an ongoing basis and when the president has been informed of trends as well as areas for corrective action.

c. Responsible for reviewing and monitoring quarterly financial analyses.

Performance is acceptable when quarterly financial reviews are published and distributed by the fortieth working day following the end of each quarter, accompanied by an executive summary highlighting major financial events.

d. Responsible for reviewing and monitoring special financial reports such as productivity analyses, overtime reports, contract labor reports, etc.

Performance is acceptable when all special reports have been monitored, when the president has been made aware of trends and when recommendations have been made for corrective action wherever called for.

e. Responsible for reviewing and monitoring the approved capital expenditure forecast.

Performance is acceptable when quarterly comparative capital expenditure reports have been reviewed within 45 days of the end of each quarter, and when the president has been advised of significant variances.

f. Responsible for reviewing the efficacy, practicability and usefulness of all computerized statistical and financial reports.

Performance is acceptable when all computerized statistical and financial reports generated by computer information services have been reviewed for accuracy, efficacy and usefulness, and when the president has been advised as to their use, add-on's or elimination.

g. Responsible for reviewing all new applications for computerized statistical and financial information systems.

Performance is acceptable when all new applications for computerized statistical and financial information have been reviewed, and when the president has been advised of the recommendations relative to implementation.

h. Responsible for reviewing the annual audited financial statements prepared by the hospital's public accountants.

Performance is acceptable when the annual audited financial statements have been reviewed, and when the president has been advised of significant changes in financial position and reasons why.

i. Responsible for reviewing the recommendations prepared by the hospital's public accountants.

Performance is acceptable when the accountants' recommendations have been reviewed, and when the president and the board of directors of Saint John's Hospital and the Health Service Corporation have been advised of their implementation or lack thereof.

j. Responsible for reviewing and monitoring all statistical and financial reports that directly affect the performance of the departments under his/her administrative jurisdiction.

Performance is acceptable when all statistical and financial reports directly impacting performance of these departments have been reviewed and monitored, and when corrective action has been taken to remove deficiencies.

3. Budgets

a. Responsible for the preparation and review of the annual operating budget and three-year capital expenditure forecast.

Performance is acceptable when the annual operating budget and three-year capital expenditure forecast have been prepared and reviewed for completeness and accuracy, when the forecasts have been reviewed with vice presidents and their respective department directors and when the forecasts have been presented for approval to the president, governing bodies and other agencies as provided for by law.

b. Responsible for the review of all lead schedules relating to significant changes in categories of expense, departmental productivity and FTEs as forecasted in the annual operating budget.

Performance is acceptable when all lead schedules have been reviewed, when the president has been advised of significant variances and their potential impact on the competitive status of the hospital in the community and when recommendations for corrective action have been submitted to the president.

4. Communication and education

a. Responsible for keeping the president informed of significant internal and external events.

Performance is acceptable when the president has been informed of significant internal or external events, their possible implications and the pros and cons of alternative solutions.

b. Responsible for keeping the department directors under his/her administrative jurisdiction informed of significant internal and external events.

Performance is acceptable when he/she meets with his/her department directors regularly and when he/she meets with employees of each of his/her departments at least quarterly.

c. Responsible for attending meetings of the administrative council, the operations committee, the board of directors, Health Services Corporation and finance committee of the Hospital Executive Council.

Performance is acceptable when meetings of the administrative council, the operations committee, etc., have been attended on a regular basis.

d. Responsible for reviewing and approving the annual operations plan, as well as the performance standards of each of the directors, assistant directors and supervisors of departments under his/her administrative jurisdiction.

Performance is acceptable when the annual operations plan, as well as the performance standards of each director, assistant director and supervisor of departments under his/her administrative jurisdiction, have been reviewed, approved and submitted to the president on a timely basis.

e. Responsible for the annual evaluation of department directors under his/her administrative jurisdiction.

Performance is acceptable when the annual evaluation of departmental directors under his/her administrative jurisdiction has been submitted to the president on a timely basis, in the format approved by the administrative council.

f. Responsible for making available educational resources to the department directors under his/her immediate supervision.

Performance is acceptable when department directors under his/her immediate supervision regularly attend I.D. meetings, special educational events sponsored internally and external educational events within the educational parameters approved by the administrative council.

5. Public relations

a. Responsible for monitoring and developing relationships with external agencies, including Colorado Hospital Commission, Blue Cross, Medicare, Department of Social Services, banks, etc.

Performance is acceptable when meetings of external agencies are attended regularly and when the president has been advised of significant developments that directly or indirectly affect the financial position of the hospital.

b. Responsible for monitoring and developing relationship with the medical staff of Saint john's Hospital.

Performance is acceptable when he/she regularly attends meetings of the executive committee.

c. Responsible for monitoring and developing relationships with the Hospital Executive Council.

Performance is acceptable when meetings of the Hospital Executive Council are attended on a regular basis, and when he/she interacts with members of the finance committee of the Hospital Executive Council on an ongoing basis.

d. Responsible for monitoring and developing relationships with the hospital's public accountants.

Performance is acceptable when he/she interacts regularly with local and national representatives of the hospital's public accounting firm.

6. Contracts

a. Responsible for the review and negotiation of all contracts and agreements underwritten by the hospital.

Performance is acceptable when all contracts and agreements have been reviewed on a timely basis and when the president has been advised of the accuracy and completeness of contracts, possible deficiencies and alternative approaches.

CHAPTER 8

Pricing strategies

Introduction

With prospective pricing policies it is more important than ever to use appropriate techniques to set rates or charges. Before prospective payment, healthcare providers established their pricing policies on the federal government's regulation of lower of cost or charges for the reimbursement of care provided to government clients. This policy tended to insure that charges were always higher than full cost as determined by accounting conventions and the Medicare cost report. It effectively prevented most major healthcare providers from engaging in market based or competitive pricing strategies.

The federal government instituted prospective pricing on a DRG basis in 1983. This does not negate the need to recover full cost, but rather it opens up a wide range of pricing strategies for healthcare providers in the long run. Failure to recover total cost still means bankruptcy or reduced ability to meet patient care demands in the future. The difference is that

Exhibit 8-1
Typical managerial decisions by
today's healthcare providers

- Where should we place our greatest efforts (and expenditures) to meet community needs and achieve satisfactory financial rewards?

- Should we accept this discount offer from the HMO, PPO, AHP?

- How much of a discount can we offer on this service?

- How much must we increase volume to break even on this service?

- What services should we stop providing?

- How to identify specific services, physicians or managers that need to be evaluated?

- What price must we establish for this procedure or service?

the government now puts a limit on how much can be charged. Providers must see that their actual costs fall within that charge limit. For example, the major pricing issues confronting most healthcare providers are presented in *Exhibit 8-1*. Answers to each of the questions in *Exhibit 8-1* require a decision on pricing strategies. The choice of pricing strategies in turn is heavily influenced by a thorough understanding of cost behavior and the determination of full costs, out-of-pocket costs, and the impact on other payers.

Determination of full cost

The full cost of any specific service, test, or provider includes the variable costs plus a fair share of all fixed costs. In this respect, all full cost models involve some subjectivity and an averaging technique. For example, in Chapter 2 total costs were defined as total fixed costs plus total variable costs.

$$TC = TFC + TVC$$

To obtain full costs on a per unit basis, all terms in the equation need to be divided through by the activity being costed. For example, the routine service charge would be determined as follows:

TFC (includes all direct and indirect fixed costs) = $10,000,000
TVC* (includes all direct and indirect variable costs) = $500,000
Total Costs = $10,000,000 + $5,000,000 or $15,000,000
Total number of Patient days = 100,000

$$\frac{TC}{pd} = \frac{TFC}{pd} + \frac{TVC}{pd}$$

Substituting the actual values in the formula gives the following computation:

$$\frac{\$15,000,000}{100,000} = \frac{\$10,000,000}{100,000} + \frac{\$50(100,000)}{100,000} \text{ or}$$

$$\$150 = \$100 + \$50$$

If all payers paid full costs and full costs included the necessary margin to provide for non-accounting costs, contingencies and asset replacement, the $150 charge would be sufficient. For the purpose of this example, let us assume that all costs are included in the $150. What rate should be established?

---

*As discussed in Chapter 2. TVC = $(VC_u)(Q)$ or in the example above $\$(50)(100,000)$ if VC_u = $50 per patient day.

Payer	Basic	% of Total Patient Days
Medicaid	80% of Accounting Costs	20%
Medicare	90% of Accounting Costs	30%
HMO, PPO	90% of Charges	10%
Blue Cross	95% of Charges	20%
Commercial and Self-Pay	100% of Accounting Costs	20%
		100%

Let us also assume that accounting costs = $125 per patient day and $25 is for other financial requirements. Therefore total accounting costs are $12,500,000 and $2,500,000 represents the required margin over costs.

The patient days per payer are computed as follows:

Medicaid Patient Days	20% × 100,000 pd =	20,000 pd
Medicare Patient Days	30% × 100,000 pd =	30,000 pd
Blue Cross	20% × 100,000 pd =	20,000 pd
HMO's, etc.	10% × 100,000 pd =	10,000 pd
Commercial, Self Pay	20% × 100,000 pd =	20,000 pd
	Total Patient Days =	100,000

Given the above information, the rates would be determined as follows:

Total Financial Requirements =		$15,000,000
Medicaid	80% × $125 × 20,000 pd =	2,000,000
Medicare	90% × $125 × 30,000 pd =	3,375,000
	Total Recovered from cost based	$ 5,375,000
	Amount remaining	$ 9,625,000
	Patient days remaining	50,000
	Charge per patient day after cost based reimbursement	$ 192.50
HMO	90% × $192.50 × 10,000	$ 1,732,500
Blue Cross	95% × $192.50 × 20,000	$ 3,657,500
	Accounting costs remaining	$ 4,235,000
	Commercial patient days	20,000
	Charge per patient day after negotiated payers	$ 211.75

The rates for each class of payers are:

Medicaid	$100.00
Medicare	$112.50
HMO	$173.25
Blue Cross	$182.88
Commercial	$211.75

Unfortunately, many third party payers do not agree with the concept of total financial requirements as presented in this text. They will pay only accounting costs, and in many circumstances, not all accounting costs are allowed. Each cost-based payer tends to determine what costs they will recognize. How does this fact affect our rate setting strategy based on full cost recovery to meet total financial requirements?

Let's assume, a healthcare provider has five types of payers who pay on the indicated basis.

The impact on the charges that were established under a cost-based system is illustrated above. Under a fixed rate payment by DRG's, the same scenario will be duplicated unless the DRG's rates are more realistically established.

Therefore, healthcare providers must be fully aware of pricing strategies which will allow the organization to meet total financial requirements.

Cost, volume, profit models

As discussed in earlier chapters, the price to be established for specific products can be determined through the use of cost, volume, profit models. The basic model as developed in Chapter 4 was:

$$PxQ = TFC \times VC_uQ + \text{Desired Margin}$$

The total fixed costs and desired margin must be allocated to the item being priced by the model. For example given the following data:

Quantity of Services	= 20,000
Total Fixed Costs	= $300,000
Variable Cost per Unit	= $ 10.00
Desired Margin	= $ 60,000

Substituting in the Cost/Volume/Profit Model

$$P(20,000) = \$300,000 + \$10(20,000) + 60,000$$
$$20,000P = \$560,000$$
$$P = \$28$$

The Cost/Volume/Profit Model is easily programmed into existing micro computer software such as LOTUS 1 2 3, MULTIPLAN, etc. Several possible scenarios on costs and volume could be used to determine the impact on the price to be charged. It should also be noted that this represents a net price to the provider unless the allowances for discounts, bad debts and free care were included in the total fixed costs or desired margin. If this condition was not met, then the price must be adjusted for the estimated allowances.

Assuming an 11% allowance account, the price would be determined as follows:

$$\text{Gross Price} = \frac{\text{Net Price}}{1 - \text{allowance percentage}}$$

$28.89 or $31.46

Other pricing techniques

The Cost/Volume/Profit Models are very useful in pricing clearly identifiable services, tests, procedures, etc. However, where a large number of individual items must be priced or where specific cost data can not be determined by test, service, or procedure, management may find it helpful to use macro approaches. In this section, three of the most common methods will be discussed.

In some departments, it is difficult to identify specific costs with individual patients, procedures, or outputs. All users of the service place a demand on the capacity of the department. The charge for this service is usually a function of the amount of capacity used by the specific service or patient or an average resource consumed approach.

For example, in operating rooms most costs are fixed and do not vary measurably with the type of procedure performed. The operating room has a certain capacity in terms of time, hours, minutes, etc. It seems reasonable that costs for the operating room should be based on the amount of time used. The time method involves estimating the types of surgical procedures to be provided, the standard amount of time by surgical procedure and the total costs of the operating room. *Exhibit 8-2* illustrates the time method.

Exhibit 8-2
"Time" method of cost allocation

Estimated Type of Surgical Procedure [1]	Standard Time Required In Minutes [2]	Standard Charge per Unit of Time [3]	Standard Charge
101	20	100	$ 33
102	30	100	$ 50
103	45	100	$ 75
104	60	100	$100

[1] Estimated by Budget process and/or planning staff.

[2] Determined by medical staff or from medical records.

[3] Based on dividing total operating room costs by estimated units of time to meet estimated demand, for example:

$$\frac{\text{Total operating room costs}}{\text{Estimated minutes required}} \quad \frac{\$4,000,000}{40,000} = \$100 \text{ standard charge per minute}$$

For some services such as lab and radiology, a standard activity base has been developed to price the output of the department. This standard activity base is called a relative value unit (RVU). Each specific output is expressed in terms of RVUs based on the complexity of the service resources needed or amount of time. In many cases, RVUs also include the capacity necessary to meet peak-load demands. The number of RVUs multiplied by the standard RVU price equals the price of the service. A sample computation is illustrated in *Exhibit 8-3.*

Exhibit 8-3
Relative value computation

Type of Test	RVU's Required	Standard Price per RVU	Price of Test
A	1	$10	$10
B	2	$10	$20
C	3	$10	$30
D	4	$10	$40

RVUs provide the opportunity for managers to monitor changes in the intensity of services provided. Many institutions are now starting to price nursing care in this manner to reflect the shift in the more seriously ill patients staying shorter periods in the hospital while the minimal care patient is now being seen on an outpatient basis.

The surcharge approach is quite useful in pricing items which are itemized in the patient bill such as pharmacy items and medical supplies. It is based on the concept that the total costs of the service department must be charged to the patient receiving the service. It is a straight forward method which assumes the total costs of the department are influenced by the activity base selected, i.e., cost of drugs or medical supplies, number of prescriptions, etc. Using the cost of drugs as an example, the surcharge would be determined in the following manner:

Total cost of drugs for department for coming year = $1,100,000
Total cost of pharmacy department = $2,200,000

$$\text{Surcharge percentage} = \frac{\text{Total Costs to be recovered}}{\text{Total Cost of drugs issued}} = \frac{\$2,200,000}{\$1,100,000} =$$

200 percent
Drug cost to patient Y = $750
Amount billed to Patient Y for drugs = 200% × $750 or $1500

The choice of pricing techniques to be used depends on the data available and the desires of management. In today's environment, the price that must be established is heavily influenced by competitive conditions and is basically a market based approach. In other cases, the price is determined by the third party reimburser; either by fiat (Medicare and/or Medicaid) or by negotiation (Blue Cross, HMO's, PPO's, etc.). Even under these circumstances, it is vital to have the best data available on the cost of providing the service.

All inclusive pricing models

In many organizations, outputs such as services, procedures, tests, etc., are priced on an all-inclusive basis. This method of pricing fits the government's current approach to pricing by DRGs. It also facilitates the development and identification of the output of the healthcare organization. For example, prior to the Tax Equity and Fiscal Responsibility Act of 1982 (TEFRA) the primary output of most healthcare organizations was expressed in terms of patient days. A per diem basis of pricing was developed. In 1982 the government mandated a case by discharge approach to pricing. A case mix measure was developed similar to the approach for DRGs demonstrated in *Exhibit 8-4* which were required by Title VI of the Social Amendment of 1983. The case mix index was designed to measure differences in the intensity of care provided by specific institutions. A hospital which specialized in the more costly procedures would have a higher index.

Using the case mix index established in *Exhibit 8-3,* a reimbursement by discharge or diagnosis could be determined for each hospital. For example, if the average cost per discharge for all hospitals was $1865.54, then a hospital with a case mix index of .89 would receive $1660.33 (.89 × $1865.64). If a diagnosis system such as DRGs were used, a similar approach could be used. Given DRG 86 and average cost of $2350, Hospital A would receive (.89 × $2350) or $2091.50.

As illustrated above, the identification of the hospital's output as either a case by discharge or case by diagnosis necessitated an all inclusive pricing model which focused on the total resources required to achieve a specific output diagnosis. However, it did not dictate which technique must be used to price individual services. Each DRG had a desired number of services, tests, or procedures associated with providing a quality output. The total costs of the DRG would be the accumulated cost of the specific services, etc. The costs of specific services would be determined by any of the earlier methods. Since total reimbursement was fixed by DRG, the government as the major third party was not concerned about the costing and allocation techniques used by the provider. This freedom offered the provider the opportunity to control pricing and profit margins to other purchasers of the services. Under the controlled average cost method of pricing used by the government in purchasing services prior to 1983, most healthcare providers were unable to establish prices to meet competition. The lower of cost or charges for government patients insured that rates were set higher than costs and costs were determined by strict cost finding methods.

Competitive pricing methods

With the removal of the average full cost approach to payment for government patients, healthcare providers are free to price their services to meet

Exhibit 8-4
Calculation of Medicare case-mix index

Hospital	Proportion of Medicare Discharges by DRG (Percent)[1]					Total (Percent)	DRG Weighted Expected Cost Per Case[2]	Case Mix Index[3]
	DRG 1	*DRG 2*	*DRG 3*	*DRG 4*	*DRG 5*			
A	2.5	27.3	10.5	41.5	18.2	100	$1660.40	.8900
B	21.0	.9	30.1	2.0	46.0	100	2401.30	1.2872
C	40.6	5.0	2.3	47.2	4.9	100	1346.30	.7227
D	5.1	18.4	62.5	10.0	4.0	100	2990.70	1.6031
E	30.4	65.0	1.0	1.6	2.0	100	929.00	.4980
Avg. Proportion for all hospitals	19.92	23.32	21.28	20.46	15.02	100	$1865.54	
DRG Cost Weight	$1000	$800	$4100	$1500	$2000			

[1] Adjusted to make these 5 DRGs hypothetically represent all 356 Medicare DRG's

[2] For hospital A, calculated as follows:
.025 (1000) + .273 (800) + .105 (4100) + .415 (1500) + .182 (2000) = $1660.40

[3] For hospital A, calculated as $1660.40 divided by $1865.54 = .8900

Source: Ernst & Whinney, "The Revised DRG's: Their Importance in Medicare Payments to Hospitals", 1983, p. 7.

market prices or community needs. Several key factors are important in developing the new pricing strategies. First, any price must at least cover variable or out-of-pocket costs if the organization is not to be worse off financially by offering the service. This method of pricing is typically called a marginal cost approach to price setting. Secondly, marginal cost pricing strategies are for short run pricing only. The short run time frame is difficult to define exactly. It depends on the financial resources of the provider, the needs of the community, and the nature of the competition. It usually should be for periods of time less than one year. For periods greater than one year but less than three to five years, a direct cost pricing approach can be developed. Direct costs are defined in this circumstance as the variable costs in the short run model plus the direct fixed costs associated with the service, etc. Depending on the point in time in which the fixed costs must be replaced, a pricing policy must be developed which insures that the direct fixed costs are recovered to allow for replacement of these assets.

In the long run, all direct costs plus a fair share of indirect costs must be recovered to continue to offer the service. *Exhibit 8-5* illustrates an example of a competitive pricing model.

Exhibit 8-5
A competitive pricing model

Given:

Variable costs $15 per test

Direct fixed costs $20,000 per month

Indirect costs $30,000 per month

Estimated number of procedures to recover full costs = 5,000

Short run competitive price $\geq$ $15

Direct cost price $\geq$ $4[1] + $15 or $19

Full cost price $\geq$ $6[2] + $4 + $15 or $25

$$^1 \quad \frac{\text{Direct fixed costs}}{\text{Estimated number of procedures}} = \frac{\$20,000}{5,000} = \$4$$

$$^2 \quad \frac{\text{Indirect costs}}{\text{Estimated number of procedures}} = \frac{\$30,000}{5,000} = \$6$$

The use of competitive pricing models requires that the manager have access to variable and fixed cost information, direct and indirect allocations, and a reliable estimate of the number of procedures to be accomplished. Most accounting systems in use today do not routinely provide these types of data.

Summary

The changing healthcare environment and a shift to prospective fixed price methods of reimbursement have presented an opportunity for healthcare providers to price their products selectively. This ability to meet price competition also means that the management must understand the various pricing strategies and assess the implications of using an average full cost approach to many specific services. The focus should be on pricing services in such a manner to maximize total revenues, considering market demands and community requirements.

Questions and problems

1. Discuss the impact on a healthcare provider's pricing strategies of the switch to a prospective pricing system by major payers.

2. Define full costs as they pertain to pricing strategies.

3. Government and other cost based payers stress that they are paying the full cost of services provided to their clients.
   Evaluate this statement in terms of impact on other payers.

4. Explain the following pricing techniques:
   Surcharge
   Weighted Average
   Average Resources Utilized

5. Explain an all inclusive pricing strategy.

6. Why was a case mix index introduced for government payers?

7. Discuss the impact of the lower of costs or charges regulation that determined reimbursement for government cost-based payers until 1983.

8. Discuss what pricing strategy might be appropriate for a healthcare provider under the following circumstances. Assume that competition is in place or anticipated:
   a. Meeting competition from a doctor's office.
   b. Meeting competition from a group practice.
   c. Meeting competiton from a free standing unit owned by:
      1. Local investors.
      2. Joint venture or medical providers.
      3. Major investor owned healthcare chain.
   d. Meeting competition from a major healthcare provider.

9. The Colorado Clinic wants to establish a rate schedule for a series of laborataory tests that will be given to patients on a routine basis. The administrator would like to know the cost of each test individually and the cost of the entire series. She estimated that approximately 1500 women would need the series which consists of 3 tests, U.V. and R. The U consists of 2 procedures; Text V, 3 procedures and Test R, 4 procedures. The accountant estimated the following cost information.

Test U	Cost Per Procedure
preprinted forms	.15
glassware breakage	.10
supplies	.19
Reagents	.23

Test V	Cost Per Procedure
disposable syringes	5.00
preprinted forms	.15
glassware breakage	.10
sterile bandages	.05
supplies	.19
Reagents	.25

Test R	Cost Per Procedure
preprinted forms	.15
glassware breakage	.12
supplies	.19
Reagents	.22

In addition, the following costs were to be directly attributable to the individual tests.

Test U	Cost Per Quarter
administration	$ 5,500
maint. utilities, janitorial	7,200
depreciation	3,180
salaries	11,120

Test V	Cost Per Quarter
administration	$ 6,500
maint. utilities, janitorial	7,200
depreciation	4,280
salaries	11,120

Test R	Cost Per Quarter
administration	$ 5,500
maint. utilities, janitorial	7,200
depreciation	3,180
salaries	11,120

The administrator believed that each test's price should be set high enough to return 10% on allocated fixed costs. He/she also estimated that allowances for free care, bad debts and discounts to HMO's would equal 15% of the billed amount.

Required:
a. Develop the rate structure for the clinic. Identify full costs, the gross price, the net price and any other important factors.
b. The administrator also believed that in the near future the clinic might lose its tax exempt status. The average tax rate currently was 30%. He/she wondered how much prices would have to be raised to maintain the same level of income if taxes had to be paid. Can you help answer this question.

10. University Hospital would like to establish a charge for the out-patient clinic which would recover all cost and contribute $120,000 to the financial resources. The following data was established by the assistant controller of the cost behavior for the next year.

Variable costs per visit $4.05.

Direct fixed expenses	100,000 per quarter
Allocated university overhead	150,000 per quarter

The estimated number of clients to be seen were 50,000 per quarter.

Required:
a. Compute the charge which would meet the hospital's objectives.
b. What other data would you like to have to develop the charge structure?

11. The administrator of the G.M. Frank Family Planning Center currently charges $20 per visit which was set to recover full costs. A recent change in state law will allow healthcare providers similar to G. M. Frank's to add an amount up to 15% of their costs to recover free care and bad debts. The Financial Vice President was reviewing the cost

data from this year to prepare new rates for next year. The following information was available.

Variable costs were established at 10% of full costs based on this year's volume and remain the same for next year. Fixed costs were $162,000 for next year. Free care, bad debts, and allowances were set at 10% of gross revenue. Estimated volume for next year was 10,000 visits.

Required:

Determine the charge that could be proposed for next year and still fall within the 15% limitation of the state regulation.

12. The administrator of the speech and hearing center, estimated the following costs for services in the department:

Service	Variable cost per service	Direct fixed
Audiological examination	$ 5	$ 30,000
Pediatric audiological evaluation	5	40,000
Pure tone—air and bone	5	5,000
Speech evaluation	3	18,000
Hearing therapy	10	27,000
Hearing and evaluation	10	10,000
Indirect fixed costs (to include administration costs, utilities, etc.)		100,000
Desired profit margin		100,000

The total volume of tests was estimated to be 25,000. The individual volumes are audiological examination, 3,000; pediatric audiological evaluation, 4,000; pure tone—air and bone, 5,000; speech evaluation, 3,000; hearing therapy, 9,000; hearing and evaluation, 1,000.

Determine a fee schedule for these services based on the cost data above. The fee should cover all costs plus the profit margin.

13. The administrator of Memorial Hospital is planning to add a new 15-bed pediatric unit to the hospital. Currently the hospital has 400 beds, and the new pediatric center will be treated as a separate cost center. You have been asked to determine the routine service charge for the new unit. The following information was collected by the assistant controller to help in your computations.

	4,000 patient days	5,000 patient days
Total direct cost		
Salaries	$48,000	$55,000
Supplies and other expenses	3,000	3,500
Total allocated costs		
Laundry and linen	2,800	3,500
Housekeeping	4,800	6,000
Dietary	12,000	15,000
Central service	840	1,050
Pharmacy	80	100
Medical records	1,920	2,400

It is not anticipated that the new unit will add significantly to the costs of the service departments.

Determine what charge you would recommend, and state any assumptions you feel were necessary to make in arriving at your decision.

References

Burik, David, "The Changing Role of Hospital Prices: A Framework for Pricing in a Competitive Environment," *Healthcare Management Review,* Vol. 8, No. 2, Spring 1983, pp. 65-71.

de Mars Martin, Pamela and Frank J. Boyer, "Product Live Costing: Developing a Consistent Method for Costing Hospital Services," *Healthcare Financial Management* Feb. 1985, pp. 30-37.

Kohlman, Herman A., "Determining a Contribution Margin for DRG Profitability," *Healthcare Financial Management,* Apr. 1984, pp. 108-110.

Jacobs, Phillip and Charles R. Franz, "Developing Pricing Policies by Diagnostic Grouping," *Healthcare Financial Management* Jan. 1985, pp. 50-52.

Saliman, Soliman Y. and William Hughes, "DRG Payments and Net Contribution Variance Analysis," *Healthcare Financial Managment* Oct. 1983, pp. 78-86.

APPENDIX 8-1

Outline of Steps Utilized by HCFA To Develop the Regional Standardized Amounts for the Federal Portion of the Prospective Payment System[1]

Using one hospital as an example, the following steps illustrate the adjustments HCFA made to each 1981 Medicare cost report. The data from one hospital was combined with all hospitals and standardized amounts were derived to establish the basis of the Federal portion of PPS. In summary, the adjustment steps are:

Step 1. Begin with total allowable inpatient Medicare costs on each hospital's cost report
Step 2. Remove:
- Capital-related costs
- Direct medical education costs
- Nursing care differential
- Costs in excess of routine limits
Step 3. Divide the net costs by number of Medicare discharges to establish operating cost per discharge
Step 4. Update for inflation for 6 months of 1981, calendar 1982, calendar 1983 and 9 months of 1984
         Standardize for:
Step 5. Case-mix differences
Step 6. Indirect medical education costs

---

[1]*Prospective Payment System-Medicare,* New York: Coopers & Lybrand, 1983, pp. 22-27 and 39-41.

Step 7.   Area wage differences (if an Alaskan or Hawaiian hospital, adjust for non-labor portion)

Step 8.   Adjust for budget neutrality and outlier payments— adjustment factors used in determination of Federal rates:
Outlier factor 0.943
Budget neutrality factor 0.969

Step 9.   Adjustment of 0.13% in recognition of non-physician costs previously billed under part B

Step 10.   Adjustment of 0.18% in recognition of FICA taxes not previously incurred.

The result is a set of standardized amounts for the Federal portion of the PPS rates broken down between urban and rural within nine regions and one overall national producing 20 standardized amounts. These standardized amounts become a component of the prospective payment rate and, following local wage and DRG weight adjustment, are combined with the hospital-specific cost base portion.

Base year cost data

Statistical Data—

- 200 Beds
- 25 FTE Interns and Residents
- FYE, June 20
- Los Angeles, California.

This example shows one hospital for purposes of illustrating the Federal-based portion. In actuality HCFA aggregated all hospitals to develop the standards. All of the hospitals, though computed separately by HCFA, were then aggregated within region and broken down between urban and rural areas to obtain the standards for the Federal-based portion of the prospective payment rate.

Step 1.	1981 Cost Report Data:		
	Total allowable Medicare inpatient costs		$10,000,000
Step 2.	Less:		
	Capital-related costs	$700,000	
	Direct medical education	600,000	
	Nursing care differential	400,000	
	Costs in excess of routine cost limits	300,000	(2,000,000)
Step 3.	Base Year Cost		$8,000,000
	divided by 1981 Medicare discharges		÷ 4,000
	Medicare Base Year Cost per discharge		$ 2,000

Step 4.   Inflation adjustment
           Inflation through HCFA fiscal year 1983
           (9/30 FYE) using actuarial estimates and
           through 9/30/84 using target rate
           percentages:

           6 mos. 1981 —
           Annual inflation rate — 15.9%
               107.66%* × $2,000   = $2,153

           1982 — annual inflation rate 15.0%
               115%* × $2,153   = $2,476

           9 mos. 1983 — annual inflation rate 11.7%
               108.65%* × $2,476   = $2,690

           3 mos. 1983 — annual target rate 7.2%
               101.75%* × $2,690   = $2,737
           9 mos. 1984 — annual target rate 6.8%
               105.06%* × $2,737   = $2,875

           Note: For a June hospital, the compounded inflation rate for the
           period 7/1/81 through 9/30/84 is 43.75% or an annual average
           rate of 11.8%.

           *Percentages obtained from HCFA.

Step 5.   CMI Adjustment
           Data from Step #4 $2,875
           Divided by the hospital's case mix index   1.0235
                                                          $2,809

Step 6.   Removal of Indirect Medical
           Education Costs

           Formula — Adjusted cost per discharge divided by [1 + (educational
           adjustment factors × intern/resident to bed ratio)] = Education ad-
           justed cost per discharge
                                     or
           Education adjustment factor = .1159 (FR 39765)
           Intern/resident to bed ratio = $\dfrac{25 \text{ interns}}{200 \text{ beds}}$ ÷ 1(FR 39764)

           Case
           $2,809 ÷ [1 + (.1159 × $\dfrac{25}{200}$ ÷ 1)] $2,454

Step 7.   Removal of Area Wage Variable
           From Step #6 $2,454
           Assumed wage index for the area
           (Los Angeles) 1.3037
           labor portion per market basket (FR 39765)   × .7915

	Labor share	$1,942
	Wage index	÷1.3037
	Wage adjusted labor share	$1,490
	plus non-labor share	+ 512
	adjusted cost per discharge	$2,002
Step 8.	Budget neutrality and outlier adjustments from Step #7	$2,002
	Budget neutrality factor	× .969
		$1,940
	Outlier adjustment factor	× .943
		$1,829
Step 9.	Non-Physician costs previously paid under part B	×1.0013
		$1,831
Step. 10.	FICA taxes not previously incurred	×1.0018
	Ultimate contribution to aggregate regional standardized amount	$1,834

This adjusted data was then summarized within the nine census divisions and broken down between urban and rural areas based upon metropolitan area definitions (not included herein).

The previous section detailed how the Federal Government arrived at the labor-related portion of regional standardized amounts and the non-labor portion of regional standardized amounts, two components of the Federal portion of the rate.   The following section illustrates the calculation of the Federal portion hospital prospective payment.

Computation of federal portion of PPS

Step 1.	Labor-related portion of regional standardized amount (Region #9 URBAN—Los Angeles) (FR 39844)	$2,220
Step 2.	Wage index (FR 39873)	×1.3037
		2,894
Step 3.	Non-labor portion of regional standardized amount (FR 39844)	+ 712
		3,606
Step 4.	Federal portion	× .25
		901
Step 5.	DRG weight factor #89	×1.1029
Step 6.	Federal portion	$ 994

Hospital-specific portion of PPS

To ease the impact of a completely new method of payment for hospital services the statute provides for a three-year transition period. Payment will be a blend of the hospital-specific portion and the Federal portion based upon the HCFA developed standards described previously.

The hospital-specific portion is determined in a manner similar to the target rate system established by TEFRA and implemented by Regulation 405.463. The computation relies on the following information:

- Base year costs—the base year is the one that precedes the year in which TEFRA applies. For example, the base year for a hospital with a June 30 year-end is subject to TEFRA for the period of July 1, 1983, through June 30, 1984. Therefore, the base year for PPS in this case is the year ended June 30, 1983. (This is not to be confused with the year HCFA used to compute the Federal portion, which was 1981.)
- Adjustments to the base year will include the following:
  - Removal of any capital-related costs
  - Removal of direct medical education costs
  - Removal of nursing care differential
  - Removal of routine costs in excess of the limits
  - Inclusion of malpractice premium costs
  - Inclusion of FICA taxes, if not previously a cost in the base year
  - Removal of kidney acquisition costs if hospital has a Renal Transplantation Center
  - Inclusion of costs of non-physician inpatient hospital services that were billed directly to part B by another supplier or the provider during the base period
  - Removal of cost increases due to changes in accounting practices aimed at raising the base
  - Adjustment for items that could have major consequences for the base year costs.

Procedure after determining base year costs

Adjusted base year costs are divided by the Medicare discharges in the base year to determine the average Medicare cost per discharge. (PPS base year adjusted cost/discharge.) The following additional steps are required:

Step 1.   Divide the adjusted base year costs per discharge by the case mix index. This, like the Federal portion, is to remove the differences in case mix complexity between hospitals.

Step 2.   Multiply the adjusted base year costs by the outlier adjustment (.943).

Step 3.   Multiply the base year cost per discharge by the updating
factor based on fiscal year-end dates. The updating factor
is a combination of adjustments both for inflation and for
budget neutrality.

Step 4.   Multiply this product by 75% (the hospital-specific portion
for year 1 of the blended rate).

Step 5.   Multiply this product by the DRG weight—(the DRG
assigned to the case—FR 39876-39886).

Example of computation of hospital-cost-based portion of PPS

(Fiscal Year-End June 30)

	PPS Base year adjusted cost/discharge	$3,000
Step 1.	Case mix index	÷ 1.0235
		$2,931
Step 2.	Outlier adjustment	× .943
		$2,764
Step 3.	Updating factor	×1.12658
		$3,114
Step 4.	Transition percentage (Hospital portion)	× .75
		$2,336
Step 5.	DRG #89 weight factor	× 1.1029
	HOSPITAL PORTION	$2,576

The hospital will compute each case in the same manner. The only
difference between each case will be the DRG weight factor.

Final computation of prospective payment

Bringing Together the Federal Portion and the Hospital-Cost-Portion

Now combine the Federal portion, which, for the first year, constitutes 25%
of the PPS, with the hospital-cost-based portion, which comprises the
remaining 75% of the payment. When these two elements are combined,
the total constitutes the prospective payment for this case, unless an outlier
situation occurs. Outliers are discussed below.

Total Prospective Payment—DRG #89

Hospital Portion	$2,576
Federal Portion	994
	$3,570

This completes the prospective payment portion of the hospital rate, without outlier adjustments and the other additional payments discussed in the following sections.

Outliers

Outliers are defined as cases that have either an extremely long length of stay (day outliers) or extraordinary high costs (cost outliers) when compared to most discharges in the same DRG.

A hospital's claim for outlier payments will be subject to a review by Utilization and Quality Control Peer Review Organizations (PROs), or Fiscal Intermediary, which will make appropriate coverage determinations. Hospitals should document cases properly so that they may qualify them as outliers. The basis for such support lies in proper physicians' medical review and certification, supported by medical records which justify the extraordinary costs and/or extra length of stay.

The statute specifies that the amount of additional outlier payment shall approximate the marginal cost of care beyond the cut-off point. HCFA has determined that the marginal cost of outlier care will be based on a 60 percent factor.

In any circumstances the total amount of additional payments may not be less than 5 percent nor more than 6 percent of the total payments to be made based on DRGs in that year. (These percentage limitations are in the aggregate. They do not apply to individual hospitals.)

There will be no rate adjustments for cases of atypically short duration.

Computation of prospective payment

Data Assumption for Model Illustration:

1. Principal Diagnosis—DRG #89
2. 450 bed general acute care hospital
3. Los Angeles, California
4. June 30 fiscal year-end
5. Base year cost $3,000

I. Calculation of Hospital-Specific Portion:

A. Formula:

$$\frac{\text{Base Year Cost}}{\text{Mix Index}} \times \text{Outlier Adjustment} \times \text{Updating Factor} \times \text{Transition Period Percentage} \times \text{DRG Weight} = \text{Hospital-Specific Portion}$$

B. Input Data and Source:

	Model	Your Hospital	Source
1. Base Year Cost—	$3,000	$_____	Hypothetical—(computed for each hospital by fiscal intermediary on HCFA Form 1007).
2. Case-Mix Index—	1.0235	_____	Hypothetical—(computed for each hospital using 1981 data (FR 39847-39870))
3. Outlier Adjustment—	0.943	0.943	Applies to all hospitals—(FR 39774)
4. Updating Factor—	1.12658	_____	(FR 39774)
5. Transition Period Percentage—	.75	.75	Applies to all hospitals with cost reporting periods beginning on or after October 1, 1984 (FR 39775)
6. DRG Weight—	1.1029	1.1029	Simple pneumonia and pleurisy, DRG #89, Table 5 of DRG weights (FR 39877)

C. Illustration:

Model $\dfrac{\$3,000}{1.0235} \times .943 \times 1.2658 \times .75 \times 1.1029 = \$2,575.76$

Your Hospital_____
Each DRG utilized by the hospital should be calculated in this manner. All that needs to be changed is the DRG weighting factor.

II. Calculation of Federal Portion:

A. Formula—

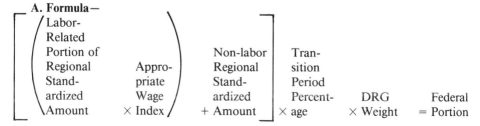

$$\left[\left(\begin{array}{c}\text{Labor-Related Portion of Regional Standardized Amount}\end{array} \times \begin{array}{c}\text{Appropriate Wage Index}\end{array}\right) + \begin{array}{c}\text{Non-labor Regional Standardized Amount}\end{array}\right] \times \begin{array}{c}\text{Transition Period Percentage}\end{array} \times \begin{array}{c}\text{DRG Weight}\end{array} = \begin{array}{c}\text{Federal Portion}\end{array}$$

B. Input Data and Source:

	Model	Your Hospital	Source
1. Regional Standardized Amount			
— Labor	$2,219.82	_____	(FR 39844)
— Non-Labor	$ 711.58	_____	(FR 39844)
2. Wage Index	1.3037	_____	(FR39875)
3. Transition Period Percentage	.25	.25	The rate will be 100% of the regional rate for discharges occuring before October 1, 1984, and will comprise 25% of the total prospective payment for cost reporting periods beginning on or after October 1, 1983 and before October 1, 1984.
4. DRG Weight	1.1029	_____	Simple pneumonia and pleurisy, DRG #89, Table #5 of DRG Weights (FR 39877)

C. Illustration:

Model $[(\$2,219.82 \times 1.3037) + \$711.58] \times .25 \times 1.1029 = 994.14$

Your
hospital $\qquad$ $\times$ $\qquad$ $+$ $\qquad$ $\times$ $\qquad$ $\times$ $\qquad$ $=$ $\qquad$

(Note: For hospitals in Alaska and Hawaii, adjust the non-labor
of the standardized amount by the appropriate cost-of-living adjustment
factor (FR 39765) and add that sum to the labor portion.)

III. Total Prospective Payment—

	Model	Your Hospital
Hospital-Specific Portion (From I)	$2,575.76	$
Federal Portion (From II)	994.14	_____
Total Payment (For DRG #89)	$3,569.90	$ _____

Each DRG utilized by the hospital should be calculated in this manner. All that
needs to be changed is the DRG wieghting factor.

CHAPTER 9

Cost allocations

Introduction

This chapter analyzes the alternative methods used for determining departmental costs in hospitals. Cost allocations are necessary because some third-party reimbursing agencies require identification of the costs of providing health services to their eligible beneficiaries. For example, RCC (ratio of charges to costs) computations rely on cost allocations. The basic goal of cost finding or cost allocation is to determine the full costs (direct costs plus allocated indirect costs) of each revenue producing center in the hospital. Full costs include salary, supply and overhead costs.

The objectives of cost allocation are:

1. to provide full cost information as a basis for establishing rates for services and to assess the adequacy of existing and proposed rates.
2. to provide information in negotiating reimbursement contracts with contracting agencies and to determine the amount of reimbursable cost.
3. to provide information for reports to hospital associations, governmental agencies and other external groups.
4. to provide information for use in managerial decision-making in areas other than rate setting[1].

This book is concerned with supplying information for management decision-making. Allocated data has the potential to mislead decision-makers in hospitals. Although cost allocations do contribute to greater awareness of costs and cost behavior pattern, the most useful information

---

[1] *Cost Finding and Rate Setting for Hospitals,* Chicago: American Hospital Association, 1968, p. 2.

for managerial decision-making will result from cost analyses or cost accounting procedures.

On the other hand, cost finding for reimbursement purposes is often a periodic, after-the-fact procedure that is used to allocate costs from nonrevenue producing centers to revenue producing centers and to nonallowable cost categories in healthcare organizations. Cost finding may also be used prospectively in estimating reimbursement rates at the beginning of a financial period (for prospective reimbursement).

The term "cost finding" is used in the first part of the chapter to designate cost allocations used primarily for reimbursement reports and calculations. Later in the chapter, cost allocations will be discussed as they affect cost accounting, rate setting, and managerial decision-making.

Cost finding is relatively limited in terms of timeliness, acceptable methodologies and relevance to ongoing managerial decisions. Cost analysis or cost accounting is much broader in scope, more timely and not as constrained as cost finding. Cost finding provides only limited information for determining cost per test or cost per procedure. In other words, cost finding is used primarily to establish total departmental costs in order to compare total costs across several departments. It is not particularly useful for identifying cost behavior patterns or cost elements within departments.

The underlying assumption or philosophy of each of these objectives is that the patients who receive particular services should pay all the costs of those services. A more limited assumption is that patients should at least be *assigned* the costs of all services necessary for their treatment. Full costs should be determined and reported to healthcare financial managers for setting rates, negotiating reimbursement arrangements and contracts and reporting on healthcare costs to external organizations. This is the philosophy of equity that requires that all services and their associated costs be assigned to the patients who have been treated. The American Hospital Association defines cost finding used for reimbursement purposes as:

> Apportionment or allocation of costs of the nonrevenue producing cost centers to each other and to the revenue producing centers on the basis of the statistical data that measure the amount of service rendered by each center to other centers[2].

Note that most healthcare organizations should strive for an understandable and meaningful cost finding technique. Cost finding should be standardized, to the extent possible, across individual reimbursing agencies and external reporting formats. Absolute standardization and uniformity can rarely be achieved, but each modification in

---

[2]*Cost Finding and Rate Setting for Hospitals,* p. 1.

cost finding should be made as an adjustment of the final results rather than as a new cost finding technique or process. The cost-benefit criterion prevails. Cost finding is usually an expensive and time-consumung process which should only be conducted when the benefits justify the efforts.

Prerequisites for cost finding

Several conditions must exist before cost finding can be implemented effectively:

1. An up-to-date organization chart separating revenue centers and cost centers.
2. A chart of accounts that is consistent with the organization structure.
3. An accurate hospital information system that is capable of providing:
   a. financial and cost data for each cost and revenue center and
   b. statistical and other nonfinancial data for each cost and revenue center.
4. An appropriate cost finding technique that will be practical and meaningful for the particular institution.

The organization structure is a key element of cost finding. Cost finding should ideally be consistent with the locus of authority and responsibility in the organization. The organization structure is analogous to a road map showing how costs are routed or transferred through different cost centers until they reach the final revenue centers. Clear lines of authority and responsibility are used to divide the organization into the organizational subunits with which costs are associated. Each hospital must identify its own unique organization chart. Revenue centers and cost centers must be clearly identified. Any nonallowable cost centers must also be identified. Revenue centers are ultimately charged with all the allowable costs of the general or service (cost) centers. Unallowable costs are shifted or reported in separate nonallowable cost centers. Therefore, the relationships between each cost center must be identified so that the services provided to other cost and revenue centers are clear. In other words, the order in which costs are distributed from one cost center to other cost centers must be delineated. Unallowable costs are usually identified early in the cost finding process. For purposes of illustration in this chapter, assume that all unallowable costs have already been eliminated.

The second important prerequisite for cost finding is that the chart of accounts be consistent with the organization structure. Many hospitals have never taken the time or the effort to modify their chart of accounts to reflect the current organization structure. Failure to maintain consistency here can result in inaccurate and deficient cost finding results. Unless the chart of accounts reflects the authority and responsibility of cost center managers, costs may be charged to the wrong cost centers and thereby be erroneously distributed under any cost finding method. An updating of the chart of accounts is the first step toward achieving an accurate information system.

The AHA, MGMA and other health service associations have formulated standardized charts of accounts. The Health and Human Services Department tried to introduce the Annual Hospital Report (AHR) system for uniform reporting which was based on a standard chart of accounts. In any event, any standardized chart of accounts is intended as a starting point for the individual healthcare organization's cost finding calculations. Each institution can modify, by dividing the standard accounts into smaller elements, the accounts recommended in a model chart of accounts. Such modifications would increase the precision and usefulness of the cost finding calculations. They would also be preliminary steps to any cost analysis.

The third prerequisite concerns the accuracy and adequacy of the hospital's information system. The information system must be capable of minimizing errors in recording and classifying data. It must be able to correctly match direct costs with the cost center incurring those costs. Revenues must also be correctly classified. Accrual accounting must be used to properly record inventories, receivables and payables. The information system must be capable of separating cash flows from accruals. It must be able to separate allowable costs from unallowable costs as defined by each reimbursing agency or department manager. In other words, the information necessary for reclassifications and adjustments must be readily available in the accounting system.

Another important aspect of the information system is the nonfinancial data. Cost finding depends on knowing the quantity of services provided by or to other cost centers. The quantity of services shared by separate cost centers is usually represented by nonmonetary statistical data which portray the activity level of service in each cost center. Each cost center, especially nonrevenue-producing cost centers, should collect and maintain at least one statistical measure of the volume of service (production). These activity measures should be clerically feasible to compile and should be meaningful measures of the most important services provided by that cost center. Examples of such nonmonetary measures include square footage, number of fulltime equivalent (FTE) employees, number of meals, pounds of laundry, etc. Dollar values may also be used as measures of activity.

The costs of collection must not exceed the benefits to be derived from the improvement in cost finding which results. The statistical measures of activity must also result in an equitable allocation of costs. They must also be applied consistently across different time periods.

Cost finding technique

Cost finding is the allocation of costs of nonrevenue cost centers to each other and to revenue centers according to some measures of the services provided by each center to the others. This allocation is used to determine the full cost of each "final" cost center (including nonallowable cost centers) and of each "final" revenue center. *Exhibit 9-1* illustrates a simplified model of how services flow between healthcare departments. Each of these flows of service could be used as a basis for cost finding. However, each method only uses some of these flows of services as the basis for cost finding.

Exhibit 9-1
Conceptual model of healthcare services

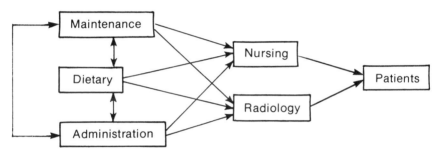

Each cost finding method starts with a determination of unallowable costs or reclassifications. Identify and eliminate any unallowable costs. Perform any necessary reclassifications. Consolidate unassigned costs. Separate any subunit costs from the costs of a parent department where each subunit will be treated as a separate cost center. Four basic methods of cost finding can be used:

1. the direct apportionment method.
2. the stepdown method.
3. the double distribution method.
4. algebraic or reciprocal methods.

The four methods differ primarily in the manner in which costs are allocated from nonrevenue-producing centers. They differ in terms of which flows are recognized as dominant. In the direct apportionment method, the costs of the nonrevenue centers are allocated directly to revenue centers or to patient care centers. This method ignores the fact that most nonrevenue centers also provide services to other nonrevenue centers as well as revenue centers. *Exhibit 9-2* illustrates the flow of cost allocations in the direct method. Costs of nonrevenue centers are allocated only to revenue centers. As noted above, this method ignores all of the services provided by administration to other departments (and vice versa).

Exhibit 9-2
Direct allocation method

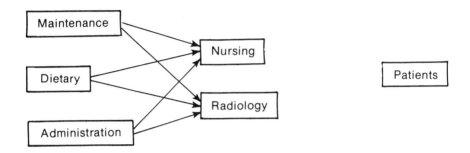

The Health Care Financing Administration (HCFA) has virtually eliminated the availability of the direct method of cost finding for Medicare purposes. This has been accomplished by requiring all hospitals certified after January 1, 1979, and all hospitals with cost reporting periods beginning after July 1, 1979, to use the "departmental method" of cost finding which generally includes the other three cost finding methods described below.

The stepdown method does compensate for some of these weaknesses in that some of the services provided by nonrevenue departments to other nonrevenue departments are recognized. *Exhibit 9-3* illustrates a simple stepdown allocation. Note that the maintenance department costs are *first* allocated to all other departments that have received maintenance service. *Second,* dietary costs (plus its share of maintenance) are allocated to the remaining departments. The maintenance department has now been "closed" for cost allocation purposes, and no additional costs are charged to it. *Third,* administrative costs are allocated to the revenue departments. At this point, all the nonrevenue departments are "closed," and all their costs have been allocated to revenue departments.

In summary, the stepdown method consists of the following steps:

1. Allocate the unassigned (nonassignable) costs to both revenue and nonrevenue centers. Use some appropriate and reasonable allocation basis to allocate the unassigned costs.
2. Allocate costs of the nonrevenue centers to other centers. This step consists of the numbered parts of *Exhibit 9-4*. As a general rule, the costs of the center that provides the greatest amount of services to other centers and receives the fewest services should be allocated first. Alternatively, the center with the largest total costs should be allocated first.

3. The order of allocation continues on this basis until the costs of all nonrevenue centers have been allocated. At this point, all the nonrevenue centers are "closed" in terms of the allocation process. "Closed" cost centers do not receive allocations from any other centers.

Exhibit 9-3
Stepdown allocation method

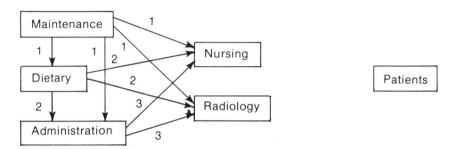

The other major approach to cost finding is called the double or multiple distribution method. The double distribution method was designed to correct one of the major weaknesses of the stepdown method: failure to account fully for interdepartmental services. As described above, departments are successively closed under the stepdown method. Under the double distribution method, each department remains "open" and costs can be reallocated to nonrevenue departments. This method may use two iterations, at which time all nonrevenue centers are "closed," or the iterations may continue successively until further iterations result in immaterial changes in the allocations. In each case, the final allocation is made successively to the revenue centers (as in the stepdown method).

The first allocation under the double distribution method is identical to the first step in the stepdown method (e.g., *Exhibit 9-3*). However, the second step may selectively exclude a few departments or it may be based on different service measures. Each iteration corresponds to the patterns of service between departments. Consequently, each institution's approach to double or multiple distribution methods will be unique at the second or third stage of the allocation process.

Double distribution methods provide a better approximation of the full costs of the revenue departments. The results are most representative of actual patterns of activities and flows of services. This allocation method more precisely represents the interaction between departments. Even though these methods are gaining in popularity, they lack some objectivity. They are ambiguous about when to stop reallocating costs to cost centers and with regard to the order of priority in which to consider the cost allocations. Any change in the order of precedence in the allocation, or a change in the stopping criteria, will change the results—perhaps significantly.

For these reasons, the algebraic or reciprocal methods are recommended as the most objective and most accurate representations of all known patterns of services and activities. The reciprocal method involves the simultaneous solution of a series of equations. This results in the most complete allocation of all costs. It is the most defensible method. Unfortunately, it is also the most complex and it usually requires the aid of a computer program. The multiple distribution approach is an approximation of the results that can be expected using the reciprocal method. Healthcare organizations that have access to computerized cost finding methods should test several alternative approaches and choose the method best suited to their particular circumstances.

Comprehensive example of cost allocation methods

A set of hypothetical data is described in *Exhibit 9-4*. These data correspond to the interrelationships between departments described in *Exhibit 9-2* and *9-3*. The flows of services between departments are represented by amounts of services provided by each of the nonrevenue-producing departments. These flows of services are converted to ratios at the bottom of *Exhibit 9-4*. Alternatively, unit cost multipliers could be computed. Note that no recognition is given to services provided by a department on its own behalf. In other words, meals consumed within the dietary department do not affect the cost allocations.

In addition, any of the cost allocation methods must allocate $900,000 of costs in nonrevenue-producing departments to revenue-producing departments. The total costs of the revenue-producing departments must always sum to the total costs, $2,000,000 in this case. In other words, cost allocations do not change the total costs except when unallowable costs must first be removed. The total costs to be allocated must equal the total costs allocated at the conclusion of the procedures.

Exhibit 9-5 illustrates the direct allocation method. Note that only the services consumed by revenue-producing departments are used to calculate the allocation bases. No interactions between the service departments are recognized. The order of allocation is irrelevant under the direct method. The costs in the nonrevenue-producing departments are transferred directly to the nursing and radiology departments. The total costs of these departments, after allocation, are shown in the last line of the exhibit. No costs remain in the nonrevenue-producing departments; the parenthesized data indicate the transfer-out of those costs.

The stepdown method of cost allocation is shown in *Exhibit 9-6*. In this case, maintenance department costs are transferred first to all the other departments. A different starting point could have been selected. The

Exhibit 9-4
Illustrative data used for cost allocation example

| | Nonrevenue-producing cost centers | | | Revenue-producing cost centers | | |
	Maintenance	Dietary	Administration	Nursing	Radiology	Total
Departmental costs before allocations	$200,000	$400,000	$300,000	$800,000	$300,000	$2,000,000
Services provided:						
by maintenance (square feet)		30,000	20,000	160,000	40,000	250,000
by dietary (meals served)	1,000		1,000	2,000	1,000	5,000
by administration (FTEs)	12	10		25	8	55
Proportions of services provided:						
by maintenance		30/250	20/250	160/250	40/250	100%
by dietary	1/5		1/5	2/5	1/5	100%
by administration	12/55	10/55		25/55	8/55	100%

Exhibit 9-5
Direct method of cost allocation

			Department			
	Maintenance	Dietary	Administration	Nursing	Radiology	Total
Departmental costs before allocation	$200,000	$400,000	$300,000	$800,000	$300,000	$2,000,000
Allocation of costs*						
Maintenance	(200,000)			160,000	40,000	
Dietary		(400,000)		266,667	133,333	
Administration			(300,000)	227,273	72,727	
Total costs of revenue-producing departments	0	0	0	$1,453,940	$546,060	$2,000,000

*Allocation bases (recalculated only for revenue-producing departments):

				Nursing	Radiology	
Maintenance				160/200	40/200	100%
Dietary				2/3	1/3	100%
Administration				25/33	8/33	100%

The unit cost multipliers are:

				Nursing	Radiology	
Maintenance				1.00	1.00	
Dietary				133.33	133.33	
Administration				9,090.91	9,090.91	

Exhibit 9-6
Stepdown method of cost allocation

	Department					
	Maintenance	*Dietary*	*Administration*	*Nursing*	*Radiology*	*Total*
Department costs before allocation	$200,000	$400,000	$300,000	$800,000	$300,000	$2,000,000
Allocation of costs:*						
Maintenance	(200,000)	24,000	16,000	128,000	32,000	
Dietary		(424,000)	106,000	212,000	106,000	
Administration			(422,000)	319,697	102,303	
Total costs of revenue-producing departments	0	0	0	$1,459,697	$540,303	$2,000,000
*Allocation bases:						
Maintenance		30/250	20/250	160/250	40/250	100%
Dietary			1/4	2/4	1/4	100%
Administration				25/33	8/33	100%
The unit cost multipliers are:						
Maintenance		.80	.80	.80	.80	
Dietary			106.00	106.00	106.00	
Administration				12,787.88	12,787.88	

allocation bases are recomputed for each successive step, reflecting only the services provided by a particular department to the remaining departments. In other words, the administration department's services reflect 25 FTEs in nursing and 8 FTEs in radiology. These two components are summed and recombined to yield the ratios 25/33 and 8/33 as the allocation bases for the administration department. Similar calculations are made for the dietary department. Again, note that unit cost multipliers could be used instead of activity ratios.

After the maintenance department costs have been allocated to the other departments, total dietary costs have increased from $400,000 to $424,000. This new total cost in the dietary department must now be allocated to the remaining departments, excluding both maintenance and dietary. The second allocation results in the second step of *Exhibit 9-6*. Similar calculations are made for each succeeding step until no costs remain in nonrevenue-producing departments.

The double distribution method is illustrated in *Exhibit 9-7*. Note that the first set of allocations is based on the original proportions of services provided. These proportions were first noted in *Exhibit 9-4*. Any other intermediate allocations could be based on the same or related data. The last allocation, which in this case is the second allocation, is based on the same proportions of service that were used for the stepdown method. In other words, the allocation ratios for the second iteration of *Exhibit 9-7* use the exact same ratios as the stepdown method in *Exhibit 9-6*.

The double distribution approach can contain as many iterations as desired, or until the costs that are being reallocated are so small as to be immaterial. In this case, for the purpose of clarifying the illustration, only two sets of allocations were made. Note that $200,000 is initially allocated away from the maintenance department. At the conclusion of the first allocation, the maintenance department has been allocated another $172,247 in costs from other departments. The first step in the next iteration reallocates the $172,247 to other departments. Since the second allocation is final, no additional costs are allocated to/from the maintenance.

The reciprocal method of cost allocation is illustrated in *Exhibit 9-8*. This exhibit is the second stage of the process because the costs that are entered on the second line of *Exhibit 9-8* must be first calculated using linear or matrix algebra. The next section illustrates the techniques that were used to obtain the second line of data, "Nonrevenue department costs recalculated using matrix algebra." These figures represent the costs that would have been charged to each nonrevenue department if all the patterns (ratios) of services provided *(Exhibit 9-4)* had been simultaneously recognized in the accounts. The essence of the solution to the reciprocal method is to obtain these "fictitious" costs using the algebraic techniques of the reciprocal method. Once these costs (second line, *Exhibit 9-8*) are obtained, the solution is straightforward in that the orginal ratios of

Exhibit 9-7
Double distribution method of cost allocation

	Maintenance	*Dietary*	*Administration*	*Nursing*	*Radiology*	*Total*
			Department			
Department costs before allocation	$200,000	$400,000	$300,000	$800,000	$300,000	$2,000,000
Allocation of costs:*						
First allocation, maintenance	(200,000)	24,000	16,000	128,000	32,000	
First allocation, dietary	84,800	(424,000)	84,800	169,600	84,800	
First allocation, administration	87,447	72,873	(400,800)	182,182	58,298	
Second allocation, maintenance	(172,247)	20,670	13,780	110,237	27,586	
Second allocation, dietary		(93,543)	23,386	46,771	23,386	
Second allocation, administration			(37,166)	28,156	9,010	
Total costs of revenue-producing departments	0	0	0	$1,464,946	$535,080	$2,000,026†

*The first allocation is made on the basis of the "original" proportions of services provided in Exhibit 8-5. Any other intermediate calculations would be based on the data in Exhibit 8-5 or on a refinement of those data. The final allocation, is based on the allocation bases used in the stepdown method (Exhibit 8-7).

†Difference due to rounding.

Exhibit 9-8
Reciprocal method of cost allocation

	Department					
	Maintenance	Dietary	Administration	Nursing	Radiology	Total
Department costs before allocation	$200,000	$400,000	$300,000	$800,000	$300,000	$2,000,000
Nonrevenue department costs recalculated using matrix algebra	(401,451)	(527,688)	(437,619)			
Allocation of costs:*						
Maintenance		48,174	32,116	256,929	64,232	
Dietary	105,538		105,538	211,074	105,538	
Administration	95,481	79,567		198,917	63,654	
Totals before adjustment	(432)	53	35	1,466,920	533,424	
Adjustment	432	(53)	(35)	(172)	(172)	
Totals after adjustment†	0	0	0	$1,466,748	$533,252	$2,000,000

*These allocations are made on the basis of the proportions of services provided by each department
†These discrepancies arise because of rounding difference in the matrix calculations. These differences are arbitrarily balanced against selected departments.

services provided *(Exhibit 9-4)* are used to allocate or spread those costs to each of the affected departments. Note that the total allowable costs remaining in the nonrevenue departments must sum to zero. No allowable costs remain "in" these departments.

The solution to the matrix calculations in the next section shows that the costs before allocation in each nonrevenue department are: maintenance, $401,451; dietary, $527,688 and administration, $437,619. These costs are then inserted into *Exhibit 9-8* and allocated to each of the affected departments. The ratios of services are obtained from *Exhibit 9-4* with no further modifications. The costs in the "final" departments therefore are:

Nursing	$1,466,748
Radiology	533,252
Total	$2,000,000

These results are more objective than the results obtained using the stepdown, direct or double distribution methods because they are based on all the data *Exhibit 9-4*. No assumptions about starting points or stopping points are made under the reciprocal method. All the interactive patterns of services that were originally identified are used as input data in the final allocation. For this reason, the reciprocal method is usually considered the most accurate of the four methods discussed in this chapter. Note also that some "straight-line" adjustment may be needed as the last step in the reciprocal method. These adjustments are due to the numerous rounding-off calculations that are made throughout the process.

Exhibit 9-9 summarizes the results obtained under each of the different methods. Each method is also described in percentage terms relative to the reciprocal method. The resulting percentage differences are minor. In this case, the double distribution method best approximates the results obtained under the reciprocal method. Foyle has suggested that in most cases, since the differences are minor, other factors such as management decisions regarding utilization of space, employees and other resources may create wider differences in the results than just the different mathematical calculations.[3]

A later paper by Howard also compares the reciprocal method with the stepdown method.[4] Howard's results show that for the six-month period

---

[3]Foyle, William R., "Evaluation of Methods of Cost Analysis," 1964 (unpublished manuscript).

[4]Howard, Thomas P., "A Comparison of Two Methods of Cost Finding," *Proceedings of the Southwestern Regional Meeting, American Accounting Association,* Houston: American Accounting Association, 1979.

Exhibit 9-9
Comparison of cost allocations under four methods

	Direct	Stepdown	Double distribution	Reciprocal
Nursing	$1,453,940	$1,459,697	$1,464,946	$1,466,920
Radiology	546,060	540,303	535,080	533,424
Exhibit source	8-6	8-7	8-8	8-9
% comparisons:				
Nursing	99.1%	99.5%	99.9%	100%
Radiology	102.4%	101.3%	100.3%	100%

of his test hospital's data, the differences in departmental costs varied by as much as 30 percent. He then compared the effect of different allocations on reimbursable costs and obtained a difference of only $517 (increase in reimbursement) under the reciprocal method. This was only a .05 percent increase in reimbursable costs. Not all cases result in such minor differences.

In any event, the management accountant in any healthcare organization must determine whether the added costs of any method are worth the expense and effort of using that method. Access to a computerized cost allocation program greatly simplifies the problems with any of these methods. However, the fees associated with such programs, or the costs of developing them, are not trivial. In all but the most complicated cases, a matrix inversion can be obtained through most computer programs (statistical packages), and the inverse of the coefficient matrix will facilitate the computations associated with the reciprocal method. The reciprocal method should not be ignored just because it looks more complicated. Given the matrix solution to the inverse, it is no more complicated than any of the other methods.

One of the advantages of the reciprocal method is that the matrix inverse is relatively permanent. As long as the pattern of service interactions does not drastically change, the same inverse of the coefficient matrix may be used repeatedly. This is an important simplification that should be recognized by healthcare organizations. In other words, once the expenses of obtaining the inverse have been incurred, they need not be incurred again until the patterns of service between departments change significantly. Consequently, the cost allocations will not change proportionately as these small changes in service patterns occur. Of course, the allocation must be performed each period using the actual costs of that period.

Matrix algebra calculations for reciprocal cost finding

Linear algebra is used to determine the cost allocations under the reciprocal method. Any healthcare organization with three or more nonrevenue departments will probably require a computer. In this case, the simultaneous solution of three equations in three unknowns is expressed in matrix terms in order to find the total costs (before allocation) in each of the three nonrevenue-producing departments. Matrix algebra is used to obtain this solution.

Let: M = total costs of maintenance department before allocation
D = total costs of dietary department after allocation
A = total costs of administration department after allocation

Total cost equations:

1. $M = 200,000 + (\frac{1}{5})D + (\frac{12}{55})A$
2. $D = 400,000 + (\frac{30}{250})M + (\frac{10}{55})A$
3. $A = 300,000 + (\frac{20}{250})M + (\frac{1}{5})D$

These total cost equations use the proportions of services provided from *Exhibit 9-4*.

Equations 1, 2 and 3 can be rearranged as follows:

1. $\quad M \quad - \quad \frac{1}{5}D \quad - \quad \frac{12}{55}A = 200,000$
2. $-\frac{30}{250}M \quad + \quad D \quad - \quad \frac{10}{55}A = 400,000$
3. $-\frac{20}{250}M \quad - \quad \frac{1}{5}D \quad + \quad A = 300,000$

This expression arranges the coefficients for each department in vertical columns relative to each other. Separating these coefficients from the parameters (M,D,A) results in a coefficient matrix [C], a vector of unknowns [X] and a vector of constants [Y].

$$\begin{bmatrix} 1 & -\frac{1}{5} & -\frac{12}{55} \\ -\frac{30}{250} & 1 & -\frac{10}{55} \\ -\frac{20}{250} & -\frac{1}{5} & 1 \end{bmatrix} \begin{bmatrix} M \\ D \\ A \end{bmatrix} = \begin{bmatrix} 200,000 \\ 400,000 \\ 300,000 \end{bmatrix}$$

These matrices can be expressed as:

$$[C][X] = [Y]$$

Since we want to obtain values for the unknown costs in each nonrevenue department (M,D,A), prior to the allocation, we set up this relationship to solve the vector of unknowns:

$$[X] = [C^{-1}][Y]$$

[C⁻¹] denotes the inverse of the coefficient matrix and is equivalent to dividing the vector of constants by the coefficient matrix. [C] may also be expressed as:

$$\begin{bmatrix} 1 & -.2 & -.218182 \\ -.12 & 1 & -.181818 \\ -.08 & -.2 & 1 \end{bmatrix}$$

The inverse of [C], [C⁻¹] may be found by either manual, mechanical or computerized techniques. The interested reader may refer to any standard reference on matrix algebra for assistance in computational methods. The authors usually recommend a computerized approach to matrix inversion. The solution to this coefficient matrix was obtained using a BASIC program as follows, where "pfn" indicates the name of a file:

```
NEW, pfn

AUTO

100 DIM 1(3,3)

110 MAT READ C(3,3)

120 MAT I=INV(C)

130 DATA 1, −.2,−.218182,−.12,1,−.181818,−.08,−.2,1

140 MAT PRINT C,1

150 END

Break

SAVE, pfn

RUN
```

The computer output from the program above, called MATFIL, using a CDC6400 time-sharing terminal, is:

```
SYSTEM: basic
OLD OR NEW FILE: old, matfil
READY.
run
79/05/16. 11.40.46.
PROGRAM MATFIL
         1          −.2       −.218182
        −.12         1        −.181818
        −.08        −.2          1

     1.05426      .26655      .278485
      .147199    1.07495      .227562
      .113781     .236314    1.06779
CP 0.072 SECS.
RUN COMPLETE.
```

The first matrix in the computer output (above) is [C] and the second is [C⁻¹]. Replacing [C⁻¹] in our original expression, we may solve for [X]:

$$[X] = [C^{-1}] \ [Y]$$

$$\begin{bmatrix} M \\ D \\ A \end{bmatrix} = \begin{bmatrix} 1.05426 & .26655 & .278485 \\ .147199 & 1.07495 & .227562 \\ .113782 & .236314 & 1.06779 \end{bmatrix} \begin{bmatrix} 200,000 \\ 400,000 \\ 300,000 \end{bmatrix}$$

Using the principles of matrix multiplication (first row times first column, second row times first column, etc.), we obtain the solution to the vector of unknowns:

$$\begin{bmatrix} M \\ D \\ A \end{bmatrix} = \begin{bmatrix} 401{,}450.70 \\ 527{,}688.40 \\ 437{,}619.00 \end{bmatrix}$$

These values are inserted in *Exhibit 9-8* as the departmental costs recalculated using matrix algebra. They are really the costs that would have been charged to each department if the full share of all other nonrevenue departments had been charged to each department. These results provide a simultaneous estimate of what these costs, before allocation, would be. Note that they sum to more than the original costs in the three departments. For that reason, they are not "real" dollars or costs, but they can be viewed as input costs in the cost finding process. Note that the result in *Exhibit 9-8* is a total cost of $2,000,000 so that the costs to be allocated equal the costs allocated. The reciprocal method has not distorted or magnified the total costs, after allocation, in any manner.

These figures represent the costs that would have been charged to each nonrevenue department if all the patterns (ratios) of services provided *(Exhibit 9-4)* had been simultaneously recognized in the accounts. The essence of the solution to the reciprocal method is to obtain these "fictitious" costs using algebraic techniques.* Once these costs (second line, *Exhibit 9-8*) are obtained, the solution is straightforward in that the original ratios of services provided *(Exhibit 9-4)* are used to allocate or spread those costs to each of the affected departments. Note that the total allowable costs remaining in the nonrevenue departments must sum to zero. No allowable costs remain "in" these departments.

---

*A simple algebraic solution for *two* nonrevenue departments can be obtained by setting up two equations in two unknowns. For example:

$$s_1 = 100{,}000 + 1/3\ s_2$$
$$s_2 = 300{,}000 + 1/6\ s_1$$

In this case, $100,000 and $300,000 are the costs originally charged to each department. The ratios 1/3 and 1/6 represent services provided by s_2 to s_1 and by s_1 to s_2. Therefore, s_1 should be charged 1/3 of the costs in s_2, and s_2 should be charged 1/6 of the costs in s_1. The simultaneous solution to this dilemma is obtained by substitution.

$$s_1 = 100{,}000 + 1/3(300{,}000 + 1/6s_1) = 200{,}000 + 1/18\ s_1$$
$$17/18s_1 = 200{,}000$$
$$s_1 = 200{,}000\ (18/17) = 211{,}765$$
$$s_2 = 300{,}000 + 1/6(s_1) = 300{,}000 + 1/6(211{,}765) = 335{,}294$$

The solutions for s_1 and s_2 would then be used in a table similar to *Exhibit 9-8* to allocate those costs to the affected departments.

Cost allocations for managers

The distinction between cost finding and cost allocation is in limiting cost finding to reimbursement procedures and calculations. As such, cost finding is usually driven and controlled by pre-printed forms and procedures manuals as determined by the reimbursement agency, e.g., Medicaid. On the other hand, cost allocations for managerial purposes are guided by usefulness and relevance criteria. Therefore, managers in healthcare organizations may choose appropriate cost allocation methods for each of the major types of decisions in their areas of responsibility.

For example, the reciprocal method may be used to allocate costs for setting rates in a particular clinic. The direct method may be used to allocate costs from maintenance to revenue producing departments. In other words, the very same cost allocation methods may be used for both reimbursement purposes as for internal managerial decision-making. The only difference is that for internal decisions, managers have flexibility as to choice of cost allocation methods and allocation bases, and to degree of complexity of the allocation methods. Problem 9 in this chapter provides an example of how the reciprocal allocation method may be used to evaluate the costs of producing services internally or contracting for services from an outside vendor.

The key point to remember in the selection between a step-down method and a reciprocal cost allocation method is the extent to which managers want to avoid arbitrary allocation criteria, such as the order of precedence, and the degree to which reciprocal services between departments is to be included. To recognize interactions between service departments a reciprocal method of cost allocation should be selected for major managerial decisions.

Software is being developed that will allocate costs to patient groups (e.g. DRG's). Ideally, such software will be based on double distribution or reciprocal cost allocation methods. Use of less sophisticated methods does not fully utilize the computer's computational capabilities and does not offer the advantages noted above.

Summary

This chapter has described the four typical approaches to cost allocation in healthcare organizations. Each method is useful in its own right. The reciprocal method is often more complicated but it is more objective. It is also more accurate because it fully uses all the available data for the services provided between departments. No information on the proportions of services provided between departments is ignored under the reciprocal method. It is the method that is recommended where the most accuracy and objectivity are required and where the expertise for its implementation is available.

Cost finding allocation techniques used primarily for rate setting and reimbursement purposes may actually lead to incorrect decisions if they figure prominently in the decisions to expand or contract a department or particular services. They may be misleading in terms of deciding whether to produce a service internally or to subcontract it to an outside vendor, for example. There are very few cost data that are useful for all purposes. Allocated costs have limited usefulness, but they are very important to healthcare organizations. The management accountant must take great care not to overemphasize allocated costs. Cost data must be used for the intended purpose. Allocated costs are not relevant to every situation where they might be applied. Caution, diligence and imagination are required.

Questions and problems

1. Define cost finding in terms of reimbursement regulations.

2. Discuss the major weaknesses of most cost finding techniques.

3. What are the prerequisites for effective cost finding analysis?

4. Refer to Medicare regulations to identify the cost allocation methods that are currently acceptable. Which do you prefer? Why? How would you choose between alternative allocation methods?

5. What are the advantages and disadvantages of the reciprocal method?

6. How does the chart of accounts affect the allocation of costs from nonrevenue departments to revenue-producing departments?

7. Cost allocation data:
   a. Using the given data, allocate the $600,000 of costs in the housekeeping, laundry and plant departments to the two revenue-producing cost centers, using the direct and stepdown methods. What are the resulting total costs in the nursing and laboratory departments under each method?
   b. Set up the cost equations for each department that would be needed for the reciprocal methods.
      Rearrange the equations so that the coefficient [C] matrix, the unknown [X] matrix and the constant [Y] matrix are apparent.
      What is the [C] matrix?
      If the inverse of this [C] matrix is assumed to be the same as the inverse derived by the computer in the section on matrix

	Nonrevenue cost centers			Revenue-producing cost centers		Totals
	House-keeping	Laundry	Plant	Nursing	Laboratory	
Direct costs for each department	$300,000	$100,000	$200,000	$1,000,000	$600,000	$2,200,000
Services provided:						
By house-keeping (square feet)	—	20,000	10,000	180,000	50,000	260,000
By laundry (pounds, wet)	20,000	—	5,000	170,000	10,000	205,000
By plant (FTEs)	10	5	—	30	10	55

algebra calculations; use that data for $[C^{-1}]$ to obtain the reciprocal cost allocations for the nursing and laboratory departments.

Optional: Invert the [C] matrix, and use the inverse in the reciprocal allocation method.

8. Cost allocation data:

	Nonrevenue cost centers		Revenue-producing cost centers		Totals
	House-keeping	Laundry	Nursing	Laboratory	
Direct costs for each department	$300,000	$100,000	$1,000,000	$600,000	$2,000,000
Services provided:					
By house-keeping (square feet)	—	20,000	180,000	250,000	
By laundry (pounds, wet)	20,000	—	170,000	10,000	200,000
FTEs	10	5	30	10	55

a. Given the data above, allocate the $400,000 of costs in housekeeping and laundry to the revenue-producing cost centers using the direct, stepdown and reciprocal methods. What are the resulting total costs in the nursing and laboratory cost centers after the respective allocations?

b. What difference would it make in part (a) if FTEs were used as the allocation base under each method?

9. The Sugarloaf Mountain Hospital (SMH) was given 35 acres of forest lands near a growing suburb of Denver. Since the hospital had been operating out of movable trailers (converted horse vans), the administration and staff enthusiastically planned their new facility. Unfortunately, at the time of construction, there was no access to electric power or utilities. Consequently, the physical plant included:

a. a water pumping and filtration system with access to a nearby spring-fed mountain lake.
b. a coal-fired boiler to generate steam for heating, and
c. an electric generating facility.

Each of these three service departments must rely on the products of other departments. Eighty percent of the water is used to produce steam, ten percent is used for other auxiliary services (housekeeping) and ten percent for direct patient care. Ninety percent of the steam is used for producing electricity, and ten percent is used for auxiliary services. Thirty percent of the electricity is used by the water plant, thirty percent for direct patient care and forty percent for other auxiliary services. Variable and fixed costs can be traced to each department:

	Fixed	Variable	Total
Water	$30,000	$ 3,000	$33,000
Steam	20,000	12,000	32,000
Electric	25,000	6,000	31,000
	$75,000	$21,000	$96,000

a. How should these costs be allocated using the reciprocal method? What are the full costs in each department?
b. If electricity were made available at 3 cents per kwh, should the SMH purchase electricity or continue to generate it? The current volume of electricity is 900,000 kwh. The electricity department manager recommends rejecting the offer because the variable costs of producing electricity are only .67 cents per kwh. What should SMH do? Why?

10. The following data pertain to the departmental costs of a hospital. Allocate the service costs to nursing and lab using the direct method:

	House-keeping	Laundry	Nursing	Laboratory	Total
Costs	200,000	110,000	510,000	600,000	1,420,00
House-keeping services		4,000*	8,000	12,000	24,000
Proportion		1/6	2/6	3/6	6/6
Laundry services	24,000		12,000	36,000	72,000
Proportion	2/6		1/6	3/6	6/6
*Labor hours					

11. Use the data in Problem 10 to calculate allocations using the stepdown method.

12. Use the data in Problem 10 to allocate costs using the double distribution method.

13. Use the data in Problem 10 to calculate cost allocations based on the reciprocal method.

14. The financial manager of Greenacre Hospital is considering adopting the reciprocal method of cost allocation. Greenacre presently used the direct method. Given the data below, calculate the reciprocal allocation and discuss its advantages.

	Direct costs before allocation	Allocated total costs direct method
Housekeeping	$125,400	
Laundry	110,000	
Nursing	694,800	$833,812
Laboratory	450,000	546,388

Fifteen percent of housekeeping services are provided to the laundry department, forty percent to nursing and forty-five percent to laboratory.

Forty-five percent of laundry services are provided to housekeeping, forty percent to nursing and fifteen percent to laboratory.

15. Case study:

Community Hospital

The Community Hospital, a 155-bed institution, completed its tenth year of operations in 1979 as a qualified institutional provider under the Health Insurance Program for the Aged. The hospital wants to receive maximum reimbursement for its allowable costs from the government. The hospital engaged you to assist in determining the amount of reimbursement due and furnished this financial and statistical information, which we reviewed and found acceptable:

a. Service revenues for the year were:

	Inpatient	Outpatient	Total
Laboratory	$1,000,000	$ 575,000	$1,575,000
Operating room	625,000	25,000	650,000
Emergency room	200,000	2,000,000	2,200,000
Routine service	3,775,000	—	3,775,000
	$5,600,000	$2,600,000	$8,200,000

b. Operating expenses for the year were:

	Salaries	Other	Total
Administrative and general	$ 300,000	$ 500,000	$ 800,000
Housekeeping	250,000	100,000	350,000
Dietary	75,000	101,476	176,476
Cafeteria		23,524	23,524
Laboratory	275,000	600,000	875,000
Operating room	200,000	175,000	375,000
Routine services	2,000,000	1,000,000	3,000,000
Emergency	1,000,000	500,000	1,500,000
Depreciation (buildings and fixtures)	—	500,000	500,000
	$4,100,000	$3,500,000	$7,600,000

c. Depreciation per books is $500,000. Depreciation for reimbursement, which includes accelerated depreciation on assets purchased prior to July 31, 1970, is $610,000.

d. Cafeteria revenue from employee and guest meals was $18,000.

e. During 1979, the hospital's fund raising expenses totalled $5,000.

f. The hospital's plant engineer completed a square footage study as of December 31, 1979. The study provided this information:

Department	Square footage
Administrative and general	50,000
Housekeeping	50,000
Kitchen	7,000
Cafeteria	3,000
Laboratory	100,000
Operating room	50,000
Routine services	250,000
Emergency room	100,000
Total	610,000

g. The supervisor of the housekeeping department prepared a study of hours spent to maintain each department. The results are:

Department	Hours
Administrative and general	10,000
Cafeteria	5,000
Operating room	53,333
Routine services	110,000
Emergency room	50,000
Laboratory	40,000
	268,333

h. The dietician reported that meals served during 1979 were:

Department	Meals
Inpatient	103,500
Guest	2,500
Administrative and general	2,500
Housekeeping	1,500
Dietary	1,500
Laboratory	1,000
Operating rooms	500
Inpatient services	7,000
Emergency rooms	1,000
	121,000

i. This information, regarding Medicare charges, was received on January 20, 1980, from the third-party intermediary:

	Inpatient	Outpatient
Number of regular days/visit	15,000	—
Regular Medicare payments	*$1,200,000	$80,000
Medicare charges by cost center:		
Operating room	$ 25,000	$10,000
Laboratory	90,000	10,000
Emergency room	10,000	90,000

*The interim per diem payment was $80. Assume there is no deductible or coinsurance.

j. Inpatient days for all patients total 45,000. All days are generated from aged, pediatric and maternity patients. All costs are to be considered as reasonable costs for this problem.

k. Per diem limits are $95 per day.

Required:

Obtain the current forms used by Medicaid or other cost-based reimbursement agencies from your instructor or from any fiscal intermediary. Use these forms to calculate allowable costs for Community Hospital.

16. The Triangle Hospice has three service departments—grounds and maintenance, general administration, and laundry. The costs of these departments are allocated by the step method, using the bases and in the order shown below:

Grounds and maintenance:
   Fixed costs—allocated on a basis of square feet of space occupied.

General administration:
   Variable costs—allocated on a basis of number of actual employees.
   Fixed costs—allocated 20% to laundry, 14% to convention center, 36% to food services, and 30% to lodging.

Laundry:
   Variable costs—allocated on a basis of number of items processed.

Fixed costs—allocated on a basis of peak period needs for items processed.

Cost and operating data for all departments in the hospice for a recent month are presented in the table below:

	Grounds and Mainten- nance	General Adminis- tration	Laundry	Grief Center	Food Services	Lodging	Total
Variable costs	-0-	$ 915	$13,725	-0-	$ 48,000	36,450	$ 99,090
Fixed costs	$17,500	12,150	18,975	$28,500	64,000	81,000	222,125
Total overhead costs	$17,500	$13,065	$32,700	$28,500	$112,000	$117,450	$321,215
Square feet of space	2,000	2,500	3,750	15,000	6,250	97,500	127,000
Number of employees	9	5	10	5	25	21	75
Laundry items processed	—	—	—	1,000	5,250	40,000	46,250
Peak period needs—items processed	—	—	—	1,500	6,500	42,000	50,000

All billing in the Hospice is done through the grief center, food services, and lodging. The Hospice executive director wants the costs of the three service departments allocated to these three billing centers.

Required:

Prepare the cost allocation desired by the executive director. Include under each billing center the direct costs of the center, as well as the costs allocated from the service departments.

References

Balachandran, V. and David A. Dittman, "Cost Allocation for Maximizing Hospital Reimbursement Under Third Party Cost Contracts," *Health Care Management Review,* Spring, 1978, pp. 61-70.

Horngren, Charles T., *Cost Accounting: A Managerial Emphasis,* 4th ed., New York: Prentice Hall, 1982.

Sahney, Vinod K. and Timothy Weddle, "Use this Model to Gauge Reimbursement," *Hospital Financial Management,* April, 1979, pp. 27-29.

CHAPTER 10

Inventory management and control

Introduction

Supplies and other materials represent significant assets, and resulting expenses, to most healthcare organizations. Inventories of supplies and other related materials often represent 10-20 percent of the hospital's assets. The supplies inventory for a clinic or public health department may represent an even larger share of total assets. Better management and control of inventories can result in significant savings because the inventories are often recycled at least three times each year. Even if inventories seem insignificant in comparison to labor costs, remember that when turnover is considered, the total resources consumed annually are often a significant component of total operating costs.

Besides saving money, better inventory control has other benefits for the hospital. Reducing stockouts or providing the right kinds of supplies at the proper time and place can result in better patient care, as well as improved relationships with physicians, patients and suppliers. Therefore, the techniques developed in this chapter should not be viewed solely as cost containment methods. They are also important ingredients in improving the quality of patient care and the efficiency and effectiveness of healthcare delivery systems.

It should also be noted that inventory control techniques are an important element of internal control. To the extent that internal control is concerned with both safeguarding physical assets and effectively using them, as inventory control is improved, so also is internal control strengthened. In addition, inventory control methods apply to any kind of inventory. For example, inventory control models can be adapted to cash balances or linen supplies. Accounts receivable also lend themselves to some of these techniques. For the purposes of clarity, most of the examples in this chapter deal with supplies of tangible items. Several of the recommended additional readings describe cash management techniques using inventory control models.

Objectives of inventory management

Many different objectives of inventory control could be listed. A local survey of supervisors of central supply departments produced this list of inventory control objectives:

1. have supplies available wherever and whenever needed
2. fully utilize existing storage space
3. never run out of supplies
4. decide which items to hold in inventory and which items to purchase on an as-needed basis
5. stock enough supplies for one week's or one month's operations and
6. provide a schedule detailing when to place (replacement) orders and how much to order.

Such a list could be almost endless. However, the overriding objective of hospital managers should be to minimize the total costs of inventory management and still maintain an acceptable level of quality of care. A decision rule that managers could follow would be to add up the costs associated with a variety of inventory management policies and to adopt that set of policies that has the *lowest* total costs. It is of little value to minimize one type of inventory cost if that action increases another type of cost. A decision rule that minimizes average purchase costs (per unit) may result in significantly larger storage and handling costs. Consequently, the emphasis must be on *total* costs. Managers must search for a set of control techniques that minimizes those total costs. Simpler decision rules, e.g., equating two kinds of inventory costs, or setting the marginal cost of X equal to the marginal cost of Y, may be correct only in limited circumstances. However, the general rule that minimizes total costs for a given level of quality is the correct criterion in almost all circumstances.

Some of the other objectives of inventory management concern the question of why to have inventories at all. Uncertainty is the primary reason for holding inventories. There are three major components of uncertainty. One reason for holding inventories deals with timing. It is impossible, in any healthcare organization, to exactly match the timing of receipt of supplies with the usage of supplies. No manager can order with such precision that physical deliveries will be made at the exact time that the materials are needed. Even if all the other internal problems of inventory management were solved, the healthcare manager could not insure the timely delivery and/or receipt of those items already ordered with promised dates of delivery. Timing is mainly concerned with external uncontrollable factors that prevent or hinder timely deliveries and receipt of materials and supplies.

The second major uncertainty factor affecting inventories is related to discontinuities between the needs of patients and the quantities of materials and supplies necessary to meet these needs. If a maternity department knew that its demand for services on a given day would be 10 normal deliveries, it could still not forecast exactly the quantities of necessary materials and supplies. There is no perfect match between patients and the materials needed to provide services to those patients. These discontinuities require inventories to help smooth out the uneven flows of supplies needed by patients or patient service departments.

The uncertainty of patient arrivals or demands is another reason for maintaining adequate inventories. Demand uncertainties prevent forecasting the exact number of patients who will need services, resulting in some of the discontinuities noted above. Demand uncertainty requires that the organization maintain a buffer between patient needs and the health services that it provides. Because of these related factors, it should be obvious that the health institution must maintain adequate supplies of backup materials. In order to minimize total inventory costs, it must also attempt to forecast patient loads, patient services and supplier responses in order to mitigate the effects of uncertainty (demand, discontinuity and timing). To the extent that these factors cannot be predicted, inventory management and control functions become even more important.

Inventory control techniques

There are three fundamental concepts that apply to inventory management and control. These three techniques form the foundation for any sound inventory control system:

1. classification: *what* kinds of materials and supplies are most susceptible to control techniques?
2. order point: *when* should supplies be reordered?
3. economic order quantity: *how many* supplies should be ordered?

These three inventory questions—what, when and how many—form the basis for a well-designed inventory control system. Each concept must be dealt with sequentially. Once the inventory control system is designed, only periodic evaluations are necessary to see that it is functioning properly.

Classification: what inventories should be controlled?

The most prevalent classification system is the ABC stratification plan. Inventory items are classified into three (or more) categories so that control techniques can be concentrated where they will be most effective.

For example, it makes little sense to design elaborate control mechanisms to monitor the use of bandages or gauze pads. On the other hand, some supply items in hospitals cost hundreds or thousands of dollars. Those items should be placed under the tightest control possible. The principle that the manager must use to decide which item to control is a subjective balancing of the costs of control versus the potential costs if an item is not closely controlled.

The ABC stratification plan can be used to help make these assessments. The following relationships between the number of items in inventory and the dollar value of the inventory are applicable to many organizations. If the hospital has 3,000 items in inventory, it may find that 300 of those items comprise over 70 percent of the total value of the inventory. Under this approach, the A category would include large, relatively expensive items used in small quantities. If one looks at total usage during the year, the A category might also include relatively cheaper supplies that are used in large quantities. The B category might comprise 600 items that represent 20 percent of the inventory value. The C category could then include the remaining 2,100 items (70 percent) that represent 10 percent of total inventory value.

Other classification criteria can also be used to establish the stratification plan. Dollar value or total cost is certainly important. Other important factors include:

1. frequency of use,
2. total usage during the year,
3. rate of obsolescence and
4. the critical requirement for an item, i.e., could a stockout create serious patient care problems?

Each of these factors must be subjectively assessed in establishing the classification plan. The real value of any ABC stratification plan is that different inventory categories are controlled and evaluated differently. That is why this is the first step in improving inventory control procedures.

Order point

The second step in an inventory control model is to determine when orders should be placed. What signals should be used to initiate the next order? If orders could be placed and supplies received instantaneously, there would be no need to be concerned about order points. Since there is usually some delay between the time an order is placed and the time the items are received, inventory control must include a time interval. This time interval is called *lead time* or the lead-time interval. Lead time is a function of the time necessary to:

1. recognize the need to place an order
2. prepare the purchase order
3. send the order
4. receive the order
5. check the items for correct quantity and quality
6. put the items in place, ready to use

As materials are used, inventory levels are depleted. When the next order is received, inventory levels rise. This pattern is illustrated in *Exhibit 10-1*.

Exhibit 10-1
Inventory usage with one-week lead time

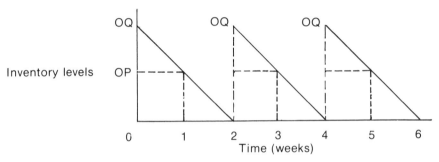

Assume that an order (OQ) had just been received at the beginning of the first week (T_0, *Exhibit 10-1*). The inventory level at the time the order came in was zero, and the amount ordered (OQ) brought the inventory level from zero to the highest point (OQ) at the beginning time period. As the supplies are used, the inventory quantity declines and, assuming a one-week lead time, a new order must be placed every other week (OP), starting with week 1 (weeks 1, 3 and 5). Once the order is placed, inventory levels continue to decline toward zero until the new order is received. This pattern continues to be repeated as long as usage is a constant rate and there are no changes in lead time.

Since most healthcare organizations cannot accurately predict these flows of materials and supplies, an additional buffer or safety stock is needed which is intended to cover those circumstances in which usage occurs at a faster than normal rate. The safety stock for any item is usually estimated from historical data adjusted for future changes. If the normal usage during the lead-time interval (one week) is 100 units and the maximum usage observed during any single week is 150, the safety stock should be 50 units. That is, the safety stock is equal to the maximum usage minus the normal usage during the lead-time interval. This relationship is shown in *Exhibit 10-2*.

With a normal usage pattern, the safety stock never drops below 50 units. In the event that it were reduced, the next period's order point could

Exhibit 10-2
Inventory usage with one-week lead time
and safety stock

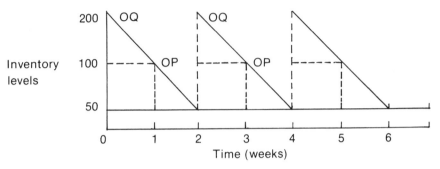

occur sooner during the week, and the order quantity would be correspondingly increased to make up any deficit in the safety stock. For example, assume that the normal quantity is 200, and 10 units of safety stock are consumed. The next order would be placed for 210 units.

Conceptually, the order point is a function of two factors: 1) usage during lead time, plus 2) safety stock.

The order point (OP) can be computed as:

OP = (usage during lead time) + (safety stock) or
OP = (average daily use) (lead-time interval) + (safety stock)

Note that safety stocks must be subjectively determined as a function of maximum levels of demand and of the acceptability of stockouts that may occur. If stockouts for a particular item would require closing the hospital, the safety stock must be large enough to satisfy any conceivable demand. If a stockout would only require deferring some elective surgery, or if it would mean an hour's delay, then safety stocks can be correspondingly reduced to bare minimums.

In any event, the general rule should be to calculate the order point (OP) based on the relationships described above. These order points should be viewed as tentative and modified according to actual experience (stockouts or excess inventories). One possible way to test any inventory policy is against historical data. The hospital financial manager can use historical demand, relative to known inventory quantities, to evaluate the effects of alternative inventory management policies. Successive adjustments, by a trial-and-error series of approximations, will often result in an appropriate order point.

One caution must be noted. In the event that the order point is reached, the quantity of the order must be adjusted by any current or anticipated shortages in inventory levels. For example, if the order point is 20 units and the inventory quantity at the time the order is placed is only 17 units, the order quantity must be increased by at least three (20 − 17) It must also be increased by any other increase in utilization during the lead-time interval.

Order quantity

Once the financial manager knows the point (OP) at which an inventory order must be placed, the next problem is to determine the optimal size of the order. The optimal order quantity (OQ) is known as the economic order quantity (EOQ) because it means trying to minimize the total (economic) cost of inventory. The costs of inventory management are frequently categorized as holding costs and ordering costs. The larger the inventory, the higher the holding costs. Therefore, to minimize holding costs, the manager must minimize inventory quantities. However, the costs of ordering are a function of the number (and frequency) of orders. To minimize ordering costs, a few very large orders should be placed each year. Examples of each type of cost are discussed in the next section.

The EOQ computation balances the conflicts between ordering costs and holding costs. It minimizes the sum of the two cost components. The total costs (TC) of the inventory, excluding the purchase price (assumed constant), is equal to holding cost plus ordering cost.

TC = (average inventory quantity) (holding cost per unit) +
$\qquad$ (number of orders) (average cost per order)

A typical pattern of costs for holding costs and ordering costs is shown in *Exhibit 10-3.*

Exhibit 10-3
Inventory holding and ordering cost

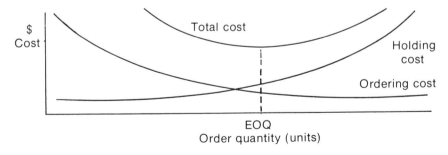

Note that the pattern of costs in *Exhibit 10-3* shows that ordering costs decrease as inventory increases. This general pattern will hold for most healthcare organizations. The shape of the relationships will differ, but the general pattern is correct. In addition, note that the minimum point of the U-shaped total cost curve *may* occur, by coincidence, at the intersection of the other two cost curves. What is important is that total costs are minimized by ordering the EOQ. This minimum point can be calculated using differential calculus (*Appendix 10-1*). The results of this differentiation can be expressed simply as:

$$EOQ = \sqrt{\frac{2(\text{annual demand}) \, (\text{costs per order})}{\text{holding costs per unit}}}$$

If annual demand is stated in terms of units, the EOQ is calculated as the quantity of units that comprise the optimal order. For example:

Annual demand = 100,000
Costs/order = $3.60
Holding costs/unit = $2.00

Then, the EOQ for this set of data is:

$$EOQ = \sqrt{\frac{2(100,000)(3.60)}{2.00}} = \sqrt{360,000} = 600 \text{ units}$$

The EOQ for this set of data is 600 units per order. We can show that this is the optimal order size by testing an EOQ of 600 relative to other order sizes (e.g., 500 or 1,000). *Exhibit 10-4,* which illustrates these computations, shows that total inventory costs are minimized at the EOQ of 600 units.

Exhibit 10-4
Costs associated with alternative order quantities

	Alternative order quantities (OQ)		
	500	*600*	*1,000*
1. Number of orders per year (Annual demand ÷ OQ)	200	167	100
2. Total ordering costs (orders per year) (cost per order)	$720	$600	$360
3. Average inventory size (OQ ÷ 2)	250	300	500
4. Total holding costs (avg. inventory) (holding costs)	$500	$600	$1,000
5. Total inventory costs (2 + 4)	$1,220	$1,200	$1,360

Note that total costs for these data do not vary greatly as the order quantity changes. In actual practice, total inventory costs are not usually sensitive to small changes in the input data. This statement can be interpreted so that minor errors in estimating any of the input costs will not significantly distort the results. The hospital financial manager is really more interested in a range of acceptable EOQs than in the precise numerical estimate of a single EOQ.

If we are interested in finding the EOQ in terms of dollars, we could simply multiply the EOQ obtained above by the purchase price (per unit). If the purchase price of the above items is $50 per unit, the dollar value of the EOQ is $30,000 (600 × $50). Alternatively, a related equation may be used to find the EOQ in terms of dollars.

$$\$EOQ = \sqrt{\frac{2 \text{ (annual demand) (cost per order) (purchase price per unit)}}{\text{holding costs per unit} \div \text{purchase price per unit}}}$$

In any event, it is easy to convert the EOQ stated in dollars to an EOQ stated in terms of units, provided that the purchase price per unit does not *vary*. If the purchase price per unit is changing drastically, the EOQ computations described above are not strictly valid. However, an approximate EOQ can still be calculated, and the computations in *Exhibit 10-4* can be expanded to include the purchase price per unit. In that case, several different order quantities can be tested to find the order quantity that reflects minimum total costs.

The objective in any inventory control or inventory management policy must be to find the best possible solution. If the calculated EOQ is within 1% to 5% of the optimal EOQ that truly minimizes all inventory costs, the financial manager has probably done better than if judgment alone had prevailed. In other words, an attempt can be made to bracket the minimum inventory costs, and an EOQ can be selected that is convenient and within that range.

Costs associated with inventory management

The costs of holding inventories and the costs of ordering inventories are the cost elements that management must be concerned with. Ordering costs are those incurred in ordering, receiving, inspection, etc. They include the variable costs of supplies and other overhead related to the purchasing function. They also include the costs of calculating and monitoring reorder points and order quantities.

Holding costs are usually much more significant. Holding costs include both the costs of carrying inventories and the costs of not carrying enough inventories. *Exhibit 10-5* identifies many different types of inventory holding costs. This list is not meant to be exhaustive and other costs could be identified.

An important point to note is that as holding costs increase, the costs of not holding enough usually will decrease. Conversely, as the costs of not having sufficient quantities increase, holding costs decrease. In addition, the management accountant must recognize that many of the costs

Exhibit 10-5
Examples of inventory holding costs

	Approximate average cost as a percentage of total inventory costs
Holding costs	
1. Obsolescence	6%
2. Handling ⎫	
3. Storage/warehouse ⎭	4%
4. Transfer and maintenance	2%
5. Property taxes and insurance	1%
6. Clerical	.5%
7. Opportunity costs of capital tied up in inventories	*
Costs of not having sufficient quantities	
1. Foregone purchase discounts	
2. Penalty costs on rush orders or quantity	
3. Added freight and purchasing cost on rush orders	7%
4. Loss of goodwill on rush orders (physicians and patients)	
5. Disruptive — scheduling (surgery, outpatient, etc.)	
Total	20.5%

*Differs depending on average cost of capital.

identified in *Exhibit 10-5* are not normally recorded in the accounting records. Opportunity costs, foregone discounts, loss of goodwill and the costs of disruptive scheduling must be estimated from data that are not usually maintained by the accountant. In most cases, these costs are larger and more significant than the holding and carrying costs that are recognized as expenses. It is very important that the management accountant not overlook these important components of inventory costs. As noted above, many of these costs must be determined subjectively, and the cost of obtaining more precise estimates must be balanced against the potential savings that may be possible with better inventory control. *Exhibit 10-5* indicates that the national average for these inventory costs is more than 20 percent of total inventory costs. This significant amount can be controlled using the concepts developed in this chapter.

Purchase price

The purchase price or the invoice price has been treated as a constant that is not subject to cost containment. Most hospital administrators recognize that potential savings due to effective purchasing can lead to impressive results. One of the most significant ways to affect the purchase price is by obtaining quantity discounts, probably through a shared or group purchasing arrangement. Savings of 20-50 percent (off list) are common under group purchasing. Many hospitals are finding that they can effectively match those prices on an individual basis by taking a more aggressive bargaining posture with suppliers.

Any group purchasing arrangement must be evaluated in total. Huge savings on a small fraction of the total inventory may not be sufficient to justify the added costs of off-site inventories, changing suppliers and not being able to control purchase and delivery dates. In any event, the most likely purchase prices, whether on a group or individual basis, must be used as the input to the order point and order quantity calculations described above.

In the event that purchase prices vary according to quantity ordered, the simplest procedure is to adjust the calculations outlined in *Exhibit 10-4* to include the foregone discount associated with each particular order quantity. For example, if a $1.00 (per unit) discount could be obtained by ordering 1,000 units or more, then the first two columns in *Exhibit 10-4* must include the additional costs due to the discount foregone by ordering less than 1,000 units. In such cases, the foregone discount is the annual demand multiplied by the associated foregone discount (per unit). As applied to the data in *Exhibit 10-4* and as shown in *Exhibit 10-6*, $100,000 (100,000 annual demand times $1.00 discount per unit) is added to each of the first two columns. This additional cost would clearly shift the EOQ to some point in excess of 999 units. Any OQ larger than 1,000 units could result in costs larger than $1,360 because storage costs are increasing faster than ordering costs are decreasing.

Exhibit 10-6
The effect of purchase price discounts of EOQ

	Alternative order quantities (OQ)		
	500	600	1,000
Total inventory costs (from Exhibit 10-4)	$1,220	$1,200	$1,360
Foregone discount ($1.00 per unit on order quantities of less than 1,000 units) (annual demand)	100,000	100,000	–0–
Total inventory outlay costs plus opportunity cost	$101,220	$101,200	$1,360

The final consideration affecting purchase price is that reductions in purchase price must be balanced against changes in other inventory costs. A quantity discount may mean fewer orders and lower ordering costs. On the other hand, a larger order quantity will result in larger inventory balances and potentially greater holding costs. It may also result in lower costs of not holding enough inventory. In summary, all these costs must be compared in order to determine whether a potential inventory price reduction is advantageous to the hospital. The provider of health services that can justify and document its evaluation of these alternative cost factors will have no problem demonstrating that it is a "prudent buyer." One of the major myths that can be demolished on the basis of inventory control policies is that purchase price reductions must be automatically accepted under the "prudent buyer" concept. The truly prudent buyer can show that all of the costs of inventory management have been evaluated and that the particular decisions that have been made are the best possible decisions under the circumstances facing that healthcare organization. Under some circumstances, the cheapest purchase price may not yield the lowest total inventory costs.

Probabilistic and uncertainty models

The discussions in this chapter have not explicitly included uncertainty. For example, a single point was selected as the expected lead time. However, there can be a variety of lead times and demands. Each of those outcomes has an associated probability of occurring. Many complicated decision models can be used to capture those probabilistic estimates of demand and lead time. A Miller-Orr model that is frequently used for cash management can also be used for any inventory control problem.[1]

A payoff matrix using expected values could also be used to identify the policy with lowest expected costs. A payoff matrix that incorporates probabilities is shown in *Exhibit 10-7*. This approach requires estimating the cost (per unit) of being understocked (out-of-stock) and relating it to the storage cost of units that are in stock. *Exhibit 10-8* adds a probability function to the various levels of demand. Using these data, an expected value of the payoff matrix is calculated. It is determined that the lowest cost order quantity is 20 units, because the stockout costs are so much higher than the storage costs for items on the shelf.

The Monte Carlo technique permits the analyst to simulate the effects of alternative inventory control policies and procedures, allowing evaluation of the effects of alternative order points and order quantities. The optimal points may be indicated by analytical procedures as noted above, while simulation then incorporates probabilities and random events to determine if the optimal solutions are feasible and realistic. Though the term "Monte Carlo" is generally associated with gambling, its use in this context refers to the uncertain or random nature of an

---

[1]Weston, J. Fred and Eugene F. Brigham, *Managerial Finance,* Hinsdale, IL: Dryden Press, 1981, pp. 355-357. Four alternative cash management models that can be adapted to inventory control problems as described.

Exhibit 10-7
Payoff matrix for alternative order quantities

Assume: Cost of being out of stock = $50 per unit
            Storage costs = $2 per unit
            Lead time = 0 days
            Alternative demand levels
            15
            16
            17
            18
            19
            20

	Actual demand					
Order quantity	15	16	17	18	19	20
15	$0	$50	$100	$150	$200	$250
16	2	0	50	100	150	200
17	4	2	0	50	100	150
18	6	4	2	0	50	100
19	8	6	4	2	0	50
20	10	8	6	4	2	0

Exhibit 10-8
Expected value of payoff matrix
for alternative order quantities

	Actual demand						
	15	16	17	18	19	20	
Probability of demand	10%	20%	30%	30%	5%	5%	
Order quantity							Totals
15	$ 0	1.00	30.00	45.00	10.00	12.50	98.50
16	.20	0	15.00	30.00	7.50	10.00	62.70
17	.40	.40	0	15.00	5.00	7.50	28.30
18	.60	.80	.60	0	2.50	5.00	9.50
19	.80	1.20	1.20	.60	0	2.50	6.30
20	1.00	1.60	1.80	1.20	.10	0	5.70

inventory control system that will be evaluated using simulation techniques.

This model does not explicitly incorporate holding costs and ordering costs. It does show how and under what circumstances stockouts occur. The financial manager must then assess the costs associated with different stockout patterns and choose the policy that will result in the optimal inventory quantities and stockouts. The advantage of a Monte Carlo simulation model is that it can be done easily by hand, or it can be converted to a computerized simulation model. In the latter case, a huge number of alternative inventory policies can be tested and a wide range of acceptable policies can be identified—at a relatively low cost.

The authors recommend using a single point estimate of demand and lead time if the relative dispersion around that point estimate is low. Alternatively, if the variance is high, a probabilistic model should be used. In other words, if the level of uncertainty is high, a model that emphasizes probabilities is preferred over a model that incorporates different cost elements. If the uncertainty is low, then the relative costs become more important to the decision, and an inventory control model that emphasizes cost is preferred.

An example[2]

Suppose that a hospital's management intuitively feels that its ad hoc approach to the problem of inventory control has led to substantial diseconomies. For purposes of illustrating the use of Monte Carlo simulation, the example will be concerned with only one item in the hospital's inventory. The management would like to determine (a) the optimal (or a near-optimal) inventory policy and (b) the extent to which deviations from this policy will result in increases in total inventory costs.

Investigation revealed that the pattern of daily demand was random and unstable, making application of the economic order quantity model inappropriate for this particular problem. Further investigation, however, disclosed that the pattern of daily demand did conform to a fairly stable probability distribution, with no detectable seasonal or secular shifts. The probability distribution of daily demand, based on historical observations, is shown in columns (1) and (2) of *Exhibit 10-9.* Notice that the distribution is not symmetric; it is skewed in the direction of high daily demand. (Thus, for example, the use of an optimization model based on the assumption of daily demand being normally distributed would not be

---

[2]This example is extracted from an article by Rodney Johnson titled "Managing Your Working Capital; Simulation: an Alternative Approach to Inventory Control," *Hospital Financial Management,* July, 1975.

appropriate.) The hospital's management also found that the lead time from placement of an order to receiving delivery varied randomly, but followed the probability of distribution given in columns (4) and (5) of *Exhibit 10-9*. These historical data did not seem to fit the assumptions of any of the better known inventory policy optimization models.

Exhibit 10-9
Data for inventory policy example

(1) Daily demand	(2) Probability	(3) Random numbers	(4) Lag time	(5) Probability	(6) Random numbers
5 units	.08	00–07	3 days	.15	00–14
6	.13	08–20	4	.40	15–54
7	.15	21–35	5	.25	55–79
8	.18	36–53	6	.20	80–99
9	.17	54–70		1.00	
10	.12	71–82			
11	.08	83–90			
12	.06	91–96			
13	.03	97–99			
	1.00				

This information—probability distributions of daily demand and lead time culled from old requisition and purchasing orders—is sufficient for some preliminary investigations of alternative inventory policies. An inventory policy is specified by two parameters: the order point and the order quantity. That is, the inventory policy will indicate at what level of existing inventory an order should be placed and the number of units that should be specified in that order.

A meeting of the hospital's top administrators was called to discuss the problem of formulating an inventory policy. Someone suggested a policy of ordering 40 units whenever the inventory at the end of a day is 35 units or less. There were some murmurings of disagreement, with varied opinions as to whether the order should be greater or less than the levels first suggested. After considerable discussion, it was agreed to evaluate the policy indicated above [denoted by (35, 40)].

They quickly agreed that it could be an expensive lesson if they followed the (35, 40) policy for a year's time and it turned out to be a very inefficient policy. Given the availability of dependable data on daily demand and lead times, however, they decided that simulation would be an appropriate technique for quickly and inexpensively evaluating the suggested (35, 40) inventory policy.

For the purpose of performing the simulation, the two-digit random numbers given in column (3) of *Exhibit 10-9* were assigned to various levels of daily demand and the random numbers in column (6) were assigned to alternative lead times. Notice that, from a long sequence of two-digit random numbers with equal probabilities of being selected, a random number in the range 00-07 should occur about 8 percent of the time; a random number in the range 08-20 should occur about 13 percent of the time, and so on. Thus the random numbers are assigned in such a way that the occurrence of random numbers should conform to the probability distribution of daily demand. Similiarly, random numbers are assigned to lead times so as to conform to the associated probability distribution.

The experience of 45 days under the (35, 40) policy is simulated in *Exhibit 10-10*. A series of two-digit random numbers, used to indicate units of daily demand, is given in column (2). The inventory at the beginning of day 1 is arbitrarily assumed to be 70 units. From *Exhibit 10-9* it is seen that the random number 71 represents daily demand of 10 units [indicated in column (4)]. The inventory at the end of day 1 is 60 units [indicated in column (5)]. The random number for day 2 corresponds to daily demand of 8 units, giving an ending inventory of 52 units. By the end of day 5, the inventory level is down to 30 units, exceeding for the first time the order point of 35 units.

At the end of day 5, an order is made to replenish the inventory. Strict adherence to the inventory policy would call for ordering 40 units. It has generally been found, however, that a preferable policy is to order the specified order quantity plus enough additional units to bring the inventory up to the order point. Following this convention, an order for 45 units is placed at the end of day 5. The random number 20 in column (6) corresponds to a lead time of 4 days. This means that delivery will be received at the end of day 9. Notice that the demand in day 9 exceeds the beginning inventory, resulting in unsatisfied demand.

This same procedure is continued for the 45 days experience shown in *Exhibit 10-10* (in actual practice, experience over a longer period of time would be simulated). The next step would be to evaluate the results of the simulation. For this purpose, management would have to estimate ordering costs, inventory carrying costs, and the costs of unsatisfied demand. These estimated costs would then be applied to the inventory experience depicted in *Exhibit 10-10* to get the total cost of the (35,40) inventory policy.

Exhibit 10-10 shows stockouts in days 9, 22, 23, 29, 30, 35, 41, 42 and 43. These frequent stockouts indicate that the order point should be raised. There were 7 orders placed during the 45 days experience. Unless inventory carrying costs are high relative to ordering costs, it probably would be advisable to also increase the order quantity. Thus a new simulation could be performed using an inventory policy of, perhaps, (50, 60). This policy could be simulated and evaluated and, based on the results, might be modified further and a new policy specified. Repeated refinement of the inventory policy would continue until management determines the inventory policy that best meets its needs.

Exhibit 10-10
Simulation for inventory policy example

(1) Day	(2) Random number	(3) Beginning inventory	(4) Daily demand	(5) Ending inventory	(6) Random number	(7) Lag time	(8) Order quantity
1	71	70	10	60			
2	39	60	8	52			
3	28	52	7	45			
4	63	45	9	36			
5	10	36	6	30	20	4 days	45
6	24	30	7	23			
7	87	23	11	12			
8	24	12	7	5			
9	53	5	8	0			
10	47	45	8	37			
11	70	37	9	28	27	4 days	47
12	33	28	7	21			
13	54	21	9	18			
14	75	18	10	8			
15	39	8	8	0			
16	43	47	8	39			
17	42	39	8	31	93	6 days	44
18	55	31	9	22			
19	45	22	8	14			
20	10	14	6	8			
21	32	8	7	1			
22	83	1	11	0			
23	57	0	9	0			
24	72	44	10	34	99	6 days	41
25	52	34	8	26			
26	61	26	9	17			
27	58	17	9	8			
28	08	8	6	2			
29	51	2	8	0			
30	00	0	5	0			
31	91	41	12	29	15	4 days	46
32	90	29	11	18			
33	01	18	5	13			
34	75	13	10	3			
35	18	3	6	0			
36	74	46	10	36			
37	51	36	8	28	91	6 days	47
38	68	28	9	19			
39	24	19	7	12			
40	82	12	10	2			
41	88	2	11	0			
42	41	0	8	0			
43	99	0	13	0			
44	66	47	9	36			
45	93	36	12	24	84	6 days	51

It should be recognized that the use of Monte Carlo simulation to determine a hospital's inventory policy yields only an approximate solution (so that an exact solution obtained by analytical evaluation is preferable when possible). Nevertheless, the approximation should be excellent if the number of simulated trials is large and the model is good. Moreover, the use of simulation allows the analyst to work with a more complex and flexible model.

This example assumed uniform demand throughout the period. With little additional effort, however, seasonal variations can be introduced into the demand pattern to make the model more realistic. The analysis of the simulation results can be modified to allow for an occasional rush shipment of an important item. The analysis might show that the expense of periodic emergency orders (so long as quality of patient care is not threatened) could be more than offset by the savings resulting from carrying small inventories. These examples illustrate the great flexibility available through the use of simulation.

Monte Carlo simulation does *not* eliminate the need to develop a model which depicts the operation of the system under study. The analytical solution is no longer a constraint and inventory control models can be developed without concern for their mathematical solvability.

It should be emphasized that while the model developed still needs to be a complete and realistic representation of all important aspects of the system under the study, it need only represent the *essential* aspects of the system. Being overly realistic means spending a great deal of effort and computer time to obtain very small improvements in the overall results. Moreover, the mass of trivial implications may obscure significant results.

Not all models are amenable to Monte Carlo simulation solution; only models in uncertain conditions can be evaluated. This is obvious because the basic premise of Monte Carlo simulation is the continued observation of the system over a long period of experience. This long history of the system's operation is, of course, a simulated rather than real history. Theoretically, the analyst draws on a large number of samples from the model and, through these observations, examines the behavior of the system. Without a random aspect to the model, all samples (or trials) would yield the same outcome.

The method used to simulate a sample is based on the use of random numbers. Random numbers are numbers selected in such a fashion that every number has an equal probability of being drawn. Once a random number is selected it is converted into an observation drawn from the probability distribution specified by the model. Random numbers can be obtained from tables of random numbers or they can be obtained by computers through the use of random number generating routines.

Zero inventory and stock-less systems

The latest developments in inventory management suggest that most inventory control problems can be shifted to suppliers who are asked to provide the capability for daily or hourly deliveries. Such a system is feasible and economically justified only where repetitive and stable services are being provided or for high cost items. In such cases, suppliers may be given annual contracts with appropriate definitions or expected performance. Where the supplier is guaranteed a certain minimum volume for an extended time period, the supplier may be willing to bear the costs and risks of inventory management. These techniques are most prevalent in high-tech electronics manufacturing, but they are being gradually incorporated into larger healthcare delivery systems. For example, multi-institutions or networked facilities may use a central warehouse with on-demand delivery capabilities so that on-site inventories are almost nil. Such procedures permit centralized inventory control so that materials, management functions become highly specialized and more complex than indicated in this chapter.

Summary

Inventory control is an important function of hospital management. In many healthcare organizations, the major inventory control technique is to take a physical count at the end of each accounting period. The use of EOQ models and optimal order points puts the focus on controlling costs before they occur. Emphasis on proper inventory control can also influence the structure of cost containment in the hospital. EOQs and optimal order points are tools that can be used to improve cost containment efforts. The financial manager must select that set of tools that improves decisions in a particular healthcare organization.

Questions and problems

1. Why are inventories necessary in a healthcare organization?

2. What are the objectives of an effective inventory management system?

3. What are the three fundamental concepts of inventory control?

4. What are the ordering costs associated with inventory management?

5. What are the carrying costs associated with inventory management?

6. Define lead time, safety stock, and order point.

7. Define economic order quantity as it pertains to healthcare organization.

8. How can group purchasing agreements and quantity discounts be used in an EOQ system?

9. How can uncertainty over future demand, lead times, prices, etc., be incorporated in an effective inventory management system?

10. The Memorial Hospital of Teller County estimated the demand for X-ray films for the coming year to be 36,500 with average daily usage to be 100 films. The purchase price of the film is estimated to be $2. The ordering costs are $20 per order, and carrying costs are estimated to be $0.40 per film per year. The lead time is 10 days, and the maximum daily usage last year was 150 films.

Required:

Compute the economic order quantity, the reorder point and the safety stock.

11. As controller of Memorial Clinic, you have been asked by the administrator to review the buying practices of the purchasing department. You find that the objective of this department has been to keep as small a quantity of each item on hand as possible, thus achieving the highest possible inventory turnover.

After extensive study, you determine that the average cost of processing an order is $9.50. This figure includes preparation of the requisition, issuance of the purchase order, processing and payment of the invoice, receipt of the merchandise and so on. You also determine that the average cost of carrying inventory is six percent of the value of the inventory on hand.

Required:
a. Explain what is meant by *economic order quantity.*
b. Illustrate the determination of EOQ for the following nonperishable items:
   Item A—Annual usage, $30,000
       Price quoted a ½ percent (.005) discount on purchases of $5,000 or more at one time

Item B—Annual usage, $800
  Price, net
Item C—Annual usage, $8,000
  Price quoted allows a one percent discount on purchases of $5,000 or more at one time

12. At the present time, purchasing at the Eastern Medical Center is decentralized. The purchasing department handles all departmental orders for items which are used by two or more departments. Other departments may order individual products themselves. These departments are radiology, pharmacy, pathology services, food services, plant operations and housekeeping. The departments initiate their own orders and maintain their own inventories. The purchasing department uses the following techniques to monitor its own performance. It attempts to turn the total inventory 12 times a year. It has a standardized committee that approves purchases of medical/surgical supplies. (Pharmacy also has a standardization committee for pharmaceutical items.)

   All purchasing is done on a competitive basis except for proprietary items and some miscellaneous items. Contracts are awarded on the basis of price and service. Two principal group purchasing arrangements are presently being used. One is a shared service arrangement with Methodist Hospital in Omaha; the second is the Hospital Purchasing Council based in Des Moines. At the present time, the purchasing department is investigating a prime vendor arrangement with American Hospital Supply, Inc.

   Required:
   a. Evaluate the current inventory ordering and control procedures.
   b. What changes would you recommend?

13. EOQ Products is a wholesale supplier of Patent Medicine. Because of the high risks in this business, the retailers to whom they sell have the common cost elements, as follows:
   S = costs per order =+ $100
   C = carrying costs = 100 percent per month
   The retailers face varying demand situations, which are highly sensitive to the availability of substitutes of given legal restrictions and are as follows (R = monthly sales):

Retail	I	II
P=$5.00	1,000	1,000
P=$4.50	1,111	1,250
P=$4.00	1,250	1,500

(Only these three prices are possible as agreed to by the trade association price ethics committee.)

EOQ Products presently sells to all retailers at the same wholesale price of $4.00 per bottle. Its variable costs are $1.00 per unit. Retailers are not allowed to sell to each other through very strict enforcement.

The new president of EOQ Products wants to increase profits. He makes the following discount from the wholesale price:

$$\$4.00 - 4 \left[\frac{R - 1{,}000}{1{,}000} \right]$$

only if the retailer agrees to a certain minimum order size (Q). If not, he/she is charged the usual $4.00 per bottle. Competition by other wholesalers has been eliminated through nonprice competition methods.

EOQ Products wants very much to increase Q because the variable costs of delivery are $500 per order. The president has narrowed his choice of the minimum order size to Q = 600, or Q = 800.

a. What are the total revenue, ordering costs, inventory costs, purchasing costs and net profits for each type of retailer prior to the discount offer?

b. If the retailer could obtain the discount price *without* the minimum Q requirement, what would his/her economic order quantity be, and his/her net profits?

c. What level of R will each type of retailer desire in order to maximize profits, given Q = 600? Given Q = 800?

d. Set up a payoff matrix for EOQ Products for Q = 600 and Q = 800, given the two types of retailers.

e. Assuming that the two types of retailers are equal in number, which Q level should EOQ products demand? Why?

f. What percentage of retailers would have to be Type 2 retailers in order for EOQ to demand that Q = 800? Why?

g. What is the maximum order size that a Type 2 retailer would be willing to make? Does this suggest something for EOQ?

14. *Assume:* Current assets for 1979 are $204,197 and current liabilities are $125,465; calculate the required amount under each set of conditions:

a. If inventories comprise $40,000 of total assets, what will be the expected current assets and current liabilities if a seven percent rate of inflation occurs?

b. If management's goal is a current ratio of 1.63, is this goal being satisfied? Why not?

c. How much must current assets increase in order for the current ratio to be 1.63?

d. How much revenue is necessary to generate this amount of current assets (part c)? Assume the bad debt ratio equals 1.66 percent of revenues.
e. If the following distribution of revenue exists, how much will rates have to be raised in each area?

Revenue center	% distribution	Patient days
Acute	30%	4,992
Long term	17%	11,356
Ancillaries	53%	$575,866*
	100	

*Last year's revenues.

15. The following information is available to Brookfield Hospital pertaining to Lab item #12.

Annual usage in units	20,000
Working days per year	365
Safety stock in units	400
Normal lead time in working days	15
Ordinary costs	$.50
Holding costs	$.75

Determine
a. The order point
b. The EOQ

16. As controller of Melbrook Hospital, you have been asked by the administrator to compute a safety level that minimizes total costs. The following information is available to you:

Probability of a stock-out	.25	.10	.04
Total actual wage during lead time	430	470	510
Expected usage provided for (reorder pt.)	380	380	380

Stock-outs if provision is also made for safety stock of:

0 units	50	90	130
50 units	0	40	80
90 units	0	0	40
130 units	0	0	0

> Stock-out cost = $1.20 per unit
> Carrying cost = $1.00 per unit
> Annual demand = 8000
> EOQ = 575

17. Shelby Cancer Research Clinic invented an injection to be used on cancer patients. It costs the clinic $85 to produce one injection (including $10 of fixed factory overhead). Set-up costs for one injection are $125. Since the injections are only effective for a short period of time, units are inspected at a cost of $1.50 per unit before they are delivered to customers. The clinic carries insurance of the injections at a cost of $.50 per injection (it is based on the average cost of inventory on hand). The rate of return required on investment in the inventory is 15 percent. Assuming on annual demand for 57,500 units, what is the economic order quantity?

18. The controller of General Hospital has given you the following information and wants you to determine the safety stock and order point for inventory item X (assume units of item X will be required evenly throughout the year).

Annual usage in units	16,425
Working days per year	365
Normal lead time in working days	35
Maximum lead time in working days	50

19. The Washington Clinic has hired you to control inventory levels of a very expensive drug that it has been using for the past year. You are given the following information:

- Cost of placing an order is $10
- The company's average (before tax) cost the capital is 12 percent
- Obsolescence and deterioration are 1 percent of average inventory per year
- Insurance and taxes on inventory are 5 percent of average inventory per year
- The storage space available in the pharmacy can accommodate 4000 units
- Additional space can be acquired at $.75 per unit
- The clinic is open 52 weeks a year, 5 days a week
- A safety stock of 100 is recommended by management
- It takes 2 weeks from the time of order to the date of delivery
- Per review of the clinic's records, usage can fluctuate from as low as 25 to as high as 70 per day

In addition to the preceding information, you obtain the following data from the purchasing dept concerning bulk purchases:

Quantity Purchased	Invoice Cost		Freight Cost	
	Unit Cost	Total Cost	Unit Cost	Total Cost
500	$100.00	$ 50,000	$2.00	$ 1,000
1000	100.00	100,000	2.00	2,000
2000	98.00	196,000	2.00	4,000
3000	98.00	294,000	1.80	5,400
4000	98.00	392,000	1.80	7,200
5000	95.00	475,000	1.75	8,750
6000	95.00	570,000	1.70	10,200.00
6500	95.00	617,500	1.70	11,050.00
13,00	90.00	1,170,000	1.50	19,500.00

Assume the maximum inventory to be computed for excess storage space is computed as follows: (order point—minimum usage) + standard quantity.

To minimize costs, what order size do you recommend?

20. Selected information relating to an inventory item carried by the Santos Hospital is given below:

Economic order quantity	700 units
Maximum weekly usage	60 units
Lead time	4 weeks
Average weekly usage	50 units

Santos Hospital is trying to determine the proper safety stock to carry on this inventory item, and the proper reorder point.

Required:
a. Assume that no safety stock is to be carried. What is the reorder point?
b. Assume that a full safety stock is to be carried.
   1. What would be the size of the safety stock in units?
   2. What would be the reorder point?

21. The Magnetic Research Corp. uses 15,000 ingots of Klypton each year. The Klypton is purchased from a supplier in another state, according to the following price schedule:

Ingots	Per ingot
500	$30.00
1,000	29.90
1,500	29.85
2,000	29.80
2,500	29.75

The Magnetic Research Corp. sends its own truck to the supplier's plant to pick up the ingots. The truck's capacity is 2,500 ingots per trip. The company has been getting a full load of ingots each trip, making six trips each year. The cost of making one round trip to the supplier's plant is $500. The paperwork associated with each trip is $30.

The supplier requires that all purchases be in round 500-ingot lots. The company's cost analyst estimates that the cost of storing one ingot for one year is $10.

Required:
a. By use of the tabulation approach to EOQ, compute the volume in which the Corp. should be purchasing its ingots. Treat the savings arising from quantity discounts as a reduction in total annual trucking and storing costs.
b. Compute the annual cost savings that will be realized if the Corp. purchases in the volume which you have determined above, as compared to its present purchase policy.

22. *Economic order quantities*

You have been asked by the administrator to review the buying practices of the purchasing department. The objective of this department has been to keep as small a quantity of each item on hand as possible, thus achieving the highest possible inventory turnover.

After an extensive study, you find that the average cost of processing an order is $7.80. This includes preparation of the requisition, issuance of the purchase order, processing and payment of the invoice, receipt of the merchandise, etc. You have also learned that the average cost of carrying inventory is six percent of the value of the inventory on hand.

The purchasing department furnishes the following information on three nonperishable items:

Item A—annual usage $20,000 (cost). Average cost is $10 per unit.
    Terms: one half percent (.005) discount on purchases of $5,000 or more at one time.
Item B—annual usage $600 (cost). Average cost is $5 per unit.
    Terms: net.
Item C—annual usage 1,000 units at $6 per unit.
    Terms: one percent discount on purchases of $5,000 or more at one time.

As an aid in making purchasing decisions, you decide to develop a framework that can be used for future ordering quantities based on the examples given.

References

Archer, Stephen H. and Charles A. D'Ambrosio, *The Theory of Business Finance*, New York: Macmillan, 1976.

Heyman, David P., "A Model for Cash Balance Management," *Management Science*, August, 1973, pp. 1407-1413.

Johnson, Rodney, "Simulation: An Alternative to Inventory Control," *Hospital Financial Management*, July, 1975, pp. 48-52.

Kirtane, Mohan and John Brinkman, "Inventory Control Is as Easy as ABC—EOQ," *Hospital Financial Management*, March, 1974, pp. 48-52.

Lusk, Edward J. and Janice Gannon Lusk, *Financial and Managerial Control, A Health Care Perspective*, Germantown, MD: Aspen Systems Corporation, 1979.

Snyder, Arthur, "Principles of Inventory Management," *Financial Excutive*, April, 1969, pp. 13-21.

Weston, J. Fred and Eugene F. Brigham, *Managerial Finance*, Hinsdale, IL: Dryden Press, 1981.

APPENDIX 10-1

EOQ formula derivation

Total costs = (costs per order) $\left(\dfrac{\text{annual quantity}}{\text{EOQ}} \right)$

$+ \left(\dfrac{\text{EOQ}}{2} \right)$(storage cost per unit)

$+$(annual quantity)(purchase price per unit)

$TC = (OC) \left(\dfrac{\text{quantity}}{\text{EOQ}} \right) + \left(\dfrac{\text{EOQ}}{2} \right) (SC) + \text{purchases}$

$TC = (OC)(\text{quantity})(EOQ)^{-1} + \tfrac{1}{2}(EOQ)(SC) + \text{purchases}$

To minimize this, differentiate total cost with respect to EOQ:

$$\frac{dTC}{dEOQ} = -1(OC)(\text{quantity})(EOQ)^{-2} + \tfrac{1}{2}(SC)(EOQ)^{0}$$

Note that purchase (costs) are constant and, therefore, they drop out of the equation.

$EOQ^{0} = 1$ and $EOQ^{-2} = \dfrac{1}{EOQ}2$ and set $\dfrac{dTC}{dEOQ} = 0$

and rearrange as follows:

$$\frac{SC}{2} - \frac{(OC)(\text{quantity})}{EOQ^{2}} = 0$$

Solving for EOQ:

$$EOQ^{2} = \frac{2(OC)(\text{quantity})}{SC}$$

$$EOQ = \sqrt{\frac{2(\text{annual quantity})(\text{costs per order})}{\text{storage costs per unit}}}$$

CHAPTER 11

Financial statement analysis

Introduction

One useful way to evaluate hospital performance is to use the comparative approach. For example, one hospital may be compared to another, or departments within a hospital might be compared with each other. One hospital may be compared to groups of other hospitals in the same city, state or region. The concept of peer grouping, establishing homogeneous comparison groups, is becoming more and more prevalent on a state and regional basis. Establishing valid comparative groups is an important ingredient of any performance evaluation.

This chapter concentrates on the use of ratios as comparative measures of performance. It presumes that valid and homogeneous data bases exist so that the resulting ratio calculations are meaningful and useful performance indicators. In other words, the garbage-in, garbage-out (GIGO) principle prevails; if the input data are worthless, the ratios will be worse than useless, they will be misleading.

Health service organizations are starting to use the traditional financial management tool of ratio analysis. Ratio analysis is a useful way to evaluate the strengths and weaknesses of many large organizations. Marc Choate was one of the first people to apply ratio comparisons to unrelated hospitals (1974). He developed consolidated financial statements, prepared on a uniform basis, for three hospitals. Choate then compared each of those hospital averages to very rough industry averages. His research was valuable in establishing an interest in comparative ratio analysis across different hospitals.

As an example of how ratio analysis can assist the financial manager, one needs only to look at the research studies that have attempted to predict bankruptcy using ratio comparisons. Everyone would accept the usefulness of ratio analysis if it can predict and prevent bankruptcy. Many different economists have used different sets of ratios to predict (ex post) bankruptcies in industrial companies, railroads, etc. Cannedy, Pointer and Ruchlin (1973) applied a series of multivariate statistical tests to a group of bankrupt hospitals and found that several factors could be used to explain or predict bankruptcy:

1. hospital size and ownership
2. total costs
3. utilization

The authors performed a pilot study on a group of four bankrupt hospitals that were closely matched to four surviving (thriving) hospitals. Four different ratios were identified that would correctly separate and identify the failed hospitals relative to the non-failed hospitals:

1. cash flow to total debt
2. total assets to FTE personnel
3. payroll expenses to FTE personnel
4. occupancy (utilization) ratios

If financial managers in health service organizations could monitor a variety of complementary ratios, they would be able to identify when the organization was thriving or in danger of failing. Ratio comparisons signal managers that correct decision behavior must be rewarded or that erroneous results must be corrected. The astute financial manager must be aware of those ratios that stimulate management to improve organizational efficiency and effectiveness.

Industry data source

Another key factor in the use of comparative financial analysis is the availability of industry data. For example, HFMA provides a Financial Analysis Service (FAS) to which healthcare organizations can subscribe. Subscribers send their audited financial statement to HFMA and receive comparative data grouped by 29 ratios into upper, medium, and lower quartile values by national, regional, and bed-size categories. There are currently over 1400 hospitals in the data sample. Another source of comparative data is the American Hospital Association's Hospital Administrative Services (HAS) Monitrend. The participating institutions submit financial, statistical and personnel data on specially designed input forms which are converted into approximately 300 operational indicators for comparative purposes. Both these sources can provide meaningful data for healthcare managers to evaluate performance and detect potential problems.

Different types of ratio comparisons

Snook and Sindell (1975) developed or identified a series of ratios to answer five basic questions:

1. Will the hospital be able to pay its current debts?
2. Is the hospital reasonably financed?

3. How likely is it that long-term debt obligations will be met?
4. Is the cash flow adequate?
5. What is the hospital's rate of return?

Fitschen (1976) also identified five major kinds of ratios:

1. solvency
2. profitability
3. collection period
4. inventory
5. debt ratios

Since there is some redundancy in these five categories, we have identified four different types of ratios that will be of use to healthcare financial managers:

1. liquidity ratios
2. turnover ratios
3. performance ratios
4. capitalization ratios

Liquidity ratios indicate the hospital's ability to remain solvent and continue to meet its financial obligations. Turnover ratios indicate how effectively the health service organization's resources are being used. Performance ratios could also be called efficiency ratios because they indicate how efficiently resources are being used. Capitalization ratios indicate how the assets were financed. They indicate the degree of leverage and the relative sources of financial capital.

Consolidated financial statements

Ratio calculations that are based on different funds in the hospital can lead to misleading or erroneous decisions. Many health service organizations are now adopting accounting systems based on a single fund. This use of only a general, or operating, fund is more consistent with normal business practice in other nonprofit organizations. Hospitals that have insignificant and immaterial assets in restricted funds, such as trusts, endowments or other fiduciary accounts, can safely ignore them in calculating ratios. However, healthcare organizations with significant resources in several operating funds, plant accounts, long-term debt accounts, etc., are only deluding themselves if they calculate ratios separately for each fund or account group.

Exhibit 11-1 illustrates a typical statement of financial position (balance sheet) for Sample Hospital's general fund and plant fund. There are significant current assets in several different asset categories. In addition,

Exhibit 11-1
Sample Hospital
Unconsolidated balance sheet

Assets		Liabilities and equities	
	General fund		
Current assets		*Current liabilities*	
Cash	$ 11,000	Accounts payable	$ 590,000
Net accounts receivable	1,700,000	Notes payable (to	
Inventory	350,000	plant fund)	150,000
Prepaid expenses	29,000	Accrued liabilities	300,000
Total current assets	$2,090,000	Total current liabilities	$1,040,000
Other assets		*Other liabilities*	
Savings	$ 1,000	Notes payable	$ 20,000
Accounts receivable	68,000	Deferred compensation	50,000
Deferred compensation	46,000	Blue Cross	100,000
Notes receivable	12,000	Total other liabilities	$ 170,000
House fund savings	150,000		
Investments	25,000	Equity	$1,184,000
Cash value of insurance	2,000		
Total other assets	$ 304,000	Total general fund	
Total general fund		liabilities and	
assets	$2,394,000	equities	$2,394,000
Current assets	**Plant fund**	*Current liabilities*	
Cash and savings	$ 21,000	Contracts payable	$ 30,000
Interest receivable	5,000	Mortgage payable	70,000
Transfers to general fund	150,000	Interest payable	20,000
Total current assets	$ 176,000	Total current liabilities	$ 120,000
Long-term assets		*Long-term liabilities*	
Plant	$4,000,000	Contracts payable	$ 70,000
		Mortgage payable	2,800,000
		Total long-term	
		liabilities	$2,870,000
		Equities	1,186,000
Total plant fund assets	$4,176,000	Total plant fund	$4,176,000

long-term debt appears in several different liability categories. Consolidation of such funds is advised. Similar assets and liabilities should be grouped together in the financial statements, unless there are legal restrictions that prohibit such consolidations. Note that commingling or reduced levels of disclosure is not advocated. All of the resources under the control of the health service organization may be consolidated into integrated, coherent financial statements. Assets with the same degree of liquidity may be grouped together and liabilities with similar maturities may also be grouped together in the financial statements.

Exhibit 11-2
Sample Hospital
Uniform consolidated fund statements

Assets		Liabilities and equities	
	Uniform consolidated general and plant fund		
Current assets		Current liabilities	
Cash and savings	$ 33,000	Accounts payable	$ 590,000
House fund savings	150,000	Notes payable	20,000
Investments	25,000	Blue Cross	100,000
Net accounts receivable	1,768,000	Accrued liability	320,000
Notes and interest		Contracts payable	30,000
receivable	17,000	Mortgage payable	
Inventory	350,000	(current portion)	70,000
Prepaid expense	29,000		
Cash value of insurance	2,000		
Total current assets	$2,374,000	Total current liabilities	$1,130,000
Long-term assets		Long-term liabilities	
Plant	$4,000,000	Contracts payable	$ 70,000
Deferred compensation	46,000	Mortgage payable	2,800,000
		Deferred compensation	50,000
Total long-term assets	$4,046,000	Total long-term	
		liabilities	$2,920,000
		Equities	2,370,000
		Total liabilities and	
Total assets	$6,420,000	equities	$6,420,000

Exhibit 11-2 illustrates the type of consolidated financial statement that is recommended for Sample Hospital. This statement is much more lucid; it is easier to interpret, and it offers the same level of disclosure as the unconsolidated statements. The AICPA, FASB and HFMA will, undoubtedly, be recommending similar types of consolidated financial statements for most nonprofit organizations. In any event, most professional accounting organizations are interested in increasing the level of disclosure and understandability of financial reports of healthcare organizations. Developments in this field will be rapid and timely in the very near future.

One final caution must be noted before calculating any ratios that use balance sheet data. The financial manager must be aware of significant changes in the structure of the balance sheet from the beginning of the year to the end of the year. If a merger has been consummated, if a large debt issue has been floated, or if any other change in financing or operating policies has occurred, the ending balance sheet is likely to be drastically different from the beginning of the year. The financial manager must assess whether some average of the two balance sheet data must be taken before calculating the necessary ratios. In some cases, a simple average or a weighted average (based on months) may be required. In other cases, the differences may be immaterial. The end-of-the-year balance sheet may also be the best indicator of future expectations. If so, no adjustments or averages are required. To illustrate the calculation of various ratios, the simplest possible assumption has been made: that no averages are required. Consequently, balance sheet data for only one point in time are presented and used in this chapter.

Liquidity ratios

Liquidity ratios indicate the degree of financial solvency of the organization. They indicate whether the hospital may have trouble meeting its current obligations. Liquidity ratios can provide clues as to how close the organization is to bankruptcy or insolvency. The balance sheet in *Exhibit 11-2* and the income statement in *Exhibit 11-3* will be used to illustrate the computation of each ratio.

Exhibit 11-3
Sample Hospital
Income statement

Operating revenues		
Daily patient services	$3,200,000	64%
Professional services	2,300,000	46
Gross revenues	$5,500,000	110
Deductions from gross revenues		
(uncollectible accounts, etc.)	$ 500,000	10
Net operating revenues	$5,000,000	100
Operating expenses		
Nursing services	$1,900,000	38
Professional services	1,800,000	36
Dietary	200,000	4
Interest	250,000	5
Fiscal and administrative	100,000	2
Depreciation	200,000	4
Insurance and other	100,000	2
	$4,550,000	91
Revenues in excess of expenses from operations	$ 450,000	9%

The current ratio is the best-known of the balance sheet liquidity ratios. The current ratio is calculated as current assets divided by current liabilities:

$$\text{current ratio} = \frac{\text{current assets}}{\text{current liabilities}}$$

The numerator contains all current assets. The denominator includes all current liabilities that will be normally liquidated within one operating cycle. The balance sheet in *Exhibit 11-2* has already been categorized according to current assets and liabilities. The calculation of the current ratio is:

$$\frac{2,374,000}{1,130,100} = 2.10$$

A general guide is that a current ratio in excess of 2.0 indicates adequate solvency. A current ratio of 4.0 or more often indicates financial mismanagement because the hospital is not matching its current resources with its current needs. A current ratio of less than 1.0 usually indicates severe financial problems. Note that no ratio, by itself, can guarantee financial health and solvency. Any ratio, or set of ratios, can only indicate problem areas or potential problems that should be investigated. A hospital with a current ratio of 1.75 is not necessarily in dire straits. Comparisons must be made to industry norms and to comparable data for hospitals with similar size, services and financial structures. For example, a county health department may operate with almost no current assets because the county treasurer pays all the bills. In this case, the current ratio for the health department would be almost zero, and it could indicate nothing about the department's ability to pay its bills.

Another liquidity ratio is the quick ratio, sometimes called the acid test. It measures short-term liquidity and the immediate capacity of the hospital to pay its current liabilities. The denominator is the same as for the current ratio. The numerator is cash, cash equivalents such as savings accounts or certificates of deposit, or any current assets that will normally become cash within one operating cycle. The quick ratio is often calculated as all current assets minus inventories. It is prefered that any accounts receivable that are more than 120 days old or that have been turned over to collection agencies be excluded from the numerator of the acid test. Hospitals often have drastically different collection procedures, relative proportions of third-party accounts and write off policies. These differences can distort the accounts receivable balance, relative to that of other hospitals, and thereby distort the quick ratio. Consequently, you should eliminate outdated ("stale") accounts that have a low probability of being collected. Assuming that no such accounts exist for Sample Hospital, the quick ratio is:

quick ratio =

$$\frac{\text{current assets} - \text{inventories} - \text{outdated accounts receivable}}{\text{current liabilities}} =$$

$$\frac{2,374,000 - 350,000 - 0}{1,130,000} = 1.79$$

A quick ratio around 1.0 is desirable. However, quick ratios around .75 are not uncommon in the health services industry.

A third liquidity ratio is the cash ratio. The numerator of the cash ratio is all current assets that are immediately convertible into cash. Consequently, it includes marketable securities, savings deposits and the cash value of life insurance policies. It may include notes receivable if they could be sold (discounted) to a bank or other financial institution. All of these items in the numerator are considered cash substitutes. The cash ratio is then calculated as:

$$\text{cash ratio} = \frac{\text{cash substitutes}}{\text{current liabilities}}$$

Assuming that the notes and interest receivable for the Sample Hospital are not cash substitutes, the cash ratio is:

$$\frac{33,000 + 150,000 + 25,000 + 2,000}{1,130,000} = .186$$

There are few current norms regarding the cash ratio, and comparable statistics for other hospitals are probably meaningless because of different preferences for cash balances. Because cash management policies differ so radically, it is probably most important to monitor the cash ratio over time, relative to the institution's experience. The authors have encountered hospitals with cash ratios ranging from .001 to over 15.0. Needless to say, there is not much comparability between such hospitals in terms of their philosophies regarding cash balances. Significant changes in the cash ratio from period to period, should be closely investigated. If they are due to temporary perturbations in collection patterns or to financing activities, there may be no cause for alarm.

A more useful way of evaluating liquidity in terms of cash substitutes is to look at the number of days that the hospital could exist with the cash and cash substitutes available. This ratio could be termed the cash on hand expressed in terms of operating days. The numerator would be the cash substitutes as used in the cash ratio. The denominator would be all expected cashflows for a period of time (e.g., week, month or year). The cash needed for this period of time could be calculated as operating expenses minus depreciation, plus payments on long-term debt plus any purchases of fixed assets. Note also that any mandatory sinking fund requirements or funded depreciation requirements must also be included in the calculation of daily cash flows. These cash flow needs would be divided by the number of days in the period to obtain a daily cash flow requirement.

$$\text{Daily cash flow} = \frac{\text{operating expenses} - \text{depreciation} + \text{debt payments} + \text{purchases of fixed assets}}{\text{days in period}}$$

$$\text{Days of cash flow available} = \frac{\text{cash substitutes}}{\text{daily cash flow}}$$

The days of cash flow available ratio indicates the real margin of safety for the hospital. Any organization should have more than one payroll period's days of cash flow available. In other words, the cash requirements for the forthcoming payroll cycle should be the minimum level of the days of cash flow available ratio.

Assuming no fixed asset purchases and a $100,000 ($30,000 + $70,000) payment outstanding debts, the days of cash flow available to the Sample Hospital would be:

daily cash flow =
$$\frac{4,550,000 - 200,000 + 100,000 + 0}{365} = \$12,192 \text{ per day}$$

days of cash flow available =

$$\frac{33,000 + 150,000 + 25,000 + 2,000}{12,192} = 17.2 \text{ days}$$

The days of cash flow available is numerically equivalent to the days of cash plus cash substitutes available. The reader may desire to verify that 17.2 days are obtained in both cases.

This ratio indicates that Sample Hospital could continue to meet its cash flow requirements for at least 17 days, even if no other cash or short-term borrowings were to become available. This is a dynamic measure that converts the other liquidity ratios to the minimal survival period. A ratio expressed in terms of days is often easier to understand and convert into operating decisions. The manager can quickly see how critical the decision needs are and what period of time is available before results must occur. This kind of margin of safety is a very important managerial indicator.

A bare minimum safety margin is to relate the daily cash flow to cash on hand. Most health service organizations should have at least one day's cash flow requirement on hand.

$$\text{days of cash available} = \frac{\text{cash (in banks)}}{\text{daily cash flow}}$$

For Sample Hospital, its cash available immediately to satisfy operating requirements would be enough for three days of operations:

$$\text{days of cash available} = \frac{33,000}{12,192} = 2.71 \text{ days}$$

Any time this ratio deteriorates to less than one day, that is a significant danger signal.

Another ratio that also indicates something about the institution's margin of safety is the times fixed charges ratio. Times fixed charges indicates the number of times that fixed charges could have been paid by the institution. For example, assume that interest charges on long-term debt are the only contractual payments that the hospital must make. Lease payments or physician compensation (e.g., radiologists) might be other examples. The financial manager would like to know what the risks are of not meeting those contractual obligations. Times fixed charges indicates the multiple or number of times that fixed commitments could have been paid out of operating revenues. Times fixed charges is calculated as:

$$\text{times fixed charges} = \frac{\text{revenues in excess of expenses from operations} + \text{fixed charges}}{\text{fixed charges}}$$

Assuming that interest is Sample Hospital's only fixed charge, its times fixed charges would be:

$$\text{times fixed charges} = \frac{450{,}000 + 250{,}000}{250{,}000} = 2.80$$

A times fixed charges ratio of 1.0 usually indicates a very low margin of safety. This ratio should be in excess of 2.0; there is really no upper limit other than the constraints that normally guide managers of nonprofit organizations.

A very important liquidity ratio, especially with regard to the probable amortization of long-term debt, is the debt service ratio. The term debt service refers to interest plus principal payments on long-term debt. The debt service ratio is related to times fixed charges because it shows how many times the debt service is protected, or covered, by all cash flows. The debt service ratio is calculated as:

$$\text{debt service ratio} = \frac{\begin{array}{c}\text{revenues in excess of expenses from operations} + \\ \text{depreciation} + \text{annual debt service requirements}\end{array}}{\text{annual debt service requirements}}$$

For Sample Hospital, the debt service ratio is calculated as:

$$\text{debt service ratio} = \frac{450{,}000 + 200{,}000 + (250{,}000 + 70{,}000)}{(250{,}000 + 70{,}000)} = 3.03$$

This a fairly secure position and is directly affected by the amount of debt amortized in any given year. Under these circumstances there is the obvious possibility of an acceleration in future debt service requirement, or perhaps some balloon payments. In that case, the debt service ratio for the current year may not be indicative of future debt service requirements or of the liquidity available to meet those requirements.

Several other liquidity ratios describe the working capital position of the hospital. The working capital growth ratio indicates whether the change in working capital is justified by changes in revenues:

$$\text{working capital growth ratio} = \frac{\text{net change in working capital}}{\text{net change in patient revenues}}$$

This ratio requires comparing this year's working capital and revenue with comparable data from last year. If revenues are increasing and working capital is not, this ratio will be close to zero. That may indicate more efficient management, or it may indicate a deterioration in liquidity. This ratio must be evaluated in conjunction with the ratios described earlier.

The last liquidity ratio deals with working capital relative to the physical plant, or capital, in the organization. Working capital per bed indicates the relative amounts of working capital required, on average, for each available bed:

$$\text{working capital per bed} = \frac{\text{working capital}}{\text{available beds}}$$

This ratio is important for any health services organization that is planning to grow or expand its services because it emphasizes the fact that working capital is a critical element of total financial requirements. If Sample Hospital were planning to add 100 beds, it would have to finance over $600,000 of additional working capital requirements:

$$(100) \frac{(2,374,000 - 1,130,000)}{200} = \$622,000$$

Minor periodic changes in this ratio are probably not too important. However, as the organization changes its scale of operations, this ratio can be used to extrapolate additional working capital requirements.

Turnover ratios

Turnover ratios are indicators of activity. They indicate the rate at which the hospital's resources are being used. Turnover relationships must be optimized by the financial manager of a health service organization. Turnover that is too fast indicates that shortages may be occurring too often. Slow turnover ratios indicate that too many resources are tied up in a particular type of asset and that the costs of maintaining those large balances, relative to needs, may be prohibitive.

Chapter 10 dealt exclusively with the turnover concept with respect to inventory management. The relationships developed in that chapter were intended to optimize the rate of inventory turnover. A fast inventory turnover ratio would result in higher ordering costs due to the increased frequency of ordering. A slow turnover ratio would mean high carrying costs. It would mean that large inventories were being maintained, and the carrying costs of those inventories would be high.

Most turnover ratios are related to operating revenues. They indicate the number of times a particular type of asset is "turned over" or cycled through operating revenues. Turnover ratios link the balance sheet and income statements in showing how particular assets are used in generating revenues or costs. Most turnover ratios can be stated in general terms as:

$$\text{turnover} = \frac{\text{periodic revenues (or costs)}}{\text{associated assets}}$$

For example, the (total) asset turnover would be:

$$\text{asset turnover} = \frac{\text{net operating revenue}}{\text{total assets}}$$

For Sample Hospital, the asset turnover ratio is:

$$\text{asset turnover} = \frac{5,000,000}{6,420,000} = .779$$

The asset turnover ratio indicates the degree of utilization of the institution's assets in generating revenues. A high ratio indicates more rapid turnover and a higher degree of utilization. A low turnover ratio may indicate that the hospital has overinvested in particular assets. Asset turnover for hospitals can range from a very low .25 to an upper extreme of 5.0. There are no industry norms because the relative age of the physical plant can drastically affect the turnover.

Most managers find that turnover is one of the more significant factors that can be affected by managerial decisions. Turnover in health services, or in any capital intensive industry, will probably be lower than corresponding ratios for manufacturing firms. Turnover ratios for public health departments, clinics and professional service departments or organizations will probably be quite high. Turnover is directly related to the capital intensity required to support the activity. As the relative mix of capital inputs to labor inputs increases, the turnover rate will decrease. It is the manager's responsibility to balance an increasing need for more capital inputs with the institution's objective of maintaining or improving turnover relationships.

A variety of other turnover ratios can be calculated:

$$\text{fixed asset turnover} = \frac{\text{net operating revenue}}{\text{fixed assets}}$$

$$\text{current asset turnover} = \frac{\text{net operating revenue}}{\text{current assets}}$$

$$\text{cash turnover} = \frac{\text{net operating revenue}}{\text{cash}}$$

$$\text{accounts receivable turnover} = \frac{\text{net operating revenue}}{\text{accounts receivable}}$$

$$\text{inventory turnover} = \frac{\text{net operating revenue}}{\text{inventory}}$$

Note that the fixed asset turnover ratio and the current asset turnover ratio are complementary. A high current asset turnover ratio implies a relatively lower fixed asset turnover. The cash, accounts receivable and inventory turnover ratios are obviously components of the current asset turnover ratio. They may not assume equal importance for all hospitals. Again, the higher the turnover, the more effective is the use of that particular asset component. Low turnover rates imply overinvestment in those particular resources.

Inventory turnover may also be evaluated relative to the costs of supplies. Rather than relating turnover exclusively to patient revenues, it can also be related to expenses. Therefore, inventory turnover may also be calculated as:

$$\text{inventory cost turnover} = \frac{\text{supplies expense}}{\text{inventory}}$$

Accounts receivable turnover may also be evaluated in several different ways. The accounts receivable turnover ratio that would be calculated for Sample Hospital would be:

$$\text{accounts receivable turnover} = \frac{\$5,000,000}{\$1,768,000} = 2.83$$

This turnover ratio indicates that accounts receivable are cycled or turned (over) into patient revenues 2.83 times each year. Another way of stating it is to say that accounts receivable of $1,768,000 are collected about 2.83 times each year. This is a relatively low turnover because the normal turnover is more than 5.0 times each year. Accounts receivable may also be evaluated in terms of average collection periods. In order to compute the average collection period, one must first calculate the average daily patient revenue:

$$\text{average daily patient revenue} = \frac{\text{net operating revenue}}{\text{number of days}}$$

The average collection period is, then:

$$\text{average collection period} = \frac{\text{net accounts receivable}}{\text{average daily patient revenue}}$$

These calculatons for Sample Hospital would be:

$$\text{average daily patient revenue} = \frac{\$5,000,000}{365} = \$13,698.63 \text{ per day}$$

$$\text{average collection period} = \frac{\$1,768,000}{\$13.698.63} = 129 \text{ days}$$

This is a relatively long collection period. Most health service organizations are striving for collection periods of 75 days or less. The average collection period can also be interpreted as the number of days revenue outstanding (not collected). The calculations for Sample Hospital indicate that 129 days of revenue from patient services are yet uncollected. These calculations can also be split into inpatient and outpatient components because the turnover rates and collection periods will usually differ markedly between these two major groups of patients. The calculations may also be split into source of payment:

1. private pay
2. Medicare
3. Medicaid
4. private insurance
5. other

Each of these payment sources has its own processing requirements and reimbursement schedules. Consequently, it is desirable to evaluate each major category separately.

Accounts receivable turnover and average collection periods are often sensitive to seasonal patterns and to changes in patient mix. To eliminate seasonal effects, the financial manager could use weighted averages, or moving averages, in computing average daily patient revenues. A simple expedient would be to use the two most recent months of patient revenues to compute the average daily patient revenue. This calculation would then roll forward each month to include the most recent month and to exclude the earliest month. Accurate, consistent cutoffs must be observed each month to insure that the data are comparable. This is an example of a situation in which a 13-month fiscal year (13 four-week periods) would insure that calendar irregularities would not distort ratio calculations.

Changes in patient mix must be considered when evaluating the accounts receivable on a periodic basis. As the mix of patients or payment sources changes, the aggregate accounts receivable ratios can be affected. The variance analysis techniques developed in Chapters 5 & 6 can be used to evaluate the different effects of changes in mix, volume and prices. Since all three factors affect accounts receivable management, it would be desirable to identify and separate those different effects.

Accounts receivable turnover and average collection periods are related. The average collection period can be derived directly from accounts receivable turnover data:

$$\text{average collection period} = \frac{\text{number of days}}{\text{accounts receivable turnover}}$$

For Sample Hospital:

$$\text{average collection period} = \frac{365}{2.83} = 129 \text{ days}$$

This shortcut method can be very useful for converting turnover rates into days, or days into turnover per year. It is not restricted to accounts receivable and can be used for other asset categories such as inventories. If inventory turnover is 12 times per year, the number of days that the hospital could operate with its current inventories is about 30 days (365 ÷ 12 = 30.4 days). It should be recognized that this type of ratio does not allow for seasonal fluctuations. During peak utilization periods, the hospital may have a smaller number of days supplies on hand. Management personnel using these figures for planning should adjust them accordingly.

The financial manager can also calculate the accounts payable payment period in a manner similar to the accounts receivable collection period. The average daily operating expenses are calculated as:

$$\text{average daily operating expenses} = \frac{\text{operating expenses}}{\text{number of days}}$$

$$\text{accounts payable payment period} = \frac{\text{current liabilities}}{\text{average daily operating expenses}}$$

For Sample Hospital:

$$\text{average daily operating expenses} = \frac{\$4,550,000}{365} = \$12,465.75$$

$$\text{accounts payable payment period} = \frac{1,130,000}{12,465.75} = 90.6 \text{ days}$$

These data indicate that Sample Hospital pays off liabilities on an average of once every 90 days, but it collects accounts receivable once every 129 days. There is an obvious need for working capital, or improved management and collection of accounts receivable, in order to equalize the financial effects of these two different turnover rates.

Performance ratios

One of the main themes underlying this text is that profits in a health services organization are necessary to continue providing quality healthcare. The financial requirements of any viable and adaptive financial organization include funds for growth, new programs, financing of working capital needs and replacement of equipment.

As shown in Chapter 1, these needs must be met out of profits, otherwise termed "revenues in excess of expenses from operations." An evaluation of performance must include an evaluation of comparative profitability. It must indicate how efficiently resources are being used. How do different aspects of the total organization contribute profits to meet the total financial requirements of the institution? The performance ratios developed in this section will help answer this question.

One of the most obvious sets of profitability ratios to calculate is to relate the expenses to revenues. The second column in *Exhibit 11-3* illustrates one such set of percentage composition ratios. They show how net operating revenues are used to meet various expenses, leaving a balance of nine percent available for future financial requirements. The net profit of total revenues may also be calculated as:

$$\text{operating margin} = \frac{\text{revenues in excess of expenses from operations}}{\text{net operating revenues}}$$

Either net or gross revenues may be used as the basis for these profitability calculations, although we prefer net operating revenues because they are not distorted by the deductions and allowances that may be necessary. The operating profit margin ratio indicates the relative amounts, out of each dollar of patient revenues, that are available for future financial requirements.

The second major performance ratio is called return on investment or, in many industries, return on assets. It is the relationship between profits and the capital used in providing health services. Return on assets is calculated as:

$$\text{return on assets} = \frac{\text{revenues in excess of expenses from operations}}{\text{total assets}}$$

This ratio indicates how efficiently capital resources are being used in making funds available for future financial requirements. It can be compared to other industries and to other hospitals. For investor-owned hospitals, it provides one indication of the attractiveness of the healthcare industry relative to other industries as potential investments.

The return on assets ratio and the net operating margin ratio are related to the asset turnover ratio:

$$(\text{asset turnover})(\text{net operating margin}) = \text{return on assets, or}$$
$$\frac{\text{net operating revenues}}{\text{total assets}} \times$$
$$\frac{\text{revenues in excess of expenses from operation}}{\text{net operating revenues}} =$$
$$\frac{\text{revenues in excess of expenses from operation}}{\text{total assets}}$$

These ratios for Sample Hospital would be:

$$\text{net operating margin} = \frac{\$\ 450,000}{\$5,000,000} = 9\%$$

$$\text{asset turnover} = \frac{\$5,000,000}{\$6,420,000} = .7788$$

$$\text{return on assets} = \frac{\$\ 450,000}{\$6,420,000} = 7.01\% = (.7788)(9\%)$$

Proving that turnover times margin does equal return on assets:

$$(.7788)(.09) = .701$$

This is a very important relationship because it shows that return on assets can be increased by increasing either turnover or the operating margin. Many health service organizations operate with relatively constant return on asset ratios. This occurs because the turnover and margin ratios may change in the opposite direction and they may be offsetting in their impact on the return on assets ratio. The desirable results would be for both relationships to improve if the hospital wants to improve its return on assets.

The relationships between turnover, margins and total returns can also be expressed in terms of return on equity. Equity is the organization's capital investment in itself. It is defined as total assets minus all liabilities. Some health service organizations identify equity as fund balances.

$$\text{Return on equity} = \frac{\text{revenues in excess of expenses from operations}}{\text{total equities}}$$

For Sample Hospital, return on equity is:

$$\text{return on equity} = \frac{\$\ 450,000}{\$2,370,000} = 19.0\%$$

This can also be expressed as turnover times net operating margin equals return on equity for Sample Hospital:

$$\frac{\$5,000,000}{\$2,370,000} \times \frac{\$\ 450,000}{\$5,000,000} = \frac{\$\ 450,000}{\$2,370,000} = 19\%$$

$$2.11 \times .09 = 19.0\%$$

These data illustrate that the equity turnover for Sample Hospital is over two times each year and that this multiplier effect more than doubles the net operating margin (9 percent) to almost a 19 percent return of equity. For an investor-owned hospital this would be a very attractive result.

These relationships are expressed in *Exhibit 11-4,* which illustrates how

Exhibit 11-4
Margin, turnover and return relationships*

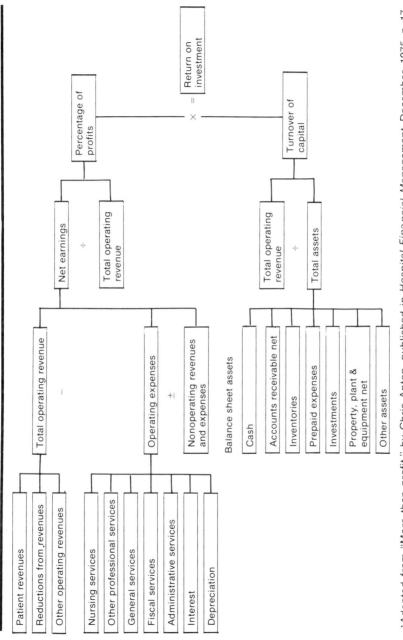

*Adapted from "More than profit," by Chris Anton, published in *Hospital Financial Management*, December, 1975, p. 17.

the financial manager can impact return on investment (either assets or equity). It shows how turnover affects returns and how operating margins affect returns. Either or both sides of this relationship can be changed if the financial manager wants to improve the organization's return ratios.

Another profitability ratio that is indicative of the return on all assets, or on all sources of capital, would be to calculate return ratios before deducting interest (or other financing costs.) For example, for a nonprofit institution, the prefinancing return on total assets is:

prefinancing return on assets =
$$\frac{\text{revenues in excess of expenses from operations} + \text{interest}}{\text{total assets}}$$

The prefinancing return on total equity is:

prefinancing return on equity and long-term debt =
$$\frac{\text{revenues in excess of expenses from operations} + \text{interest}}{\text{total equities} + \text{long-term debt}}$$

Further adjustments in these ratios are required for organizations that are subject to income taxes. The interested reader is referred to any standard accounting or finance text, e.g., Anthony and Reese (1979; see references at the end of this chapter). These two prefinancing ratios can be compared with the organization's average interest costs (interest expense ÷ long-term debt). In the event that average interest costs exceed either of the prefinancing return ratios, financial theory states that negative leverage exists. The presence of long-term debt usually connotes the existence of leverage, but negative leverage means that the community or the institution is borrowing money and investing it at lower returns than the cost of borrowed funds. Some hospitals and health service organizations cannot avoid negative leverage, but hospitals in that unhappy circumstance should be very careful about evaluating and approving new capital investments.

Other performance ratios relate to average costs per unit of service or per unit of input factor. A unit of service refers to an output unit such as patient days, admissions or laboratory tests. An input factor refers to hours of labor services, numbers of full-time equivalent (FTE) employees or pounds of laundry. Average costs per unit of input factor are much more reliable than costs per output unit of service. The deficiencies of using patient days as the unit of service are well-known and discussed elsewhere. Health planners and other regulatory agencies should be extremely cautious about evaluating the performance of health service organizations solely on the basis of patient day measures. As stated above, average costs per input factor have higher reliability than many output units of service. They are easier to understand, and it is easier to demonstrate the effects of managerial decisions by using a set of input factor performance ratios. The differential effects of mix, volume and prices are easier to separate for departments or responsibility centers if input factor performance ratios are used.

One problem that financial managers may encounter is how to select from the almost limitless set of input factor performance ratios that are available. The department manager has a restricted scope because he/she is concerned with only one or a few departments, and many different input factor performance ratios will be regularly evaluated at the departmental level. However, at the upper levels of managerial responsibility and at the regulatory or governmental level, information overload can easily occur if all possible input factor performance ratios are computed and reported. The problem is to limit one's search and review to input factor performance ratios that reflect the essential elements of hospital or departmental operations. Many ratios are redundant, and the financial manager usually has only enough time and energy to evaluate and utilize relevant, nonredundant information. Most managers develop an informal and intuitive heuristic to eliminate redundant input factor performance ratios. It is the purpose of this chapter to only indicate what some of those alternative ratios are. The manager or regulatory agency that may wish to use a statistically valid technique to eliminate redundant ratios is referred to Neumann's article in the *Journal of Accounting Research* (1979; see references at the end of this chapter). The essential point is that managers can use both judgment and statistics to eliminate redundant ratios.

Examples of input factor performance ratios are shown in *Exhibit 11-5*. This set of ratios is not meant to be exhaustive, and it should be noted that many of the departmental ratios indicated in *Exhibit 11-5* can be further segregated into fixed and variable (cost) components. This separation is desirable whenever fixed costs are material in amount or significant to performance evaluation.

An important ratio that relates liquidity and performance is the allowance ratio. This ratio measures the deductions that occur from gross patient revenue for contractual allowances, bad debts, or charity care. Allowances are an important factor for managers to control because they have a direct impact on charges and cash flow to the organization. Charges that are not collected must be added to the charges of other payers if total financial requirements are to be net. The allowance ratio is computed as follows:

$$\text{Allowance ratio} = \frac{\text{contractual allowances} + \text{bad debts (charity care)}}{\text{Gross Patient Revenue}}$$

For Sample Hospital, the allowance ratio would be

$$\frac{\$\ 500,000}{\$5,500,000} = .09$$

In summary, performance ratios should be identified and calculated for

Exhibit 11-5
Selected input factor performance ratios

Laundry per pound $= \dfrac{\text{laundry expenses}}{\text{pounds processed (wet or dry)}}$

Dietary per meal $= \dfrac{\text{dietary expenses}}{\text{meals served}}$

Wages per manhour $= \dfrac{\text{payroll expenses}}{\text{total manhours}}$ or $\dfrac{\text{payroll expenses-salaries}}{\text{total hours reported by hourly employees}}$

Nursing wages per hour $= \dfrac{\text{nursing salaries}}{\text{nursing hours}}$

Lab tests per admission $= \dfrac{\text{laboratory tests}}{\text{total admissions}}$

Revenue per bed $= \dfrac{\text{net operating revenues}}{\text{licensed beds}}$

Total assets per bed $= \dfrac{\text{total assets}}{\text{licensed beds}}$

Long-term debt per bed $= \dfrac{\text{total long-term debt}}{\text{licensed beds}}$

FTE per bed $= \dfrac{\text{total full-time equivalent employees}}{\text{licensed beds}}$

Square feet per bed $= \dfrac{\text{usable square feet floor space}}{\text{licensed beds}}$

Revenue per FTE $= \dfrac{\text{net operating revenues}}{\text{FTE employees}}$

Total assets per FTE $= \dfrac{\text{total assets}}{\text{FTE employees}}$

Payroll per FTE employee $= \dfrac{\text{payroll expenses}}{\text{FTE employees}}$

any aspect of operations that the manager wishes to evaluate. As compared to the other three kinds of ratios, the definitions of performance ratios are not as restricted, and the manager has much more latitude in selecting different performance ratios that reflect controllable decisions or events. Performance ratios that reflect noncontrollable events are often irrelevant and should be ignored if more appropriate ratios can be identified and calculated.

Capitalization ratios

Capitalization ratios indicate how the hospital's assets are financed. They indicate how effectively the organization is using external funds to finance its total financial requirements. The most usable capitalization ratios are composition ratios that indicate the relative sources of financing. Debt ratios and/or debt equity ratios are subject to confusion and misunderstanding. However, capitalization composition ratios are effective substitutes for debt ratios, and they can be quickly transformed into debt ratios whenever necessary. A capitalization composition ratio simply indicates the relative percentage of one type of financing to total assets. For example, the capitalization composition ratios for Sample Hospital are shown in *Exhibit 11-6*. These data show that 45.5 percent of Sample Hospital's assets are financed by long-term debt and 36.9 percent are financed internally.

Exhibit 11-6
Capitalization composition ratios for Sample Hospital

	Amounts	Capitalization composition ratios
Current liabilities	$1,130,000	17.6%
Long-term liabilities	2,920,000	45.5
Equities	2,370,000	36.9
Total	$6,420,000	100.0%

A health service organization would like to have its fixed assets financed by permanent capital (long-term debt plus equities) and its current assets financed by short-term credit. It would also like to balance its long-term debt and equity position. Most lenders would prefer to see the capitalization composition ratios for long-term debt and equity at about equal levels. Alternatively, a desirable result would be for the long-term debt ratio to approximate 100 percent.

$$\text{long-term debt ratio} = \frac{\text{long-term debt}}{\text{total equities}} = \frac{2,920,000}{2,370,000} = 1.23$$

Exhibit 11-7
Summary of ratios

1. Liquidity

$$\text{Current ratio} = \frac{\text{current assets}}{\text{current liabilities}}$$

$$\text{Quick ratio} = \frac{\text{current assets} - \text{inventories} - \text{outdated accounts receivable}}{\text{current liabilities}}$$

$$\text{Cash ratio} = \frac{\text{cash substitutes}}{\text{current liabilities}}$$

$$\text{Daily cash flow} = \frac{\text{operating expenses} - \text{depreciation} + \text{debt payments} + \text{purchases of fixed assets}}{\text{days in period}}$$

$$\text{Days of cash flow available} = \frac{\text{cash substitutes}}{\text{daily cash flow}}$$

$$\text{Days of cash available} = \frac{\text{cash (in banks)}}{\text{daily cash flow}}$$

$$\text{Times fixed charges} = \frac{\text{revenues in excess of expenses from operations} + \text{fixed charges}}{\text{fixed charges}}$$

$$\text{Debt service ratio} = \frac{\text{revenues in excess of expenses from operations} + \text{depreciation} + \text{annual debt service requirements}}{\text{annual debt service requirements}}$$

$$\text{Working capital growth ratio} = \frac{\text{net change in working capital}}{\text{net change in patient revenues}}$$

$$\text{Working capital per bed} = \frac{\text{working capital}}{\text{available beds}}$$

2. Turnover ratios

$$\text{Asset turnover} = \frac{\text{net operating revenue}}{\text{total assets}}$$

$$\text{Fixed asset turnover} = \frac{\text{net operating revenue}}{\text{fixed assets}}$$

$$\text{Current asset turnover} = \frac{\text{net operating revenue}}{\text{current assets}}$$

$$\text{Cash turnover} = \frac{\text{net operating revenue}}{\text{cash}}$$

Accounts receivable turnover $= \dfrac{\text{net operating revenue}}{\text{accounts receivable}}$

Inventory turnover $= \dfrac{\text{net operating revenue}}{\text{inventory}}$

Average daily patient revenue $= \dfrac{\text{net operating revenue}}{\text{number of days}}$

Average collection period $= \dfrac{\text{net accounts receivable}}{\text{average daily patient revenue}}$

Average daily operating expenses $= \dfrac{\text{operating expenses}}{\text{number of days}}$

Accounts payable payment period $= \dfrac{\text{current liabilities}}{\text{average daily operating expenses}}$

3. Performance ratios

Operating margin $= \dfrac{\text{revenues in excess of expenses from operations}}{\text{net operating revenue}}$

Return on assets $= \dfrac{\text{revenues in excess of expenses from operations}}{\text{total assets}}$

Return on equity $= \dfrac{\text{revenues in excess of expenses from operations}}{\text{total equities}}$

Prefinancing return on assets $=$

$$\dfrac{\text{revenues in excess of expenses from operations} + \text{interest}}{\text{total assets}}$$

Prefinancing return on equity and long-term debt $=$

$$\dfrac{\text{revenues in excess of expenses from operations} + \text{interest}}{\text{total equities} + \text{long-term debt}}$$

Allowance ratio $= \dfrac{\text{contractual allowances} + \text{bad debts} + \text{charity care}}{\text{gross patient revenue}}$

4. Capitalization ratios

Long-term debt ratio $= \dfrac{\text{long-term debt}}{\text{total equities}}$

Fixed asset capitalization ratio $= \dfrac{\text{fixed assets}}{\text{long-term debt plus equities}}$

A further condition would be for the fixed asset capitalization ratios to be less than 100 percent:

$$\text{fixed assets capitalization ratio} = \frac{\text{fixed assets}}{\text{long-term debt plus equities}}$$

For Sample Hospital:

$$\text{fixed asset capitalization ratio} = \frac{4,046,000}{2,920,000 + 2,370,00} = 76.5\%$$

This indicates an effective balance between long-term sources of capital and short-term sources of capital financing. Note that composition ratios may also be calculated for the asset side of the balance sheet.

A number of the ratios discussed earlier in this chapter are also directly related to capital structure. Times interest earned, debt service ratios and leverage ratios all indicate something about the capital structure of the institution. No single category of ratios may be calculated independently of the other ratios that may be related. Therefore, it is sufficient to state that capitalization and the effectiveness of the capital structure must be evaluated in conjunction with the other categories of ratios discussed earlier. Note also that a whole set of ratios that may be relevant to investor-owned hospitals have not been discussed. Stock-related ratios, such as earnings per share, dividends per share, payout ratios, book value per share, etc., are all beyond the scope of this chapter, and the interested reader can, again, refer to any standard finance text. *Exhibit 11-7* presents a summary of the ratios contained in this chapter.

Summary

This chapter identified four different sets of ratios that are useful from the manager's perspective. Comparative evaluation, across different healthcare organizations or across years, will permit managers to evaluate critical areas of concern. Trend analysis is an essential component of ratio analysis. An even more important component is the manager's assessment of future financial performance as a result of this period's ratio analysis.

An additional input that managers might consider is HFMA's Financial Analysis Service. This service encompasses 29 key ratios that partially overlap the coverage in this chapter. The Financial Analysis Service provides a User's Guide that completely explains each ratio in terms of how it is calculated and how it can be interpreted. The major advantage of the Financial Analysis Service is that it performs the calculations from audited financial statements and identifies median ratios for a variety of possible peer group comparisons. The financial manager who wants to avoid some computational drudgery and/or wants to obtain additional data from similar hospitals should consider a subscription to the Financial

Analysis Service. This chapter provides a comprehensive framework that can be used in any type of ratio analysis.

Questions and problems

1. How can ratio analysis help the hospital financial manager?
   a. What are the first steps to take before computing any particular ratio?

2. Explain the following categories of financial ratios:
   a. liquidity
   b. turnover
   c. performance
   d. capitalization

3. Why should consolidated financial statements be made before financial ratios are computed?

4. When should year-end financial statements' amounts be used to compute the ratios?

5. What ratios would you compute as an aid in determining
   a. the financial solvency of a healthcare organization?
   b. the managment of the use of resources?
   c. the relationship of revenue and expenses and total investment?
   d. the financial structure of the healthcare organization and the relative risk involved?

6. The Navajo Mission Hospital financial statements indicate the following amounts:

| | Dec. 31 (in thousands) | | |
	19X1	19X2	19X3
Net patient service revenues	18,859	20,742	23,890
Patient accounts receivable	3,813	4,266	4,760

Required:
   a. Calculate the number of days charges in receivable (average collection period) and the accounts receivable turnover.
   b. What judgment would you make about the management of patient receivable?

7. Using the data that follows, evaluate each of the following requirements.
   a. The hospital's financial manager is concerned about how well the hospital can meet its current obligations. Determine and evaluate the 1) current ratio, 2) quick ratio and 3) cash ratio.
   b. How can we determine the risks of not meeting those obligations? (Hint: calculate the times fixed charges and debt service ratios.)

Balance sheet

Assets			Liabilities and equities	
Current assets:			Current liabilities:	
Cash and savings	$	28,000	Accounts payable	$ 404,000
Investment		60,000	Notes payable	123,000
Net accounts				
receivable		1,895,000	Accrued expenses	37,000
Inventory		450,000	Mortgage payable —	
			current portion	40,000
Prepaid expenses		21,000		
Total current assets		$2,454,000	Total current liabilities	$ 604,000
Long-term assets:			Long-term liabilities:	
Plant and equipment		4,200,000	Notes payable	460,000
			Mortgage payable	1,600,000
			Total long-term liabilities	$2,060,000
			Equities	3,990,000
Total assets		$6,654,000	Total liabilities and equities	$6,654,000

Income statement

Operating revenues		
Daily patient services	$3,700,000	
Professional services	1,300,000	
Gross revenues	$5,000,000	
Deductions (uncollectible		
accounts, etc.)	500,000	
Net operating revenues		$4,500,000
Operating expenses		
Nursing services	$1,855,000	
Professional services	1,050,000	
Dietary	320,000	
Interest	265,000	
Fiscal and administrative	250,000	
Depreciation	125,000	
Other	125,000	
		3,990,000
Net revenue		$ 510,000

c. The hospital is considering expanding its facilities from 1,200 to 2,000 beds. Calculate 1) the daily cash flow, 2) the working capital ratio, and 3) determine their importance in making the final decision.

d. The financial manager is wondering if an increase in the collection of accounts receivable may improve their position. Determine and discuss the accounts receivable ratios.

e. Calculate the return on assets assuming the operating margin = 11.33% and the asset turnover = .67%. How can we improve the return on assets?

f. Determine and evaluate the hospital's return on equity.

8. You have been recently hired as the controller of the Manchester County Hospital. The administrator hs asked you to review the financial statements for the organization (*Exhibits A-E*). He is particularly interested in determining any problem areas that might be identified from the financial management area.

Required:

Using the information contained in the financial statements, what report would you make to the administrator about the financial condition of the Manchester County Hospital? (Assume that all restricted funds are properly disclosed.)

Exhibit A

Balance sheets — unrestricted fund
Manchester County Hospital
June 30, 1980, 1979 and 1978

	1980	1979	1978
Assets			
Current assets			
Cash	$ 420,105	$ 367,086	$ 212,848
Receivables from patients and third-party payers, less allowances for contractual adjustments and doubtful accounts (1980 — $266,000; 1979 — $421,000; 1978 — $237,895)	1,486,172	1,449,656	1,592,934
Inventories	192,347	138,712	63,069
Deferred cost reimbursement — current portion	118,000	—	—
Prepaid expenses	91,171	33,605	20,434
Due from plant expansion fund	67,799	15,352	59,507
Due from endowment fund	—	236	—
Total current assets	$ 2,375,594	$ 2,004,647	$1,948,792
Other assets			
Cash (1980—$549; 1979—$705; 1978 — $41,582) and investments designated by Board for plant replacement	$ 1,414,348	$ 511,404	$ 145,667
Other investments	28,372	32,086	26,577
Investment in and advances to Paoli Memorial Medical Building Corporation	111,963	76,987	60,724
Deferred cost reimbursement	187,300	169,200	145,500
Bond issue expenses, less amortization	361,718	387,219	227,112
Land and building—held for sale	84,511	84,511	—
	$ 2,188,212	$ 1,261,407	$ 605,580

Property, plant and equipment	$ 8,210,063	$ 7,424,079	$5,930,828
Funds held by trustee			
Cash	$ 562	$ 526,915	$ 38,644
Certificates of deposit	867,425	1,740,982	438,000
U.S. Treasury notes	186,927	110,275	145,016
Accrued interest	19,140	46,765	7,591
	$ 1,074,054	$ 2,424,937	$ 629,251
	$13,847,923	$13,115,070	$9,114,451

Liabilities and fund balance

Current liabilities			
Accounts payable and accrued			
expenses	$ 259,551	$ 181,305	$ 184,814
Employee compensation	477,473	181,282	138,947
Advances from third-party			
payers	64,345	61,225	52,845
Due to endowment fund	—	—	1,417
Total current liabilities	$ 801,369	$ 423,812	$ 378,023
Liabilities payable from funds held			
by trustee			
Accounts payable—construction	$ 34,660	$ 430,910	$ 68,344
Accrued interest on hospital			
gross revenue bonds	212,608	212,608	125,587
	$ 247,268	$ 643,518	$ 193,931
Hospital gross revenue bonds	$ 7,037,700	$ 7,212,700	$4,725,000
Fund balance	5,761,586	4,835,040	3,817,497
	$13,847,923	$13,115,070	$9,114,451

Balance sheets — restricted funds
Manchester County Hospital
June 30, 1980, 1979 and 1978

	1980	1979	1978
Assets			
Plant expansion fund			
Cash	$ 183,251	$ 26,795	$ 35,505
Due from investment custodian	5,693	—	—
Certificates of deposit	—	—	800,000
Investments	784,447	558,155	—
Pledges receivable, less allow-			
ance for estimated uncollectible			
amounts (1980 — $64,000; 1979			
— $39,000; 1978 — $47,000)	80,130	249,129	424,452
Accrued interest receivable	26,499	9,439	12,305
	$1,080,020	$843,518	$1,272,262

Exhibit A (cont.)

Balance sheets — restricted funds
Manchester County Hospital
  June 30, 1980, 1979 and 1978

	1980	1979	1978
Endowment fund			
Cash	$ —	$ 797	$ 3,601
Investments	63,391	63,358	70,935
Due from unrestricted fund	—	—	1,417
	$ 63,391	$ 64,155	$ 75,953
Liabilities and fund balances			
Plant expansion fund			
Accounts payable	$ —	$ 59,587	$ —
Due to unrestricted fund	67,799	15,352	59,507
Fund balance	1,012,221	768,579	1,212,755
	$1,080,020	$843,518	$1,272,262
Endowment fund			
Due to investment custodian	$ 245	$ —	$ —
Due to unrestricted fund	—	236	—
Fund balance	63,146	63,919	75,953
	$ 63,391	$ 64,155	$ 75,953

Exhibit B

Statements of revenues and expenses — unrestricted fund
Manchester County Hospital
  Years ended June 30, 1980,
  1979 and 1978

	1980	1979	1978
Patient service revenue:			
Inpatient	$ 9,037,633	$7,161,553	$5,205,051
Outpatient	1,929,392	1,471,850	1,025,577
	$10,967,025	$8,633,403	$6,230,628
Allowances and uncollectible			
accounts	1,553,794	1,374,451	825,919
Net patient service revenue	$ 9,413,231	$7,258,952	$5,404,709
Other operating revenue	85,499	60,255	21,272
Total operating revenue	$ 9,498,730	$7,319,207	$5,425,981

Exhibit B (cont.)

Statements of revenues and expenses — unrestricted fund
Manchester County Hospital
Years ended June 30, 1980,
1979 and 1978

	1980	1979	1978
Operating expense:			
Nursing services	$ 2,124,173	$1,787,695	$1,357,954
Other professional services	2,971,586	2,454,258	1,779,551
General services	1,293,735	1,049,552	741,008
Fiscal and administrative services, including interest (1980 — $424,551; 1979 — $253,191; 1978 — $235,581)	1,900,178	1,433,404	1,150,725
Depreciation and amortization	483,858	389,258	331,638
Total operating expense	$ 8,773,530	$7,114,167	$5,360,876
Earnings from operations	$ 725,200	$ 205,040	$ 65,105
Nonoperating revenue:			
Unrestricted gifts	$ 42,803	$ 102,575	$ 34,424
Unrestricted income from endowment funds	2,877	6,098	8,605
Interest income	103,604	24,672	34,534
Gain on early retirement of hospital gross revenue bonds	23,961	—	—
Gain on sale of securities	35,427	—	—
Gain (loss) on sale of equipment	(10,889)	838	(818)
Equity in net loss of Manchester County Medical Building Corporation	(7,392)	(21,279)	(22,549)
	$ 190,391	$ 112,904	$ 54,196
Excess of revenues over expenses before cumulative effect on prior years of a change in accounting method	$ 915,591	$ 317,944	$ 119,301
Cumulative effect on prior years (to June 30, 1980) of a change in accounting method for vacation expense	(78,684)	—	—
Excess of revenues over expenses	$ 836,907	$ 317,944	$ 119,301
Pro forma excess of revenues over expenses assuming the new method of accounting for vacation expense is applied retroactively	$ 915,591	$ 292,181	$ 120,219

Exhibit C

Statements of changes in fund balance — unrestricted fund
Manchester County Hospital
Years ended June 30, 1980,
1979 and 1978

	1980	1979	1978
Balance at beginning of year, as previously reported	$4,835,040	$3,817,497	$2,305,925
Restatement of balance at July 1, 1977, for inclusion of funds held by trustee	—	—	1,796,257
Balance at beginning of year as restated	$4,835,040	$3,817,497	$4,102,182
Additions:			
Excess of revenues over expenses	$ 836,907	$ 317,944	$ 119,301
Donation of property	—	—	75,000
Transfers from plant expansion fund	22,724	626,754	170,804
Income from investments of funds held by trustee, net of amounts applied against construction costs (1980—$24,682; 1979—$137,082; 1978—$62,370)	66,915	72,845	34,822
	$ 926,546	$1,017,543	$ 399,927
Deduction:			
Transfers to plant expansion fund	$ —	$ —	$ 684,612
Balance at end of year	$5,761,586	$4,835,040	$3,817,497

Exhibit D

Statement of changes in fund balances — restricted funds
Manchester County Hospital
    Years ended June 30, 1980,
    1979 and 1978

	1980	*1979*	*1978*
Plant expansion fund			
Balance at beginning of year	$ 768,579	$1,212,755	$ 550,066
Restricted contributions and interest	251,516	178,989	153,208
Gain on sale of investments	14,850	3,589	—
Transfers from funds held by trustee	—	—	684,612
Campaign expenses	—	—	(4,327)
Transfers to unrestricted fund, including, in 1980, $554,594 to funds held by trustee	(22,724)	(626,754)	(170,804)
Balance at end of year	$1,012,221	$ 768,579	$1,212,755
Endowment fund			
Balance at beginning of year	$ 63,919	$ 75,953	$ 75,609
Contributions	—	—	238
Restricted investment income	—	—	106
Loss on sale of investments	(733)	(12,034)	—
Balance at end of year	$ 63,186	$ 63,919	$ 75,953

Exhibit E

Statements of changes in financial position — unrestricted fund
Manchester County Hospital
Years ended June 30, 1980,
1979 and 1978

	1980	1979	1978 Restated
Funds provided.			
Earnings from operations	$ 725,200	$ 205,040	$ 65,105
Add (deduct) items included in operations not affecting funds: Depreciation and			
amortization	483,858	389,258	331,638
Deferred cost reimbursement	(18,100)	(23,700)	(80,500)
Funds derived from operations	$1,190,958	$ 570,598	$ 316,243
Cumulative effect on prior years of change in accounting principle	($ 78,684)	$ —	$ —
Nonoperating revenue	190,391	112,994	54,196
Donation of interest in real estate	—	(80,090)	—
Gain on early retirement of bonds	(23,961)	—	—
Equity in net loss of Manchester County Medical Building Corporation	7,392	21,279	22,549
	$ 95,138	$ 54,183	$ 76,745
Total from operations and nonoperating revenues	$1,286,096	$ 624,781	$ 392,988
Decrease in funds held by trustee	1,350,883	—	1,206,953
Proceeds from gross revenue bonds—series of 1978	—	2,502,700	—
Donation of property	—	—	75,000
Transfers from plant expansion fund	22,724	626,754	170,804
Income from investments of funds held by trustee, net of amounts applied against construction costs	66,915	72,845	34,822
	$2,726,618	$3,827,080	$1,880,567

Exhibit E (cont.)

Statements of changes in financial position — unrestricted fund
Manchester County Hospital
    Years ended June 30, 1980,
    1979 and 1978

	1980	1979	1978 Restated
Funds used			
Additions to property, plant and equipment, net	$1,252,834	$1,867,108	$ 804,242
Retirement of bonds	142,546	—	—
Transfers to plant expansion fund	—	—	684,612
Increase in funds held by trustee	—	1,795,686	—
Decrease (increase) in amounts payable from funds held by trustee	396,250	(449,587)	78,580
Advances to Manchester County Medical Building Corporation	42,369	37,542	22,449
Bond issue expenses	—	175,507	—
Increase in board designated assets	902,944	365,737	8,739
Other	(3,715)	25,021	26,577
	$2,733,228	$3,817,014	$1,625,199
Increase (decrease) in working capital	(6,610)	10,066	255,368
Working capital at beginning of year	1,580,835	1,570,769	1,315,401
Working capital at end of year	$1,574,225	$1,580,835	$1,570,769
Changes in components of working capital			
Increase (decrease) in current assets:			
Cash	$ 53,019	$ 154,238	($ 131,756)
Receivables	36,516	(143,278)	548,103
Inventories	53,635	75,643	10,714
Deferred cost reimbursement — current portion	118,000	—	—
Prepaid expenses	57,566	13,171	7,395
Due from plant expansion fund	52,447	(44,155)	16
Due from endowment fund	(236)	236	—
	$ 370,947	$ 55,855	$ 434,472

Exhibit E (cont.)

Statements of changes in financial position — unrestricted fund
Manchester County Hospital
Years ended June 30, 1980,
1979 and 1978

	1980	1979	1978 Restated
Increase (decrease) in current liabilities:			
Accounts payable and accrued expenses	$ 78,246	($ 3,509)	$ 85,485
Employee compensation	296,191	42,335	39,357
Advances from third-party payers	3,120	8,380	52,845
Due to endowment fund	—	(1,417)	1,417
	$ 377,557	$ 45,789	$ 179,104
Increase (decrease) in working capital	($ 6,610)	$ 10,066	$ 255,368

9. You have recently been appointed chairperson of the Memorial Medical Center finance committee. The Board of Trustees has asked you to evaluate the financial condition of the center and to make recommendations to the board on the financial performance of the administrator during the five years she has held the job.

Required:

From the financial statements (*Exhibits F-I*), prepare the report to the Board of Trustees.

Exhibit F
Memorial Medical Center
Balance sheet — June 30, 1980, 1979, 1978, 1977 and 1976

	1980	1979	1978	1977	1976
Assets					
Current assets:					
Cash	$ 143,032	$ 504,233	$ 366,257	$ 238,148	$ 237,525
Accounts receivable, less reserve for uncollectible accounts of $660,000 in 1980, $620,000 in 1979, $580,000 in 1978, $384,000 in 1977 and $350,000 in 1976	3,456,004	2,542,593	2,331,201	2,197,084	1,864,766
Estimated settlements receivable in connection with third-party reimbursement contracts	—	85,834	48,449	—	—
Inventories, at cost (note 1)	362,859	320,788	284,251	239,343	180,475
Prepaid expenses	234,598	176,917	112,114	109,720	74,775
Total current assets	$ 4,196,493	$ 3,630,365	$ 3,142,272	$ 2,784,295	$ 2,357,541
Board-designated funds, at cost, which approximates market (note 1)	$ 200,000	$ 750,000	$ 500,000	$ 650,000	$ 950,000
Plant and equipment, at cost (notes 1 and 2):					
Land and improvements	$ 1,673,048	$ 1,260,246	$ 1,135,828	$ 1,135,828	$ 1,135,828
Buildings	7,085,715	7,064,014	7,071,056	6,551,458	6,546,769
Equipment and furnishings	10,427,118	9,603,537	9,143,615	8,064,325	7,742,588
	$19,185,881	$17,927,797	$17,350,499	$15,751,611	$15,425,185
Less — reserve for depreciation	6,258,587	5,499,491	4,798,206	4,146,940	3,560,806
	$12,927,294	$12,428,306	$12,552,293	$11,604,671	$11,864,379

Exhibit F (cont.)
Memorial Medical Center
Balance sheet — June 30, 1980, 1979, 1978, 1977 and 1976

	1980	1979	1978	1977	1976
Construction in progress, at cost (see note 2)	$ 527,655	$ 20,790	$ .90,067	$ 1,010,093	$ —
Specific purpose fund assets (note 1)	$ 436,000	$ 350,141	$ 323,622	$ 418,153	$ 328,632
	$18,287,442	$17,179,602	$16,608,254	$16,467,212	$15,500,552
Liabilities and fund balances					
Current liabilities:					
Current portion of long-term debt	$ 216,168	$ 201,000	$ 126,600	126,600	$ 126,600
Accounts payable	481,891	422,103	404,695	353,932	313,518
Salaries, wages and accrued vacation (note 5)	673,776	561,168	332,639	249,839	89,589
Payroll taxes withheld and accrued	17,540	15,218	13,816	9,436	51,692
Accrued pension contribution payable	—	125,204	—	—	—
Advance payments under Medicare program	—	—	—	—	176,000
Estimated settlements payable in connection with third-party reimbursement contracts	117,795	—	—	264,500	55,127
Contract retainage payable	—	6,779	12,038	97,286	—
Total current liabilities	$ 1,507,170	$ 1,331,472	$ 889,788	$ 1,101,593	$ 812,526

Exhibit G
Memorial Medical Center
For the years ended June 30, 1980, 1979, 1978, 1977 and 1976

	1980	1979	1978	1977	1976
Patient service revenues:					
Daily care services	$ 8,719,055	$ 7,168,098	$ 6,578,039	$ 5,495,775	$ 4,936,760
Patient supporting services	3,018,948	2,337,948	2,026,492	1,831,447	1,610,442
Professional services	6,885,264	5,997,253	4,828,739	3,936,008	3,630,273
	$18,623,267	$15,503,299	$13,433,270	$11,263,230	$10,177,475
Deductions from patient service revenues:					
Contractual adjustments (note 1)	$ 1,069,253	$ 702,889	$ 864,276	$ 1,086,919	$ 950,107
Provision for bad debts and charity service	564,931	459,345	434,609	276,941	425,403
Policy discounts	31,284	32,565	22,535	15,124	19,914
	$ 1,665,468	$ 1,194,799	$ 1,321,420	$ 1,378,984	$ 1,395,424
Net patient service revenues	$16,957,799	$14,308,500	$12,111,850	$ 9,884,246	$ 8,782,051
Other operating revenues:					
Cafeteria sales	$ 258,750	$ 220,453	$ 219,010	$ 184,880	$ 154,738
School of nursing	141,241	142,903	134,147	136,049	145,907
Purchase discounts	20,252	22,979	22,828	20,280	17,143
Management fees and other	97,024	125,634	52,703	48,280	84,480
	$ 517,267	$ 511,969	$ 428,688	$ 389,489	$ 402,268
Total operating revenues	$17,475,066	$14,820,469	$12,540,538	$10,273,735	$ 9,184,319

Long-term debt, less current portion included above:					
First mortgage bonds, 7¾%, secured by plant and equipment, net of reserve funds of $781,559 in 1980, $733,232 in 1979, $558,795 in 1978, $409,574 in 1977 and $260,118 in 1976 (note 2)	$ 4,804,441	$ 5,065,768	$ 5,314,605	$ 5,463,826	$ 5,613,282
Real estate contract, 8½%, secured by certain land and improvements, payable in monthly installments of $1,000, including principal and interest to 1995	$ 98,763	$ —	$ —	$ —	$ —
Deferred Medicare liability (note 1)	$ 835,000	$ 733,000	$ 650,000	$ 560,000	$ 440,000
Fund balances, per accompanying statement:					
General fund (note 1)	$10,606,068	$ 9,699,221	$ 9,430,239	$ 8,923,640	$ 8,306,112
Specific purpose funds (note 1)	436,000	350,141	323,622	418,153	328,632
	$11,042,068	$10,049,362	$ 9,753,861	$ 9,341,793	$ 8,634,744
	$18,287,442	$17,179,602	$16,608,254	$16,467,212	$15,500,552

The accompanying notes to financial statements are an integral part of this balance sheet.

Operating expenses:					
Departmental —					
Nursing services	$ 2,737,952	$ 2,988,529	$ 3,887,028	$ 4,587,785	$ 5,312,539
Professional services (laboratory, radiology, pharmacy, etc.)	2,079,890	2,325,083	3,067,043	3,826,887	4,346,838
General services (dietary, housekeeping, laundry and plant operation)	1,538,837	1,680,166	2,147,500	2,403,899	2,811,250
Administrative and fiscal services	776,731	873,210	1,118,464	1,310,047	1,581,511
Nursing education	182,200	202,307	234,587	246,409	279,775
Nondepartmental —					
Employee benefits (note 4)	487,881	584,460	689,019	981,667	1,129,654
Depreciation (note 1)	536,927	604,947	651,266	706,290	759,096
Interest	465,000	465,000	465,000	465,000	461,934
Vested vacation benefits (note 5)	—	151,360	18,271	169,632	63,958
Total operating expenses	$ 8,805,418	$ 9,875,062	$12,278,178	$14,697,616	$16,746,555
Net operating revenue	$ 378,901	$ 398,673	$ 262,360	$ 122,853	$ 728,511
Nonoperating revenue, primarily interest income	$ 48,057	$ 121,080	$ 101,548	$ 146,414	$ 144,960
Revenues over expenses	$ 426,958	$ 519,753	$ 363,908	$ 269,267	$ 873,471

The accompanying notes to financial statements are an integral part of this statement.

Exhibit H
Memorial Medical Center
Statement of changes in fund balances
For the years ended June 30, 1980, 1979, 1978, 1977 and 1976

	1980		1979		1978		1977		1976	
	General fund	Specific purpose funds	General fund	Specific purpose funds	General fund	Specific purpose funds	General fund	Specific purpose funds	General fund	Specific purpose funds
Balance, beginning of year	$ 9,699,221	$350,141	$9,430,239	$323,622	$8,923,640	$418,153	$8,306,112	$328,632	$7,880,990	$246,870
Revenues over expenses per accompanying statement	873,471	—	269,267	—	363,908	—	519,753	—	426,958	—
Contributions restricted for property additions	—	100,896	—	26,560	—	28,823	—	162,241	—	62,135
Investment income	—	6,134	—	4,675	—	7,449	—	10,858	—	5,554
Federal grant for student loans	—	15,000	—	9,812	—	13,316	—	20,036	—	16,524

Unrealized gain (loss) from changes in market value of investments	—	(631)	—	1,080	—	1,167	—	(2,840)	—	(771)
Transfers between funds — cash	33,376	(33,376)	204	(204)	142,691	(142,691)	97,775	(97,775)	—	1,836
Other	—	(2,164)	(489)	(15,404)	—	(2,595)	—	(2,999)	(1,836)	(3,516)
Balance, end of year	$10,606,068	$436,000	$9,699,221	$350,141	$9,430,239	$323,622	$8,923,640	$418,153	$8,306,112	$328,632

The accompanying notes to financial statements are an integral part of this statement.

Exhibit I
Memorial Medical Center
Statement of changes in financial position
For the years ended June 30, 1980, 1979, 1978, 1977 and 1976

	1980	1979	1978	1977	1976
Sources of funds:					
Provided from operations —					
Revenues over expenses per accompanying statement	$ 873,471	$ 269,267	$ 363,908	$ 519,753	$ 426,958
Noncash charge for depreciation	759,096	706,290	651,266	604,947	536,927
Additional Medicare reimbursement due to use of accelerated depreciation (note 1)	102,000	83,000	90,000	120,000	159,000
	$1,734,567	$1,058,557	$1,105,174	$1,244,700	$1,122,885
(Increase) decrease in board-designated funds	550,000	(250,000)	150,000	300,000	(950,000)
Transfers (to) from specific purpose funds	33,376	204	142,691	97,775	(1,836)
Real estate contract payable, net	98,763	—	—	—	—
Total sources of funds	$2,416,706	$ 808,761	$1,397,865	$1,642,475	$ 171,049

Uses of funds:

Purchases of plant and equipment, net	$1,258,084	$ 420,625	$ 351,986	$ 345,239	$ 223,752
Costs incurred in connection with construction of new facilities	506,865	92,401	326,876	1,010,093	—
Reduction in long-term portion of first mortgage bonds	261,327	248,837	149,221	149,456	133,518
Other	—	489	—	—	—
	$2,026,276	$ 762,352	$ 828,083	$1,504,788	$ 357,270
Net increase (decrease) in working capital (see summary below)	390,430	46,409	569,782	137,687	(186,221)
Total uses of funds	$2,416,706	$ 808,761	$1,397,865	$1,642,475.	$ 171,049

Summary of changes in working capital:

Increase (decrease) in current assets —

Cash	($ 361,201)	$ 137,976	$ 128,109	$ 623	$ 36,915
Accounts receivable, net	913,411	211,392	134,117	332,318	(99,282)
Estimated settlements receivable in connection with third-party reimbursement contracts	(85,834)	37,385	48,449	—	—
Inventories	42,071	36,537	44,908	58,868	19,356
Prepaid expenses	57,681	64,803	2,394	34,945	3,968
	$ 566,128	$ 488,093	$ 357,977	$ 426,754	($ 39,043)

Exhibit I (cont.)
Memorial Medical Center
Statement of changes in financial position
For the years ended June 30, 1980, 1979, 1978, 1977 and 1976

	1980	1979	1978	1977	1976
(Increase) decrease in current liabilities —					
Current portion of long-term debt	($ 15,168)	($ 74,400)	$ —	$ —	$ —
Accounts payable	(59,788)	(17,408)	(50,763)	(40,514)	(24,287)
Salaries, wages and accrued vacation payable	(112,608)	(228,529)	(82,800)	(162,250)	(35,206)
Payroll taxes withheld and accrued	(2,322)	(1,402)	(4,380)	42,256	(4,562)
Contract retainage payable	6,779	5,259	85,248	(97,286)	—
Accrued pension contribution payable	125,204	(125,204)	—	—	—
Advance payments under Medicare program	—	—	—	176,000	(25,896)
Estimated settlements payable in connection with third-party reimbursement contracts	(117,795)	—	264,500	(207,273)	(57,227)
	($ 175,698)	($ 441,684)	$ 211,805	($ 289,067)	($ 147,178)
Net increase (decrease) in working capital	$ 390,430	$ 46,409	$ 569,782	$ 137,687	($ 186,221)

The accompanying notes to financial statements are an integral part of this statement.

Memorial Medical Center notes to financial statements June 30, 1980, 1979, 1978, 1977 and 1976 (Exhibits F-I)

1. **Summary of significant accounting policies:**
   a. *Fund accounting.* The Medical Center records its activities using two funds, as follows:
      General fund. This fund is used to account for all medical center operations, including the plant and equipment, but excluding the specific purpose funds below.
      Specific purpose funds. These funds are restricted as to use and consist of United States Public Health Service student loan fund, building endowment fund and other specific purpose trust funds.

   b. *Depreciation.* For financial reporting purposes, depreciation is provided on the straight-line method using guidelines set forth by the American Hospital Association.

   c. *Deferred Medicare liability.* In determining allowable costs for Medicare purposes, the medical center computes depreciation on assets acquired pior to 1972 using an accelerated method while using the straight-line method for financial reporting purposes. The resulting additional Medicare reimbursement represents additional proceeded which will be offset in future years. This additional reimbursement has been reflected as a deferred liability in the accompanying balance sheet.

   d. *Contractual adjustments.* The medical center provides care to patients covered by various third-party reimbursement programs. Charges at normal billing rates for all patients are included in patient service revenues, and provisions (contractual adjustments) are made to reduce such charges to the estimated amounts to be realized as reimbursement to the medical center from the third parties.

   e. *Inventories.* Inventories are substantially valued at the lower of first-in, first-out cost or market.

   f. *Board-designated funds.* Periodically, the medical center's board of directors has designated cash resources not needed for the day-to-day operations of the medical center as funded depreciation. These funds are invested in appropriate income-producing investments and will be used to replace existing facilities, to expand facilities as necessary in the future and to continue the health services provided by the medical center.

2. **First mortgage bonds and proposed financing.** The first mortgage bond indenture provides, among other things, for the retirement of the balance of the outstanding bonds through the operation of a sinking fund. Annual deposits to the sinking fund vary from $213,000 in 1981 to $579,000 in 1994. The medical center is also required to maintain a reserve fund for early redemption of the bonds and for possible debt service requirements.

The medical center is currently planning to construct an addition to its present facilities. This project will provide additional space for revenue-producing departments and supportive services. Construction costs, excluding interest during construction, are estimated to be $13,000,000 and would be financed primarily through the issuance of hospital revenue bonds of approximately $21,750,000 in fiscal 1981. The proceeds from the issuance of the bonds in excess of estimated construction costs would be used to establish certain debt service reserves, pay costs of the financing and interest during construction and redeem the outstanding first mortgage bonds. In connection therewith, the medical center would be required to pay a call premium on the early retirement of the bonds of approximately $290,000 which would be recognized as a charge to operations, net of the third-party reimbursement benefit, in fiscal 1978.

The medical center would also be required to deposit the difference between $1,000,000 and the amount of the projected construction costs incurred at the date of delivery of the bond proceeds into a construction fund to be used for payment of construction costs.

3. **Line of credit.** The medical center has an established unsecured line of credit for $1,000,000 with a local bank. As of June 30, 1980, the medical center had not used any of this line of credit.

4. **Pension plan.** The medical center has a pension plan covering substantially all of its full-time employees. The cost to the medical center for current service costs and amortization of prior service costs was $390,699 in 1980, $337,604 in 1979, $163,200 in 1978, $163,200 in 1977 and $103,200 in 1976. As of the date of the most recent actuarial valuation, the vested benefits were not in excess of the fund's assets.

The Employee Retirement Income Security Act (ERISA) requires the medical center to amend its pension plan to conform with certain provisions of the Act, which became effective for plan years beginning after December 31, 1978. The most recent actuarial valuation indicates that the effect on annual pension costs and vested benefits resulting from this amendment will not be significant. Upon amendment of the plan, vested benefits will not exceed the value of the pension fund's assets.

5. **Vested vacation benefits.** Effective June 30, 1977, the medical center adopted a vacation policy to provide for vesting of vacation benefits on the employee's anniversary date. The effect of this change was to reduce revenues over expenses, as reflected in the accompanying statement of revenues for the year ended June 30, 1977, by approximately $86,000 net of the third-party reimbursement benefit.

   During the year ended June 30, 1979, the medical center amended its vacation policy to provide for current vesting of vacation benefits as the services are provided by the employees. The effect of this amendment was to reduce revenues over expenses by approximately $87,000 for the year ended June 30, 1979, net of the third-party reimbursement benefit.

6. **Pending litigation.** The medical center and others have been named as defendants in two related actions seeking damages for negligence. The amount claimed in these actions is approximately $4,700,000 for compensatory damages and $250,000 for punitive damages. It is the opinion of the medical center's legal counsel that the possibility of an award for damages against the medical center is these actions is remote. In addition, damages awarded, if any, would be well within the coverage provided by malpractice insurance, except that the claim for punitive damages may not be covered by the existing malpractice policy. However, in the opinion of the medical center's legal counsel, the claim for punitive damages is without merit.

7. **Professional liability insurance coverage.** During the year ended June 30, 1979, the medical center changed its professonal liability insurance coverage from a claims-incurred basis policy to a claims-made policy. Claims based on occurrences prior to the change are insured under the former policy. Should the present claims-made policy not be renewed or replaced with equivalent insurance, any claim based on occurrences during its term, but asserted subsequently, would be uninsured. However, the medical center's present claims-made policy provides an option to purchase an endorsement which would provide coverage for claims asserted subsequent to termination of the policy. The cost of this endorsement would be based on the prevailing rate in effect at that time.

10. The financial statements for Castile Laboratories, Inc., are given below:

CASTILE LABORATORIES, INC.
Balance Sheet
May 31, 19X4

Assets		
Current assets:		
Cash		$ 6,500
Accounts receivable, net		35,000
Inventory		70,000
Prepaid expenses		3,500
Total current assets		115,000
Property and equipment, net		185,000
Total assets		$300,000
Liabilities and Stockholders' Equity		
Liabilities:		
Current liabilities		$ 50,000
Bonds payable, 10%		80,000
Total liabilities		130,000
Stockholders' equity:		
Common stock, $5 par value	$ 30,000	
Retained earnings	140,000	
Total stockholders' equity		170,000
Total liabilities and equity		$300,000

CASTILE LABORATORIES, INC.
Income statement
For the Year Ended May 31, 19X4

Revenues	$420,000
Less cost of materials	292,500
Gross margin	127,500
Less operating expense	84,500
Net operating income	43,000
Interest expense	8,000
Net income before taxes	35,000
Income taxes (40%)	14,000
Net income	$ 21,000

Account balances on June 1, 19X3, were: accounts receivable, $25,000; and inventory, $60,000. All sales were on account.

Required:

Compute financial ratios as follows:
a. Current ratio.
b. Net working capital.
c. Debt-to-equity ratio.
d. Accounts receivable turnover in days.
e. Inventory turnover in days.
f. Times interest earned.
g. Asset turnover.
h. Net profit margin.

11. Comprehensive case problem

Background information

Memorial Hospital has been in operation for approximately 15 years. It has grown from a relatively small hospital operated by its founder to a large, general purpose, 420-bed hospital. It is the only hospital in a rural Colorado city of approximately 70,000 persons. The primary industry in town is agriculture, and a large state university is nearby.

There is very little turnover among the hospital staff, and all the key supervisors have at least five years of experience in their positions. The administrator, Bill Collins, has been with Memorial seven years. The chairman of the board of trustees is president of the largest bank in town and a prime contributor to hospital fund drives.

Recently the board of trustees have been complaining about the level of costs in the hospital. They have also indicated some displeasure at the recent 15 percent increase in room rates as well as the increases in charges for several other services offered by the hospital. At a recent meeting of the board, Bill Collins argued that Memorial's costs are no higher than costs in comparable hospitals in other communities. The board grudgingly accepted this explanation, but Collins knew he would have to come up with a more detailed cost analysis to satisfactorily answer the board's questions about cost increases.

Analysis of financial statements

Your goal is to analyze Memorial Hospital's most recent financial statements. *Exhibits 1 through 5* contain data for your analysis. The administrator has asked for the following information to be included in your analysis:

a. List your major findings.
b. Indicate areas of strength and areas of weakness.
c. Indicate where action or further investigation is required.
d. Wherever applicable, delineate methods of measurement or comparison.
e. State clearly any assumptions which you feel are necessary.

In your analysis of the problems at Memorial Hospital your analyses and recommendations may be broader than the areas covered by the case. What other hospital departments or activities would you recommend be studied? Why?

Exhibit 1
Financial statement information

1. Blue Cross pays billed charges rather than a per diem rate.

2. County welfare pays a negotiated per diem rate which at present is total cost less depreciation.

3. There is no outpatient clinic.

4. Supply prices are up approximately five percent from 19Y1.

5. A general salary increase, averaging four percent, went into effect January 1, 19Y2. At the same time, all room and nursery charges were raised $1.50 per day.

6. A new air conditioning system was completed early in 19Y2. Among the 19Y2 equipment purchases was an autoanalyzer for the laboratory. Equipment retirements for the year were nominal.

7. The three-year school of nursing earned its accreditation in March, 19Y2. One of the accreditation requirements was the reduction of student hours of service by approximately 10 percent and an increase in classroom hours.

8. There are no anesthetists on the hospital payroll.

9. The housekeeping department provides a checkout service upon discharge of patients. This service includes stripping the bed, washing the furniture, making the bed, cleaning the toilet and wet-mopping the floor.

10. An analysis of the increase in plant fund balance shows:
    a. Miscellaneous donations for equipment totaling $7,500 and
    b. interest earned on plant fund investments totaling $8,486.

11. Attached exhibits:
    a. Comparative balance sheets (Exhibit 14-9)
    b. Income statement (Exhibit 14-10)
    c. Miscellaneous statistics (Exhibit 14-11)
    d. Departmental reports (Exhibit 14-12)

Exhibit 2
Memorial Hospital
Comparative balance sheets
December 31, 19Y2 and 19Y1

	19Y2	19Y1	Increase (decrease) Amount	Percent
Unrestricted Fund				
Current assets:				
Cash on hand and in checking	$ 127,699	$ 198,333	$(70,634)	(35.6)%
Cash in savings	30,000	25,000	5,000	20.0
Accounts receivable —patients	1,087,792	959,744	128,048	13.3
Allowance for uncollectibles	(90,322)	(77,739)	(12,583)	16.2
Accounts receivable —other	10,400	15,128	(4,728)	(31.3)
Inventories—general stores	76,752	71,001	5,751	8.1
—drugs	69,106	65,878	3,228	4.9
Prepaid expenses	29,622	35,051	(5,429)	(15.5)
Total current assets	$1,341,049	$1,292,396	$ 48,653	3.8 %
Plant assets:				
Land and improvements	$ 120,540	$ 120,540	$ —	— %
Accumulated depreciation	(30,057)	(25,236)	(4,821)	19.1
Buildings	7,602,696	7,587,462	15,234	.2
Accumulated depreciation	(1,859,219)	(1,707,165)	(152,054)	8.9
Equipment	2,225,400	1,991,043	234,357	11.8
Accumulated depreciation	(987,928)	(875,976)	(111,952)	12.8
Cash	9,865	16,525	(6,660)	(40.3)
Investments	162,820	180,938	(18,118)	(10.0)
Total plant assets	$7,244,117	$7,288,131	$ (44,014)	(.6)%
Total unrestricted fund assets	$8,585,166	$8,580,527	$ 4,639	Neg.
Current liabilities:				
Accounts payable	$ 118,336	$ 126,265	$(7,929)	(6.3)%
Salaries and wages payable	113,811	99,240	14,571	14.7
Other current liabilities	32,523	31,122	1,401	4.5
Total current liabilities	$ 264,670	$ 256,627	$ 8,043	3.1 %
Mortgage payable	340,000	400,000	(60,000)	(15.0)
Total liabilities	$ 604,670	$ 656,627	$(51,957)	(7.9)%
Current fund balance	1,076,379	1,035,769	40,610	3.9
Plant fund balance	6,904,117	6,888,131	15,986	.2

Exhibit 2 (cont.)
Memorial Hospital
Comparative balance sheets
December 31, 19Y2 and 19Y1

	19Y2	19Y1	Increase (decrease) Amount	Percent
Total unrestricted fund liabilities and fund balances	$8,585,166	$8,580,527	$ 4,639	Neg.
Endowment Fund				
Cash	$ 22,017	$ 21,171	$ 846	4.0 %
Investments	86,624	86,624		
Total assets	$ 108,641	$ 107,795	$ 846	.8 %
Endowment fund balance (restricted)	$ 108,641	$ 107,795	$ 846	.8 %

Exhibit 3
Memorial Hospital
Income statement for years ended
December 31, 19Y2 and 19Y1

	19Y2	19Y1	Increase (decrease) Amount	Percent
Routine service—inpatients	$2,905,126	$2,633,744	$271,382	10.2 %
Revenue from ancillary services	2,751,087	2,679,361	71,726	2.6
Revenue from emergency room	95,370	94,333	1,037	1.1
Gross operating revenue	$5,751,583	$5,407,438	$344,145	6.4 %
Less adjustments and allowances	253,069	234,004	19,065	8.1
Net operating revenue	$5,498,514	$5,173,434	$325,080	6.3 %
Operating expenses				
Administration and general	$ 570,675	$ 525,196	$ 45,479	8.7 %
Dietary	510,618	475,535	35,083	7.4
Household and property	753,951	709,561	44,390	6.3
Nursing service	1,480,633	1,397,447	83,186	6.0
Emergency room	61,606	58,299	3,307	5.7
Other professional care	1,841,900	1,708,339	133,561	7.8
Depreciation	270,827	256,122	14,705	5.7
Total operating expenses	$5,490,210	$5,130,499	$359,711	7.0 %

Exhibit 3 (cont.)
Memorial Hospital
Income statement for years ended
December 31, 19Y2 and 19Y1

	19Y2	19Y1	Increase (decrease) Amount	Percent
Gain from operations	$ 8,304	$ 42,935	$ (34,631)	(80.7)%
Other revenue	50,805	47,234	3,571	7.6
Total	$ 59,109	$ 90,169	$ (31,060)	(34.4)%
Less interest expense	18,500	21,500	(3,000)	(14.0)
Net income	$ 40,609	$ 68,669	$ (28,060)	(40.9)%

Exhibit 4
Memorial Hospital
Miscellaneous statistics for years ended
December 31, 19Y2 and 19Y1

	19Y2	19Y1	Increase (decrease) Amount	Percent
Number of beds	420	420		
Number of bassinets	40	40		
Patient days				
—adults and children	136,437	133,371	3,066	2.3 %
—newborn	10,658	10,952	(294)	(2.7)
Discharges				
—adults and children	17,952	18,023	(71)	(.4)
—newborn	2,175	2,191	(16)	(.7)
Outpatient visits or procedures:				
Emergency room (visits)	21,096	20,885	211	1.0
Radiology (procedures)	28,071	26,372	1,699	6.4
Laboratory (procedures)	32,447	31,594	853	2.7
Others (visits)	4,561	4,433	128	2.9
Average daily census:				
Adults and children	374	365	9	2.5
Newborn	29	30	(1)	(3.3)
Total personnel	747	723	24	3.3
Total payroll	$3,128,692	$2,950,210	$178,482	6.0

Exhibit 5
Memorial Hospital
Departmental reports for years ended
December 31, 19Y2 and 19Y1

	19Y2	19Y1	Increase (decrease) Amount	Percent
Administration:				
Salaries	$ 252,850	$ 240,815	$ 12,035	5.0 %
Supplies, printing, postage	26,438	25,422	1,016	4.0
Telephone and telegraph	32,829	32,119	710	2.2
Dues and memberships	4,333	3,820	513	13.4
Institute and education	3,925	4,014	(89)	(2.2)
General insurance	15,235	12,625	2,610	20.7
Other	21,810	20,444	1,366	6.7
Total	$ 357,420	$ 339,259	$ 18,161	5.4 %
Employee benefits:				
Health insurance	$ 33,741	$ 32,727	$ 1,014	3.1 %
Life insurance	5,424	5,272	152	2.9
Retirement plan	25,664	25,285	379	1.5
FICA	128,405	103,575	24,830	24.0
Workmen's Compensation	9,586	8,860	726	8.2
Other	10,435	10,218	217	2.1
Total	$ 213,255	$ 185,937	$ 27,318	14.7 %
Personnel	56	56		
Dietary:				
Salaries	$ 209,223	$ 192,882	$ 16,341	8.5 %
Raw food	266,321	248,666	17,655	7.1
Other	35,074	33,987	1,087	3.2
Total	$ 510,618	$ 475,535	$ 35,083	7.4 %
Personnel	72	69	3	4.3 %
Meals served	395,667	373,438	22,229	6.0
Housekeeping:				
Salaries	$ 230,665	$ 221,142	$ 9,523	4.3 %
Supplies and other	43,964	41,831	2,133	5.1
Personnel	75	74	1	1.4
Laundry:				
Salaries	$ 101,901	$ 89,548	$ 12,353	13.8 %
Supplies and other	18,574	15,941	2,633	16.5
Personnel	36	33	3	9.1
Pounds of laundry processed	2,387,650	2,147,730	239,920	11.2
Linen service:				
Salaries	$ 7,339	$ 7,071	$ 268	3.8 %
Supplies and other	45,192	40,935	4,257	10.4
Personnel	3	3		

Exhibit 5 (cont.)
Memorial Hospital
Departmental reports for years ended
December 31, 19Y2 and 19Y1

	19Y2	19Y1	Increase (decrease) Amount	Percent
Supplies and other expense	129,631	118,602	11,029	9.3
Personnel	20	19	1	5.2
Diagnostic exams	42,398	40,690	1,708	4.2
Therapy treatments	15,197	14,543	654	4.5
Laboratories:				
Revenue	$ 558,082	$ 538,855	$ 19,227	3.6 %
Salaries	132,914	130,319	2,595	2.0
Professional fees	98,222	95,449	2,773	2.9
Supplies and expense	49,185	45,608	3,577	7.8
Personnel	27	28	(1)	(3.6)
Exams	243,704	237,760	5,944	2.5
Pharmacy:				
Revenue	$ 571,791	$ 558,390	$ 13,401	2.4 %
Salaries	46,768	44,121	2,647	6.0
Drugs	203,530	189,294	14,236	7.5
Other expense	1,088	1,056	32	3.0
Personnel	9	9		
Inhalation therapy:				
Revenue	$ 116,735	$ 112,788	$ 3,947	3.5 %
Salaries	31,640	30,134	1,506	5.0
Supplies and expense	20,454	18,939	1,515	8.0
Personnel	7	7		
Physical therapy:				
Revenue	$ 84,430	$ 82,658	$ 1,772	2.1 %
Salaries	43,678	41,401	2,277	5.5
Supplies and expense	2,355	2,252	103	4.6
Personnel	8	8		
Treatments	22,819	22,155	664	3.0
Central service:				
Salaries	$ 85,738	$ 78,746	$ 6,992	8.9 %
Supplies and expense	3,932	3,672	260	7.1
Personnel	24	23	1	4.3
Medical-surgical:				
Revenue—supplies	$ 141,012	$ 140,247	$ 765	.5 %
Revenue—IV solutions	113,204	110,298	2,906	2.6
Cost of supplies	90,953	82,460	8,493	10.3
Cost of IV solutions and supplies	60,225	55,972	4,253	7.6

Exhibit 5 (cont.)
Memorial Hospital
Departmental reports for years ended
December 31, 19Y2 and 19Y1

	19Y2	19Y1	Increase (decrease) Amount	Percent
Medical records:				
Salaries	$ 48,388	$ 46,172	$ 2,216	4.8 %
Supplies and expense	4,225	4,098	127	3.1
Personnel	12	12		
School of nursing:				
Salaries	$ 94,622	$ 83,902	$ 10,720	12.8 %
Supplies and expense	29,560	29,209	351	1.2
Personnel	16	15	1	6.7
Students	157	163	(6)	(3.7)
Nurses' residence:				
Salaries	$ 6,771	$ 6,492	$ 279	4.3 %
Supplies and expense	3,078	3,290	(212)	(6.4)
Personnel	2	2		

Exhibit 5 (cont.)
Memorial Hospital
Departmental reports for years ended
December 31, 19Y2 and 19Y1

	19Y2	19Y1	Increase (decrease) Amount	Percent
Plant operations and maintenance:				
Salaries	$ 97,675	$ 93,559	$ 4,116	4.4 %
Supplies	34,619	33,034	1,585	4.8
Fuel	39,280	40,122	(842)	(2.1)
Water and sewage	18,338	18,103	235	1.3
Electricity	63,018	57,186	5,832	10.2
Purchased services	43,537	41,307	2,230	5.4
Total	$ 296,467	$ 283,311	$ 13,156	4.6 %
Personnel	23	23		
Nursing service:				
Daily patient service revenue	$2,905,126	$2,633,744	$271,382	10.2 %
Salaries	1,305,277	1,236,058	69,219	5.6
Supplies and other expense	51,174	48,278	2,896	6.0
Personnel	281	270	11	4.1
Emergency room:				
Revenue	$ 95,370	$ 94,333	$ 1,037	1.1 %
Salaries	46,588	44,118	2,470	5.6
Supplies and other expense	15,017	14,181	836	5.9
Personnel	10	10		
Visits	21,096	20,885	211	1.0
Operating rooms:				
Revenue	$ 322,850	$ 320,285	$ 2,565	.8 %
Salaries	212,870	202,734	10,136	5.0
Supplies and other expense	83,228	77,206	6,022	7.8
Personnel	53	49	4	8.2
Operations	9,928	9,820	108	1.0
Delivery room:				
Revenue	$ 75,831	$ 76,182	$ (351)	(.5)%
Salaries	63,403	60,098	3,305	5.5
Supplies and other expense	9,521	9,094	427	4.7
Personnel	13	13		
Deliveries	2,198	2,213	(15)	(.7)
Anesthesia:				
Revenue	$ 97,167	$ 96,301	$ 866	.9 %
Supplies and other expense	42,916	40,602	2,314	5.7
Radiology:				
Revenue—diagnostic	$ 539,188	$ 517,952	$ 21,236	4.1 %
—therapy	130,797	125,405	5,392	4.3
Salaries	110,382	100,898	9,484	9.4
Professional fees	266,654	229,412	37,242	16.2

References

Altman, Edward, "Financial Ratios, Discriminant Analysis and the Predictions of Corporate Bankruptcy," *The Journal of Finance,* September, 1968, pp. 589-608.

Altman, Edward, "Predicting Railroad Bankruptcies in America," *Bell Journal of Economics and Management Science,* Spring, 1973, pp. 184-211.

Beaver, William, "Financial Ratios as Predictors of Failure," *Empirical Research in Accounting,* 1966, pp. 71-112.

Cannedy, Lloyd L., Dennis D. Pointer and Hirsch S. Ruchlin, "Viability and Hospital Failure: Methodological Considerations and Empirical Evidence." *Health Services Research,* Spring, 1973, pp. 27-35.

Choate, C. Marc, "Financial Ratio Analysis," *Hospital Progress,* January, 1974, pp. 49-57, 67.

Cleverley, William O., "Financial Flexibility: A Measure of Financial Position for Hospital Managers," *Hospital and Health Service Administration* Vol. 29, Number 1, Jan/Feb 1984, pp. 23-37.

Cleverley, William O., "How Hospitals Measure Liquidity: A Survey Report," *Healthcare Financial Management,* Nov. 1983, pp. 66-72.

Cleverley, William O., "Volunteer: Its Impact on Accounting Measures of Income and Return on Capital," *Healthcare Management Review,* Vol. 8, No. 2, Spring 1983, pp. 51-63.

Edmister, Robert O., "An Empirical Test of Financial Ratio Analysis for Small Business Failure Prediction," *Journal of Financial and Quantitative Analysis,* March, 1972, pp. 1147-1493.

Elam, Rick, "The Effect of Lease Data on the Predictive Ability of Financial Ratios," *Accounting Review,* Vol. 50, January, 1975, pp. 25-43.

Fitschen, Fred, "Look to Ratios to Measure Financial Health," *Hospital Financial Management,* November, 1976, pp. 45-48.

Neumann, Bruce R., "An Empirical Investigation of the Relationship Between an AID Hospital Classification Model and Accounting Measures of Performance," *Journal of Accounting Research,* Spring, 1979, pp. 123-139.

Snook, I. Donald and William B. Sindell, "Financial Ratio Analysis," *Hospital Financial Management,* June, 1975, pp. 16-19.

Weston, J. Fred and Eugene F. Bringham, *Managerial Finance,* Hinsdale, IL: Dryden Press, 1981.

CHAPTER 12

Capital investment decisions and relevant costs

Introduction

There is no more important factor in insuring the long run viability of a healthcare organization than its capital investment decision process. Capital investment decisions typically involve the investment of large sums of money for long periods of time. A poor capital investment process can lead the organization toward an over-investment in the wrong kind of facilities, a high fixed cost structure and an inability to react to changes in its environment.

It is becoming increasingly clear to healthcare decision-makers, both providers and regulators, that one of the best ways to control healthcare costs in the long run is to control capital investment decisions. The pass through of capital related costs such as interest and depreciation charges is under serious study by the federal government, American Hospital Association and Health Care Financial Management Association, to list a few. Congress has dictated that the capital component of healthcare costs will be included in the DRG rate no later than 1986. Numerous methodologies have been proposed, but there is currently no clear choice between the proposals. One thing seems to be clear; the amount of funding will be reduced in the future. This means healthcare managers must pay increasing attention to the evaluation of capital investment decisions.

What is a capital investment?

A capital investment is generally considered to be an expenditure that, under generally acceptable accounting principles, is not properly chargeable as an expense of the current year. In other words, the expenditure is expected to benefit more than one operating period.

Capital investment requirements should primarily flow from the institution's objectives. These objectives should be reflected in the healthcare facility's comprehensive (growth) plan, which should be based on such factors as community needs, the competitive market and technological advances. Within the general framework of the hospital objectives, most capital investment proposals will be initiated by individual department heads. Properly motivated supervisors are in the best position to identify and set priorities for their departmental needs.

The capital budgeting process

There will typically be more capital investment proposals submitted than there are available funds. Therefore, a formal review process that evaluates and ranks the proposals must be instituted. A formalized capital budgeting system is a necessity in most hospitals. Such a system should include a standardized set of worksheets to help in the identification and justification of financially feasible projects, an approval and review process, and a timetable for the submission, review and approval process.

The department supervisor should be able to request the help of qualified staff personnel in completing the forms. For example, the materials manager or purchasing agent can help in identifying the capabilities and relative costs of equipment alternatives. The maintenance engineer can assist in estimating modification and installation costs; the controller can help in preparing cost estimates and completing the evaluation process. The completed capital budgeting documents should represent the best expert advice available to assist in evaluating the proposal.

A framework for analysis

There will always be both qualitative and quantitative aspects in the analysis of capital investment proposals. The first and most important will be qualitative issues. Such factors as quality of care, improved employee morale and other intangible benefits are decided on subjective grounds. However, most proposals also have a quantitative side. It is the analysis of the quantitative factors that is beginning to play a more important role in the evaluation of capital projects. Every capital investment proposal should require information on five quantitative factors:

1. the cash outflows
2. the cash inflows
3. the economic life
4. the opportunity cost for hospital funds
5. the impact of taxation and/or cost-based reimbursement

Graphically, some of these factors are diagrammed, for a single project, in *Exhibit 12-1*. Similar graphs or diagrams for alternative projects can be used to represent other alternative opportunities. The relative impact of taxation or cost-based reimbursement must be reflected in the cash flow patterns.

Exhibit 12-1
The capital investment framework

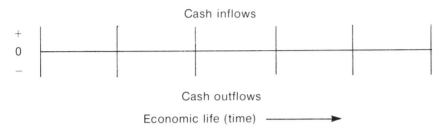

Cash inflows

Cash outflows

Economic life (time) ⟶

Each of these critical decision variables is explained in greater detail in this chapter. The cash outflows include the amount of cash required to acquire or initiate the investment proposal. They should include the purchase cost, installation costs and any other out-of-pocket costs that are associated with this decision. They should also include the cash outflows required to operate and maintain the project.

The cash inflows consist of the incremental revenues or expense reductions (on a cash basis) associated with the capital project. They also include the effects of reimbursement. Periodic cash inflows are often netted against periodic cash outflows; only the net difference each year needs to be entered into the subsequent analysis.

The economic life of the proposal should be consistent with the cash outflows and inflows. The economic life can be defined as the period of time the hospital is expected to receive the benefits and/or incur the costs. It should not be confused with the physical life of the project or the depreciation period established by the Internal Revenue Service or third-party payers. However, either of these two periods may set the upper limit on how long the project will continue.

Opportunity cost refers to the benefits received from the next best alternative use of the investment funds. Some healthcare organizations use the interest rate on invested funds or a weighted average cost of available funds (the cost of capital concept). The cost of capital concept will be discussed in detail later in this chapter. Basically, no matter what technique is used, it is, in the end, a subjective estimate by management of what rate to use.

In the case of proprietary hospitals, the tax rate will affect any benefits realized from the investment proposal. In similar fashion, the percentage of cost-based reimbursement will also affect the net effect of any operating benefit from the investment proposal. The shift to a prospective rate will eliminate this surrogate tax approach to many non-profit healthcare providers.

Methods of analysis

Once estimates have been made of the major factors discussed above, the evaluation process can begin. There are two problems in evaluating capital investment decisions. The first is a screening problem: does the investment meet the minimum return on investment criterion of the organization? The second is a problem of ranking; given the number of investment proposals, how do we set priorities for them? This is particularly sensitive when there are more projects than the available funds can support (capital rationing).

Several evaluation or analytical techniques are currently in use. They are:

1. the accounting rate of return (sometimes called the unadjusted rate of return)
2. the payback method
3. the net present value method
4. the time adjusted rate of return (sometimes called the internal rate of return)

Each of these techniques has different strengths and weaknesses and should be thoroughly understood if it is to be used effectively.

The accounting rate of return was used extensively in the past because it relies on information that normally appears in financial statements. The net income of the project (as reported in the statement of revenue and expenses) is divided by either the total or average book investment required for the project. The resulting rate of return is compared with the desired rate of return to decide whether to accept the investment. This technique, although easy to understand and compute, has a serious conceptual weakness. It does not consider the time value of money in assuming that a dollar at some point in the future is considered to represent the same economic value as a dollar today. The accounting rate of return can be computed by using the formula in *Exhibit 12-2*.

The payback method refers to the amount of time it takes to recover the initial cash outflow for the investment from future cash inflows. This method is quite easy to compute and understand, but it has two major weaknesses: it ignores the time value of money and disregards the cash inflows after the payback period is completed.

$$\frac{\text{Initial cash outflow}}{\text{Average annual cash inflow}} = \frac{O_{t_0}}{I_a} = \text{payback period (years)}$$

Exhibit 12-2
Accounting rate of return

$$\frac{\text{Average annual increase in income}}{\text{Initial investment required to obtain the increase in income}^*} \ \bigg| = \frac{I_a}{O_{t_o}} = \text{accounting rate of return}$$

*Alternatively, the average investment may be used in the denominator. The average investment would be calculated by summing the net investments in the project (at year-end) and dividing by the number of years.

Note that both the first two methods ignore the time value of money. That is, dollars at different points in time are treated equally. This can be particularly troublesome in the capital investment process when cash outflows occur early in the investment time frame and the cash inflows occur later. The time value of money attempts to correct this deficiency by using discounting techniques to put all future cash flows on an equivalent basis.

Discounting may be more easily understood if we first consider the compounding of interest techniques with which most individuals are familiar. Interest is computed on the principal for the given time period and then added to the principal on which interest will be computed for the next time period. For example, $10,000 at 10 percent per year would earn $1,000 the first year. This $11,000 ($10,000 + $1,000) would earn $1,100 the second year, so the total value would be $12,100 at the end of the second year. To test your understanding of the concept, calculate how much you would have at the end of the fourth year. This can be computed using the normal compound interest formula of $(1 + i)^n$ where n equals the period of time and i equals the interest rate paid by the savings and loan company. For managers who do not want to actually compute this formula, tables are available which solve the compounding equation. The most frequently used tables are included in Appendix 12-1. *Exhibit 12-3* presents the solution to the above problem.

Exhibit 12-3
Compounding of a single sum

Amount of investment today	$10,000
Future value of $10,000 in 4 years at 10 percent	
(Future value factors from Appendix 1, Table 3	1.464
Future value	$14,640

The relationship of compounding to discounting can be illustrated in the following manner. Assume that hospital management wanted to replace a piece of equipment in four years that will cost $14,641. How much should be invested today to realize $14,641 in four years? In this case, we are interested in the present value of a future sum. This problem is the complement of the first problem where the financial manager wanted to know the future value of a present sum. The formula for computing the present value of the future sum is:

$$\frac{1}{(1 + i)^n}$$

The present value formula is the reciprocal of the compounding formula. Tables have also been constructed to facilitate this type of computation and are included in Appendix 12-1. *Exhibit 12-4* illustrates the solution to this type of problem.

The relationship between compounding and discounting should now be clear. The same relationship exists for any type of problem where annual sums are to be invested or received. For example, consider the data in *Exhibit 12-5*. Instead of a $10,000 initial investment, plan on investing $2,500 a year for each of the next four years. How much will be in the savings account if 10 percent is earned on the investment?

Exhibit 12-4
Present value of future amount

Amount needed at the end of the 4th year	$14,641
Present value factor 10 percent, 4 years	
(Present value factor from Appendix 1, Table 1)	.683
Present amount that must be invested today	$10,000

Exhibit 12-5
Future value of an annuity

Amount invested each year for 4 years	$ 2,500
Compounding factor 10 percent, 4 years	
(Future value factor from Appendix 12-1, Table 4)	4.641
Future value of savings account, 4 years	$11,603

To consider a similar problem involving the concept of a present value, determine how much would be paid *today* for the right to receive $2,500 a year for four years, assuming the opportunity cost of any comparable investment is 10 percent (*Exhibit 12-6*).

In other words, *Exhibit 12-6* indicates that the right to receive $2,500 a year for four years in the future is worth $7,925 if the return from an alternate, but comparable, investment is 10 percent. Since the present value concept is the most appropriate technique that can be used to evaluate capital investments, we will focus attention on the present value technique for the remainder of this chapter.

Exhibit 12-6
Present value of an annuity

Amount to be received for 4 years	$2,500
Discount factor 10 percent, 4 years	
(Present value factor from Appendix 12-1, Table 2)	3.17
Present value of $2,500 each year for 4 years	$7,925

Given the preceding discussion of the time value of money, we can continue our development of discounted cash flow analysis of capital investments. The net present value and the time adjusted rate of return techniques are both discounted cash flow methods. The net present value approach to evaluating capital investment decisions computes the difference between the discounted cash outflows and the discounted cash inflows of the decision. This amount can be either negative or positive. A positive net present value indicates that the investment return is financially feasible because the investment meets the desired or criterion discount rate. A negative net present value indicates the opposite. *Exhibit 12-7* illustrates a sample problem. Given the cash inflows and outflows for the project in *Exhibit 12-7,* this capital investment returns less than 15 percent.

Exhibit 12-7
Net present value technique
Project data

Initial cash outflows	$20,000
Annual cash inflows for 10 years	$ 3,500
Opportunity cost for hospital	15%

Year	Cash	Amount	×	Factor	=	Present value
0	Outflows	$20,000	×	1.0	=	$20,000
1-10	Inflows	3,500	×	5.018	=	17,563
	Net present value (inflows − outflows = $I_{pv} - O_{pv}$) =					($ 2,437)

Exhibit 12-8
Net present value technique

Year	Cash	Amount	×	Factor	=	Present value
0	Outflows	$20,000	×	1.0	=	$20,000
1-10	Inflows	4,500	×	5.018	=	22,581
Net present value (inflows − outflows = $I_{pv} - O_{pv}$)					=	$ 2,581

Assume the cash inflows can be increased to $4,500 per year for the project in *Exhibit 12-7*: what happens to the net present value? *Exhibit 12-8* shows that with the cash inflows increased to $4,500, the project now returns more than 15 percent.

An alternative discounted cash flow method (to the net present value method) is the time adjusted rate of return. This method is conceptually very similar, except that it calculates the actual rate of return for each capital investment project. Based on the preceding discussion, we can identify the actual rate of return to be the rate of return at which the net present value is zero. This computation is shown in *Exhibit 12-9.*

Exhibit 12-9
Computation of time adjusted rate of return

Year	Cash	Amount	×	Factor	=	Present value
0	Outflows	$20,000	×	1.0	=	$20,000
1-10	Inflows	3,500	×	??*	=	20,000
				Net present value	=	$ 0

*?? equals 20,000 ÷ 3,500, or 5.714.

We need to solve for the factor that will equate the future cash inflows to a present value of $20,000. This can be accomplished by dividing the initial investment ($20,000) by the future cash inflow ($3,500 per year) so that 20,000 ÷ 3,500 = 5.714. Using this calculated factor, we enter Table 2 in Appendix 1 on the 10-year row and proceed across the row until we reach the factor nearest to 5.714. Reading from the column heading, we can obtain the approximate rate of return for this proposal—12 percent. This 12 percent is the annual yield on the project. It is also called the internal rate of return. Caution: note that the assumption used here is that each annual yield is equal.

Using the revised cash inflows of $4,500 (*Exhibit 12-8*), we obtain an estimated factor of 4.44 = $20,000 ÷ $4,500. This equates to an internal rate of return of approximately 18 percent as shown in *Exhibit 12-10.*

Exhibit 12-10
Selected present value factors

	10%	15%	18%	20%
10 years	6.144	5.018	4.494	4.192

Both the net present value method and the time adjusted rate of return method incorporate the time value of money concept. Both are effective as screening techniques when the required (target) rate of return is known. However, when ranking of priorities becomes the major problem, the time adjusted rate of return becomes the more commonly used method. This is primarily due to the fact that decision-makers find it easier to rank investments according to a rate of return criterion. Ranking by net present values will usually result in equivalent rankings, but it is not as well understood and is not used as much.

If the net present value amount is to be used as a ranking criterion, it typically is converted into a profitability index which incorporates investment base (cash outflows) and the present value of the cash inflows. This technique is demonstrated in *Exhibit 12-11*. Capital investments with the highest profitability indexes reflect more desirable investments from a discounted cash flow point of view.

Exhibit 12-11
Profitability index*

$$\frac{(\text{Present value of cash inflows})}{(\text{Present value of cash outflows})} = \frac{I_{pv}}{O_{pv}} = \text{profitability index}$$

*Only valid for mutually exclusive projects

Sample problem

Let's assume a hospital administrator is confronted with two capital investment proposals and only one can be accepted. *Exhibit 12-12* describes each project.

Exhibit 12-12
Two competing capital investments projects

New radiology equipment	Project A	Project B
Cost including installation	$60,000	$55,000
Estimated additional revenue and cost savings	$15,000/year	$13,000/year
Estimated economic life	5 years	5 years

The authorized depreciation method is straight-line for both proposals, and the controller estimates the opportunity cost for alternative investments at 16 percent. Using the four methods of analysis discussed in the preceding section, the results obtained in *Exhibit 12-13* can be calculated.

Each of the evaluating methods ranked Project A as best. Therefore, as ranking devices, each was successful. However, if we were concerned with screening the proposals, we would have to establish our criteria for the accept/reject decision. This is typically done by establishing a criterion equal to the opportunity cost concept at the minimum desired rate of return. The rate was stated as 16 percent in the sample problem. Clearly, neither Project A nor Project B was close to this rate of return. The 16 percent rate of return may be too high for a typical hospital. Therefore,

Exhibit 12-13
Four capital investment methods for sample problem

Accounting rate of return

Project A		Project B
$15,000	*Additional income*	$13,000

$$\frac{12,000}{\$\ 3,000} = (\frac{60,000}{5})$$ *Depreciation expenses* $$(\frac{55,000}{5}) = \frac{11,000}{\$\ 2,000}$$

Change in net income based on total investment

$$\frac{3,000}{60,000} = .05 \qquad\qquad \frac{2,000}{55,000} = .036$$

Based on average investment

$$\frac{3,000}{30,000} = .10 \qquad\qquad \frac{2,000}{27,500} = .072$$

Payback computations

$$\frac{60,000}{15,000} = 4 \text{ years} \qquad\qquad \frac{55,000}{13,000} = 4.23$$

Net present value

Project	Year	Amount	Factor			Present value
A	0	60,000	×	1.0	=	(60,000)
	1–5	15,000	×	3.274	=	49,110
			Net present value		=	(10,890)
			Profitability index			$\frac{49,110}{60,000}$ = .82
B	0	55,000	×	1.0	=	(55,000)
	1–5	13,000	×	3.274	=	42,562
			Net present value		=	(12,438)
			Profitability index			$\frac{42,562}{55,000}$ = .77

Time adjusted rate of return

Project	Year	Amount	Factor			
A	0	60,000	×	1.0	=	60,000
	1–5	15,000	×	4.0	=	60,000
			Net present value		=	0
			Rate of return		=	8%
B	0	55,000	×	1.0	=	55,000
	1–5	13,000	×	4.23	=	55,000
			Net present value		=	0
			Rate of return		=	6%

each organization must establish its own cutoff rate, or hurdle rate, as it is sometimes called. In the next section, we develop some methods designed to help establish the hurdle rate.

Cost of capital concept

Several approaches have been used to establish the discount rates or hurdle rates for capital investment decisions. One approach is to have a group of high level managers subjectively establish a rate. Another method is to establish the hurdle rate at the same amount as is earned on current investments in savings accounts or securities.

Although the latter method approaches the opportunity cost concept, it does not allow for the fact that funds for investment come from various sources, including debt, donations, grants and retained earnings from prior periods. A conceptual approach to resolving this issue is called the cost of capital. The cost of capital approach is well accepted in business finance, and the reader is encouraged to review standard finance texts for a more in-depth understanding.[1]

Basically, the cost of capital for any organization is considered to be the weighted average cost of all funds used, or expected to be used. The concept is easy to comprehend, but determining the actual figures is exceedingly difficult. To do so, the financial manager must make the following estimates for the healthcare organization:

1. *An optimum financial structure for the future financial viability of the hospital.* Capital structure identifies the various sources of funds and how much of each should be obtained. It also affects the costs of acquiring capital funds from each source. For example, an administrator may decide that 40 percent is the maximum amount of funding that can come from debt sources. The remaining 60 percent must come from other sources available to the hospital. The financial structure would appear as: debt—40 percent and other sources—60 percent. This would mean that a hospital with $20,000,000 of total capital funds would need $8,000,000 in debt funds and $12,000,000 from other sources. Ideally, this is based on the forecasted capital structure and not on the historical composition ratios. An alternative approach is to use the current structure, but base the relative proportions on their market values.

2. *The cost of the various sources.* The cost of debt poses no particular problem, since this would be the average interest rate

---

[1]J. Fred Weston and Eugene F. Brigham, *Managerial Finance,* 5th ed., Hinsdale, IL: Dryden Press, 1981, Chapter 16.

on the debt. It must also include expected future interest costs of any new debt funds included in the optimal capital structure. The impact of cost-based reimbursement for interest payments will be covered later. The much more difficult task is estimating the cost of the other sources of capital funds. Some hospital administrators consider these other sources, such as donations and retained earnings, to be free. However, it would seem logical that there is at least an opportunity cost equal to the amount that could be earned in savings accounts or U.S. Treasury securities. If a market-based financial structure is used, costs of the sources should reflect the current .rates. Once the estimated costs are computed, the entire framework (Step 3) can be completed.

3.

Weighted average cost of capital			
Capital source	*Optimum fraction*	*Average cost*	*Weighted cost*
Debt	.40	8%	.032
Other sources	.60	9%	.054
Total weighted average cost			.086 = 8.6%

The computation in Step 3 would indicate that the hospital should earn an average return of 8.6% on all its investments. If it accomplishes this goal, it will recover the average cost of the debt sources of funds. This is verified in *Exhibit 12-14.*

Exhibit 12-14
Reconciliation of the cost capital

Average assets	$20,000,000
Average return	.086
Annual return	$ 1,720,000

This return would be allocated in the following manner, to each source of capital funds:

Debt	$ 8,000,000 × .08	$ 640,000
Other sources	12,000,000 × .09 =	1,080,000
	Dollar return	$1,720,000

The weighted average cost of capital requires that the financing decision, where the funds come from, should be separated from how the capital funds are used. Although it may be possible to obtain 100 percent debt financing for some proposals, this high proportion of debt is feasible only because equity or other sources of capital are used for other projects. It should be clear that using all debt capital for one project will require that some other project must obtain all of its financing from other sources.

Unless the distinction between sources of capital and uses of capital is maintained, capital investment decisions will not hinge on the relative merits of each proposal, but rather on the type of financing available. When cheap funds are available, poor projects may be accepted. In the worst case, the institution could end up in a position where all available debt funds have been committed and no further debt is available for essential projects.

Impact of cost-based reimbursement

The cost-based payment mechanisms of the third-party payers have had a major impact on the capital investment process. Depreciation and most interest payments are reimbursable, which adds to the cash flow of the project. However, in a manner similar to tax mechanisms, third-party payers also share in any cost savings that occur through the investment process. The pending switch to a prospectively determinant reimbursement rate will meliorate many of the problems of the past. It should be recognized, however, that the cost based mentality still influences decisions.

Lease versus buy decisions

In many capital investment decisions, the administrator is confronted with the choice of leasing the equipment instead of purchasing it. If equipment is purchased, depreciation is a reimbursable cost, as are the associated interest payments. If equipment is leased (in the case of an operating lease), the entire lease payment can become a reimbursable cost.[2] The net present value analysis of the lease/buy financing decision is shown in *Exhibit 12-15*. This analysis assumes that the equipment has already been justified. The analysis in *Exhibit 12-15* only addresses the question of which source of financing is most attractive. The decision whether to acquire the equipment must be based on the relative benefits and costs, excluding financing costs of the equipment.[3] The lease/buy decision is merely the selection of the cheapest form of financing available for an otherwise acceptable project.

The analysis in *Exhibit 12-15* would indicate that the lease, as a source

---

[2]Financial Accounting Standards: Pronouncement as of July 1, 1978. FASB Statement No. 13, Financial Accounting Standards Board, High Ridge Park, Stamford, CT 06905, pp. 868-869.

[3]In the evaluation of financing decisions, the cost of capital criterion must shift to the rate associated with the most favorable financing available. For example, the rate of interest on currently available debt financing must be used as the criterion rate for evaluating alternative financing options.

Exhibit 12-15
Net present value of lease versus buy financial decision (with no salvage or residual values)

Assume $60,000 purchase cost with a 5 year economic life

Cost of Capital = 15%
Debt interest rate = 10%
Lease payments $18,000 per year
Depreciation and interest reimbursement included in prospective rate

OPTION 1: lease the equipment
lease payments $18,000 for 5 years at beginning of each year.

NPV of lease payment	
year 1 (payment at beginning of year)	$18,000
year 2-5 $18,000 × 2.855 (factor 15%, 4 years)	$51,390
Total NPV of lease payment	$69,390

OPTION 2: purchase equipment from plant fund for $60,000

NPV of purchase (payment at beginning of year 1) $60,000

OPTION 3: Purchase equipment with chattel mortgage, one-third down, level principal payment of $10,000 plus interest for 4 years.

NPV
YEAR			
1	20% down payment beginning of year	=	$20,000
1	first year principal payment 10,000 × .869	=	8,690
1	first year interest (10% × 49,000) × .869	=	3,476
2	second year principal 10,000 × .756	=	7,560
2	second year interest (10% × 30,000) × .756	=	2,268
3	third year principal 10,000 × .657	=	6,570
3	third year interest (10% × 20,000) × 657	=	1,314
4	fourth year principal 10,000 × .571	=	5,710
4	fourth year interest (10% × 10,000) × .571	=	571
	NPV of borrowing		$56,159

of financing, is the most expensive. All other factors being equal, under these conditions, the lease would be selected.

Relevant cost concept

Relevant costs are costs that influence the decision being made. For example, costs are the same between two alternatives, they are not relevant to the decision being made. Relevant costs are sometimes called incremental costs or out-of-pocket costs. All of these concepts refer to the changes in cash flow which will occur from choosing one decision over another.

Relevant costs are particularly important in capital investment decisions. Costs such as salvage value, investment tax credit allowances, overhauls, installation costs, etc., must be included in the decision analysis. They are relevant because they will have an impact on future cash flows. All of these factors can be included in the basic framework presented earlier in this chapter.

Summary

Capital investment decisions are a vital part of the management function in healthcare organizations. Only by properly evaluating alternative proposals and selecting those that meet the qualitative and quantitative objectives of the hospital will the administrator maximize the quality of healthcare provided.

Questions and problems

1. Define a capital investment decision for a healthcare organization.

2. Define the capital screening problem.

3. Define the capital ranking problem.

4. What five factors must be considered in the capital budgeting process?

5. Define the cash inflows for a healthcare investment decision.

6. Define the cash outflows for a healthcare investment decision.

7. What is the cost of capital concept as it pertains to a healthcare organization?

8. Name and explain the four quantitative methods for evaluating capital investment decisions.

9. The board of trustees has decided that Memorial Trust Hospital must have a computer if it is to render the best possible service. The only decision facing the board is whether to purchase or rent. The useful life of the computer is estimated to be 10 years. Because of the newness of this type of machine and its complexities, it is essential that a factory maintenance and inspection contract be in effect. Such a contract costs $200 per year. However, this contract is included in the rental fee. The alternative actions are:

Rental (includes maintenance and inspection)	
1st year	$5,000
2nd year	5,000
3rd year	4,000
4th year	4,000
5th year	3,000
6th year	3,000
7th year	2,000
8th year	2,000
9th year	1,000
10th year	1,000

The annual rent can be paid in 12 equal monthly installments.
Purchase. Because of lack of sufficient funds, it will be necessary to purchase the computer on an extended payment basis. The best terms that can be arranged are:
Down payment—$5,600.
Each year thereafter—$1,600 for 9 years.
Interest at the rate of 6 percent on the unpaid balance must be added to the principal payments.

Required:

Prepare a schedule which compares the effect on operating expenses and on cash requirements under the rental plan with the effect under the purchase plan for each of the 10 years of the computer's life. The hospital uses straight-line depreciation. In this case, the rate would be 20 percent. Indicate comparative cost under rental and purchase method. Both the lease and the purchase options would be treated the same for reimbursement purposes. The administrator would also like to know which of the options would be best for the long-range financial condition of the hospital. The cost of capital for the hospital has been estimated at 10 percent by the controller.

10. Compute the net present value of the following capital investment decisions. (Assume a 15 percent discount factor.)

Cash outflow	Cash inflows by year			
	1	2	3	4
(A) (2,000)	1,150	0	1,150	0
(B) (2,000)	1,150	0	0	1,150
(C) (2,000)	0	1,150	1,150	0

11. Compute the internal rate of return for each of the following independent investments.

Cash outflow	Cash inflows by year			
	1	2	3	4
(A) (3,000)	1,575	0	1,735	
(B) (3,000)	1,500	1,780	0	
(C) (3,000)	0	1,700	1,690	

12. Community Hospital is considering the purchase of a new piece of diagnostic equipment costing $100,000 for its nuclear medicine laboratory. It is anticipated that the new asset will bring an incremental increase in cash flow of $35,000 for each of the next four years. At the end of the four years the machine will be obsolete and discarded. The opportunity cost of funds for Community has been computed to be 15 percent. Ignore taxes and the impact of cost-based reimbursement.

Required:

Compute the:
a. payback period
b. accountant's rate of return
c. net present value of the investment
d. internal rate of return

13. Using the data from Problem 12, assume that 60 percent of patient care is reimbursed on the basis of costs which include straight-line depreciation. Compute the following:
a. payback period
b. accountant's rate of return
c. net present value of the investment
d. internal rate of return

14. The Central City Medical Center has recently learned of a new gamma computer which can be purchased for $60,000 cash. This new

computer can be added to the camera the center now owns for an additional cost of $40,000. This adaptation will not affect the remaining four-year useful life of the camera or its estimated salvage value of $10,000. Variable costs of using the equipment would increase by 10 cents per test.

The current income statement for the camera operation is:

Revenues (100,000 tests at $4)		$400,000
Variable costs	$180,000	
Fixed costs*	120,000	
Total costs		$300,000
Excess of revenues over expenses		
before taxes		100,000
Income taxes		40,000
Net revenue after taxes		$ 60,000

*All fixed costs are directly allowable to the processing of the tests and include depreciation on equipment of $20,000 calculated on a straight-line basis of 10 years.

Market research has disclosed three important findings relating to the new computer. First, the local nonprofit hospital will certainly purchase the computer if the center does not. If this were to happen, the medical center's demand for tests would fall to 70,000 per year. Second, if no increase in the selling price is made, Central City Medical Center could expect to accomplish 90,000 additional tests with the new computer. Third, it is anticipated that because of rapid technology changes in the area, the new computer will be obsolete at the end of four years.

Required:

Prepare a schedule which shows the after-tax cash flows for the two alternatives. Assume that the Central City Medical Center will use the sum-of-the-years digits method for depreciating the costs of the computer.

Using present value techniques, should Central City buy the new computer? Assume the cost of capital is 20 percent and there are no cost-based payers for this test.

15. The Rocky Mountain Institute is a nonprofit healthcare organization which engages in research projects to advance medical science. It is entirely supported by donation and earnings on endowment funds. The director is confronted with the purchase of a small scientific

computer which costs $800,000 and will reduce administrative costs by $150,000 per year. The computer will cost $20,000 per year to operate and will last 10 years before it is obsolete.

Required:
a. What rate of return is earned by the computer?
b. It may be possible to use some endowment earnings to buy the computer which have been invested in 15 percent securities. Would it be better to buy the computer outright and use $20,000 per year for the operating costs or to make annual withdrawals of $170,000 for the 10 years?

16. Rainbow Pharmacy is investigating the purchase of a new drug dispensing machine that is capable of dispensing several different types of medication/drugs at one time. The machine costs $20,000. It will have an eight-year useful life and a $2,000 scrap value. The machine falls in the 5-year property class. The company will use straight-line depreciation. The following annual operating results are expected if the machine is purchased:

Increase in annual revenues		$14,000
Increase in expenses:		
Cash operating expenses	$7,000	
Depreciation	4,000	11,000
Net income before taxes		3,000
Income taxes (30%)		900
Net income		$ 2,100

Rainbow Pharmacy expects an after-tax return of 18 percent on all equipment purchases.

Required:
a. What is the after-tax payback period on the new machine? If the company has a required payback period of three years or less, should the machine be purchased?
b. What is the after-tax simple rate of return on the new machine? Is it an acceptable investment?
c. The president is uneasy about the results obtained by the simple rate of return, and would like some further analysis done.
   1. What is the net annual cash inflow before taxes promised by the new machine?

2. Using discounted cash flow, determine whether the machine will provide the minimum 18 percent after-tax return required by the company.
3. Compute the new machine's internal rate of return.

17. The Sweetwater Clinic would like to buy a new machine that would automatically "dip" film as it is taken in the development process. The "dipping" operation is presently done largely by hand. The machine the company is considering costs $115,000 new. It would last the company 12 years but would require a $4,500 overhaul at the end of the 7th year. After 12 years, the machine could be sold for $8,000.

The company estimates that it will cost $12,000 per year to operate the new machine. The present method of developing costs $30,000 per year. In addition to reducing operating costs, the new machine will increase output by 6,000 films per year. The company realizes a contribution margin of $1.50 per film. The company requires a 20 percent return on all investments.

Required:
a. What are the annual cash inflows that will be provided by the new dipping machine?
b. Compute the new machine's net present value.
c. Compute the internal rate of return for the machine.

18. On Jan. 1, 1984 Belleview Hospital purchased a new machine for $200,000 with an estimated useful life of five years and no salvage value. The straight line method of depreciation will be used for both book and tax purposes. The machine is expected to produce annual cash flows from operations, before income taxes, of $40,000. Belleview uses a time adjusted rate of 12% and assumes its income tax rate is 40% for all years. What is the net present value of the machine?

19. Jackson Clinic purchased new x-ray equipment on July 1, 1984. The cost of the equipment was $150,000 and is to be depreciated, using the straight line method, over 5 years with a salvage value of $10,000. The equipment is expected to produce cash flow from operations of $42,500 in each of the next 5 years. Assume a full years depreciation is taken in the year of purchase. What is the payback period?

20. Southside Hospital is considering the purchase of new emergency room equipment. The cost of the equipment is $450,000 and will be depreciated over 6 years using the straight line method. Assume a full

years depreciation in the year of acquisition. It is expected that the equipment will produce cash flows (net of income taxes) of $112,500 a year over the next six years. What is the accounting rate of return on the initial investment?

21. Woodside Nursing Homes purchased heart monitor equipment which will be depreciated on the straight line method over 7 years. The equipment is expected to generate cash flows of $95,000 in each of the following seven years. Assuming a negative net present value of $16,860, what is the cost of the equipment?

22. Marcus Hospital purchased equipment for $950,000 with a useful life of 8 years and no salvage value. Expected cash flows from the equipment are estimated at $200,000 while the equipment is being depreciated on the straight line method. Assume Marcus uses a time adjusted rate of return of 12%. Ignoring income taxes, what is the net present value?

23. Greendale Hospital currently owns ventilation equipment that was purchased three years ago for $85,000. The equipment has a remaining useful life of six years, however, it will require a major overhaul at the end of three more years of life at a cost of $15,000. The disposal value is currently $25,000 and in six years its disposal value is expected to be $12,000, assuming the $15,000 major overhaul is done on schedule. Cash operating costs of the equipment are expected to be $45,000 annually.

   The hospital has recently been approached by a local electrical contractor offering to sell the hospital new ventilation equipment. The new equipment will cost $64,000 or $44,000 plus the old equipment. The new machine will reduce operating costs by $15,000 annually, will have a useful life of 6 years, will have a salvage value of $3000 (after 6 years) and will not require any major overhauls.

   Assuming a required rate of return of 12%, determine which alternative should be chosen using the net present value method.

References

Chae, Young M., James D. Suver and David Chou, "Goal Programming as a Capital Investment Tool for Teaching Hospitals," *Healthcare Management Review,* Vol. 10, Number 1, Winter 1985, pp. 27-35.

Cleverley, William O. and Joseph G. Filkner, "Capital Budgeting Techniques," *Healthcare Management Review,* Vol. 9, Number 3, 1984, pp. 45-55.

Fitz, Thomas E., Jr., "Debt Capacity Analysis is Critical to Planning," *Healthcare Financial Management* Jan. 1983, pp. 52-58.

Horwitz, Ronald M., "Accounting Management Impact of FASB 13," *Hospital Financial Management,* August, 1979, pp. 16-20.

Long, Hugh W. and J.B. Silvers, "Medicare Reimbursement is Federal Taxation of Tax-Exempt Providers," *Healthcare Management Review,* Winter, 1976, pp. 9-23.

Magee, John F., "How to Use Decision Trees in Capital Investment," *Harvard Business Review,* September-October, 1964, pp. 79-96.

Neumann, Bruce R. and Joyce V. Kelly, "The Three Components of a Prospective Capital Reimbursement System," *Healthcare Financial Management* July 1984, pp. 92-100.

Oszustowicz, Richard J., "A Capital Equipment Acquisition Process," *Healthcare Financial Management* April, 1982, pp. 12-33.

Shaul, Roger L., Jr. and Curtis P. McLaughlin, "A Second Look at Leasing," *Healthcare Management Review,* Spring, 1977, pp. 55-63.

Vraciu, Robert A., "Three Rules for Selecting Capital Financing Options," *Healthcare Financial Management* April, 1980, pp. 38-46.

Weston, J. Fred and Eugene F. Brigham, *Managerial Finance,* Hinsdale: Dryden Press, 1981.

Wacht, Richard F. and David T. Whitford, "A Goal Programming Model for Capital Investment Analysis in Nonprofit Hospitals," *Financial Management,* Summer, 1976, pp. 37-45.

Zimmerman, Martin E., "Accounting for Leases," *Hospital Financial Management,* June, 1979, pp. 26-29.

Present value and compound interest tables

Table 1
Present value of $1:

$$P_{n,i} = \frac{1}{(1+i)^n}$$

n	Rate of interest, i%										
	1.0	1.5	2.0	5.0	6.0	8.0	10.0	15.0	20.0	25.0	30.0
1	.990	.985	.980	.952	.943	.925	.909	.869	.833	.800	.769
2	.980	.970	.961	.907	.890	.857	.826	.756	.694	.640	.592
3	.970	.956	.942	.863	.839	.793	.751	.657	.578	.512	.455
4	.961	.942	.923	.822	.792	.735	.683	.571	.482	.409	.350
5	.951	.928	.905	.783	.747	.680	.620	.497	.401	.327	.269
6	.942	.914	.888	.746	.705	.630	.564	.432	.334	.262	.207
7	.932	.901	.870	.710	.665	.583	.513	.375	.279	.209	.159
8	.923	.887	.853	.676	.627	.540	.466	.326	.232	.167	.123
9	.914	.874	.836	.644	.591	.500	.424	.284	.193	.134	.094
10	.905	.861	.820	.613	.558	.463	.385	.247	.161	.107	.073

11	.056	.085	.134	.214	.350	.428	.526	.584	.804	.848	.896
12	.043	.068	.112	.186	.318	.397	.497	.556	.788	.836	.887
13	.033	.055	.093	.162	.289	.367	.468	.530	.773	.824	.878
14	.025	.044	.077	.141	.263	.340	.442	.505	.757	.811	.870
15	.020	.035	.064	.122	.239	.315	.417	.481	.743	.799	.861
16	.015	.028	.051	.106	.217	.291	.393	.458	.728	.788	.852
17	.012	.022	.045	.092	.197	.270	.371	.436	.714	.776	.844
18	.009	.018	.037	.080	.179	.250	.350	.415	.700	.764	.836
19	.007	.014	.031	.070	.163	.231	.330	.395	.686	.753	.827
20	.005	.011	.026	.061	.148	.214	.311	.376	.673	.742	.819
21	.004	.009	.021	.053	.135	.198	.294	.358	.659	.731	.811
22	.003	.007	.018	.046	.122	.183	.277	.341	.646	.720	.803
23	.002	.005	.015	.040	.111	.170	.261	.325	.634	.710	.795
24	.002	.004	.012	.034	.101	.157	.247	.310	.621	.699	.787
25	.001	.003	.010	.030	.092	.146	.233	.295	.609	.689	.779
26	.001	.003	.008	.026	.083	.135	.219	.281	.597	.679	.772
27	.001	.002	.007	.023	.076	.125	.207	.267	.585	.669	.764
28	.001	.001	.006	.020	.069	.115	.195	.255	.574	.659	.756
29	.001	.001	.005	.017	.063	.107	.184	.242	.563	.649	.749
30	.000	.001	.004	.015	.057	.099	.174	.231	.552	.639	.741
35	.001	.000	.001	.007	.035	.067	.130	.181	.500	.593	.705
40	.000	.000	.000	.003	.022	.046	.097	.142	.452	.551	.671
45	.000	.000	.000	.001	.013	.031	.072	.111	.410	.511	.639
50	.000	.000	.000	.000	.008	.021	.054	.087	.371	.475	.608

Table 2
Present value of an annuity of $1 per period:

$$P_{n,i} = \frac{1 - \left[\frac{1}{(1+i)n}\right]}{i}$$

Rate of interest, %

n	1.0	1.5	2.0	5.0	6.0	8.0	10.0	15.0	20.0	25.0	30.0
1	.990	.985	.980	.952	.943	.925	.909	.869	.833	.800	.769
2	1.970	1.955	1.941	1.859	1.833	1.783	1.735	1.625	1.527	1.440	1.361
3	2.911	2.912	2.883	2.723	2.673	2.577	2.486	2.283	2.106	1.952	1.816
4	3.902	3.854	3.807	3.546	3.465	3.312	3.169	2.855	2.588	2.361	2.166
5	4.853	4.782	4.713	4.329	4.212	3.992	3.796	3.352	2.990	2.689	2.436
6	5.795	5.697	5.601	5.075	4.917	4.622	4.355	3.784	3.325	2.951	2.643
7	6.728	6.598	6.472	5.786	5.582	5.206	4.868	4.160	3.604	3.161	2.802
8	7.651	7.485	7.325	6.463	6.209	5.746	5.334	4.487	3.837	3.328	2.925
9	8.566	8.360	8.162	7.107	6.801	6.246	5.759	4.771	4.031	3.463	3.019
10	9.471	9.222	8.982	7.721	7.360	6.710	6.144	5.018	4.192	3.570	3.092
11	10.367	10.071	9.786	8.306	7.886	7.139	6.495	5.233	4.327	3.656	3.147
12	11.255	10.907	10.575	8.863	8.383	7.536	6.813	5.420	4.439	3.725	3.190
13	12.133	11.731	11.348	9.393	8.852	7.903	7.103	5.583	4.532	3.780	3.223
14	13.003	12.543	12.106	9.898	9.295	8.244	7.366	5.724	4.610	3.824	3.249
15	13.865	13.343	12.849	10.379	9.712	8.559	7.606	5.847	4.675	3.859	3.268

16	14.717	14.131	13.577	10.837	10.105	8.851	7.823	5.951	4.729	3.887	3.283
17	15.562	14.907	14.291	11.274	10.477	9.121	8.021	6.047	4.774	3.090	3.295
18	16.398	15.672	14.992	11.689	10.827	9.371	8.201	6.128	4.812	3.927	3.304
19	17.226	16.426	15.678	12.085	11.158	9.603	8.361	6.198	4.843	3.942	3.311
20	18.015	17.168	16.351	12.462	11.469	9.818	8.513	6.259	4.869	3.953	3.316
21	18.857	17.900	17.011	12.821	11.764	10.016	8.648	6.312	4.891	3.963	3.320
22	19.660	18.620	17.658	13.163	12.041	10.200	8.771	6.358	4.909	3.970	3.323
23	20.455	19.330	18.292	13.488	12.303	10.371	8.883	6.398	4.924	3.976	3.325
24	21.243	20.030	18.913	13.798	12.550	10.528	8.984	6.433	4.937	3.981	3.327
25	22.023	20.719	19.523	14.093	12.783	10.674	9.077	6.464	4.947	3.984	3.328
26	22.795	21.398	20.121	14.375	13.003	10.810	9.160	6.490	4.956	3.987	3.330
27	23.559	22.067	20.706	14.643	13.210	10.935	9.237	6.513	4.963	3.990	3.330
28	24.316	22.726	21.281	14.898	13.406	11.051	9.306	6.533	4.969	3.992	3.330
29	25.065	23.376	21.844	15.141	13.590	11.158	9.369	6.550	4.974	3.933	3.331
30	25.807	24.015	22.396	15.372	13.764	11.257	9.426	6.566	4.978	3.995	3.331
35	29.408	27.075	24.998	16.374	14.498	11.651	9.614	6.616	4.991	3.998	3.331
40	32.834	29.915	27.355	17.159	15.046	11.924	9.779	6.641	4.996	3.999	3.331
45	36.094	32.552	29.490	17.774	15.455	12.108	9.862	6.654	4.998	3.999	3.331
50	39.196	34.999	31.423	18.255	15.761	12.233	9.914	6.660	4.999	3.999	3.331

Table 3
Compounded amount of $1 :
$A_{n,i} = (1 = i)^n$

Rate of interest, $i\%$

n	1.0	1.5	2.0	3.0	4.0	6.0	8.0	10.0
1	1.010	1.015	1.020	1.030	1.040	1.060	1.080	1.100
2	1.020	1.030	1.040	1.060	1.081	1.123	1.166	1.210
3	1.030	1.045	1.061	1.092	1.124	1.191	1.259	1.331
4	1.040	1.061	1.082	1.125	1.169	1.262	1.360	1.464
5	1.051	1.077	1.104	1.159	1.216	1.338	1.469	1.610
6	1.061	1.093	1.126	1.194	1.265	1.418	1.586	1.771
7	1.072	1.109	1.148	1.229	1.315	1.503	1.713	1.948
8	1.082	1.126	1.171	1.266	1.368	1.593	1.850	2.143
9	1.093	1.143	1.195	1.304	1.423	1.689	1.999	2.357
10	1.104	1.160	1.219	1.343	1.480	1.790	2.158	2.593

11	1.115	1.177	1.243	1.384	1.539	1.898	2.331	2.853
12	1.126	1.195	1.268	1.425	1.601	2.012	2.518	3.138
13	1.138	1.213	1.293	1.468	1.665	2.132	2.719	3.452
14	1.149	1.231	1.319	1.512	1.731	2.260	2.937	3.797
15	1.161	1.250	1.345	1.558	1.800	2.396	3.172	4.177
16	1.172	1.269	1.372	1.604	1.873	2.540	3.425	4.595
17	1.184	1.288	1.400	1.652	1.947	2.692	3.700	5.054
18	1.196	1.307	1.428	1.702	2.025	2.854	3.996	5.559
19	1.208	1.327	1.456	1.753	2.106	3.025	4.315	6.115
20	1.220	1.346	1.485	1.806	2.191	3.207	4.661	6.727
21	1.232	1.367	1.515	1.860	2.278	3.399	5.033	7.400
30	1.347	1.563	1.811	2.427	3.243	5.743	10.062	17.449
40	1.488	1.814	2.208	3.262	4.801	10.285	21.724	45.259

Table 4
Compounded amount of an annuity of $1 per period:

$$A_{n,i} = \frac{(1+i)^n - 1}{i}$$

Rate of interest, i%

n	1.0	1.5	2.0	3.0	4.0	6.0	8.0	10.0
1	1.000	1.000	1.000	1.000	1.000	1.000	1.000	1.000
2	2.010	2.015	2.020	2.030	2.040	2.060	2.080	2.100
3	3.030	3.045	3.060	3.090	3.121	3.183	3.246	3.310
4	4.060	4.090	4.121	4.183	4.246	4.374	4.506	4.641
5	5.101	5.152	5.204	5.309	5.416	5.637	5.866	6.105
6	6.152	6.229	6.308	6.468	6.633	6.975	7.335	7.715
7	7.213	7.323	7.434	7.662	7.898	8.393	8.922	9.487
8	8.285	8.432	8.583	8.892	9.214	9.897	10.636	11.435
9	9.368	9.559	9.754	10.159	10.582	11.491	12.487	13.579
10	10.462	10.702	10.949	11.463	12.006	13.180	14.486	15.937
11	11.566	11.863	12.168	12.807	13.486	14.971	16.645	18.531
12	12.682	13.041	13.412	14.192	15.025	16.869	18.977	21.381
13	13.809	14.236	14.680	15.617	16.626	18.882	21.495	24.522
14	14.947	15.450	15.973	17.086	18.291	21.015	24.214	27.975
15	16.096	16.682	17.293	18.598	20.023	23.276	27.152	31.772

16	17.257	17.932	18.639	20.156	21.824	25.672	30.324	35.949
17	18.430	19.201	20.012	21.761	23.697	28.212	33.750	40.544
18	19.614	20.489	21.412	23.414	25.645	30.905	37.450	45.599
19	20.810	21.796	22.840	25.116	27.671	33.760	41.446	51.159
20	22.019	23.123	24.297	26.870	29.778	36.785	45.762	57.275
21	23.239	24.470	25.783	28.676	31.969	39.992	50.422	64.002
22	24.471	25.837	27.299	30.536	34.248	43.392	55.456	71.402
23	25.716	27.225	28.845	32.452	36.617	46.995	60.893	79.543
24	26.973	28.633	30.421	34.426	39.082	50.815	66.764	88.497
25	28.243	30.063	32.030	36.459	41.645	54.864	73.105	98.347
26	29.525	31.514	33.670	38.553	44.311	59.156	79.954	109.181
27	30.820	32.986	35.344	40.709	47.084	63.705	87.350	121.099
28	32.129	34.481	37.051	42.930	49.967	68.528	95.338	134.208
29	33.450	35.998	38.792	45.218	52.966	73.639	103.965	148.630
30	34.784	37.538	40.568	47.575	56.084	79.058	113.283	164.494
35	41.660	45.592	49.994	60.462	73.652	111.434	172.316	271.024
40	48.886	54.267	60.402	75.401	95.025	154.762	259.056	442.592
45	56.481	63.614	71.892	92.719	121.029	212.743	386.505	718.904
50	64.463	73.682	84.579	112.796	152.667	290.335	573.770	1163.908

APPENDIX 12-2

Cost of capital*

Increasingly, hospitals see debt as an almost costless source of capital. With interest charges reimbursed by third party cost-based payers, the net cost of an eight percent loan under 100 percent cost-based reimbursement can be reduced to zero for the hospital.

Yet this notion is misleading. It fails to consider all the consequences of large amounts of debt—such as restricting management action.

Most organizations, including hospitals, have upper limits to their debt capacity. This means that once the debt limits are reached, the cost of debt may skyrocket or, at the extreme, lenders may no longer loan funds. This could mean that some necessary projects could not be funded only because they were approved after the debt capacity was reached and additional debt funding was not available. In this case, the failure to include future costs (opportunity costs) in the original capital budgeting decision may understate the true cost of capital funds.

This section suggests a method for determining more realistic costs of capital in healthcare institutions. Current practice requires a subjective estimate of the cost of retained earnings; here we develop a much more realistic cost of capital rate using a return on asset criterion. We maintain that a viable financial position must be a major objective of any healthcare organization. Failing to correctly consider the impact of short-run factors on capital investment decisions can lead to a deterioration in healthcare services, to a reduction in quality or even to bankruptcy. Unless the long-run nature of the cost of the various sources of capital financing is made explicit, future capital needs may be extremely costly or impossible to obtain.

The concept of cost of capital

The concept of cost of capital is a useful managerial tool. The cost of capital to a hospital can be defined as the cost of obtaining and using

*Reprinted with permission of Hospital Financial Management Association from *Hospital Financial Management,* February 1978. ©1978.

capital funds for operating and capital expenditures. It can also be viewed as the target return that investors or the community would like to receive on their investment in the hospital. For example, if the average cost of obtaining funds from all sources is eight percent and the hospital earns eight percent on its assets, then the community's expectations are realized. This overly-simplified example ignores many real-world issues such as quality of care, uncertainty and risk. But the cost of capital concept will help hospital financial managers to better cope with community expectations. It allows for the inclusion of debt capacity and other capital costs in the capital budgeting decision process. The remainder of this article will focus on developing the concept in greater detail.

The profit sector has developed and used the "optimum financial structure" to minimize the cost of obtaining capital from various sources. It has not been used to any great extent in the healthcare environment. Basically, this concept means determining the types of funding sources available to the institution, the relative proportion of each source in the

Table 1
Sources of capital available to institutional providers by ownership status

source of capital	nonprofit	for-profit	government
retained earnings	yes	yes	yes
equity	no	yes	no
philanthropy	yes	no	yes
grants	yes	no	yes
taxes	no	no	yes
loans	yes	yes	yes
taxable bond	yes	yes	no
revenue bond (exempt)	yes	no	yes
general obligation bond (exempt)	no	no	yes

Table 2
Cost of capital worksheet for XYZ Hospital

capital source	relative amount from each source	cost of each source	weighted cost
debt	50%	_____	_____
fund balances: retained earnings	30%	_____	_____
donations	10%	_____	_____
grants	10%	_____	_____
	100%	average cost of capital	_____

total capital structure, and the cost of obtaining funds from each source. *Table 1* summarizes the sources of capital financing available to most hospitals.

The average cost of capital depends on the proportion of various types of capital funds and their respective costs. It is important to recognize that *every* source of capital funds has some cost. This cost is determined by the outlays made by the hospital to obtain the capital funds. It is also affected by the alternative opportunities that range from available but unpurchased equipment, to other kinds of investments that may be made. *Table 2* illustrates a worksheet that might be used to compute the cost of capital for a typical hospital.

Determining the capital structure

Although determining the optimum financial structure is subjective at best, it is a decision that all managers make, either by conscious effort or by default. It should be stressed that the decision must be forward-looking, based on the best available evidence as to the financial conditions confronting the hospital. In the future, such things as debt capacity are determined by predicted cash flows, the credit rating of the organization, and the financial community's support of the hospital. On the other side of the question is the new requirement for funds. Most of this data should be contained in the three-year budget or other long range planning documents.

The cost of capital approach isolates financial decisions from the individual capital project. For example, it might be possible to borrow 90 percent of the funds needed for a specific project. However, typically the fact that the hospital is able to borrow at such a high level is due to the earning power of the assets already owned by the institution. It is very difficult to find a lender who will furnish a high percentage of funds for a specific investment without some commitment of resources from the borrower and a proper earning/repayment record in the past. The increasing reliance on commercial debt sources will only serve to make the earning record of the institution even more important in future financial transactions. (The worksheet in *Table 2* assumes a 50 percent split between long-term debt and equity sources of capital. This mix of capital will continue to be used in the examples throughout this paper, but it should be realized that each hospital must determine its own optimum mix depending on the factors listed above.)

How to determine capital costs

There are several ways to measure capital costs. This section suggests one, but hospital financial managers are encouraged to explore other alternatives. The cost of debt can usually be measured objectively.

Current interest rates may be used to provide estimates of future interest rates. Investment bankers may be consulted for advice. It is important to note that it is expected *future* interest costs that should be used in calculating the cost of capital.

If the hospital anticipates no major changes in its debt structure, risk or interest costs then the current interest costs may be used to compute the cost of debt capital. However, interest costs are extremely sensitive to the debt capacity of the hospital and to the relative amounts of cost-based reimbursement. If the hospital is near its level of debt capacity, expected interest costs should be adjusted to reflect higher interest rates in the future. The hospital could try to estimate this cost directly, or an expedient adjustment could be used. For example, if the hospital is above or anticipates moving above its debt capacity, a simple adjustment would be just to *double* the expected interest costs. This doubling would reflect a penalty cost associated with operating beyond the normal debt capacity level.

The relationship of interest costs to reimbursement levels must also be considered because the effective cost of interest is much lower to a hospital that is being reimbursed for interest costs. To illustrate these computations, assume that this cost includes all types of available financing such as bank loans, mortgage bonds, tax exempt revenue bonds, etc. Because interest cost is a reimbursable expense, the presence of third party payers will influence the determination of the effective interest costs. *Table 3* shows the effect of cost-based reimbursement under several levels of reimbursements.

The data in *Table 3* assume no significant timing differences between the payment of interest and reimbursement of interest costs from third parties. Under advance funding arrangements, it does not appear that this should be a significant factor. It is clear that the net effect of third party payers is to make debt a very low cost option for securing funds. The use of this "net of reimbursement effect" can lead to the misleading decision that debt has no cost, but as discussed earlier this does not reflect reality.

Table 3
Effect of cost-based reimbursement on the effective interest cost

% of cost-based reimbursement	0%	40%	80%	100%
amounts of debt	$1,000,000	$1,000,000	$1,000,000	$1,000,000
interest rate (8%)	80,000	80,000	80,000	80,000
less reimbursement	—0—	32,000	64,000	80,000
net cost to hospital	80,000*	48,000	16,000	—0—
	8%	4.8%	1.6%	—0—

For this reason, another approach could be used to estimate the cost of debt. The actual interest rate would be used on the cost of capital work sheet and the reimbursed interest charges would be considered as an inflow of funds during the investment analysis. In this respect, it could be included with the reimbursable depreciation charges and used to determine the return on investment for the specific decisions. All capital investments would be credited for the following cash flows:

- excess of revenues over expenses reimbursed
- depreciation expense
- reimbursed interest expense

The use of this method would stress the interest cost of debt and be particularly useful in evaluating cost saving investments in which the revenues are decreased by the amount of the cost savings. We will use this concept, but either method will provide a useful cost of capital rate if used consistently in the investment decision.

The next step in the process is to estimate the opportunity cost of fund balances. Determining these opportunity costs requires subjective estimates by the hospital financial manager. One approach is to assign a cost to the fund balances based on what could be earned through investing the funds in bonds or stocks. For example, current returns on these kinds of investment would yield 5-10 percent. This would be the minimum possible return at the minimum level of risk.

Our opinion is that there are higher opportunity costs than the bond investment rates in most hospitals. The theory of business finance suggests that the institution must really search out the "next best alternatives" to construct the cost of capital for equity fund balances. For example, if the hospital is able to measure the true benefits of its projects it may find that the total return ratios are in the neighborhood of 20-30 percent. This requires quantifying the benefits of each project to the community and comparing such benefits to the total costs of each project.

Since most hospitals do not have the time nor the inclination to go through the process of determining total costs and benefits for each project, we suggest an alternative approach to determining the cost of equity fund balances. The cost of obtaining funds from donations and grants could be estimated by taking the average yield on tax-free municipal bonds, currently around eight percent. To recognize the fact that administrative costs average 10-20 percent of each fund drive, an adjustment factor of 1 or 2 percent could be added to the bond yield, making the cost of obtaining funds through donations and grants approximately 9-10 percent. (Ten percent will be used in examples here and the amounts of donations and grants in the cost of capital computation will be shown net of the administrative and fund raising costs.)

The basic opportunity cost for retained earnings could be considered the rate that could be earned by investing the funds externally. This would be approximately the eight percent discussed for fund drives. Another method would be to assign to the retained earnings the opportunity cost for internally-generated investments. This could approximate the 20-30 percent discussed earlier. Regardless of the method used, the key concept is that retained earnings, similar to other sources of capital, has a cost and it must be included in determining an average cost of capital to the hospital.

To illustrate how the cost of capital computations would be made, a worksheet similar to *Table 4* could be used.

Table 4
Cost of capital worksheet
for XYZ Hospital

capital source	relative amount from each source	×	cost of each source	=	weighted cost
debt	50%		8.0%		4.0%
fund balances:					
retained earnings	30%		30.0%		9.0%
donations	10%		10.0%		1.0%
grants	10%		10.0%		1.0%
	100%		average cost of capital		15.0%

This resulting total of 15 percent is the weighted average cost of capital. It is also the target rate of return or the criterion that can be used to evaluate alternative capital investment proposals. For example, a hospital with $10 million in capital funds (debt plus fund balances) must receive $1.5 million in cash flows in order to meet its long-run target rate of return. The 15 percent can be also used as an investment criterion so that an optional project can be required to yield operating savings or cash flows in excess of 15 percent each year. Projects that do not yield 15 percent can be recognized as projects that must be jusitified on other factors rather than return on investment.

Illustrating the use of cost of capital

To test this concept, let us work the following example. The computations in *Table 5* indicate that a return on total assets of approximately 15 percent would cover the required costs of each source of capital. These costs were:

debt	8.0%
retained earnings	30.0%
donations	10.0%
grants	10.0%

The approximate total amounts in each category for a hospital with $10,000,000 in total assets would be:

debt	50% (10,000,000)	$ 5,000,000
retained earnings	30% (10,000,000)	3,000,000
donations	10% (10,000,000)	1,000,000
grants	10% (10,000,000)	1,000,000
	total assets	$10,000,000

If our cash flows from net operating income, reimbursable charges from depreciation and interest expense equal 15 percent on total assets of $10,000,000, we would have $1,500,000 in funds. These earnings would be divided in this manner:

debt	5,000,000 × 8.0% =	$ 400,000
retained earnings	3,000,000 × 30% =	900,000
donations	1,000,000 × 10% =	100,000
grants	1,000,000 × 10% =	100,000
		$1,500,000

The $1,500,000 in cash flow would just equal the expected costs of each source of capital. If we were to use the 15 percent as a cut-off rate for all investments, we would just cover the required rate of return on all assets and costs of the various sources of capital.

Cost of capital evaluation

Another way to evaluate whether the calculated cost of capital is reasonable is to adopt an external standard. For example, Hugh Long suggests that the minimum cost of capital for hospitals should be in the 10-15 percent range *(Table 5)*. He justifies this rate by adding the cost of several external factors to develop an average rate of return. The average return (4.5 percent after taxes) on the equity of all US industries for a 40-year period is then added to the basic rate to obtain a target rate of return of about 14.5 percent.

By working backwards through *Table 6,* the weighted cost of retained earnings is computed at 8.5% (14.5% − 4.0% −1.0% −1.0%). Dividing through (8.5% ÷ 30.0%), the estimated cost of retained earnings is calculated to be 28 percent. This is approximately the same as the 30 percent cited above for the sample computation. If these two figures are

Table 5
Required rate of return on total assets*

basic factor	estimated required rate of return on assets
inflation	5.5%
technology	2.0%
expansion of existing services	1.0%
alternatives of services	1.0%
recession, economic controls	0.5%
subtotal	10.0%
average rate of return or equity for major U.S. industries (past 40 years)	4.5%
	14.5% average required rate of return on assets

*Long, Hugh W. "Valuation as a criterion for not-for-profit decision making," *Health Care Management Review*, Summer 1976, pp. 34–46.

Table 6
Hypothesized determination of cost capital on retained earnings

capital source	relative amount of each source	cost	weighted cost
debt	50	8.0%	4.0%
fund balances:			
retained earnings	30%	28.0%	8.5%
donations	10%	20.0%	1.0%
grants	10%	20.0%	1.0%
	100%	Cost of capital	14.5%

reasonably close, the hospital financial manager has some assurance that realistic expectations are embodied in the estimated cost of capital.

Summary

This section stresses the need for calculating a realistic rate of return on hospital assets. How many boards of directors or hospital administrators consider 15 percent as the required return on hospital assets? Evidence indicates that even half of this amount is somehow considered unethical.

Failing to consider the total capital costs of hospitals will ultimately lead to a reduction in the quantity or quality of medical care. Plant and equipment must eventually be replaced, new technology must be exploited if quality of care is to be maintained and improved.

The techniques suggested in this article are easy to apply. They should be recognized as approximations to the actual costs (obtaining more accurate data may cost more than the benefits received).

If hospitals are to remain financially viable, more consideration must be given to what is the proper return on hospital assets.

Regression analysis of cost behavior patterns

Introduction

In Chapter 3 we introduced the concept of statistical analysis of cost behavior patterns. This chapter extends that discussion through an extensive presentation of regression analysis. All the caveats and preliminary steps discussed in Chapter 3 also apply to regression analysis. Simple and multiple regression analyses represent the most typical statistical approaches to the identification of cost behavior patterns. Correlation analysis, discriminant analysis, cluster analysis and principal components analysis are beyond the scope of this text. Chapter 13 describes both manual and computerized regression calculations. It discusses the assumptions that must be met in order to use regression analysis. Finally, the last sections of this chapter present an actual regression analysis of cost behavior patterns for a group of eight hospitals.

Least squares calculations

Assuming that the manager or analyst has used the techniques described in Chapter 3 to identify any possible errors or inconsistencies in the data base, and assuming that a linear cost behavior relationship is to be tested, the next step is to use the least squares mathematical computations to obtain the coefficients of the line that best fits the observed data. The coefficients describe the computed cost behavior equation. The least squares method assures an objective, unbiased fit, and the calculations are relatively simple and straightforward. The least squares method will provide the information necessary to construct a univariate (one dependent variable) cost behavior equation of the form:

$$y = a + bx,$$
where y = criterion (dependent) variable
x = predictor (independent) variable
a = intercept
b = slope or variable cost

Assume that the departmental manager wants to investigate the relationship between supply costs and manhours. The data for eight payroll periods are displayed and plotted in *Exhibit 13-1*. The scatter diagram in *Exhibit 13-1* illustrates how the "a" and "b" coefficients of an approximate linear relationship can be interpreted. These coefficients are approximate because the line was obtained by the visual fit method. Consequently, it may be biased, and there is no measure of error. The analyst or manager who wants to identify a more precise relationship would use the least squares method to obtain the best available cost behavior equation. Note that each of the data points in *Exhibit 13-1* is paired, and this association must be maintained throughout the calculation.

Exhibit 13-1
Departmental supply costs and manhours

Period	Supply costs (y)	Manhours (x)
1	$3,500	1,000
2	4,500	1,200
3	4,000	1,100
4	4,800	1,350
5	3,200	950
6	5,100	1,500
7	4,700	1,300
8	4,400	1,150

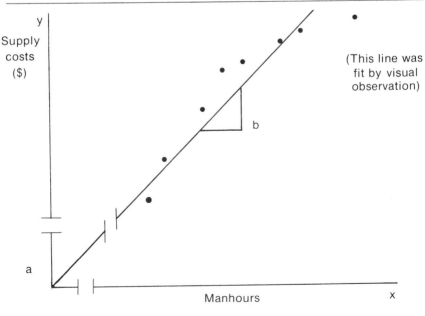

The least squares technique will result in a line that is the smallest (squared) distance from all the data points. The least squares (smallest squared distance) criterion has several desirable mathematical properties. *Exhibit 13-2* illustrates the final least squares regression line superimposed on the data points, and the regression line is minimized. No other linear relationship would result in a smaller sum of squared deviations. Note that these are the vertical deviations relative to the horizontal axis; they are not the deviations perpendicular to the regression line. The fact that these are the vertical deviations and that the regression line represents the best fit, statistically, will provide measures of the relative goodness of the fit and how much error is associated with the predicted costs. In other words, the least squares calculations result in desirable statistical properties that permit comparison with other alternative cost behavior equations. They also will provide an estimate of the potential error so that the manager can determine how much confidence to place in the cost predictions. This deviation can be expressed mathematically as:

$$\Sigma (y - y^1)^2, \text{ where}$$
$$y = \text{observed (cost) data, and}$$
$$y^1 = \text{predicted (cost) data}$$

Exhibit 13-2
Illustration of least squares criterion

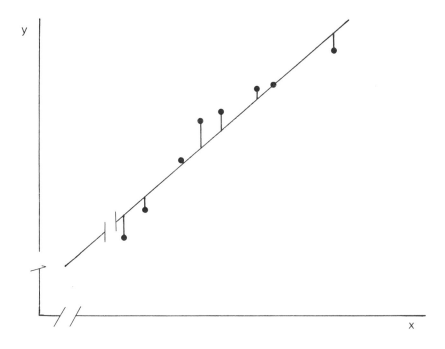

The least squares calculation minimizes $(y - y^1)^2$ by calculating the "a" and "b" coefficients from a set of normal equations. The normal equations are:

$$na + (\Sigma x) b = \Sigma y, \text{ and}$$
$$(\Sigma x)a + (\Sigma x^2)b = \Sigma xy$$

In this case, "n" is the number of data observations, and the summation expressions for the "x" and "y" values are calculated from the observed data. *Exhibit 13-3* illustrates these calculations. The summations indicated in *Exhibit 13-3* are then substituted into the two normal equations. This results in two equations in two unknowns:

$$8a + 9,550b = 34,200, \text{ and}$$
$$9,550a + 11,637,500b = 41,640,000$$

These relationships can be solved by first solving for "a" and "b" and then substituting the obtained value in the other equation. For example:

$$8a + 9,550b = 34,200$$
$$8a = 34,200 - 9,550b$$
$$a = (34,200 - 9,550b) \div 8$$
$$a = 4,275 - 1,193.75b$$

Substituting the expression for "a" into the other equation permits calculation of the "b" coefficient:

$$9,550a + 11,637,500b = 41,640,000$$
$$9,550(4,275 - 1,193.75b) + 11,637,500b = 41,640,000$$
$$40,826,250 - 11,400,312.5b + 11,637,500b = 41,640,000$$
$$237,187.5b = 813,750$$
$$b = 3.4308$$

Replacing the calculated value for "b" into the expression for "a" results in:

$$a = 4,275 - 1,193.75b$$
$$a = 4,275 - 1,193.75(3.4308)$$
$$a = 4,275 - 4,095.5175$$
$$a = 179.4825$$

The resulting cost prediction equation is obtained by substituting the calculated values for each of the coefficients into the equation for a straight line:

$$y^1 = a + bx$$
$$y^1 = 179.483 + 3.4308x$$

If the manager now wants to prepare a flexible budget for supply costs at 1,000 hours of activity and at 1,600 hours of activity, the cost prediction equation can be used for those calculations. For example, the cost prediction equation could be used to predict supply costs of $3,610 at 1,000 manhours. At 1,600 hours, predicted costs are almost $5,670. These calculations are summarized below:

$$y^1{}_{1,000} = 179.483 + 3.4308(1,000) = 3,610.28$$
$$y^1{}_{1,600} = 179.483 + 3.4308(1,600) = 5,668.76$$

The cost prediction equation can be used to predict supply costs at y activity level within the relevant range. Note that slightly different values for "a" and "b" may be obtained because of differences due to rounding. For example, the precise coefficients obtained with a computer for the data in *Exhibit 13-1* are:

$$a = 179.467 \text{ and } b = 3.4308$$

These differences are indeed slight.

Since few of the original data points fit exactly on the regression line (*Exhibit 13-2*), it is important to have some measure of the dispersion around the regression line. Any cost behavior equation derived from real data represents an average relationship. The regression line calculated with the least squares computation only estimates costs relative to activities.

Exhibit 13-3
Least squares calculations

Period	Supply costs (y)	Manhours (x)	x^2	xy
1	$3,500	1,000	1,000,000	3,500,000
2	4,500	1,200	1,440,000	5,400,000
3	4,000	1,100	1,210,000	4,400,000
4	4,800	1,350	1,822,500	6,480,000
5	3,200	950	902,500	3,040,000
6	5,100	1,500	2,250,000	7,650,000
7	4,700	1,300	1,690,000	6,110,000
8	4,400	1,150	1,322,500	5,060,000
	$\Sigma y = 34,200$	$\Sigma x = 9,550$	$\Sigma x^2 = 11,637,500$	$\Sigma xy = 41,640,000$
	$\overline{y} = 4,275$	$\overline{x} = 1,193.75$		

Measures of dispersion

Measures of dispersion provide information about the extent of possible errors in the predicted costs. If all the observed data points fit precisely on a single straight line, the hospital financial manager would be reasonably certain that next period's predicted costs would also fit on the same line. Since this happy coincidence rarely occurs, the analyst must allow for possible errors or deviations. The dispersion measures provide a statistical description of these deviations. They also permit calculation of a range of possible predicted costs in which the analyst can be reasonably confident that actual future costs will fit.

Another way of looking at dispersion is to ask how much of the total variation in the observed data can be attributed to chance. How much of the variation is due to a random relationship between the predictor variable and the criterion variable? The least squares regression model permits the analyst to separate the total variation into two components: the amount of variation that is random and the amount of variation that is due to a relationship that can be used to predict costs.

The average value $(\bar{y})$ of the criterion variable serves as a baseline for evaluating variation. In other words, if the only information that the analyst had to predict costs was $\bar{y}$, the prediction would be at the average level. *Exhibit 13-3* shows that $\bar{y}$ is at \$4,275 for the original data in *Exhibit 13-1*. In the absence of any other data, the best possible prediction of future costs would be the average costs \$4,275. However, the analyst also has all the information in *Exhibit 13-1* and has calculated the regression coefficients described above. How much better is the prediction based on the regression coefficients than a prediction based solely on the mean (average)? Least squares regression analysis is based on an implicit comparison between averages $(\bar{y})$ and predictions (y^1).

Exhibit 13-4 illustrates the two components of the total variation. The regression coefficient would provide a cost prediction of almost \$5,500 at 1,540 hours. Coincidentally, actual costs at 1,540 hours were slightly higher at \$5,700. The total variation of \$1,425 can be separated into the two components of that portion that is unexplained $(y - y^1 = 200)$ and that portion that is explained by the regression $(y^1 - \bar{y} = 1,225)$. These two components fully account for all the observed variation.

Similar measurements of variation of dispersion can be calculated for all of the data points originally plotted in *Exhibit 13-1*. One summary measure of dispersion describes how close the regression line is to the actual data. Deviations from the mean are squared and summed. For example, the total deviation of \$1,425 $(y - \bar{y})$ is first squared and then added to all such deviations for the remainder of the actual data (see *Exhibit 13-5*):

$$\Sigma (y - \bar{y})^2 = (3,500 - 4,275)^2 + (4,500 - 4,275)^2 + \ldots$$
$$+ (4,400 - 4,275)^2 = 3,035,000$$

These squared deviations represent the total sum of squares for the entire variation between actual costs and average costs. The squared deviations are then compared to the squared deviations that are explained by the regression line:

$$\Sigma (y^1 - \bar{y})^2 = (3,610.28 - 4,275)^2 + (4,296.44 - 4,275)^2 + \ldots$$
$$(4,124.90 - 4,275)^2 = 2,829,337.95$$

Exhibit 13-4
Two components of total variation

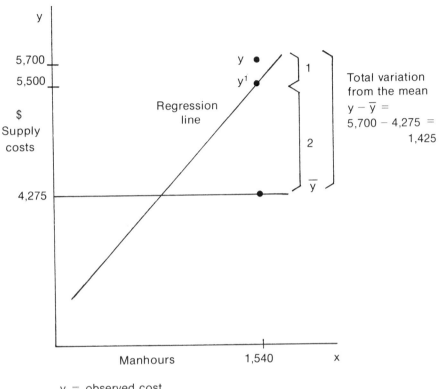

y = observed cost
y^1 = predicted cost $(179.467 + 3.4308[1,540]) \approx 5,500$
$\bar{y}$ = average cost
$1 = y - y^1$ = variation not explained by (x) activity
   $= 5,700 - 5,500 = 200$
$2 = y^1 - \bar{y}$ = variation explained by (x) activity
   $= 5,500 - 4,275 = 1,225$

In similar fashion, the sum of the squared deviations that are not explained by the regression line are computed (see *Exhibit 13-5*):

$$\Sigma (y - y^1) = (3,500 - 3,610.28)^2 + (4,500 - 4,296.44)^2 + \ldots$$
$$+ (4,400 - 4,124.90)^2 = 243,162.05$$

Exhibit 13-5
Dispersion calculations

Period	$y - \bar{y}$	$(y - \bar{y})^2$	y^1	$y - y^1$	$(y - y^1)^2$
1	-775	600,625	3,610.28	-110.28	12,161.68
2	225	50,625	4,296.44	203.56	41,436.67
3	-275	75,625	3,953.36	46.64	2,175.29
4	525	275,625	4,811.06	-11.06	122.32
5	-1075	1,155,625	3,438.74	-238.74	56,996.79
6	825	680,625	5,325.68	-225.68	50,931.46
7	425	180,625	4,639.52	60.48	3,657.83
8	125	15,625	4,124.90	275.10	75,680.01
		$\Sigma(y - \bar{y})^2 = 3,035,000$			$\Sigma(y - y^1)^2 = 243,162.05$

The computations necessary for dispersion analysis are usually a standard output of a computerized regression program. The separate computations for each month's data are added to determine the total explained and unexplained deviations. Again, if all the data fell on a single straight line, there would be no unexplained deviations ($[y - y^1]^2 = 0$). Since this result only occurs in textbooks the analyst then compares the sum of the unexplained deviations against the total deviations:

$$\frac{\Sigma(y - y^1)^2}{\Sigma(y - \bar{y})^2} = \frac{\text{unexplained variation}}{\text{total variation}} = \frac{243,162.05}{3,035,000} = 8.01\%$$

This calculation can be interpreted so that 8.01 percent of the total dispersion is due to random variation, random errors or variables not included in the model. The remaining variation of 91.99 percent (100 percent - 8.01 percent) is due to the variation in costs that can be attributed to differences in manhours.

A statistical measure of the explained variance is called the coefficient of determination (r^2). This measure is typically used as a measure of how well the regression line explains the total variance between actual costs and average costs. It is a summary measure of the "goodness of fit" of the regression. It is calculated as the complement of the total variation versus that portion not explained by the regression:

$$r^2 = 1 - \frac{\text{unexplained variation}}{\text{total variation}} = 1 - \frac{\Sigma (y - y^1)^2}{\Sigma (y - \bar{y})^2}$$

$$= 1 - \frac{243,162.05}{3,035,000} = 1 - .0801$$

$$= 100\% - 8.01\% = 91.99\%$$

Of the total variation (100 percent), almost 92 percent is explained or accounted for by the regression line. A coefficient of determination larger than 70 percent is usually considered to be quite acceptable.

The square root of the coefficient of determination ($\sqrt{r^2} = r$) is called the coefficient of correlation:

$$r = \pm \sqrt{1 - \frac{\Sigma (y - y^1)^2}{\Sigma (y - \bar{y})^2}}$$

where the $\pm$ is determined by the sign of the coefficient "b" in the regression equation. For the data above:

$$r = \sqrt{r^2} = + \sqrt{.9199} = .9591$$

The correlation coefficient indicates that manhours are positively, and highly, correlated with costs. The coefficient of correlation, a measure of the relationship between two variables, can vary between 0 and ± 1.0. A negative correlation coefficient indicates that a positive change in one variable is accompanied by a negative change in the other variable (or vice versa). Note also that the correlation coefficient provides no direct information about the degree of error attributed to the regression equation; only r^2 provides that information.

Another measure of dispersion is the standard error of the estimate (s_e). The standard error of the estimate is a measure of dispersion around the regression line. A measure of this dispersion will help the analyst evaluate the accuracy of the regression line as a basis for predicting costs. The standard error of the estimate indicates the degree of scatter of the actual costs around the regression line. It indicates the relative scatter in a scatter diagram. The standard error of the estimate is calculated as:

$$s_e = \sqrt{\frac{\Sigma (y - y^1)^2}{n - 2}}, \text{ where the size of the sample is "n."}$$

For the data discussed above:

$$s_e = \sqrt{\frac{243,162.05}{8 - 2}} = \sqrt{40,527.01} = 201.31$$

A similar computation, particularly where pocket calculators are used to calculate the regression coefficients, is:

$$se = \sqrt{\frac{\Sigma y^2 - a\Sigma y - b\Sigma xy}{n - 2}}$$

Using the data from Exhibit 13-3 (where $\Sigma y^2 = 149,240,000$):

$$s_e = \sqrt{\frac{149,240,000 - 179.467(34,200) - 3.4308(41,640,000)}{8 - 2}}$$

$$= \sqrt{\frac{243,716}{6}} = \sqrt{40,619.33}$$

> = 201.542, which is almost equivalent, except due to
> arithmetical rounding, to s_e = 201.31

The standard error of the estimate is useful because any regression equation calculated from actual data is only an estimate of the true regression equation that could be calculated from the entire population. In other words, any set of observed data is probably a sample from a much larger population. The healthcare financial manager usually does not have the resources to fully explore or obtain the entire population. Consequently, a sample is used to identify an estimated equation that can be used to predict costs. The standard error of the estimate can be used to identify boundaries or limits within which the predicted cost will actually occur on a certain percentage of trials. If several important statistical assumptions (discussed later in this chapter) that pertain to regression analysis are met, the number of standard errors of the estimate are related to probabilities as follows:

Number of standard errors	Probability
$1s_e$	66⅔%
$2s_e$	94 %
$3s_e$	99 %

Therefore, at a level of 1,540 manhours, the analyst would estimate that supply costs would be around $5,462.90, or 179.467 + 3.4308(1,540), with a range of $\pm 2s_e$, or 2(201.543) = 403.09. Therefore, the analyst would predict that actual costs (at 1,540 hours) would be between $5,059.81 and $5,865.99 with a 94 percent chance of being correct.

The lower the standard error for the estimate (s_e), the better the regression equation. In other words, a low standard error will permit the hospital financial manager to make more accurate predictions. If the standard error can be reduced, the prediction can be improved. Therefore, the standard error of the estimate describes the dispersion around the regression line and allows us to predict the relative dispersion of predicted costs.

The standard error of the estimate is a measure of dispersion for the entire regression equation. However, each of the coefficients in the regression equation also has an associated error rate or measure of dispersion. The standard errors of the regression coefficients help assess the relationship between a sample and the entire population. Remember that any cost prediction model is based on a sample of actual observations. The population of all observations is much larger and can never be fully determined. The financial manager is usually trying to assess whether the sample data accurately represent the population and whether they can be used to predict something about the population.

The standard errors of the regression coefficients are used to determine whether the regression coefficient is significant in terms of the unknown population parameter. In other words, by pure random coincidence, does a regression coefficient indicate some relationship between a predictor variable and a criterion variable, when, in fact, there is no such relationship in the population? Are the calculated coefficients a function of chance (random), or do they indicate a "real" relationship that is consistent with the relationships that occur within the real world (population)? The standard error, for each regression coefficient, is used to help answer these questions.

To do so, the analyst sets up an implicit hypothesis that the true regression coefficient in the population is really zero. If this hypothesis can be rejected on the basis of the sample data, the analyst has some assurance that a significant relationship exists. Each standard error of a regression coefficient is a measure of the sample error associated with that coefficient. Consequently, the standard error of a regression coefficient is related to the standard error of the estimate (described above). For example, the standard error(s_b) of the slope (b) coefficient is calculated as:

$$s_b = \frac{s_e}{\sqrt{\Sigma (x - \bar{x})^2}} = \frac{s_e}{\sqrt{\Sigma x^2 - \bar{x} \Sigma x}}$$

Either term may be used to compute the standard error of b (s_b), although the second expression is easier to compute. Note that in each expression, the denominator indicates the dispersion of the observed data around the mean. Therefore, the standard error of a regression coefficient helps measure the dispersion of the components of the regression equation, while the standard error of the estimate measures the dispersion of the entire equation. For the data in *Exhibit 13-3,* the standard error of b is calculated as:

$$s_b = \frac{201.543}{\sqrt{11,637,500 - (1,193.75)(9,550)}} = \frac{201.543}{\sqrt{237,187.5}}$$

$$= \frac{201.543}{487.019} = .4138$$

The standard error of the regression coefficient must be evaluated relative to the original coefficient. The analyst uses the standard error to determine whether the regression coefficient is due to random chance. To accomplish this objective, the standard error is used to compute the number of standard errors that the calculated coefficient is away from a "real" coefficient of zero. For example, the regression coefficient (b), calculated earlier, is 3.4308. This calculated value is more than 8 (8.291 = 3.4308 ÷ .4138) standard error units away from a population coefficient equal to zero. This calculation of the number of standard errors away from a population coefficient equal to zero is called a t-value. The t-value is computed as:

$$t = \frac{\text{regression coefficient}}{\text{standard error of the regression coefficient}} = \frac{3.4308}{.4138} = 8.291$$

A t-value in excess of 2.0 is usually considered sufficient. In other words, the chances that a deviation as great as two standard errors could occur (randomly), with a population coefficient equal to zero, are about five percent. The chances that a t-value as great as eight standard errors could similarly occur are almost zero. One could refer to a table of t-values

Exhibit 13-6
Table of student's distribution (values of t)

Degrees of freedom (df)	Level of significance					
	.2	.1	.05	.025	.01	.005
1	1.376	3.078	6.314	12.706	31.821	63.657
2	1.061	1.886	2.910	4.303	6.965	9.925
3	.978	1.638	2.353	3.182	4.541	5.841
4	.941	1.533	2.132	2.776	3.747	4.604
5	.920	1.476	2.015	2.571	3.365	4.032
6	.906	1.440	1.943	2.447	3.143	3.707
7	.896	1.415	1.895	2.365	2.998	3.499
8	.889	1.397	1.860	2.306	2.896	3.355
9	.883	1.383	1.833	2.262	2.821	3.250
10	.879	1.372	1.812	2.228	2.764	3.169
11	.876	1.363	1.796	2.201	2.718	3.106
12	.873	1.356	1.782	2.179	2.681	3.055
13	.870	1.350	1.771	2.160	2.650	3.012
14	.868	1.345	1.761	2.145	2.624	2.977
15	.866	1.341	1.753	2.131	2.602	2.947
16	.865	1.337	1.746	2.120	2.583	2.921
17	.863	1.333	1.740	2.110	2.567	2.898
18	.862	1.330	1.734	2.101	2.552	2.878
19	.861	1.328	1.729	2.093	2.539	2.861
20	.860	1.325	1.725	2.086	2.528	2.845
21	.859	1.323	1.721	2.080	2.518	2.831
22	.858	1.321	1.717	2.074	2.508	2.819
23	.858	1.319	1.714	2.069	2.500	2.807
24	.857	1.318	1.711	2.064	2.492	2.797
25	.856	1.316	1.708	2.060	2.485	2.787
26	.856	1.315	1.706	2.056	2.479	2.779
27	.855	1.314	1.703	2.052	2.473	2.771
28	.855	1.313	1.701	2.048	2.467	2.763
29	.854	1.311	1.699	2.045	2.462	2.756
30	.854	1.310	1.697	2.042	2.457	2.750

to make the exact computations. (See *Exhibit 13-6.*) These computations are illustrated below; the hospital financial manager can usually be satisfied if the calculated t-value is at least 2.0.

The corresponding calculations for the intercept (a) of the regression equation are:

$$s_a = (s_e)\sqrt{\frac{1}{n} + \frac{\bar{x}^2}{\Sigma(x - \bar{x})^2}} = (s_e)\sqrt{\frac{1}{n} + \frac{\bar{x}^2}{\Sigma(x^2 - \bar{x}\,\Sigma\,x)}}$$

For the sample data in *Exhibit 13-5,* the resulting calculations are:

$$s_a = (.4138)\sqrt{\frac{1}{8} + \frac{(1,193.75)^2}{11,637,500 - (1,193.75)(9,550)}}$$

$$= (.4138)\sqrt{\frac{1}{8} + \frac{(1,193.75)^2}{237,187.5}} = (.4138)\sqrt{\frac{1}{8} + 6.0081}$$

$$= .4138\sqrt{6.1331} = .4138(2.4765) = 1.0248$$

The t-value for the intercept is then calculated by dividing the standard error of "a" into the original value of the intercept:

$$t_a = \frac{179.467}{1.0248} = 175.12$$

Such a high t-value means that the true intercept could equal zero only under the most unusual circumstances.

Note that similar computations are possible if there is more than one predictor variable. The higher the t-value, the more confidence the financial manager has in using that particular coefficient as a predictor variable. A regression coefficient with a low t-value is a candidate for exclusion from the cost prediction model.

The standard error of a regression coefficient can also be used to evaluate the probability that the population parameter is within certain limits. These limits, called confidence intervals, are computed using the standard error of the regression coefficient. Values from a table of t-statistics are also used to compute the confidence limits:

confidence limit = regression coefficient $\pm$ (t-value probability) (s_b)

The t-value for a particular probability is obtained from a table of t-statistics. For example, *Exhibit 13-6* illustrates one such table for many degrees of freedom. Degrees of freedom relate to the sample size of the original observations. A regression equation with one predictor variable and one criterion variable has $n-2$ degrees of freedom (where n is the total number of observations). The associated probability depends on how much confidence the analyst desires. A probability of one percent indicates a much wider range, and lower confidence, than a probability of .5 percent. A probability of 10 percent is interpreted to mean that there is a 10 percent chance that the true population parameter could be outside the calculated confidence limits. There is a 90 percent chance that the population parameter is within the confidence limit calculated from t-values associated with a 10 percent probability.[1]

The confidence limits for the sample data (slope), a probability of .01 and six degrees of freedom (8–2) are:[2]

$$\text{confidence limits}_b = b \pm (t_{.01})(s_b)$$
$$= 3.4308 \pm (3.143)\,(.4138)$$
$$= 3.4308 \pm 1.3006$$
$$= 2.1302 \text{ and } 4.7314$$

Therefore, the 98 percent confidence limits are 2.1302 to 4.7314. The analyst is 98 percent confident that the population parameter for the slope (b) is somewhere between these values. A lower level of confidence will result in a narrower range of values. The higher the confidence and its associated probability, the farther apart are the extremes of the confidence limits. Note that these confidence limits do not include zero, and, again, we are able to reject the hypothesis that the population parameter is equal to zero.

In summary, measures of dispersion can be used to determine:

1. how much of the variation in all the data is explained by the regression equation (r^2)
2. the relative dispersion around the regression line (s_e)
3. the standard errors of the regression coefficients (s_b and s_a)
4. the probability that the calculated coefficients of the regression line occurred by chance (t-values and confidence limits)

These different measures of dispersion are useful for determining the usability of the regression data. They improve the analyst's understanding of the relationship of hospital costs to activity and permit the financial manager to better predict costs. There are no precise guidelines governing the required accuracy of predicted costs. As the financial manager gains experience and confidence with the use of regression data, the trade-offs between different types of errors and dispersion will become more meaningful.

---

[1] Statistical purists might quibble with our choice of terminology in this section and assert, correctly, that 90 percent of the confidence limits calculated from representative sample data will include the population coefficient. We prefer the more intuitive statements of the probability of correctly estimating a coefficient that can be used for predictive purposes. In our judgment, financial managers are more concerned with reasonable predictive ability than statistical purity.

[2] The probability of .01 represents 1 percent on each side of a two-tailed distribution. Please note that the t statistics in *Exhibit 13-6* also represent a one-tailed distribution.

Statistical assumptions of regression analysis

A healthcare financial manager cannot blindly apply the statistical techniques that have been discussed. In many cases, the data may not be appropriate for regression analysis. A naive application of a computerized regression analysis may actually mislead the analyst. The results must be subjected to a careful analysis to determine that the underlying assumptions are satisfied. If not, the financial manager must search for other, more appropriate tools or perhaps reevaluate the data base using the techniques described. The brief survey of regression analysis in these chapters only qualifies the financial manager of a healthcare organization to better evaluate the usefulness of cost behavior models. If difficulties that may violate these statistical requirements are encountered, the assistance of a professional statistician may be necessary.

Six different assumptions underlying regression analysis must be tested and evaluated. They are:

1. stable relationships
2. linear relationships
3. homoscedasticity (uniform dispersion)
4. absence of serial correlation
5. absence of multicolinearity
6. normal distribution

Testing of these regression assumptions is often called specification analysis. Specification analysis is used to determine that the calculated regression coefficients (a and b), which are based on a limited sample of observed data, are unbiased, efficient estimators of the "true" regression coefficients in the entire population. Fortunately, most computer programs provide data that permit relatively quick and easy specification analyses. Many of the detailed tests of serial correlation, normality, etc., are automatically available as part of the regression output. However, the manager's judgment is still required in specification analysis because it is rare that the results are completely consistent and unambiguous. Some of the statistical assumptions may not be as strong as others, and the analyst must carefully weigh the conflicting evidence.

The first assumption that must be evaluated is whether the relationship between the predictor variable(s) and the criterion variable is stable. Will the relationship persist? Are the historical data used to predict costs useful for predicting future costs? Because of the need for a continuing and stable relationship between the regression variables, regression analysis is most successfully applied to repetitive activities. Consequently, laboratories, dietary departments and other ancillary departments are excellent candidates for determining cost behavior equations through regression analysis. If the first assumption or requirement is not met, there is probably little reason, outside of intellectual curiosity, to continue the regression analysis. For example, if the hospital or the department anticipates a merger or some other type of reorganization, the regression equation probably cannot be used directly to predict future costs. On the other hand, the historical data can be used to establish a baseline measure of what the costs would have been, hypothetically, in the absence of the organizational change.

The second assumption pertains to linearity within the relevant range. Simple regression attempts to fit a linear equation of the form:

$$y = a + bx, \text{ which can be restated as}$$
$$y = a + bx + u$$

The "u" term, called the disturbance term or error term, indicates the deviation of the actual data from the regression line. Consequently, $u = y - y^1$ as discussed earlier in this chapter. The expected value of the error term is expected to be zero. Error arises from the fact that the regression equation is calculated from sample data because the entire population is not known and therefore not included in the regression calculations. Therefore, some error will occur. If the relationship is linear, the financial manager would expect the average error to be zero.

In the case of simple regression, linearity can be easily checked by evaluating a scatter diagram of the data as discussed in Chapter 3. This test should never be omitted. Of equal importance is the necessity of assessing the width of the relevant range. The relationship may be linear within the anticipated relevant range, while it may be nonlinear outside of that range (see *Exhibit 3-4*). If shifts in volume or activity are anticipated, the analyst must be careful about extrapolating the regression results outside the limits of the relevant range. In any event, both linearity and the relevant range must be simultaneously evaluated. A stable linear relationship within a reasonable relevant range of historical activity is a sound basis for pursuing the best cost behavior model. Note also that linearity does not usually apply to multiple regression analysis.

The third assumption that must be evaluated concerns homoscedasticity or constant variance. This condition requires that the standard deviation and variance be constant for all the error terms (u) of the observed data (x). Homoscedasticity indicates that data are uniformly dispersed around the regression line.[3] For example, *Exhibit 13-7* indicates constant variance in the first graph and decreasing variance in the second. Violation of the homoscedasticity assumption can be tested by calculating the standard deviation and variance for each quartile (or half) of the data base. If the standard deviations and variances from each partition of the data are not approximately equal, the constant variance assumption has been violated.

---

[3]The absence of homoscedasticity is called heteroscedasticity.

Exhibit 13-7
Illustration of homoscedasticity and heteroscedasticity

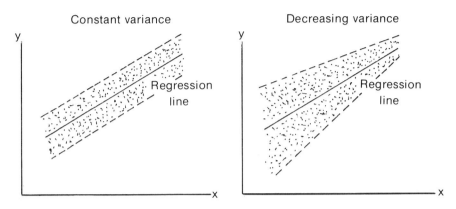

If so, the analyst can place less confidence in the slope (b) coefficient of the regression line. In other words, the absence of homoscedasticity can bias the "b" coefficient. This is likely to happen with typical cost data in healthcare organizations, and the financial manager must determine if the bias is significant enough to distort the cost predictions. Unfortunately, this is where judgment plays an important role; there is no rule that can indicate when the bias resulting from a violation of the homoscedasticity assumption will overwhelm the usefulness of the cost predictions.

The fourth statistical assumption that must be evaluated is whether serial correlation is present. This condition exists when any single disturbance term (u) is related to any other disturbance term. The error terms should be independent, and the size of one deviation or disturbance should not influence any other deviation. This condition is also called autocorrelation, and the analyst should test to determine whether the autocorrelation is significant.

This is, again, likely to happen with cost data from healthcare organizations. For example, cost increases may be variable with respect to increases in some activity level while decreases in the same activities may not lead to proportionate decreases in costs. For example, some costs are quite "sticky" or slow to decrease because managers are reluctant to fire people and close down departments (or beds) as volume declines. Many costs are related to time and to inflation over time, and the error terms of time-related costs are often serially correlated. Most computer programs do permit the analyst to test for the degree of serial correlation. The Durbin-Watson statistic is often used to evaluate serial correlation; most analysts agree that a Durbin-Watson statistic around 2.0 indicates almost no serial correlation.

If the error terms are not independent, this can lead to several problems with statistical measures of dispersion. These problems include:

1. underestimation of the standard errors of the regression coefficients (s_a and s_b)
2. overestimation of the sampling variances of the regression coefficients
3. greater dispersion among the predicted costs than would be ordinarily expected

Simply stated, the standard errors will be underestimated and the variance of the coefficients (and the standard errors) will be overestimated because the deviations in the observed data (u) are not independent. There are just not enough independent observations in the data to permit valid and usable cost predictions.

The fifth assumption concerns the absence of multicolinearity. This condition pertains only to multiple regression, which is discussed in the last section. Multiple regression requires more than one predictor variable, and multicolinearity would indicate that these predictor variables are highly correlated. Multicolinear predictor variables lead to unreliable and unstable regression coefficients. The calculated coefficients are highly dependent on the sample observations, and the addition or deletion of a few observations will usually cause large shifts in the regression coefficients. The prediction of costs may still be quite feasible and valid, but the individual coefficients will provide unreliable evidence about the marginal effects of each separate predictor variable.

Fortunately, the presence of multicolinearity is relatively easy to observe. A correlation table can usually be obtained as part of any computerized regression program. The analyst should consider excluding a predictor variable if it is highly correlated with another predictor variable. The analyst's judgment is used to assess which variable is less important. The less important variables that are highly correlated with other, more important, variables should be excluded. Of course, separate analyses should be conducted with those excluded variables to confirm that they really are not important. Generally, correlation coefficients greater than .70 or .80 indicate variables that may be excluded from the regression equation.

The multicolinearity test is also consistent with the general objective of parsimony. The financial manager of a healthcare organization would like to use a regression equation that is as simple as possible and uses as few predictor variables as possible. Why monitor and collect 20 different variables when sufficient accuracy and reliability can be obtained with two or three variables? By eliminating some of the variables that are highly correlated with each other, the analyst is fully using all the information captured by the remaining variables. Redundant variables should always be eliminated, and a parsimonious model should be used for cost prediction purposes. The multicolinearity tests merely help achieve this objective; they can certainly be used to reduce what would otherwise be a multiple regression model into a simple regression model.

The final statistical assumption that must be evaluated concerns the distribution of points around the regression line. The statistical measures of dispersion discussed earlier in this chapter rely on a normal, or almost normal, distribution of the sample data around the regression line. This is exactly the same as testing whether the disturbance terms (u) are normally distributed. A normal distribution is a symmetrical bell-shaped curve. The error terms can actually be plotted to observe the shape of the distribution. The normality assumption is generally considered to be the least important statistical requirement; most analysts are satisfied if the distribution of the error terms is roughly symmetrical around a single mode (not bimodal or multiple modes).

Each statistical assumption described above must be successively tested and evaluated. The analyst, working together with the financial manager, must assess whether the statistical assumptions are met sufficiently to justify using the regression equation for cost prediction. In most cases, several of the statistical requirements will be strongly satisfied while others are only marginally satisfied. The financial manager of a healthcare organization must have some idea of the probable impact of any unsatisfied statistical requirements, and the manager will then be able to revise, probably downward, the level of confidence and assurance that may be placed in the results.

Possible misuse of regression analysis

This chapter has repeatedly emphasized the necessity for the financial manager to apply judgment and thought regarding the results of regression analysis. There are frequently alternative cost prediction models that all meet the statistical criteria described above. How does the manager or analyst choose between alternative predictor variables or between alternative cost prediction models? The best criterion for making this choice is to choose the cost prediction model that provides the best possible prediction at the lowest possible cost and with the minimum possible error. Three possible errors should be avoided:

1. measurement errors
2. analytical error
3. errors in judgment

The total error of any cost prediction can be expressed as the sum of these three components. The total error should be minimized; therefore, it is generally good practice to minimize each component of the total error.

Measurement errors are errors in the data base. They include errors in data collection, coding and input, as well as errors of classification and definition. The techniques to avoid these errors were described previously. Analytical errors are errors of calculation. Not all computer programs yield the same results for equivalent input data. Specification errors are analytical errors. They were described in the preceding section of this chapter in terms of the statistical assumptions of regression analysis.

The most important and crucial error that is usually made in using regression analysis is error in judgment. A very important error in judgment is often due to omitted variables. The analyst must be aware of possible explanatory variables that would be useful and significant if included in the data base. These variables may be extremely important, but no one thought to collect or include them. Minor increments in data collection costs can often significantly improve cost prediction models. Unfortunately, there are no guides or signals to indicate when some significant variables have been omitted.

Another very crucial judgment error is introduced when the cost prediction is just not plausible. The relationships between the criterion variable (costs) and predictor variables must make "good economic sense." The predictor variables must be subject to managerial control, or else it is useless to identify the cost prediction model. Each of the predictor variables must also be logically defensible. There must be some reason why they were chosen.

The final error in judgment concerns the tests of "goodness of fit." Ideally, the cost behavior model that satisfies all of the above criteria will also be the one that best fits the observed data. The coefficient of determination (r^2) should be as high as possible. The t-values for the regression coefficient should exceed 2.0. The standard error of the estimate (s_e) should be low relative to the predicted costs. The sign of the slope (b) coefficient should be consistent with the expected sign. That is, if the plausible economic model has a positive sign upward sloping to the right on b, then a calculated b with a negative sign would be sufficient cause to reevaluate alternative models. In any event, the financial manager cannot just choose that model that has the highest r^2. Blind faith in high r^2 has led many unwary analysts to nonsensical cost predictions.

Further thought concerns possible negative signs on the intercept (a) coefficient that might be obtained through regression analysis. Does a negative intercept indicate that the results are unusable? Does a negative intercept mean negative fixed costs? Not necessarily. The answers to these questions depend on the relevant range. *Exhibit 13-8* illustrates a regression line with a negative intercept (and positive slope). The fixed costs are certainly not negative within the relevant range. In fact, to obtain a more accurate estimate of fixed costs, the intersection of the (lower) relevant range and the regression line must be extended to the vertical axis. The horizontal dotted line illustrates how the fixed costs would be read from a graph. Similar calculations could be made using the regression equation and the appropriate value of the criterion (x) variable.

Exhibit 13-8
Illustration of a negative intercept

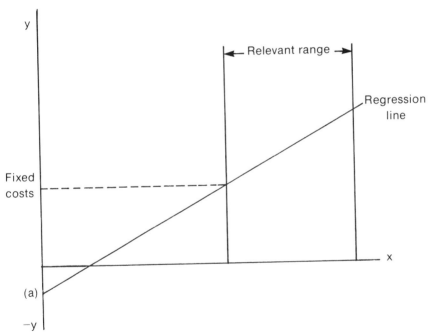

Note also that a true variable cost, with no fixed component, should be expected to have an intercept (a) of almost zero. The intercept (a) should also have a very low t-value because the analyst would then be interested in accepting the hypothesis that the intercept was not significantly different from zero.

Computerized regression analyses

This chapter has so far described the manual approach to regression computations. The early part of the chapter presented the normal equations that would be used to manually calculate the regression coefficients. Measures of dispersion could also be manually calculated and the various assessments of error made without the aid of a computer or calculator. However, as the number of data points increases, the associated calculations become more cumbersome (and tiresome). It is fortunate that most computer installations provide ready and easy access to an algorithm that will quickly calculate all, or most, of the regression coefficients and statistics. This section presents the computer output from an interactive regression algorithm (STATPKG) where the various analyses and statistics are calculated according to the analyst's responses to the computer's questions. A batch processing algorithm known as SPSS (Statistical Package for the Social Sciences) or Minitab could have been used to provide similar outputs. Any of these regression algorithms is convenient to use and interpret. The most difficult problem usually is to put the data in a format the computer can accept.

This section illustrates the concepts discussed earlier in this chapter regarding statistical analysis of cost behavior. An interactive (prompting) computer program is used to obtain:

1. A description of the data base (*Exhibit 13-9*)
2. Descriptive statistics on 15 variables (*Exhibit 13-10*)
3. A regression analysis of monthly costs as a function of time (Variable 15 months, see *Exhibit 13-11*)

Exhibit 13-9
Variable descriptions, ALLCA data file

Variable #	Description
1	Month number
2	Year
3	Calendar month (1 = January)
4	Total costs
5	Adult beds
6	Patient days
7	Percent debt financed
8	Outpatient visits
9	Percent cost-based reimbursement
10	Fulltime equivalent employees
11	Surgery minutes
12	Critical care beds
13	Physicians
14	Square feet
15	Total costs ÷ 1,000

4. Four plots of monthly costs relative to time, patient days, square feet and beds (*Exhibit 13-12,* a-d)
5. A multiple step-wise regression of hospital costs as a function of 12 possible predictor variables

The first step in the use of any computer-assisted decision model or statistical analysis package (e.g., STATPKG) is to make sure that the computer is reading the data file correctly. Alternatively, small data bases can be manually entered directly from the terminal. The first page of computer output merely tells the computer to read the data in a particular format. The 15 variables are described to aid in interpreting the resulting output (*Exhibit 13-9*). This data file contains 30 rows of data for 30 months (numbered from 1 through 30) on eight different hospitals. Some data are missing for several hospitals; consequently, only 168 rows of data have been entered in the data file.

STATPKG is then asked to perform an "Elementary Statistics" analysis. This analysis provides the mean, standard deviation and various other measures of dispersion (*Exhibit 13-10*).

Exhibit 13-10
Descriptive statistics, ALLCA data file

```
WHAT ANALYSIS DO YOU WISH TO PERFORM *
? ELEMENTARY STATISTICS

DO YOU WISH TO USE THE SAME DATA *
? YES
```

VAR.	MEAN	STANDARD DEVIATION	ESTIMATED STD. DEV.	EST STD ERR OF THE MEAN	MAXIMUM	MINIMUM
1	15.548	8.270	8.295	.640	30.000	1.000
2	1976.792	.731	.733	.057	1978.000	1976.000
3	6.048	3.419	3.429	.265	12.000	1.000
4	2063544.315	908368.164	911083.769	70291.639	3882175.000	658628.000
5	312.345	115.936	116.283	8.971	452.000	108.000
6	6744.905	2828.782	2837.238	218.898	11631.000	2192.000
7	.460	.184	.185	.014	.760	.080
8	3888.321	1503.240	1507.734	116.324	7079.000	1201.000
9	.488	.135	.135	.010	.735	.327
10	293066.560	627462.424	629338.250	48554.500	1792960.000	381.000
11	44496.685	18361.648	18416.541	1420.867	89677.000	7429.000
12	26.506	18.881	18.938	1.461	60.000	7.000
13	160.012	158.079	158.552	12.233	540.000	10.000
14	275550.560	181905.171	182448.984	14076.245	541000.000	5.000
15	2063.544	908.368	911.084	70.292	3882.175	658.628

A regression analysis is then conducted to test the effect of time (month number) on hospital costs. Even though a high t-value is obtained, the correlation coefficient is so low (.30) that the analyst would conclude that time and inflationary factors are having a modest effect on costs for these eight hospitals (*Exhibit 13-11*).

Exhibit 13-11
Regression analysis of costs as a function of month (total costs)

```
WHAT ANALYSIS DO YOU WISH TO PERFORM *
? REGRESSION

DO YOU WISH TO USE THE SAME DATA *
? YES

SPECIFY THE COLUMN NUMBER OF THE DEPENDENT VARIABLE *
? 15

SPECIFY THE COLUMN NUMBER OF THE INDEPENDENT VARIABLE *
? 1

INTERCEPT....................    1543.55710
REGRESSION COEFFICIENT.......      33.44481

STD. ERROR OF REG. COEF. ....       8.120
COMPUTED T-VALUE.............        4.119

CORRELATION COEFFICIENT......         .304
STANDARD ERROR OF ESTIMATE...       870.433
```

ANALYSIS OF VARIANCE FOR THE REGRESSION

SOURCE OF VARIATION	D.F.	SUM OF SQ.	MEAN SQ.	F VALUE
ATTRIBUTABLE TO REGRESSION	1	12851776.8689	12851776.8689	16.9626 .
DEVIATION FROM REGRESSION		166125770520.1772	757653.7360	
TOTAL		167138622297.0461		

The four plots (*Exhibit 13-12*) are fairly self-explanatory and would be used to further refine the analysis. The analyst should search for clusters or data partitions that are not immediately evident. In addition, scatter diagrams (plots) that have absolutely no pattern would be excluded from further analysis.

The multiple "step-wise regression" first asks the analyst to specify the dependent (criterion) variable. Any or all of the remaining variables could serve as predictor variables. In this case three variables are deleted and the computer starts cranking out the regression results (*Exhibit 13-13*). Since a step-wise regression analysis was specified, the STATPKG will select the variable with the largest explanatory power (#5). By itself, adult beds (#5)

Exhibit 13-12(a)
Plot of total cost vs. time (month)

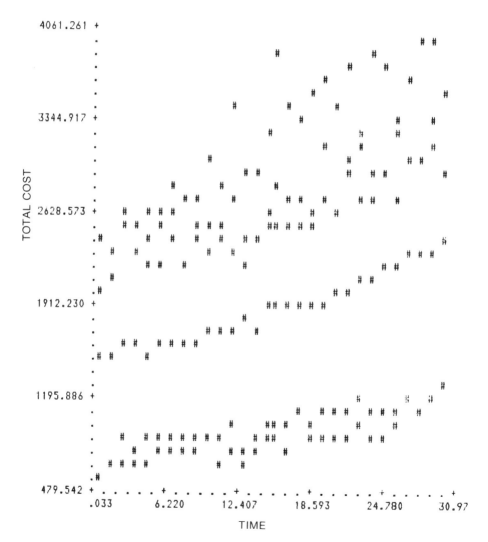

DO YOU WISH TO USE THE SAME DATA *
? YES

SPECIFY COLUMN NUMBERS OF HORIZONTAL (X) AND VERTICAL (Y) VARIABLES
IN THE FORM XX/YY
? 1/15

SPECIFY A 1 CHARACTER PLOT SYMBOL
? #

DO YOU WISH TO PLOT MORE VARIABLES *

Exhibit 13-12(b)
Plot of total cost vs. patient days

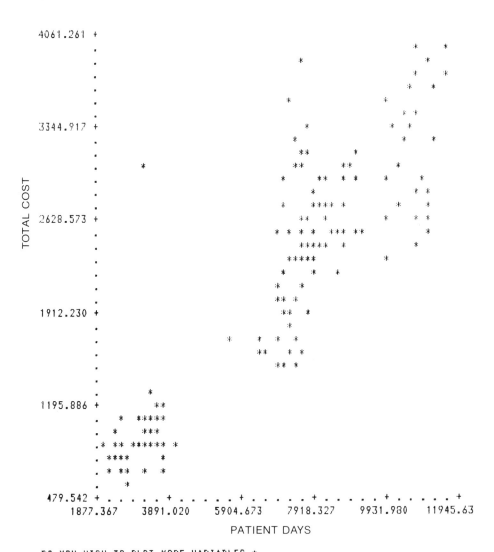

```
SPECIFY COLUMN NUMBERS OF HORIZONTAL (X) AND VERTICAL (Y) VARIABLES
IN THE FORM XX/YY
? 6/15

SPECIFY A 1 CHARACTER PLOT SYMBOL
? *
```

DO YOU WISH TO PLOT MORE VARIABLES *
? YES

SPECIFY COLUMN NUMBERS OF HORIZONTAL (X) AND VERTICAL (Y) VARIABLES
IN THE FORM XX/YY

Exhibit 13-12(c)
Plot of total cost vs. square feet

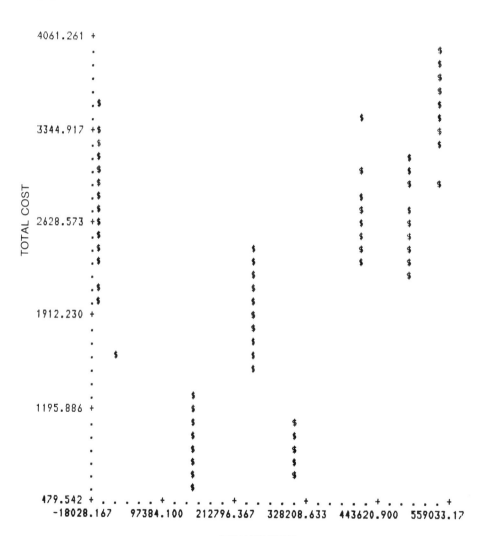

```
SPECIFY COLUMN NUMBERS OF HORIZONTAL (X) AND VERTICAL (Y) VARIABLES
IN THE FORM XX/YY
? 14/15

SPECIFY A 1 CHARACTER PLOT SYMBOL
? $
```

SQUARE FEET

Exhibit 13-12(d)
Plot of total cost vs. beds

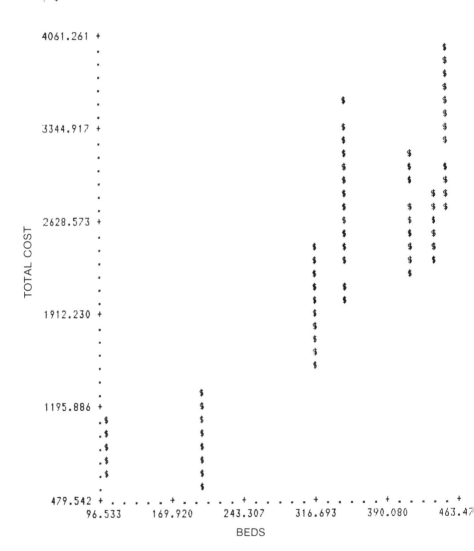

? 5/15

SPECIFY A 1 CHARACTER PLOT SYMBOL
? $

DO YOU WISH TO PLOT MORE VARIABLES *
? YES

is able to explain 81.1 percent of the variance in monthly costs. The F- and t-values are extremely high, and the analyst would not even need to consult any reference tables to know that the productive ability of this particular equation is relatively high. However, the standard error of the estimate is high relative to average monthly costs ($397,602 \div 2,063,544 = 19\%$). This indicates that further analyses should be pursued to try to reduce the standard error.

By the time that three more variables have entered the equation (#9, #1, and #11), the r^2 has increased to 96.7 percent and the standard error of the estimate has been reduced to 168,577. This is much lower relative to average costs ($168,577 \div 2,063,544 = 8\%$), and the analyst may reasonably conclude with the four predictor variables. The cost prediction equation at this stage is:

Total costs = $-1486.3 + 5.99$ (Beds) + 2179.51 (Cost-based percent) + 28.5 (Month) + $.004$ (Surgery minutes).

Note that the t-values on each of the predictor variable coefficients are all larger than 2.0. Note also that step #4 has not improved the various statistical indicators relative to step #3. In this case, from the standpoint of a parsimonious model, the analyst may prefer the reduced model from step #3 (*Exhibit 13-13*).

The analyst may also check out a series of related regression equations where departmental or service variables are predicted first and then total costs are predicted from the departmental or service variables. In summary, the process of conducting regression analysis and of building cost prediction models requires creative and artful thought. There is no manual or text that can possibly anticipate all the steps or all the problems that financial managers may encounter.

Summary

This chapter focused on the statistical methods that can be used to obtain estimates of cost behavior patterns. Regression models offer considerable help to the hospital management team when applying the management accounting techniques discussed earlier in this book. Like all statistical tools, regression analysis cannot be applied blindly, especially when computer applications are used. The effective manager understands both the strength and weakness of the tools he/she uses.

Exhibit 13-13
Multiple regression analysis of total costs

```
WHAT ANALYSIS DO YOU WISH TO PERFORM *
? STEP-WISE REGRESSION

DO YOU WISH TO READ NEW DATA *
? NO

SPECIFY THE COLUMN NUMBER OF THE DEPENDENT VARIABLE *
? 15

DO YOU WISH TO DELETE ANY VARIABLES *
? YES

HOW MANY VARIABLES DO YOU WISH TO DELETE *
? 3

SPECIFY THE COLUMN NUMBERS OF THE VARIABLES TO BE DELETED IN THE FORM
XX/XX/...
? 2/3/4/

STEP  1

VARIABLE SELECTED..... 5

SUM OF SQUARES REDUCED IN THIS STEP....*2379766.882
PROPORTION OF VARIANCE OF Y REDUCED....      .811
F FOR THIS VARIABLE (D.F.=1,166) ......    710.871

CUMULATIVE SUM OF SQUARES REDUCED......*2379766.882
CUMULATIVE PROPORTION REDUCED..........      .811  OF138622297.046

MULTIPLE CORRELATION COEFFICIENT....   .900   (ADJUSTED R =    .900)
F FOR ANALYSIS OF VARI.(D.F.= 1,166) 710.871
STANDARD ERROR OF ESTIMATE.......... 397.602   (ADJUSTED SE= 397.602)

VARIABLE   REG.COEF.   STD.ERROR-COEF.   COMPUTED T   BETA COEF.
    5       7.05458          .26459       26.6622       .90038

INTERCEPT   -139.91903

STEP  2

VARIABLE SELECTED..... 9

SUM OF SQUARES REDUCED IN THIS STEP....11985861.929
PROPORTION OF VARIANCE OF Y REDUCED....      .086
F FOR THIS VARIABLE (D.F.=1,165) ......    138.719

DO YOU WISH TO ENTER THIS VARIABLE IN THE REGRESSION *
? YES
```

STEP 3

VARIABLE SELECTED..... 1

SUM OF SQUARES REDUCED IN THIS STEP.... 9354605.966
PROPORTION OF VARIANCE OF Y REDUCED....   .067
F FOR THIS VARIABLE (D.F.=1,164) 312.961

DO YOU WISH TO ENTER THIS VARIABLE IN THE REGRESSION *
? YES

CUMULATIVE SUM OF SQUARES REDUCED......*3720234.776
CUMULATIVE PROPORTION REDUCED..........   .965 OF138622297.046

MULTIPLE CORRELATION COEFFICIENT....   .982   (ADJUSTED R =   .982)
F FOR ANALYSIS OF VARI.(D.F.= 3,164)1491.217
STANDARD ERROR OF ESTIMATE.......... 172.889   (ADJUSTED SE= 173.934)

VARIABLE	REG.COEF.	STD.ERROR-COEF.	COMPUTED T	BETA COEF.
5	6.52494	.11705	55.7438	.83279
9	2045.33759	100.60526	20.3303	.30326
1	28.58276	1.61569	17.6907	.26022

INTERCEPT   -1417.66616

STEP 4

VARIABLE SELECTED.....11

SUM OF SQUARES REDUCED IN THIS STEP.... 269907.828
PROPORTION OF VARIANCE OF Y REDUCED....   .002
F FOR THIS VARIABLE (D.F.=1,163) 9.498

DO YOU WISH TO ENTER THIS VARIABLE IN THE REGRESSION *
? YES

CUMULATIVE SUM OF SQUARES REDUCED......*3990142.604
CUMULATIVE PROPORTION REDUCED..........   .967 OF138622297.046

MULTIPLE CORRELATION COEFFICIENT....   .983   (ADJUSTED R =   .983)
F FOR ANALYSIS OF VARI.(D.F.= 4,163)1178.738
STANDARD ERROR OF ESTIMATE.......... 168.577   (ADJUSTED SE= 170.112)

VARIABLE	REG.COEF.	STD.ERROR-COEF.	COMPUTED T	BETA COEF.
5	5.98769	.20837	28.7362	.76422
9	2179.51065	107.32311	20.3079	.32315
1	28.04798	1.58492	17.6968	.25535
11	.00403	.00131	3.0818	.08142

INTERCEPT   -1486.29866

```
CUMULATIVE SUM OF SQUARES REDUCED......*4365628.810
CUMULATIVE PROPORTION REDUCED..........     .897  OF138622297.046

MULTIPLE CORRELATION COEFFICIENT....   .947   (ADJUSTED R =    .947)
F FOR ANALYSIS OF VARI.(D.F.= 2,165) 719.675
STANDARD ERROR OF ESTIMATE......... 293.946   (ADJUSTED SE= 294.830)

VARIABLE   REG.COEF.   STD.ERROR-COEF.   COMPUTED T   BETA COEF.
   5         6.64510          .19868       33.4468        .84812
   9      2014.28884       171.02286       11.7779        .29866

INTERCEPT     -995.64162
```

Questions and problems

1. List the assumptions underlying regression analysis.

2. What is the purpose of specification analysis?

3. Why is the financial manager's judgment necessary in conducting regression analyses?

4. Why is regression analysis most successfully applied to repetitive activities?

5. Name some ways that linearity of the data can be evaluated.

6. How can we test homoscedasticity?

7. Why is it important to test for autocorrelation?

8. How would you evaluate a correlation coefficient of .785 determined through multiple regression? What should be done next?

9. How does the financial manager choose between various cost prediction models?

10. Identify the components of total error. What can the financial manager of a healthcare organization do about each type of error?

11. The following six monthly observations of healthcare costs are to be used as a basis for a budget formula. A scatter diagram indicates behavior in the form $y = a + bx$.

Month	Supply usage	Healthcare costs
Jan.	800	$2,000
Feb.	400	1,100
March	700	2,100
April	1,200	2,600
May	1,000	2,300
June	600	1,500

Using least squares, compute the variable and fixed costs for the budget equation.

12. The following observations of supply costs and patient level are to be used to develop a budget formula. A scatter diagram indicates the data fit to a linear equation.

Period	Patient level	Supply costs
1	1,100	$ 8,710
2	1,200	9,400
3	1,500	11,270
4	900	7,580
5	1,100	8,840

a. Determine a least squares regression equation.
b. Calculate the predicted supply costs given a level of 1) 1,300 patients and 2) 1,450 patients.

13. Metropolitan General Hospital has collected the following supply cost data from the prior four periods for the outpatient department. The departmental manager wants to investigate the relationship as a basis for future budgets.

Period	Supply costs	Patient level
1	$350	800
2	350	1,200
3	150	400
4	550	1,600

a. Draw a scatter diagram.
b. Using the high-low method (Chapter 12), calculate the budget equation.
c. Using least squares analysis, calculate the budget equation.
d. Compute the coefficient of determination.
e. Compute the standard error of estimate.
f. Calculate a 95 percent confidence limit for the slope of the regression line.

14. The healthcare departmental manager wishes to investigate the relationship between supply costs and service level. Below are the data for the last five periods.

Period	Service level	Supply costs
1	250	$2,600
2	210	2,150
3	230	2,500
4	200	2,100
5	260	2,700

a. Draw a scatter diagram.
b. Using least squares analysis, compute the equation of the line.
c. Calculate the unexplained and explained portions of the total variation at a level of 230 patients.
d. Calculate and explain the coefficient of determination.
e. Describe how well the service levels correlate with supply costs.
f. Calculate and explain the standard error of estimate.
g. Calculate a 99 percent confidence limit for the slope of the cost line.

15. An administrator at Hillside Health Center wants to prepare a budget for the outpatient department. Below are the supply costs and related patient levels for the past six quarters.

Quarter	Patient level	Supply cost
1	600	$1,300
2	900	2,000
3	800	1,400
4	1,100	2,500
5	1,200	2,700
6	1,000	2,100

a. Is a linear equation appropriate?
b. Calculate the regression equation, using least squares analysis.
c. Determine the explained and unexplained portions of the total variation at a level of 1,000 patients.
d. Calculate the coefficient of determination.
e. Compute the standard error of estimate.
f. Determine a 95 percent confidence limit for the slope of the budget line.

16. *Problem related to identification of the appropriate use of linear versus nonlinear models.*

You have been given the following monthly cost data representing feeding and maintenance costs for research animals at the Institute of Genetic Research Division of Metropolitan State University Medical Center. You are to examine the cost data and prepare a formula to be included as part of a comprehensive computer program used to predict future costs of operating the Institute of Genetic Research.

Month	Feeding and maintenance costs	Number of animals
January	$11,500	100
February	14,725	115
March	17,376	126
April	18,924	132
May	23,109	147
June	27,964	158
July	19,996	136
August	16,141	121
September	22,236	144
October	25,216	154
November	28,725	165
December	31,084	172

Required:
a. Identify the criterion variable related to research animal feeding and maintenance costs.
b. Identify the predictor variable related to research animal feeding and maintenance costs.
   1. Can time be used as a predictor variable of research animal feeding and maintenance costs? Why or why not?
   2. Can time ever be used as a predictor variable in identifying hospital cost behavior patterns? Why or why not?
c. Is the prediction of animal feeding and maintenance costs best suited for prediction by a linear or a nonlinear model?
   1. Mathematically support your answer.
   2. Support your answer by preparing a scatter diagram. Explain how the scatter diagram supports your answer.

17. *Problem related to methods of confirming the logical knowledge technique of identifying cost behavior patterns.*

   As the chief cost analyst for your state's regulatory commission for hospitals, you are asked by the chief administrator of the commission to develop an estimate of the annual average fixed cost for radiology departments of the seven hospitals in the greater metropolitan area of Sand Silica.

   You immediately begin to review all standard required quarterly reports on file with the commission for Sand Silica area hospitals. You find that the only statistics and cost data required and on file related to radiology departments are total radiology department costs and number of X-rays processed per quarter. For example, the costs and statistics for Sand Silica Memorial Hospital for the previous four quarters were:

Quarter	Total radiology department costs (C)	Number of X-rays processed (N)
1st quarter	$ 94,765	2,225
2nd quarter	157,165	4,175
3rd quarter	128,525	3,280
4th quarter	116,685	2,910

You are also able to find this information for the six other hospitals in the greater metropolitan area of San Silica. You believe that if you can adequately calculate the fixed costs for each hospital using the above available information, a simple arithmetic average of the calculated fixed costs for each of the seven hospitals would be a sufficient estimate for the commissioners to use at their meeting in the morning. You begin working with the Sand Silica Memorial Hospital data.

Required:

Using the data available for Sand Silica Memorial Hospital, calculate the total annual fixed costs related to the radiology department.

18. In developing a budget formula, the following healthcare data for the last six months were collected. The least squares analysis will be used.

Total costs Σy	$3,600
Average costs $\bar{y}$	$ 600
Total usage Σx	900 units
x^2	3,240,000
xy	5,760,000

a. Determine the budget formula.
b. What are the fixed costs?
c. What are the variable costs?
d. Calculate total costs given a usage of 162 units.

19. A healthcare departmental manager has collected the data below for the last 12 months. He wants to determine a budget formula using least squares analysis.

Σy Total costs	$19,320
y Average costs	$ 1,610
x Total patients	2,400
$\Sigma\bar{x}$ Average patients	200
$\Sigma(y - y^1)^2$ Unexplained variation	107,324
$\Sigma(y - \bar{y})^2$ Total variation	1,393,818
Σx^2	484,000
Σxy	3,869,000

For the month of June that patient level was 130 with total costs of $1,580.00.
a. Determine the budget equation.
b. Calculate the explained and unexplained portions of the total variation at a level of 130 patients.
c. Calculate and explain the coefficient of determination.

20. The following cost data are from the last 10 weeks at GMG Hospital. In determining a budget equation, the financial manager has decided to use the least squares method.

Total costs	$5,600
Average costs	$ 560
Total patient level	1,500
Average patient level	150
Σxy	3,716,000
Σx^2	848,000
Standard error of estimate	5,044

a. Calculate the budget formula.
b. At the patient level of 1,320, determine 1) fixed costs, 2) variable costs, and 3) total costs.
c. Calculate the 95 percent confidence limit for the slope of the regression line.

21. The data below have been collected from hospitals for the last 10 weeks. Examine the information and evaluate the statistical results.

Weeks	Laboratory costs	Patient level	y^1
1	$4,700	440	4,662.44
2	5,010	472	4,915.24
3	4,300	460	4,820.44
4	4,850	425	4,543.94
5	4,410	411	4,433.44
6	4,500	420	4,504.44
7	4,970	466	4,867.84
8	5,050	475	4,938.94
9	4,200	390	4,267.44
10	4,350	405	4,385.94
Total supply costs			$46,340.00
Total patients			4,364.00
Average supply costs			$ 4,634.00
Average patients			436.4
Variable costs			$ 7.90

Fixed costs	$ 1,186.44
Coefficient of determination(r^2)	56.41%
Standard error of estimate (s_e)	224.69
99 percent confidence limit for variable costs:	
between $16.13 and $−0.33	

References

Cooper, William D. and Charles D. Mecimore, "Statistical Sampling: Its Use in Hospital Decision Making," *Healthcare Financial Management,* Jan. 1984, pp. 66-70.

Griffith, John R., *Quantitative Techniques for Hospital Planning and Control,* Lexington, MA: Lexington Books, 1972.

Horngren, Charles T., *Cost Accounting: A Managerial Emphasis,* New York: Prentice-Hall, 1982.

Shuman, Larry J., R. Dickson Speas, Jr. and John A. Young, *Operations Research in Health Care,* Baltimore, MD: Johns Hopkins University Press, 1975.

Warner, D. Michael and Don C. Holloway, *Decision Making and Control for Health Administration,* Ann Arbor, MI: Health Administration Press, 1978.

CHAPTER 14

Management information systems*

Introduction

This chapter summarizes some of the important issues concerning management information systems (MIS), decision support systems (DSS), microcomputer applications, and the movement toward more widespread computer utilization. Several actual applications in healthcare organizations are also described.

Healthcare financial managers have the responsibility to plan, direct, coordinate, budget, and control the activities within the organization, as well as to manage the resources of the institution in a way that is both effective and efficient. All decisions made by management are based on the best available information; more information should lead to better decisions. It is also management's responsibility to ensure that the institution's information systems and processes are adequate for effective decision-making.

There are at least three categories of information systems: clinical or medical information systems, information systems that support administrative operations, and management planning and control systems. Clinical or medical information systems are used primarily to support direct patient care activities in a hospital. Operational administrative systems, often called accounting information systems, have been designed to aid management in the daily non-patient care activities of the hospital. Management planning and control systems, often called Management Information Systems (MIS), assist in making strategic policy decisions that involve planning, controlling, and evaluating activities. A fourth information system may overlay these systems as a data base management system, which is a collection of

---

*This chapter was prepared with the assistance of former health administration students Stuart Bramer and the late Carolyn Kragh.

Exhibit 14-1
An integrated data base for hospital information systems*

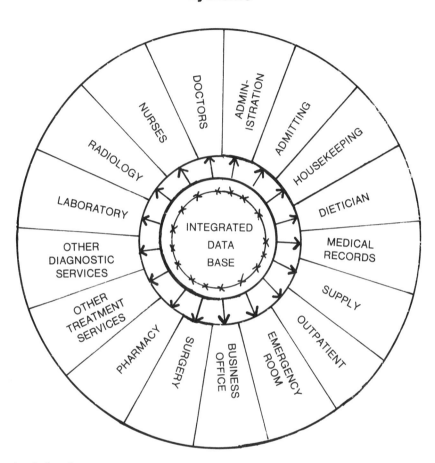

1. Online data entry, retrieval, and display on specialized terminals
2. Program-controlled message switching for communicating information through-out the hospital
3. Integral part of the hospital's day-to-day operations
4. Fully integrated system design

*Charles Austin, *Information Systems for Hospital Administration*, (Ann Arbor: Health Administration Press, 1979)

interrelated data stored with as little redundancy as possible, independent of the programs which use the data and a general format for retrieval and formatting special reports.

In addition to individualized systems or components, fully integrated information systems have been developed that facilitate communication between the various departmental entities and the previously described systems. With an integrated system, data is entered at the source and stored in data files that can be retrieved at strategic locations by authorized personnel. This capability virtually eliminates the redundancy of information data entry and should significantly decrease the need for many data entry personnel, increasing the efficiency and effectiveness of operations. A model that illustrates this integrated data base concept can be seen in *Exhibit 14-1.*

Hospitals are increasing the size and complexity of this data processing and management information system. 50 percent of all hospitals surveyed in 1981 and 1984 had increased their data processing budgets by more than 55 percent, and 25 percent had increased budgets by more than 114 percent (Packer, et. al., 1985 p. 115). The median data processing budget rose from $350,000 to $610,000 during this interval at an average compound growth rate of 18 percent per year. The relative budgets for different sizes of hospitals are shown in Panel A of *Figure 14-2.* Panel B indicates that more than 46 percent of all hospitals responding to the survey are using shared services. Another 44 percent are using in-house systems (Packer, et. al., 1985, p. 117).

More important than these growth curves is the shift to new applications involving patient care systems and strategic management systems. *Exhibit 14-2,* Panel C, indicates that almost all hospitals surveyed now have patient billing, receivable, and general ledger systems. Meanwhile, the growth in financial planning, DRG analysis systems, medical records, order-entry, and admissions systems have been phenomenal. Many of these systems are now integrated, or at least linked, so that patient data can be tied to financial planning models.

Much of the growth in data processing budgets and applications, as well as shifts in data processing approach used, can be explained as hospitals' attempts to meet the challenges of the current, turbulent, healthcare environment. Hospitals are giving significant attention and dollars to tracking patient utilization (e.g., number of tests being provided, length of stay, discharge planning). They are attempting to ensure the cost effectiveness of services provided through the use of cost accounting systems, flexible budgeting, and other applications.

To continue providing quality care at a competitive price, hospitals need to get maximum mileage out of their data. A large percentage of hospitals are merging their financial and clinical information. In the future, market-based information from consumers and payers also may be integrated with these financial and clinical data. Such manipulations would help the hospital to

Exhibit 14-2

Panel A
Average data processing budgets by bed-size, (000 omitted).

	1981	*1984*
Hospitals		
50-200 beds	$ 188.3	$ 304.4
201-350 beds	412.7	668.4
351-500 beds	651.3	1,104.3
More than 500 beds	1,462.5	2,433.1

Panel B
Hospitals' primary approach to data processing.

	1981	*1984*
In-house	47.1%	43.9%
Turnkey	9.4	7.6
Facility management	5.9	2.3
Shared service	37.6	46.2

Panel C
Percentage of hospitals with selected applications.

	1981	*1984*
Financial management systems		
Patient billing/accounts receivable	92.8%	100.0%
General ledger	89.2	98.8
Inventory	46.4	57.1
Patient care systems		
Admissions	51.1	78.5
Order/entry	13.0	40.4
Medical records	28.5	59.5
Strategic management systems		
Financial planning	35.7	48.8
DRG analysis	0.0	65.4

better realize its strengths, weaknesses, areas of potential market dominance, and effective new marketing strategies. (Packer, et. al., 1985, p. 118).

MIS in a healthcare environment

Most healthcare organizations are labor intensive. Hence, if a new information system is going to pay for itself, it will probably have to reduce some labor costs.

Healthcare organizations are information intensive, and in order to achieve effective delivery of services, a variety of information must be managed. Accurate, timely, and useful information must be readily available; management information systems provide a means to accomplish this.

Many clinical and non-clinical departments must interact in an effective and efficient manner if high-quality patient care is to be provided and effective operations is going to be maintained. Management information systems provide the means to enhance communications between departmental entities. A variety of goals may be established to achieve these diverse ends (*Exhibit 14-3*).

Exhibit 14-3
Potential hospital information system goals*

1. To improve departmental communications.
2. To provide operational controls over systems applications.
3. To minimize late, lost and incorrect charges.
4. To provide accurate, complete, and timely processing of physicians' orders.
5. To improve provider and patient satisfaction with the healthcare delivery process.
6. To improve proficiency of personnel in use of the system.
7. To improve the delivery of timely and accessible quality patient care.
8. To provide comprehensive financial, resource, and budgeting data reporting for management control based upon responsibility reporting concepts.
9. To plan structured implementation of systems and applications to facilitate optimum utilization of hospital resources.
10. To enhance ongoing cost containment efforts.
11. To provide useful, accurate, complete and timely demographic, financial and statistical data.
12. To provide systems flexibility to adapt to changing needs and to interact to other potential computer systems or modules.
13. To provide useful, accurate, complete, and timely patient and hospital activity and patient care statistics to meet the requirements of the various agencies requiring such data.
14. To increase user participation in healthcare operations.
15. To reduce clerical time.

*William F. Andrew and Associates, "Guide to Hospital Information Systems," Winter Haven, Florida, 1981.

The flow of information in a healthcare environment is complex and multi-faceted. *Exhibit 14-4* illustrates some of these information flows, which may be either manual or computerized. *Exhibit 14-5* illustrates a possible configuration of terminals, printers, storage devices, and a mainframe that will permit the communication flows shown in *Exhibit 14-4*.

Exhibit 14-4
An example of information flow

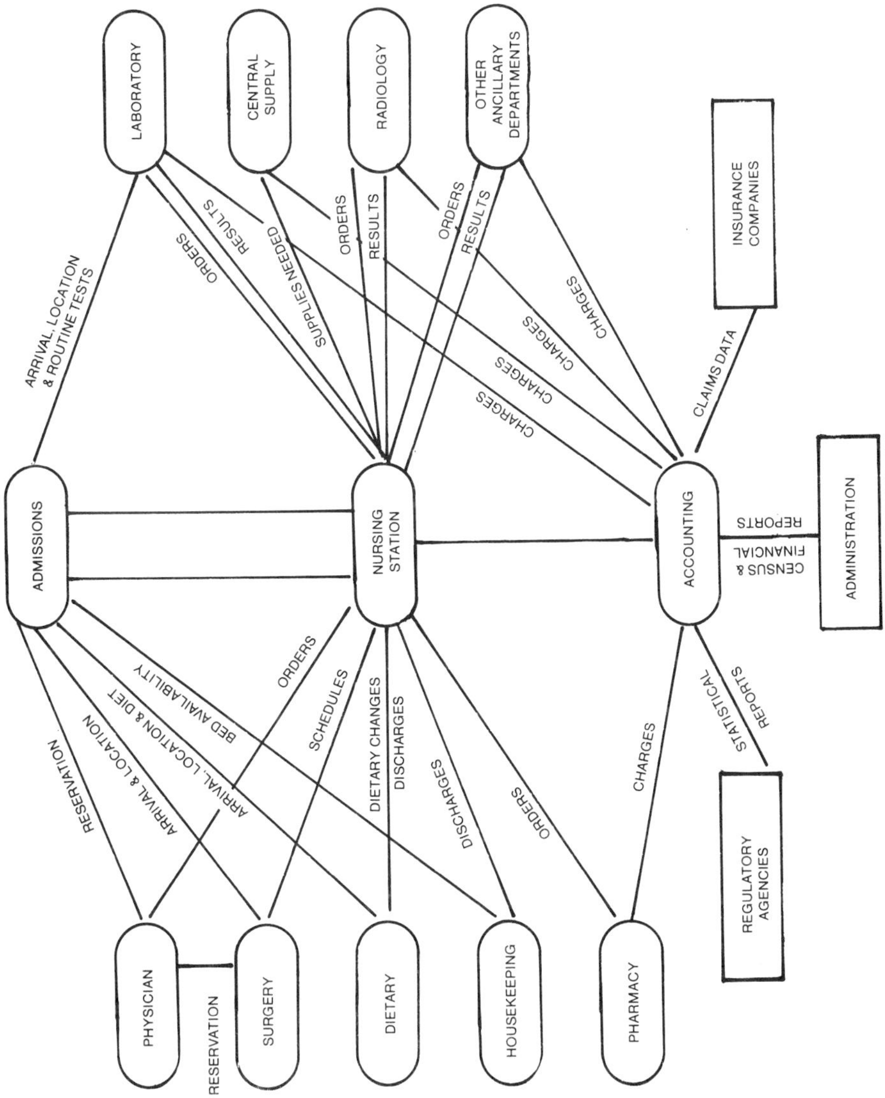

Exhibit 14-5
An example of a hospital information system EDP configuration

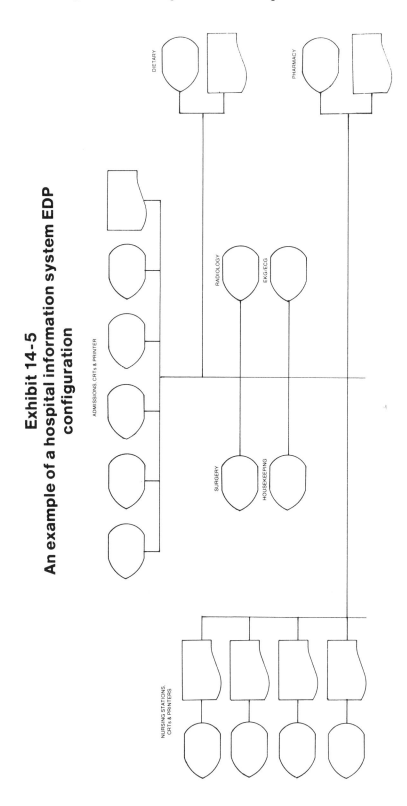

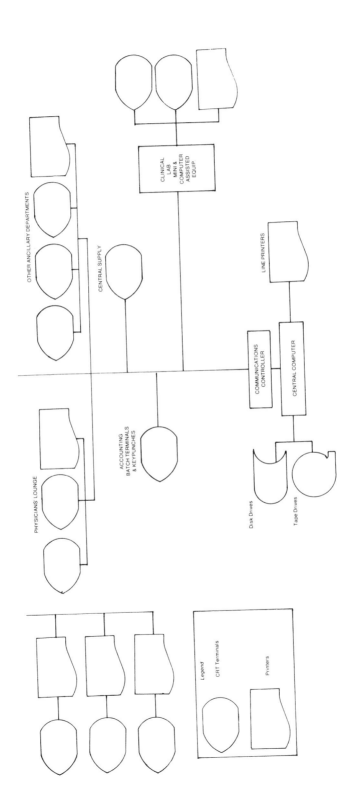

Cost-benefit analysis of MIS

Any implementation or reorganizing of a healthcare MIS should be preceded by a cost-benefit analysis of the proposed system compared to the existing system. Both qualitative and quantitative costs and benefits should be included.

The primary quantitative dimension relates to the economic impact that the proposed information system would have on various healthcare personnel, presumably leading to a reduction in patient care costs. For example, a new MIS could perform many of the clerical activities that are now the responsibility of management and clinical personnel. This could lead to an increase in productivity as personnel concentrate to a greater extent on providing health services rather than clerical activities. Through job restructuring, it is conceivable that a reduction in personnel could be achieved in the long run.

Inventories and accounts receivables could be more effectively managed because of the increased availability of current, accurate, and useable information. Better decisions may be made as a function of more timely, accurate and useable financial, statistical, and demographic information. The ability to retrieve such information in a variety of formats could positively influence decision-making processes of physicians, nurses, and other clinical staff. With improved information, clinical managers may make more informed decisions and have greater control over departmental and hospital wide operations.

A qualitative benefit of an MIS that may also have quantitative implications relates to quality of patient care and its impact on risk management. For example, a satisfied patient is less likely to sue a hospital. If an assumption can be made that an effective information system can positively influence quality of care (e.g., by providing readily accessible, useful, accurate, and timely information, allowing better clinical decisions to be made), then hospital administration may see a reduction in dissatisfied patients and the law suits they bring.

The change to an automated system is not without costs and potential problems. Economic costs of the system are great. They include the installation fees (including training costs), operating expenses and maintenance costs. Future costs also should be considered. These might include costs associated with updating the system in terms of additional hardware and software. The opportunity costs associated with implementing a totally integrated system are high and patient revenue may be lost by not developing new revenue producing services. Interest earnings are also forfeited by not investing the MIS purchase cost in interest-bearing financial instruments. However, a fully integrated system should pay for itself in a number of ways, e.g., by reducing lost, late, and misapplied charges, by providing more accurate billing information, and by increasing the productivity of personnel through more effective and

Exhibit 14-6
Cost-benefit dimensions of MIS

Quantitative Dimensions

1. Impact on departmental and overall financial goals.

2. Economic impact on each department.
   a. On lost, late or misapplied charges, billing accuracy
   b. Personnel productivity and staffing levels
   c. Effectiveness and efficiency of operations (reduction of data redundancy using data base management systems)
   d. Reducing clerical activities of management and staff
   e. Better inventory and accounts receivable management
   f. Impact on operating equipment requirements and costs
   g. Information systems costs (installation, operations, and maintenance)
   h. Opportunity costs associated with MIS implementation
   i. Impact on reimbursement (on cost-based and prospective payments)

3. Impact on accuracy, timeliness and useability of demographic, financial and statistical data.

4. Risk management implications.

5. Impact of system on length of stay.

Qualitative Dimensions

1. Impact on departmental, hospital and societal goals.

2. System impact on the decision-making processes and decision makers (e.g., a. physicians, b. top management, c. operating management, d. clinical staff, e. technical staff, and f. operating personnel.)

3. Impact on the structure, process, outcome, and quality of care.

4. Impact on physicians' time, convenience and referral patterns.

5. Impact on operations and patients relating to equipment failures and/or downtime.

6. Effect of the change process on personnel behavior (e.g., aggressive, projection and avoidance behaviors).

7. Impact on personnel and data availability where data entry occurs at the point of service.

8. Effect on public relations.

efficient operations. *Exhibit 14-6* summarizes the important qualitative and quantitative dimensions of the costs and benefits of an MIS.

Potential problems that should be considered prior to system implementation relate to dysfunctional personnel reactions to change. Three common dysfunctional behaviors, aggression, projection and avoidance, may occur among personnel when new information systems are installed. These reactions occur differentially among three different work groups (operating personnel, operating management, and top management) as shown in *Exhibit 14-7*.

Even though there is no single solution to behavioral problems associated with MIS, being cognizant of potential dysfunctional behaviors and performing appropriate institutional diagnoses during the design stage, prior to system implementation, are two steps that could minimize these problems. *Exhibit 14-7* describes some of the reasons that resistance to information system acceptance may occur. Possible ways to meliorate these behavioral effects include creating an atmosphere that opens lines of communication between the different levels of management and between management and staff. Try to instill a cooperative spirit in personnel by assuring them that they will not lose their jobs to a computer. Participation in system design and implementation at all levels of the organization encourages cooperation by giving staff members a sense of control. Clarify the purpose and characteristics of any new MIS. If a synergistic relationship between people and machines can be formed, then personnel acceptance should come easier.

A new information system's capabilities to reduce clerical tasks and increase patient care, particularly for managers and clinical personnel, should be emphasized. For example, by reducing the pharmacists' clerical tasks, they can spend more time reviewing patient profiles. The system should be designed to fulfill the needs of the user by providing managers with essential informatin and not just providing them with more reports. It should be emphasized that creation of an appropriate atmosphere could mean the difference between a system that helps to improve operations and one that actually worsens them. In a good behavioral climate, benefits can be enhanced; costs and potential problems can then be minimized.

Research on MIS costs and benefits

Battelle Corporation conducted one of the few comprehensive studies of the effects of MIS. They performed an extensive economic evaluation of the impact of a fully integrated hospital information system developed by Technicon Medical Information Systems at El Camino Hospital (California). Their findings:

1. The overall impact of the Technicon Medical Information System (TMIS) on total direct expenses (which includes systems costs)

Exhibit 14-7
Behavioral factors associated with MIS*

	Operating (nonclerical)	Operating (clerical)	Operating Management	Top Management
Dysfunctional Behavior				
Aggression	X		X	
Projection		X	X	
Avoidance			X	X
Possible Reasons for MIS Resistance				
Threats to economic security		X	X	
Threats to status or power		X	X*	
Increased job complexity	X		X	X
Uncertainty or unfamiliarity	X	X	X	X
Changed interpersonal relations or work patterns		X*	X	
Changed superior-subordinate relationships		X*	X	
Increased rigidity or time pressure	X	X	X	
Role ambiguity		X	X*	X
Feelings of insecurity		X	X*	X*

X* = The reason has a strong possibility of being the cause of resistance.

*G. W. Dickson and John Simmons, "The Behavioral Side of MIS," *Business Horizons*, August, 1970.

was to increase expenses per patient by 1.7 percent and expenses per patient day by 3.2 percent.

2. TMIS reduced the expense per patient day for medical care (nursing and ancillary services) only *if* the costs of the operating system are excluded.

3. A large comparative increase in total direct expenses per patient for support services was encountered, but was not necessarily due to the TMIS.

4. TMIS reduced patients' average length of stay when compared to other hospitals in the area. Other impacts on quality of patient care were not quantified. (Barrett, Heresch, and Caswell, 1979).

Evaluation of the TMIS:

1. Management information systems may not necessarily reduce the overall costs of hospital care (when systems costs are taken into account). Further research is necessary to assess more of the quantitative and qualitative benefits of TMIS.

2. The net benefits of TMIS implementation may vary as a function of clinical and ancillary utilization.

3. A benefits realization program may be required if the full benefits of TMIS are to be realized. This would include identification of how jobs can be restructured so that personnel productivity can be increased, with a consequent reduction in personnel levels and expenses.

Ten major guidelines for a healthy MIS

This section summarizes ten practical guides to help achieve and maintain productive and effective MIS regardless of size, cost, or organizational complexity.

1. Know the vendor's reputation[1]
   —length of time in business
   —ability to sustain warranty service
   —dealer commitment to customer service
   —check references and financial status
2. Know the vendor's experience
   —experience in similar healthcare organizations
   —ability to customize hardware and software

---

[1]This material is based on an article by Warren S. Reid, "Ten Commandments to Ensure a Healthy Computer System," *Los Angeles Business Journal,* Aug. 23, 1982.

      —prior experience with specific configuration

      —specific personnel who will work with your organization

3. Know which features are needed

      —off-the-shelf vs. customized system

      —are modifications needed, at what cost?

      —specialized staff required to operate/maintain system

4. Know the true costs

      —base costs

      —supplies, training, power, space, maintenance, and insurance

      —communications requirements

      —total long-run cost (3-5 years)

      —growth capacity

5. Examine the vendor's proposal

      —issue request for proposal (RFP) or request for information (RFI)

      —degree of completeness relative to RFP

      —understanding of MIS objectives and requirements

      —astuteness of vendor questions

      —quality of vendor recommendations

      —incorporate RFP and vendor responses into the final contract

6. Know and test the system's design quality

      —adaptability to growth and change

      —ability to follow/trace source code

      —universal or unique structure and architecture

      —documentation of programming

      —conduct a "test drive"

      —conduct a sequenced examination of all system features in the order and magnitude needed by your organization ("string-test")

      —conduct a test of one month's recent financial statements ("parallel test")

      —test security and "crash-proofness" of system ("bullet test")

      —test garbage responses

      —pull power plug and test restart/recovery procedures

7. Know the system's performance and reliability

      —speed, response time, peak load limits

      —back-up support

      —average time between failures

      —length of time on market

      —repair availability and procedures

      —parts availability

      —restrictions or concerns of other users regarding hardware and software

      —software track record, who/where/how are bugs eliminated?

8. Know who's going to install MIS
   —determine space, wiring, and climatic requirements
   —review installation manual or plan
   —who/how will convert existing data?
   —adequacy/availability/costs of training
   —amount of vendor on-site support during installation/
     conversion
9. Be sure of ongoing support
   —ongoing maintenance of hardware
   —ongoing maintenance of software
   —commitment and effectiveness to maintenance
   —access by telephone or service call
   —demand and load at service facilities
   —enhancements, updates, changes
   —put service/support details in contract
10. Is the vendor willing to negotiate
    —adaptation to standard contract
    —periodic payments, phased to installation schedule
    —protect both vendor and client
    —incentives to assure satisfactory performance
    —negotiate for discounts off list price
      (15 - 20 percent discounts are usually obtained)

These recommendations should help attain a happy and healthy update of an organization's MIS. Failure to consider all of the points noted above can lead to more operating costs, delays, absolute reduction in usage, or, in the worst case, sabotage of the MIS. The qualitative implications of not considering these implementation guides can result in a net decrease in healthcare efficiency and effectiveness. The overall implication of these "ten commandments" is that the healthcare provider can't know all the details about acquiring and installing an MIS. Reliance on vendors and/or consultants is essential. But a careful and unhurried RFP, followed by prudent negotiations can only enhance the ultimate reliability and usefulness of the MIS.

The microcomputer option

With the advent of powerful microcomputers (low cost, large storage, user-friendly), healthcare financial managers are starting to develop many new decision tools independently of the primary information system. Software is generally available that can provide a decision support system operated and maintained by the user, rather than by technicians in the data processing department.

Microcomputers can help hospital financial managers generate intelligent decisions based upon sound analysis within short time frames.

They can increase the quality of decision-making and professional productivity. Microcomputers which operate with easy-to-use, ready-made software can frequently produce numeric analysis very quickly. These primary attributes enable microcomputers to outperform a centralized data processing center.

A microcomputer has the same components as a larger computer: a means to enter data (terminals), some way to process it (memory), somewhere to store it (disks or floppy disks), and a hard copy display (printer).

Enchanced microcomputers may serve as terminals or they may approach the capacities of small minicomputers with an ability to save large amounts of data in files, an ability to manipulate large data bases, and reduction of time-sharing connect charges. The memory capabilties of a personal computer are based upon the memory utilized by the internal operating systems, a particular program, and a particular data set.

Ready-made or "canned" software packages have become more prevalent as the microcomputer industry attempts to meet business needs. Canned software is available for most types of microcomputers at often nominal prices. The rule of thumb to follow relative to software is the old cliche: "Don't try to re-invent the wheel". Canned software packages can easily accommodate many of the financial manager's needs, in a cost effective manner. When buying software applications for the personal computer, it's important to analyze the package in terms of its appropriateness to the task and ease of use. It also is important to verify that the program has been tested and documented.

Case study of microcomputer MIS application

Five applications of the microcomputer were implemented at Memorial Hospital.

(1) Budget Worksheet: The finance department wanted to provide historically-based projections of expense for budgeting purposes. They also wanted to budget at a much finer level of expense than in prior years. Budgeting occurred at the object code level with the use of a data base software program. Expense data from the prior eight months of the fiscal year was entered into the computer for each object code category. A formula was entered to straight-line the expense data to the end of the year, as well as sum across object codes. The rest of the printout was developed as a worksheet for the departmental manager to define budgets. A column was made for the deletion of one-time expenses from the budget base. Another space was offered on the worksheet for explanation of unusual increases in expense in the request budget. Each one of the hospital's accounts (approximately 100) were prepared as a file on diskette. Each account consisted of an average eighteen object code categories.

In general, the budget worksheets were well received. The calculations made in this particular application were fairly minimal, though. The strength of this application was that it created a more participative and orderly tone to the budgeting process.

(2) Operating Expense and Workload Analysis: Once the request budgets were submitted by each department, a methodology was needed to analyze expense figures. Many "electronic worksheet" software programs can compute redundant calculations with relatively few keystrokes. This allows for variance analysis of total operation expense dollars and work load. More specifically, net budgeted dollars were compared to the request budget, net budgeted dollars. Percentage change between years was also indicated. A historically-based, straight line projection of actual operating expense was included as a reference figure. Workload data projections were compared.

The accounts within the hospital were aggregated in two different ways:

— Accounts were combined together in four generic types of expense: Inpatient, Outpatient, Medical Support and Non-Medical Support.

— Accounts were also combined in terms of administrative responsibility. This allowed each administrator to see the total impact of their particular accounts request budgets. Accounts were sub-totaled in the four generic expense categories for each administrator.

A summary sheet was prepared that indicated variances in each of the four generic expense categories across the hospital. This allowed each administrator to compare the extent of contribution his or her accounts made to increases or decreases in the hospital's total operating expense. The data provided was used to make final decisions relative to budgeting.

(3) Employee Attitude Survey: The results of the Hospital Finance Employee Attitude Survey were analyzed in terms of:
— total respondents to each specific question
— the number of responses to each multiple-choice category
— the average response and the mode

(4) Payer Mix Comparison Charts: Changes in payer mix between two years were displayed in a pie chart format, with the use of a graphics program.

(5) Labels: Distribution lists were developed into files. Labels for the printer were obtained. Distribution with preprinted labels has improved efficiency of the finance office. Lists can be updated easily by "blanking" out matrix cells.

In addition, future applications may include:
— Multiple regression analysis of expense
— Pro forma balance sheets and income statements
— FTE data on vacancies, transfers, terminations

—Fixed and variable expense analysis
—Identification of inventory, inventory costing
—Contribution margin analysis by responsibility center
—Economic ordering quantity analysis
—Seasonality of workload analysis
—Productivity analysis
—Graphic representations of accounts receivable trends
—Analyses of changes in indigent patients
—Lease versus buy worksheet

Several general recommendations may enhance the utilization of microcomputers at Memorial Hospital:

1. Provide a general orientation to hospital finance staff which includes a demonstration of software applications.
2. Consult with hospital finance staff about their application projects.
3. Develop a sign-up sheet, access, and general procedures manuals.
4. Develop a reference library of texts, journals, and articles.
5. Evaluate microcomputer applications on a regular basis.
6. Formalize the responsibilities of data entry by developing a personnel position description and allocating a half-time accounting technician for data entry.
7. Begin planning future projects.

This case has shown some first steps that were actually taken at a finance and budget department of Memorial Hospital to increase the use of microcomputers. These applications can be significantly expanded. Don't forget to consider the possibility that a microcomputer may not be right for your department. Here's why.

Six Reasons Not To Buy a Microcomputer[2]

#1 Your Acquaintances All Have Microcomputers or "Keeping Up With the Jones"

Good for them, and good for you. Now you are assured the vicarious pleasure of owning a microcomputer, and unless you've thought through the whole process of acquiring and using a micro in the business, enjoying it through someone else's experience may be the better way. In other words, don't let bandwagon psychology become your prime reason for buying. It's tough to resist the ads and the sales statistics. They're impressive. Sales of small computers are expected to reach $23 billion by 1985, according to

[2]Reprinted by permission of Alexander Grant & Company, accountants and management consultants, Chicago, IL.

International Data. For example, United Technologies recently ordered 5,000 and Ford bought 4,500. There's an important message here for smaller organizations: large companies, with their super-powerful mainframe computers and platoons of programmers and troubleshooters, are buying micros to fill little niches in the data processing landscape. They're buying micros for departmental use—"to do *VisiCalc* planning and projecting, not for accounting," says an analyst at International Resource Development, Inc. By contrast, the allure of micros to small organizations is for mainline management functions—accounting, bookkeeping, billing, recordkeeping, etc. So while the sale charts show micros shooting off the top, bear in mind where the shipments are going and how the equipment is being used. The passing parade may not be going your way.

#2 Your Bookkeeping and Financial Systems Are a Shambles

That's bad news. But if you're counting on a micro to tidy up the mess, forget it. Computers are dumb critters. They grow smart, efficient, and powerful as you do, no faster. If you feed incompetence into one end of a computer it will come out incompetence at the other end—faster, perhaps, but otherwise no different. You must have heard the computerese that describes this phenomenon: "Garbage in, Garbage out"—GIGO, for short. To understand why a micro is incapable of straightening out your business problems, consider what those problems are. James Senn, Professor of management information systems at the State University of New York, Binghamton, lists these common difficulties:

- Insufficient operating data and information
- Inaccurate, untimely, or irrelevant data
- Inadequate monitoring of operations
- Unknown costs, margins, and profits
- Failure to project the results of change
- Failure to capture, maintain, or use historical and trend data
- Inefficiency
- Reactive planning and firefighting

Now ask yourself how many of these problems can be solved by a microcomputer alone. Of course, none of them. Solving or even reducing these problems by computer requires not only hardware but proper software selected as a result of careful analysis and planning by management. "The biggest mistake first-time users make is computerizing before they have their manual systems organized," says Tim McMahon, manager of the computer group at Venture Development Corp., Wellesley, Massachusetts. The right time to consider computerization, say McMahon and other advisers, is when your manual operation is organized and controlled—but overloaded.

#3 Microcomputers Are Cheap, and They're Getting Cheaper

The ads say—take-it-home-and-plug-it-in; a turnkey system for only five hundred bucks. What have you got to lose? Considering only the dollar side of the question, the cost is likely to be a lot higher than you're led to believe.

While it's true that $500 will buy a console with memory, a video display unit, a cassette drive, and connecting cables, systems suitable for business invariably need upgrading. The cassette tape drive, for example, though perfectly adequate for a computer hobbyist, is too slow and too limited for most decision applications. Almost certainly, the main memory and output of a $500 system will be inadequate for business use. Unless you're buying the micro as a toy, be prepared to upgrade an inexpensive system. How much will that cost? Bare-bones: $1,500 to $2,500, with the knowledge that you'll probably spend twice as much before you are mildly content. To extract greater value from the system, you may have to spend $5,000 to $10,000 for a microcomputer system (hardware, software, installation support) with adequate flexibility, interconnect ability, and growth potential. If the biggest mistake first-time users make is computerizing before they're organized, the second biggest is *underestimating* the total cost. And the manufacturers, relishing prospects of a mass market for micros as personal computers, aren't doing much to clarify that misunderstanding.

#4 You've Tried the Micro Yourself and It Works Beautifully

It's a funny thing about microcomputer demonstrations. Prospective buyers demand a lot less than they do when, for example, they're buying a car. Micro buyers seldom sit down at the keyboard and take a "test ride" themselves, for the obvious reason that few know how to "drive" a microcomputer. So while they may think they've taken the micro out for a spin, they've probably just gone for a ride. The salesperson has done the driving—and taken you where he or she wanted to go. And the salesperson is, after all is said and done, more interested in selling equipment than solving your data processing problems. Therefore, if the answers to your specific questions about how the micro will serve your particular situation seemed ever so slightly suspect (e.g., "Yes, I know one user who does it that way . . . as I recall he made some modifications . . . but most users think this standard format works even better—after they get used to it") there is reason to seek independent outside advice. Where can you get it? From consultants who understand both data processing and your healthcare environment— and are not selling equipment.

#5 There's a Software Package for Everything You Need To Do

True—the software catalogs grow larger and less expensive every day. Competition is steadily improving the product and driving down the price. But the proliferation of software creates the impression that off-the-shelf packages are practically the same as custom software. That's not true, and it probably never will be. In order to take advantage of even the most flexible software package, you'll have to adapt your operations to fit the characteristics (and limitations) of the package. Unwilling to change your way of doing things? Then your alternatives are either to modify a software package to meet your specific needs or write custom software tailored to your operations. Either alternative requires know-how beyond that of most first-time users and under any circumstances adds to the total cost of the system. How much? That depends on the individual case, and general rules don't apply. Software, and the attendant training, data conversion, and start-up costs, can run from 50 percent to 300 percent of the cost of hardware. It's the *most frequently underestimated* component of the total cost to computerize.

#6 Your Bookkeeper Is Ready, Willing, and Able

There's always a rosy glow about the prospect of computerizing. This is bound to color people's attitudes, at least superficially. But it is erroneous to leap to conclusions about employee acceptance of computer-based systems. The error, he says is "to assume that employees will accept and use these systems if they are shown the advantages of using computers and the output they produce." In other words, though logic may run a computer, it's usually not enough to ensure employee support. Employees worry about things that never occur to machines, like whether the machine is going to replace them, or make them look slow and inefficient by comparison, or so drastically change work routines that it just won't be the same job anymore. This fear of, and resistance to, computers is well documented and the subject of serious study. In the *Harvard Business Review,* (September-October 1982) James L. McKenny and F. Warren McFarlan write: "Organizations change much more slowly than technology." The authors recount four phases in the process of "assimilating" technology. First is the decision to invest and install; second, learning how to use the new technology to perform more tasks than originally proposed; third, the development of precise controls to ensure that future system design and installation is more cost efficient than the original; and fourth, the spread of this new technology throughout the organization. Experienced observers tell us this process applies universally, from the simplest microcomputer installation to the most sophisticated mainframe. It can derail anyplace along the continuum, and when it does the reason is just as likely to be people failure as machine failure. What's more, the burden may rest more heavily on management's failure to manage the process than on employees' failure to carry it out. How do you avoid people breakdowns? We recommend a time-tested process called communication. Everyone involved in a computerization project should be involved in decision-making early on.

Encouraging employee participation by soliciting ideas and comments, even if the ideas are naive or unrealistic and the comments are negative, can be most useful. Getting impressions and fears out on the table is always preferable to wondering what they are and who has them. All of this is designed to reduce the chances of foot-dragging or even outright sabotage—not physical sabotage, which is rare, but sabotage by subterfuge, furnishing wrong or incomplete information and the like, both during and after installation. It happens more often than people care to admit.

Another important factor may lie in selecting your software option not just on cost or features but on the ability of the vendor to help train your people, help them through the cultural shock of conversion, and provide trouble-shooting support after installation. It may cost more, but the added cost could pay enormous dividends in employee support. *Exhibit*

14-8 summarizes the important factors to consider as part of the microcomputer purchase decision.

Exhibit 14-9 provides a summary of the various linkages in a comprehensive MIS. Its overall structure and approach provides a sound design for an MIS in any healthcare organization.

Exhibit 14-8
Microcomputer comparison form*

A. List the specific functions you now perform manually which are to be computerized (e.g., accounts receivable, inventory, time-keeping, word processing, mailing list). For each function, indicate the number of daily and monthly transactions. Capacity is expressed in bytes, or characters of information. The memory size of microcomputers averages 128K-256K bytes; on-line storage averages 200K bytes.

Name of Business Function		Volume of Transactions		Total Required Capacity (bytes)
	Daily	Monthly		
A	_____	_____	_____	
B	_____	_____	_____	
C	_____	_____	_____	Memory
D	_____	_____	_____	Size ____
E	_____	_____	_____	
F	_____	_____	_____	On-Line
G	_____	_____	_____	Storage ____
H	_____	_____	_____	

B. Identify the off-the-shelf software packages available to perform the functions listed above. Capacity should be enough to serve your immediate needs plus a factor for expansion. Be sure to check references supplied either by the retail vendor or the software maker. Indicate whether outside maintenance is available. If not, identify staff personnel who will maintain software.

SOFTWARE

Name of Package	Capacity	References	Maintenance?
_____	_____	_____	_____
_____	_____	_____	_____
_____	_____	_____	_____
_____	_____	_____	_____
_____	_____	_____	_____
_____	_____	_____	_____
_____	_____	_____	_____
_____	_____	_____	_____

C. Identify hardware that fits your software choices. If more than one hardware configuration will work, price may be the determining factor. Identify necessary output devices, such as dot-matrix printer, letter-quality printer, graphics plotter.

With Software Name & Model No.	Cost	Required Output Method
A		
B		
C		
D		

Estimated Cost

Central Processor	$ _____			
Monitor	$ _____			
Diskette drive(s)	$ _____	Maintenance	$ _____
Hard-disk drive	$ _____			
Output device(s)	$ _____	Maintenance	$ _____
Software	$ _____	Post-installation	
Installation support	$ _____	support	$ _____
INITIAL COST	$ _____	ANNUAL COST	$ _____

D. Determine whether the software vendor has a charge for user documentation; offers user training, and at what cost; and provides assistance in converting files and records to the new system, and at what cost. Also determine whether the maintenance contract includes trouble-shooting services that are not hardware- or software-related, and if so at what cost.

One-time costs:	System Documentation	$ _____
	User training	$ _____
	Conversion support	$ _____
Annual costs:	(including post-installation support)	$ _____

E. At today's prices and state of the art, a microcomputer system should not cost more than $10,000-$15,000 initially. If the total is significantly more, consider a microcomputer. In any case, financial justification goes beyond the initial outlay. The payback period indicates more about financial justification than any other factor.

Another important question is how the proposed system will affect management control. Ask a data processing consultant to help evaluate this critical final step. It's not unheard of to decide there is no justification to computerize and to continue existing systems.

Financial Justification

_____

_____

_____

_____

Exhibit 14-9
Overview of relationships among conceptual content areas of an integrated MIS*

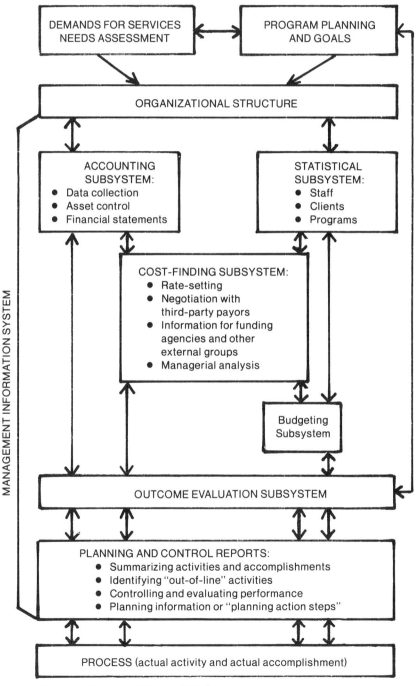

*Sorensen, Hanbery, & Kucic (1983).

Questions and problems

1. What behavioral factors should be considered in planning for a change in the MIS?

2. Choose a healthcare delivery system with which you are familiar. Identify several key information subsystems and identify their objectives. Are there trade-offs between overall objectives and sub-system objectives? How might they affect the MIS?

3. When is the patient record the primary source for clinical and analytical computer applications in healthcare? When isn't it?

4. What is meant by the term "patient data computerization"? Develop a list of examples in acute and ambulatory care settings.

5. What is the difference between computer users and user-managers? Why is this difference important?

6. As a change agent for MIS in a healthcare organization, what knowledge and skills are required?

7. Outline the steps in the processing cycle of information flow through a computer system (data entry thru data output). Compare your flow diagram with an actual application.

8. What are the benefits of data base management systems?

9. Do you think a healthcare provider should develop its own software? Why? In what areas could a provider develop software?

10. Why is it important for MIS user-managers to direct and participate in system testing activities?

11. What are the advantages and disadvantages of acquiring computer equipment by renting, leasing, or purchasing? Identify circumstances where one method may be preferred.

12. How will patient privacy be protected in clinical data systems? What policies might be considered to enhance confidentiality?

13. What is the current impact of MIS in medical care?

14. What are some of the exogenous influences on the development of MIS? On healthcare data systems? On patient data computerization?

15. What quality controls and requirements should be implemented in patient data systems? How does this compare to administrative systems?

References

Ahituv, Niv and Seev Neumann, *Principles of Information Systems for Management*, Dubuque, IA: Wm. C. Brown Company Publishers, 1982.

Austin, Charles, *Information Systems for Hospital Administration*, Ann Arbor: Health Administration Press, 1979.

Barrett, James, Philip Heresch and Robert Caswell, *Evaluation of the Impact of the Implementation of the Technicon Medical Information System at El Camino Hospital: Part II-Economic Trend Analysis: Final Report*, National Center for Health Sciences Research, Hyattsville, MD, May 14, 1979.

Cerullo, Michael, "Smoothing of Management Information Flow with Systems Analysis," *Hospital Financial Management*, 33, August 1979, 12-14.

Christensen, William W. and Eugene I. Stearns, *Microcomputers in Health Care Management*, Rockville, MD: Aspen Systems Corp., 1984.

Dickson, G.W. and John Simmons, "The Behavioral Side of MIS," *Business Horizons*, August 1970, 59-71.

Moscove, Stephen A. and Mark G. Simkin, *Accounting Information Systems: Concepts and Practice for Effective Decision Making*, New York: John Wiley & Sons, 1981.

Packer, C.L. and Shared Data Research staff, "Historical Changes in Hospital Computer Use," *Hospitals*, January 16, 1985, pp. 115-119.

Paden, Barbara, "Micro Software Purchase Tips," *Journal of Accountancy*, February, 1985, pp. 108-109.

Priest, Stephen L., *Managing Hospital Information Systems*, Rockville, MD: Aspen Systems Corp., 1982.

Sorensen, James E., Glyn W. Hanbery, and A. Ronald Kucic, *Accounting and Budgeting Systems for Mental Health Organizations*, Rockville, MD: Mental Health System Reports, Public Health Service, DMHS Publication No. (ADM) 83-1046, 1983.

Tilley, Bruce, "MIS To Contain Hospital Costs," *Computers in Hospitals*, March/April 1982, 36-41.

Warner, D. Michael, and Kyle L. Grazier, *Decision Making and Control for Health Administration: The Management of Quantitative Analysis*, Ann Arbor: Health Administration Press, 1984.

Waters, Kathleen A. and Gretchen F. Murphy, *Systems Analysis and Computer Applications in Health Information Management*, Rockville: Aspen Systems Corporation, 1983.

Weinberger, George and Aaron Tenenbaum, "The Evolution of Health Care Computer Systems," *Computers in Hospitals*, January/February 1982, 40.

Index

288–294
units of input and output, 96–98,
  324–325
univariate models of cost behavior,
  33, 35, 45
  least squares, 409–413

V

variable costs
  defined, 18
  estimating, 22–24
  see also fixed and variable;
    semivariable
variable and direct costs contrasted,
  22
variance defined, 86. *see also*
  analysis
variance analysis. *see* analysis of
  variance

volume
  and costs, summarized, 18–25
  and flexible budgeting, 53–54
  and static budgeting, 50–53
  variance, 93, 130

W

weighted units of measurement,
  97–98
worksheet
  labor, 157–159
  for revenue budgeting, 157
  statistical, 155–156

Z

zero-base budgeting, 163, 202–207
  sample decision packages,
    208–219